A Companion to the
Book of Common Prayer

A Companion to the Book of Common Prayer

Gerald Bray

James Clarke & Co.

JAMES CLARKE & CO.

P.O. Box 60
Cambridge
CB1 2NT
United Kingdom

www.jamesclarke.co
publishing@jamesclarke.co

Hardback ISBN: 978 0 227 17931 4
Paperback ISBN: 978 0 227 17930 7
PDF ISBN: 978 0 227 17932 1
ePub ISBN: 978 0 227 17933 8

British Library Cataloguing in Publication Data
A record is available from the British Library

First published by James Clarke & Co., 2023

Table of Contents

Preface and Acknowledgements

One of the more remarkable developments of recent years has been the return of the 1662 Book of Common Prayer (BCP) to the forefront of Anglican self-awareness. For the first 300 years of its existence, the 1662 prayer book was virtually unchallenged as the supreme manifestation of Anglican devotional piety, even though by the early twentieth century various revised forms of it had been produced and were increasingly being used, especially outside England. In some places, like Scotland and the United States, an alternative prayer book tradition had been in existence for centuries, and the 1662 book was less influential, but they were exceptions to the rule, and partial ones at that. Elsewhere, the liturgy adopted after the restoration of the monarchy in Britain in 1660, slightly modified and expanded from the one that had been suppressed in 1645, was the standard text, universally recognised as such and frequently praised as a monument of English literature. As late as 1965, it was still possible for Stella Brook to publish *The Language of the Book of Common Prayer*, a study of the way in which the prayer book had established itself as a literary classic.[1] Mrs Brook knew that major liturgical revision was on the way but that it had not yet progressed very far, and her readership was still familiar with the cadences of the seventeenth-century text.

A generation and a half later, the world that she inhabited has disappeared. Today it is mostly only worshippers over 70 who are intimately familiar with the 1662 rite, and many of them have forgotten large parts of it. To younger people it is often an alien relic, not unlike the King James Bible, which they may hear intoned from time to time but with which they are only noddingly acquainted. It is not so much the content

---

1. S. Brook, *The Language of the Book of Common Prayer* (London: Andre Deutsch, 1965).

that is unfamiliar as the style and language in which it is presented. The 'thees' and 'thous' of the original, still lovingly preserved in early and mid-twentieth-century revisions, have disappeared and, with them, the sense of religious 'otherness' that had both attracted and repelled the generations that grew up with them.

The linguistic changes that have occurred in the past several years have made the greatest impression, because they are so obvious and (to those who know the original texts by heart) disconcerting. However, more important have been the theological changes, many of which have gone unnoticed by the undiscerning, which have taken us away from our Reformation moorings. The 1662 prayer book is not above criticism, nor is it immune to possible improvement, as its seventeenth-century critics already pointed out. Nevertheless, for all its defects – real and imaginary – it conveys the Gospel message in scriptural tones to a degree that none of its proposed substitutes has been able to equal. It is the desire to recapture that emphasis that has driven the recent urge to recover it for modern use; and it is for that reason, above all, that it ought to be restored to the regular worship of the Church.

In the early twentieth century, when discontent with the 1662 prayer book was starting to impact the Church of England, two clergymen, Charles Neil (1841-1924) of St Mary's, Stamford Brook, and James Mason Willoughby (1867-1918) of St Luke's, West Hampstead, collaborated to produce *The Tutorial Prayer Book*.[2] They recognised that they had inherited two generations of liturgical study, much of it learned, some of it biased in favour of a militant Anglo-Catholicism, but virtually all of it inaccessible to the general reader. They saw the need for something more serviceable, which they described as follows:

> The aim of the present undertaking, as the title indicates, is to act in the capacity of a private tutor, whose duty it is to help the reader over difficult stiles, to furnish him with essentials, to elucidate the subject in a systematic manner, to keep him well abreast of the latest investigations, and throughout to consider his interests as a student.[3]

---

2. C. Neil and J.M. Willoughby (eds), *The Tutorial Prayer Book: For the Teacher, the Student, and the General Reader* (London: The Harrison Trust, 1912).
3. Ibid., p. v.

The Tutorial Prayer Book appeared in 1912 and was an immediate best-seller, with 5,000 copies sold in ten months. A second edition was called for and was published in 1913, happily embracing a number of suggestions that had been made to the authors in the meantime. That edition was periodically reprinted for half a century and is now available once more in a print-on-demand format. Those who know of it find it invaluable but, although its aims have stood the test of time, it must be admitted that much of it is now out of date. The controversies of that era have either disappeared or changed character so much that it is hard for the uninitiated to follow some of their arguments. The Church is no longer torn by debates over the true meaning of the prayer book's rubrics, for example, and, although some notice must be taken of them, they no longer occupy centre stage in the way that they once did.

It also has to be recognised that the 1662 book can no longer be used quite as readily as it was a century ago, even by those who are able to overcome the (greatly exaggerated) barriers of language. Furthermore, what was originally designed for the Church of England cannot be transposed into a worldwide Anglican Communion without some adjustment, nor can the theological and liturgical research of the past century be ignored. One obvious example of the 1662 book's datedness can be seen in its baptismal rites, of which it contains no fewer than three. The first is the rite for the public baptism of infants, the second is one for their private baptism and the third – added almost as an afterthought in 1662 – is for the baptism of those who are 'of riper years'. It was included partly because the upheavals of the English Civil War had left a number of children unbaptised and partly because overseas expansion had led to the conversion of natives in other parts of the world.

Today, the private baptism of infants is discouraged and the public baptism of professing adults has become much more common, even in the lands of historic Christendom. More importantly, though, we now acknowledge that, in theological terms, the baptism of professing believers is primary and that its application to infants must be seen in that light. The 1662 order of priorities has been inverted, not by liturgical revision or advance, but by historical studies that have recovered the practice of the Early Church and made it normative for subsequent generations. Of course, none of this affects the basic doctrine of baptism, which remains unchanged. Much the same can be said for the rest of the prayer book. The underlying message is still the same today but circumstances have often made it necessary (or at least desirable) to present it in a different way.

The basic problem we face is that the 1662 rite has become frozen over time. It is embedded in the law of England and, short of dis-establishment, that situation is unlikely to change. In other parts of the world, conditions are now so different that English usage is no longer appropriate or even possible. This is most obvious in the prayers for the Sovereign and the royal family, which abound in the prayer book but are inapplicable in non-Commonwealth countries, where there are now large numbers of Anglicans. There are also other archaisms that crop up here and there which puzzle the uninitiated and sometimes lead to curious anomalies. Perhaps the most famous of these is the rubric in the service of Holy Communion that requires the celebrant to stand at the 'north end' of the table. This made sense when the table was spread lengthwise down the church but is odd when it is removed to the place traditionally occupied by the medieval altar. Why should the celebrant stand to the left of the table (the 'north end') instead of behind it, facing the congregation (the so-called 'westward' position)? Of course, that is what most celebrants now do; but it is contrary to the strict guidelines of the prayer book and there are still some parishes that adhere to them, even though common sense would recommend otherwise.

In the liturgical controversies of the late nineteenth and early twen-tieth centuries, observances of this kind were matters of contention between the warring parties, with defenders of the 1662 book tending to insist that no change of any kind should be allowed, while others moved progressively away from a modest updating of the text towards something quite new. Nowadays it is safe to say that everybody accepts that some degree of change is overdue, that new prayers and forms of worship should be permitted, and that a certain reordering of the material is desirable. Can this be achieved without disturbing the fundamental principles on which the 1662 book was constructed?

Recently an attempt to do just that has been undertaken in the United States by Samuel Bray and Drew Keane, who have worked in the context of a divided American Anglicanism. They have recognised the central importance of the 1662 Book of Common Prayer for the Church as a whole and have produced an International Edition that is specifically designed to address these difficulties and resolve them.[4] It is still too early to tell whether their effort will succeed. However, they have demonstrated that modest and sensitive revision is possible and that the classical text can be recovered for modern use if it is handled properly. At the very least, they have shown what can be done and paved

---

4. S.L. Bray and D.N. Keane, *The 1662 Book of Common Prayer: International Edition* (Downers Grove, IL: InterVarsity Press, 2021).

the way for others who may want to develop their work further. In the meantime, their achievement has provided the inspiration for a modern guide to the 1662 book that will make it more accessible to our present generation in the way that the authors of *The Tutorial Prayer Book* did for theirs.

In seeking to achieve this aim, this *Companion* follows the order of the 1662 book, beginning with the prefatory material and following that with the daily offices (Morning and Evening Prayer), the order for the Lord's Supper (Holy Communion or the Eucharist), the rites of Christian initiation (baptism, catechism, confirmation), the occasional pastoral services, the accession service and the Ordinal. The last two are not officially part of the Book of Common Prayer but, as they are almost always printed with it, it seems wrong to exclude them.[5] The history of the prayer book at the beginning and the Bibliography at the end are completely new, although older works that are still of value have been included in the latter. It is beyond the scope of any reasonably sized guide to the 1662 book to include all the many liturgical developments that have occurred in the past century or more, especially those that have taken place outside England. Some attention has been given to the more important of them, especially those that impinge on the prayer book in some way, but a comprehensive study of these modern texts must await a different volume.

My thanks for preparing this *Companion* go first to the Latimer Trust, which sponsored the project from the beginning, and to Adrian Brink of James Clarke & Co., who kindly agreed to publish it. I owe a considerable debt to Dorothy Luckhurst, my copy-editor, who corrected a number of errors and made some invaluable suggestions for improving the text. I am also full of admiration for the professionalism of Samuel Fitzgerald, who has seen the volume through the press and greatly improved the style and presentation at numerous points. Finally, I must mention my longsuffering students at Beeson Divinity School, who unconsciously acted as guinea pigs when I was preparing the material and who made me aware of what was needed to make it truly useful to those who love the Prayer Book and want to study it seriously. It is to them – Benjamin Bisgrove, Colby Brandt, Zachary Clemmons, Jacob Collins, Teal Cuellar, Chase Edgar, Eric Henningfeld, Cody Prewitt, Lukas Stock, Jason Varnadore, Jared Willett and Damien Zink – that this *Companion* is dedicated with affection and deep gratitude.

---

5. The accession service is not included in the International Edition.

Chapter 1

History of the Book of Common Prayer

What Is the Book of Common Prayer?

The Book of Common Prayer, or simply the prayer book, is the name given by Anglicans to the principal liturgical resource that they use in the public (and sometimes also in the private) worship of God. As such it is not a single book, but a collection of different volumes that have emerged over time as successive generations and independent Anglican Churches have adapted them for their own use. Having said that, there is a definite family resemblance among them and a genealogy that can be traced back to the first prayer book, which appeared in 1549. Since that time, the book has evolved along different lines, which may be classified as follows:

The mainstream tradition. This encompasses the revision of the 1549 Book of Common Prayer that was undertaken almost immediately and led to a second edition in 1552. Within the Churches of England and Ireland the 1552 prayer book is the direct ancestor of all the subsequent revisions. The first of these occurred in 1559, the second in 1604 and the third in 1662. The 1662 Book of Common Prayer has remained the definitive standard in the Church of England and has been more widely influential in the Anglican world than any other version. In recent years it has come to be recognised as the 'classical' Anglican liturgy that sets the benchmark for all those that have followed. This is particularly important for matters concerning church doctrine, which often depend on the 1662 prayer book for illustration.

The alternative tradition. This also harks back to 1549 but treats it as an independent source of liturgy. One or two features of 1549 were incorporated into the 1559 prayer book, and thus became part of the mainstream tradition, but they did not affect its essential character, which was squarely based on 1552. The first liturgy that effectively bypassed 1552 was the Scottish liturgy of 1637. The 1637 prayer book was stillborn as far as actual use was concerned but elements from it were incorporated into the 1662 rite and it was also used for later Scottish and American liturgies. To this day, the liturgical tradition of the Scottish Episcopal Church and of the American Episcopal Church (with its various offshoots) descends directly from 1549 and is less influenced by 1552/1662 than are the prayer books of most other Anglican Churches, although this independence should not be exaggerated. It is only since 1911 in Scotland, and 1928 in the USA, that the prayer book of the Episcopal Churches in those countries has diverged significantly from the 1662 rite, and that is at least as much the result of modern liturgical studies as it is of any traditional adherence to 1549 or 1637.

The local adaptations. For the most part, these are translations of the 1662 book and/or modifications of it that have been made in the twentieth and twenty-first centuries. In England, 1662 remains the official standard and all subsequent liturgies are supplementary to it. Elsewhere, local Anglican Churches have been able to replace the 1662 book with prayer books of their own but, with few exceptions, these are mainly derived from 1662, which continues to form a backdrop to them.

Until the 1960s liturgical revision in the Anglican world was generally conservative and the 1662 prayer book was familiar, or at least easily recognisable, to the majority of Anglicans worldwide. In the past generation, regular use of the 1662 book has declined dramatically, even in England, where relatively few people now use it as the basis for their daily or weekly worship. Unfortunately, this change has led to a situation in which most Anglicans are no longer at home with one of the basic texts of their tradition, with the result that different branches of the Anglican world have become more distant from one another. The forces of liturgical 'renewal', often ecumenical in nature, combined with theological developments, and even (in some cases) a nationalism disguised as 'contextualisation' or 'indigenisation', have conspired to drive Anglicans away from 1662 and apart from each other. Many congregations have despaired of formal liturgy altogether and have composed their own services which may range from being some variation or combination of an approved rite or rites to a free pattern that may appear to be quite 'non-liturgical'. A simple return to 1662 is no longer possible and probably not desirable either. Modern traditionalists too easily forget that the 1662 prayer book was not universally accepted at the time it was produced, that pressure for revising it continued for some years and that it was largely because of the fear of further division, coupled with inertia, that it survived and dominated the field for as long as it did.

Today the seventeenth-century English attracts some but repels others, creating new fault lines that are difficult to overcome. It is hard to generalise but, on the whole, it seems that those who cling to the older forms of language are less inclined to appreciate the theology that the prayer book articulates, whereas those who would accept the latter in principle want to express it in more contemporary ways. Translated versions of the 1662 book escape this problem to some extent, because they are not bound to the forms of the original. A comparison might be made with something like John Calvin's *Institutes of the Christian Religion*, which is readily available in modern English translations, but not in French ones. This is because Calvin wrote in both Latin and French, which makes it difficult to modernise the latter without running the risk of altering what he originally intended. The result is that French-speakers are forced to read Calvin in sixteenth-century prose, whereas English-speakers can make him our linguistic contemporary. Something analogous to this is also the case with translations of the 1662 prayer book; what sounds archaic to an English-speaker does not come across that way in other languages, which are free to update their translations as and when they wish. This is one reason why versions of the 1662 book used in parts of the developing world do not come across as 'old-fashioned' and the demand for modernisation is not felt as strongly as it can be in the English-speaking world.

Having said that, English remains the working language of the Anglican Communion, which means that the original text retains an influence that it might not otherwise have. This confronts commentators with a particular challenge. It makes no sense to study a modernised version of the 1662 text in detail, especially since the modernisations are not great enough to constitute a different language, but, at the same time, students must be alerted to archaic linguistic phenomena that may interfere with their understanding. This problem is compounded by different levels of education and exposure to the language. Native speakers who have studied classical English literature (like Shakespeare, for example) will not have the same difficulties as those who have not. Those who have mastered English as a second language may be perfectly at home in its modern form but unfamiliar with earlier stages to which they have not been exposed. There is a dilemma here that cannot easily or satisfactorily be resolved in a way that will satisfy everyone. The only practical approach for a companion of this kind is to stick with the original text and explain its difficulties as they arise, proposing alternative forms only when they are clearly necessary. This is not meant to encourage a kind of seventeenth-century fundamentalism that resists all change as a matter of principle, but rather to ensure that such changes as are made retain (as far as possible) the spirit of the original. It is with that aim in view that the present *Companion to the Book of Common Prayer* has been written.

Before the Reformation

The Jewish Legacy

The 1662 prayer book is the heir of a long tradition of worship that goes back to the earliest days of Christianity and, even before that, to the cultic practices of ancient Israel. In very early times devotion to God was associated with the prayers and sacrifices made by prominent individuals, notably, by the patriarchs Abraham, Isaac and Jacob. They bequeathed the memory of their activities to subsequent generations but there was no official pattern of worship that the later Israelites were expected to follow. That did not emerge until the time of Moses and Aaron, respectively, the lawgiver and his elder brother, the high priest, who received detailed instructions from God about how the people should worship him. The bulk of these instructions focussed on what would later, in the time of King Solomon, become the Temple at Jerusalem. The first Temple, built in the tenth century BC, was destroyed by the Babylonians in 586 BC but rebuilt 70 years later. This second Temple became the uncontested centre of the Jewish world until it too was destroyed, this time by the Romans, in AD 70.[1] This was the Temple that we find in the New Testament, where Jesus preached and where his disciples, the first Apostles, worshipped. Even the Apostle Paul went to the Temple when he was in Jerusalem, which shows that that must have been a common practice among Jewish Christians as long as the building survived.[2]

Having said that, it is clear from the New Testament that Temple worship had been superseded by the coming of Christ, who identified

---

1. The Temple was actually completely rebuilt by Herod the Great (40-44 BC) but it is never referred to as the 'third' Temple.
2. Acts 21:26-30.

his body with the Temple and interpreted its rituals as types of his own suffering and atoning death.[3] The destruction of the physical Temple therefore had little direct impact on the Christian Church, which had already incorporated its functions into its own spiritual life. Jesus Christ had combined in his own person the role of both the high priest and the sacrificial victim, thereby making atonement not only for the sins of Israel but for the whole world – past, present and future. What had previously been done once a year in symbolic form was now accomplished once and for all in eternity. There would be no more sacrifice for sin and no further need of a Temple or its priesthood. Instead of that, the Christian Church focussed its worship on remembering what Christ had accomplished and on bringing that home to those who wished to follow him. In this vital respect, Christian worship is quite different from its Jewish predecessor, although that difference has not always been appreciated in the way that it should be.

Many early Christians interpreted the Old Testament less as a historical prelude to the coming of Christ and more as a typological representation of his eternal sacrifice within a time and space framework. That way of thinking made it possible for them to assimilate their own worship to that of the ancient Israelites. As time went on, the Church created its own priesthood which mirrored, if it did not completely replicate, that of Aaron. The parallel was never exact and it took many centuries to develop fully but, by the time of the Reformation, there was a functioning priesthood that was physically distinct from the rest of God's people and that performed the main acts of worship on their behalf.[4] The memorial of Christ's atoning death had evolved into a re-presentation of his sacrifice, made possible by the 'miracle of the altar', which was the transubstantiation of bread and wine into the Lord's body and blood.

In this respect, the New Testament priesthood was considered to be far superior to that of the Old. Whereas the descendants of Aaron were forced to search for spotless lambs that could fulfil the sacrificial demands of the law, Christian priests were able to produce their own sacrifices by consecrating the sacred elements whenever it was necessary to do so. Far from being obliged to concentrate on an annual re-enactment of Christ's death in a single place, they were able to remember him on a daily basis wherever there was a venue suitable

---

3. John 2:19-22.

4. The Old Testament priesthood was vested in the tribe of Levi and inherited; but its New Testament replacement was sworn to celibacy.

for the purpose. Interestingly, this did not diminish the sense of mystery that surrounded the ancient Temple rites but intensified it, by bringing the 'miracle' closer to the people and making it more readily available to them. However, equally important, this diffusion of the sacred did not necessarily bring Christians any closer to God. Many of them felt unworthy to partake of so great a blessing and actual Communion was usually much less frequent than it should have been. Leaving aside the priests themselves, most laymen partook of the sacrament only a few times a year at most. The Church tried to make Christmas, Easter and Pentecost (Whitsun) occasions when Communion was expected but, although they had some success with that, it was a far cry from the regular (weekly?) celebrations that we find in the New Testament.

The Reformers wanted to recover a sense of worship as the work of the whole people of God, rooted in the Old Testament as it had been fulfilled and superseded in Christ. That did not mean abandoning the Old Testament as Scripture, rather reinterpreting it in the light of the new covenant. Instead of concentrating on the ceremonial aspects of Israelite worship, which had been abolished by the coming of Christ, their focus was on the law and the prophets. The law was the moral and spiritual standard that God expected of his people, which was more important than ritual acts and even independent of them. The Old Testament is full of warnings about hypocrisy in worship and about priests who betrayed their calling by their inconsistent behaviour. That did not invalidate what they did in the Temple and elsewhere but placed it in context. The prophets reminded the people (and the priests if they were listening) what God required of them and pointed out that it was impossible to rise to His standards separately from repentance and the grace that would accompany that. If the Lord did not build the house, those who laboured at trying to build it were wasting their energy.[5]

It is essential to understand how the Reformers viewed the Old Testament if we are to appreciate the use they made of it in composing the prayer book. On the one hand, in the liturgy of the Lord's Supper they were extremely careful to emphasise the once-and-for-all sacrifice that Christ made on the Cross and that was not in any way re-presented or repeated in the Communion service. On the other hand, it explains their inclusion of the Ten Commandments, not in the shorter form known as our Lord's summary of the law but in the full text of Exodus 20:2-17, as well as their extensive use of prophetic texts in the call to worship at the beginning of the daily offices. Of the eleven Bible verses given

---

5. See Psalm 127:1.

there, three come from the prophets (Ezekiel 18:27, Joel 2:13 and Daniel 9:9-10), four from the Psalms (51:3, 51:9, 51:17 and 143:2) and one from both Jeremiah 10:24 and Psalm 6:1. By contrast, only three are taken from the New Testament.[6]

The range of prophets cited reveals the importance that the Reformers attached to their oracles. However, there can be no doubt that the psalter claims pride of place in the prayer book's use of the Old Testament. Many of the suffrages (or intercessory petitions) in the daily offices are taken from it; and the entire psalter itself was assigned for monthly reading, a great increase on what had gone before. The Psalms had always been popular; but it was not until 1549 that they were included in full in daily worship and regulated in a way that provided for such frequent repetition. In earlier times the psalter had been used selectively and often thematically, and that tradition was not wholly eclipsed in the prayer book, as we can see from the inclusion of Psalm 95 in Morning Prayer and of Psalm 100 as an alternative canticle in Evening Prayer. However, what had been eclectic before 1549 now became systematic. Why?

The psalter was the song book of ancient Israel and of the Early Church. Frequent quotations from it in the New Testament attest to its familiarity. It stands out among the books of the Hebrew Bible for the way in which it expresses the entire range of human emotion in the worship of God. Many Christian commentators claimed that it was the voice of the incarnate Christ, who took on human flesh in all its dimensions, and that, in singing it, worshippers were uniting themselves with him. There is some justification for this in the way that Jesus used Psalm 22 on the Cross but this does not seem to have been the main motivation for the Reformers. What they wanted was to expose the Church to what they called 'the whole counsel of God', revealed in the Scriptures but put into the mouths of God's people in the Psalms. Only by becoming familiar with all of them would it be possible to absorb the fullness of the divine revelation, and this was the Reformers' guiding principle. So successful were they in this aim that in later revisions of the prayer book there was popular resistance to updating the psalter by providing a more accurate translation, such as was done with the Epistles and Gospels read on Sundays and holy days. Even in modern times, the pattern of the monthly reading of the Psalms and the desire to retain as much of the original translation as possible can still be felt in the prayer books

---

6. Matthew 3:2, Luke 15:18-19 and 1 John 1:8-9.

that have supplemented and in places superseded the traditional Book of Common Prayer.[7]

The Early Church

The influence of the New Testament on the composition of the prayer book is most obvious in the Epistles and Gospels mentioned above and there is a tendency to present the biblical texts in some kind of order, particularly in the Sundays after Trinity that occupy roughly half the year. Portions of the Pauline Epistles from Romans to Colossians are read consecutively, and there are generous selections from Matthew, which was traditionally regarded as the first of the Gospels to have been written. By contrast, there is almost nothing from Mark, though both Luke and John are well represented. The Acts of the Apostles are also frequently found in lieu of an Epistle, and there are some selections from Revelation, though very few from Hebrews, which is surprising, given the liturgical relevance of that Epistle. These gaps were made up for in the lectionary, which covered almost all of the New Testament, but few ordinary worshippers would have been exposed to it because they did not attend church on a daily basis.

The most obvious use of the New Testament occurs in the institution narrative of the Lord's Supper, where a large part of 1 Corinthians 11, along with passages from the Gospels, are incorporated more or less *verbatim*. The canticles in Luke's Gospel also find a place in the daily offices, with the *Magnificat* and the *Nunc dimittis* being provided at Evening Prayer. By far the most frequently used New Testament text is the Lord's Prayer, which occurs, sometimes more than once (both with and without the doxology) in virtually every service in the prayer book. It is the ultimate call to prayer and reflects the petition of Jesus' disciples, who are recorded as having asked him how they should pray. In response, Jesus is said to have given them the prayer that we now use, though there is some indication from the shorter alternative found in Luke 11:2-4 that the Matthaean text represents a developed form designed for liturgical purposes. The presence of this version, complete with the doxology, in the *Didache*, a very early Christian manual that is almost contemporary with the apostles, reinforces that view.[8] Whether Jesus himself elaborated it, or whether his disciples put it together from

---

7. Some modern prayer books have replaced (or supplemented) the 30-day cycle with a 60-day one, but the principle remains the same.

8. *Didache* 8:2.

his words we cannot say but, either way, the Lord's Prayer brings us as close to his teaching on prayer as we are able to get.

How far the pattern of worship of the earliest Christian communities foreshadowed liturgical developments in later times is impossible to determine, because concrete evidence is lacking. The Reformers wanted to be as 'biblical' as possible but they had little to go on beyond some basic principles. These included regular meeting for worship, the celebration of the Lord's Supper, the singing of Psalms and prayer, much of which seems to have been *ex tempore*. Within those parameters there would have been a fair degree of uniformity across the Church, but the guidelines are so general that it is unlikely that there was anything resembling a standard form of service of the kind that we would recognise today.

We know that the Early Church had a trinitarian pattern of questions that were asked of candidates for baptism and examples of these have been preserved from many different places. It is often thought that there is a relationship between these baptismal questions and the creeds, in particular the so-called Apostles' Creed, embryonic forms of which can be traced as far back as the late second and early third centuries. The Apostles' Creed is included in the daily offices in the prayer book, but this is because it found its way there in the time of Charlemagne (747-814) by which time its original connection with baptism had been forgotten.

Here we come up against a phenomenon that characterises the Book of Common Prayer and that must be understood if its relationship to the Early Church is to be properly appreciated. It was the boast of many leading Anglo-Catholic liturgists in the nineteenth century that the Book of Common Prayer contains prayers and other liturgical elements that go back to earliest times, and in a sense that is true. However, the relationship between the origin of a prayer and its later use is not always what it might appear to be on the surface. Just as it is possible to find stonework in houses and other buildings that was taken from medieval monasteries when the latter were dissolved, so we can detect elements from the pre-Reformation Church that have been incorporated into the prayer book, though often in ways that bear little resemblance to their sources. Sometimes, as with the Apostles' Creed, the Reformers simply continued earlier practices without enquiring too deeply into their provenance, of which both they and their contemporaries were largely ignorant. On other occasions, they quarried from the rich resources of medieval times, often modifying and reshaping their material to suit their own purposes. We must not be surprised that they did so, since people tend to work with what they have to hand, but neither should we be misled, as some of the early Anglo-Catholics were, into positing a continuity with the pre-Reformation Church that is more apparent than real.

On the whole, the Reformers were glad when they found evidence in the Early Church for what they believed – but they did not hesitate to ignore or discard what did not fit their agenda. Devotion to ancient forms of the kind that might nowadays be called 'patristic fundamentalism' is a modern phenomenon that was largely unknown to them, despite their eagerness to probe the sources of Christian teaching and practice. Their only canonical authority was the Holy Scriptures and anything that could not be found in them, or justified by them, could freely be dismissed or altered on the ground that it had fallen away from the pure standards of God's revelation. This observation is particularly pertinent because much of the criticism that has been levelled against the prayer book in recent times has concentrated on the evidence of early liturgies that modern enthusiasts have promoted as being somehow more 'authentic' than the sources used by the Reformers.

Thomas Cranmer (1489-1556) and his contemporaries were aware of many of these ancient liturgies and, like others in the sixteenth century, they took them at face value. Thus, we find that Cranmer borrowed a prayer from the liturgy of St Chrysostom, which is still the one most frequently used in the Eastern Orthodox Churches today. He put it at the end of the litany and later on it was added to both Morning and Evening Prayer as well. John Chrysostom (347-407) was a great preacher and teacher in his day, who paid with his life for his opposition to the emperor and his court. He was very popular with the Reformers, who saw him as a model for their own ministries; and it may be for that reason that Cranmer was inclined to borrow from him. Today, however, we know that the liturgy that bears his name was a later composition and we also know that the same prayer can be found in the less well-known liturgy of St Basil, which almost certainly was composed by Basil of Caesarea (329-79) and may therefore have been known to Chrysostom. In other words, the material itself is ancient but the prayer book's attribution of it to John is misleading.

Complexities of this kind abound when studying ancient liturgies and great caution is required before making pronouncements about them. Eighteenth-century critics of the prayer book relied heavily on the so-called Clementine liturgy, supposedly composed by Clement of Rome before AD 100 and transmitted to us in the eighth book of the *Apostolic Constitutions*, which claim a similarly primitive origin. We now know that this is false and that the material in question has heretical tendencies associated with fourth-century Arianism, but this knowledge did not stop it from having an influence on early revisions of the prayer book. Similarly, in more recent times, some liturgists have made great play of the so-called *Apostolic Tradition*, which they attributed to Hippolytus of Rome (early third century), although this theory is now hotly contested and rejected by most mainstream scholars. However, as with the *Apostolic Constitutions* before it, 'Hippolytus' has been allowed to influence modern liturgical revision to an extraordinary degree and it is difficult to undo that now. The sixteenth-century Reformers, motivated (as they were) more by theological than by historical or liturgical criteria, were largely spared such embarrassments and their ignorance of such 'facts' meant that they influenced their compositions far less than might have been the case had they adopted the 'patristic fundamentalism' of more recent times.

The Middle Ages

With the adoption of Christianity as the official religion of the Roman Empire in the late fourth century, the rather free and often informal patterns of worship that had been common up to then gave way to increasingly elaborate and public ceremonial. The liturgy of St Basil was an example of this but there were many others. Not surprisingly, the forms adopted in the major centres – Constantinople, Alexandria, Antioch and Rome – exercised considerable influence in their respective regions and were often seen as models to be imitated. The Roman rite, in particular, enjoyed a prestige in the West that was unmatched and it gradually superseded more local usages. When Augustine of Canterbury went to England in 597, he must have taken Roman customs with him but he was not expected to impose them on the newly formed English Church. The historian Bede tells us that Augustine did not know what form of public worship to adopt and that he wrote to Pope Gregory I (590-604) for advice on the subject. Far from telling Augustine to be content with the Roman order, Gregory advised him to look around and take the best from different Churches in order to produce a new and satisfactory rite for the English.[9]

Whether Augustine actually did that is unclear but we do know that, as the evangelisation of the country progressed, the Roman mission came into conflict with Celtic customs that had survived and developed independently in the centuries after the withdrawal of the

---

9. Bede, *Ecclesiastical History of the English People*, 1.27.

Roman legions from Britain in 410. The English Church had to resolve the issue in order to maintain its inner cohesion and, at the synod of Whitby in 664, it opted for Rome. Not everybody acquiesced in that decision immediately, and some of the Celtic Churches retained their customs for up to a century or more afterwards, but the direction of travel was clear and by 800 the Roman tradition was dominant virtually everywhere, not only in the British Isles but across Western Europe.

However, if Roman customs triumphed in general terms, the rite itself was modified and adapted to local needs. Spain, in particular, developed traditions of its own, some of which have come down to us in the so-called Mozarabic rite. Within the English Church there were many different rites, or uses as they are generally known, which developed in different places.[10] Over time some of the smaller dioceses adopted the use of another cathedral church but, even as late as the sixteenth century, complete uniformity had not been attained. Thomas Cranmer recorded in his preface to the 1549 prayer book that there were at least five uses known to him – those of Salisbury (Sarum), Hereford, Bangor, Lincoln and York.[11]

Of these, the uses of Hereford, Lincoln and York are well attested but, as time went on, it was Salisbury use, better known to us as the Sarum rite, that became something of a standard for England as a whole. The English cathedrals were evenly divided between monastic and secular foundations, and some historians have assumed that the former provided the pattern for the latter. However, all five of the cathedrals listed by Cranmer were secular, so that theory must be abandoned. York was the metropolitan see of the northern province but it was the only secular cathedral in the north and its influence did not spread much beyond its own diocese. In the southern province of Canterbury, we know of uses from Exeter and London (both secular cathedrals), in addition to Hereford, Lincoln and Salisbury. The London use seems to have been somewhat idiosyncratic and largely confined to St Paul's. Lincoln was the largest English diocese and might be thought to have wielded more influence than it did, but Hereford and Exeter were both relatively remote. Of the other secular English cathedrals, there is some evidence for a use of Wells, which was part of the mixed diocese of Bath

---

10. 'Rite' and 'use' can be used more or less interchangeably, as they are here, though technically speaking, 'rite' has a wider application, being sometimes employed to designate particular services, whereas 'use' is restricted to the overall pattern found in a particular place.
11. This preface is printed in the 1662 prayer book as 'Concerning the Service of the Church'.

and Wells, but none for Lichfield (also a mixed diocese, combined with Coventry) or Chichester.[12] The Welsh dioceses were something of an anomaly, although Cranmer knew of a use of Bangor, which remains unidentified and may never have existed as such.[13]

Salisbury was not a particularly prominent diocese, however from its foundation in 1075 it was ruled by some gifted bishops who took a real interest in the structure of public worship. It seems to have been that, more than anything else, that led to the later prominence of its liturgy. Rightly or wrongly, most medieval English churchmen came to see the Sarum rite as superior to the others and, by the time printing was invented, its dominance was assured. It was not until 2 March 1543 that it was formally imposed on the province of Canterbury as a uniform pattern of worship but, by then, it had effectively attained that status on its own. Certainly, as far as the Book of Common Prayer is concerned, it is the Sarum rite that was its principal pre-Reformation antecedent and it must be read in that light.

The development and spread of more carefully defined uses depended to a large degree on the books that were produced to disseminate them. It was impractical, if not entirely impossible, for all the liturgical materials needed for public worship to be contained within a single volume and so, from a very early time, they were spread across several more manageable books, of which each individual church would possess a collection. The individual volumes were arranged thematically as follows:

1. The **missal**. This consisted of what were originally five separate books, all of which focussed on the celebration of the Mass or Lord's Supper. Its constituent parts were:

    a. the sacramentary (*sacramentarium*), which contained the canon of the Mass, the collects and whatever was said by the celebrant. It formed the core of the missal, which developed over time by the addition of supplementary material. The sacramentary also contained material proper to Sundays, Wednesdays and Fridays (the *temporale*) and also for saints' days (the *sanctorale*). (See below.)

---

12. 'Mixed' because Bath and Coventry were monastic foundations, whereas Wells and Lichfield were secular ones.
13. For the history of medieval English uses, see R.W. Pfaff, *The Liturgy in Medieval England: A History* (Cambridge: Cambridge University Press, 2009).

b. the epistle-book (*lectionarium*), which was given to the subdeacon, who read the Scripture passages selected for the Epistle of the Sunday or holy day.

c. the gospel-book (*evangelium*), given to the deacon to read, which contained the gospel lessons that were co-ordinated with the collect and Epistle of the day.

d. the gradual (*graduale*), also known as the *antiphonarium Missae* or as the *cantatorium*, which was given to the choir and contained the scriptural parts of the Mass.

e. the troper (*troparium*), which included the non-scriptural parts of the Mass and was also given to the choir. As time went on, there was a tendency to put material from the troper into the gradual.

f. the sequencer (*sequentiarium*), which contained versicles and responses sung by the choir. Over time, the sequencer was often merged with the troper.

Beyond these basic elements, missals varied enormously in their contents. They often included prayers and services that were used in a particular monastery or even by private individuals who owned them. Only with the invention of printing was there a drive towards standardisation but that was never achieved in the medieval period.

2. The **breviary**, also known as the *portiforium* or *portuis* when produced in a portable format, and as the 'coucher' when made for the lectern in a church.[14] It contained the material used for the daily offices or canonical hours, which were said at different times of the day. The first three (Nocturns, Matins and Lauds) came early in the morning and over time tended to be combined as a single service. Then came the hours of Prime (first), Terce (third), Sext (sixth) and None (ninth), calculated according to the solar clock. Finally, in the evening there were Vespers and Compline, the former used at sunset and the latter just before bedtime. Like the missal, the breviary was also composed of distinct elements:

a. the psalter, containing the Psalms and canticles

b. the legend, or *legendarium*, containing the Biblical passages, homilies and hagiographies that were read as lessons

14. 'Coucher' from the French *coucher* ('to lay down').

     c. the antiphonal, containing the musical elements of the services
     d. the hymnal, usually contained within the antiphonal
     e. the collectar, containing Scripture verses and the collects which were said by the main officiant
     f. the ordinal, which was essentially an index to the component parts of the breviary[15]
     g. the consuetudinary, which set out the ceremonial and allocated the duties of the various ministers in the service
     h. the 'pie', or perpetual calendar, also called the *directorium*, which provided for all the variants made possible by the shifting dates of the Easter cycle.[16]

3. The **manual**, sometimes called the sacerdotal or the ritual.[17] This contained the occasional offices, like baptism, matrimony and burial, which were reserved for the priest. Some manuals also included confirmation and the canon of the Mass for convenience.

4. The **pontifical**, also called the benedictional. This contained the services reserved for the bishop, like ordinations, confirmation, the consecration of churches and various episcopal blessings.

5. The **processional**. This contained material used in processions and was made up of liturgical elements taken from elsewhere. For that reason, processionals were not really required and often other liturgical books were used instead.

    Within these main groupings another distinction must be observed. The missal, the breviary and the processional (in particular) were subdivided into 'permanent' parts and 'variable' ones. The permanent parts, which were usually put in the middle of the book in question, were those parts of the service that did not change. The variable parts, which were usually placed either at the beginning or at the end (or both), were of three types:

---

15. This ordinal must not be confused with the Ordinal that contains ordination services performed by a bishop. They were included in the pontifical (see below).
16. 'Pie' was a nickname (from 'magpie'), adopted because the book was printed in black and white and not in red.
17. In Continental Europe it was called the *agenda*.

a. the variants related to the different seasons of the church year, known as the *propria de tempore* or *temporale*
b. the variants required for saints' days, the *propria de sanctis* or *sanctorale*
c. the variants used for particular types of saints (apostles, martyrs etc.) and sometimes also for little known saints, which were common to their group, the *communia sanctorum* (in the plural) or *commune sanctorum* (in the singular).

Occasionally, variables that we might think belong in one of these groupings are in fact found in another. This is true, for example, of the saints' days commemorated between Christmas and the Epiphany, which are normally placed in the *temporale* and not (as one might expect) in the *sanctorale*. There was also some confusion regarding St Andrew's Day (30 November) because it could fall before, on or after the first Sunday in Advent, which was the start of the Church's year. It was normally placed at the beginning of the *sanctorale*, however, a custom that is followed in the prayer book.

Over time there appeared another set of books intended mainly for the laity. Prominent among them were psalters, often accompanied by canticles, the creeds, the Lord's Prayer and the *Gloria* as appendices. These expanded as time went on to include private devotions to the Virgin Mary, the litany, the different services for the dead (like the *Placebo* and the *Dirige*) and so on. When these became too numerous to be included in a single book, they were split off from the psalter and published separately as *horae* ('hours'), which came to be referred to as the primer.[18] Primers appeared in Latin in the thirteenth century and in English from the fourteenth century onwards. They included selections of Psalms that were used for particular purposes or on particular occasions, and it was from them that most lay people became familiar with the psalter.

To get a sense of how widespread these books were and how dominant the Sarum rite became in the province of Canterbury, we may consider the figures for printed texts that appeared between 1479 and 1549:[19]

---

18. Pronounced as 'primmer', not as 'prime'.
19. The figures are those given by G.J. Cuming, *A History of Anglican Liturgy*, 2nd edn (London: Macmillan, 1982), p. 14. The other uses were never printed.

	Sarum	York	Hereford
Missal	51	5	1
Breviary	42	5	1
Manual	13	2	0
Processional	11	1	0
Ordinal (pontifical)	4	1	0
Primer	184	5	0
Total	305	19	2

The Book of Common Prayer contains elements of four of the five service books (all but the processional) in a single volume that was greatly simplified. The order of presentation is that the breviary comes first (the daily offices), followed by the missal (the collects, Epistles and Gospels as well as the canon of the Lord's Supper) and the manual (the occasional offices, apart from confirmation, which was in the pontifical). The modern Ordinal, which was also derived from the pontifical, was not part of the 1549 prayer book and remained distinct even in 1662, though it is now always printed with the prayer book and may be regarded as part of it for practical purposes. The primers also exerted a certain influence on the Book of Common Prayer, especially in the matter of translation, because it was in them that the first English-language liturgical texts appeared.

It must always be remembered that, while the pattern of service books was common to the Western Church as a whole, the details the books contained varied considerably from place to place. This was even more true of the primers, which did not acquire a settled form in England until Henry VIII authorised one in 1545, only a few years before the 1549 book appeared.[20] Convergence was fostered for many different reasons but uniformity only came after the Reformation. It was obviously more convenient for travelling clergy to be familiar with the forms of worship they would be likely to meet in different places;

---

20. See E. Burton, *Three Primers Put Forth in the Reign of Henry VIII* (Oxford: Oxford University Press, 1834). This volume contains the texts of *A Goodly Prymer*, first published in 1535, *The Manual of Prayers, or the Prymer in English*, 1539, and *King Henry's Primer*, 1545. On the history of the primers, see C.C. Butterworth, *The English Primers (1529-1545): Their Publication and Connection with the English Bible and the Reformation in England* (Philadelphia: University of Pennsylvania Press, 1953).

and the invention of printing made widespread diffusion of identical materials possible for the first time. Ecclesiastical provinces could further their internal unity and cohesion by adopting a common use and, by logical extension, it could be assumed that eventually the whole of the Western Church would coalesce around a single form, perhaps with minor local variants.

It was the Reformation that completed the drive towards uniformity, although in a way that could hardly have been envisaged around 1500 or so. The emergence of different confessions that held sway in different areas made it necessary to define matters of doctrine and practice to a degree that had not previously been necessary. Deviation from the standard could easily be seen as heresy, or at least as rejection of the ecclesiastical settlement in a given territory. Churches had to ensure that their personnel were singing from the same hymn sheet, as we might say today, which meant that they had to be carefully examined for their beliefs and practice. Examination also implied a norm by which success could be measured and so uniformity became a matter of necessity. This was true of the Roman Catholic Church just as much as it was of any Protestant body. The Council of Trent (1545-63), summoned to rescue the Church from the various dissenters that assailed it, managed to produce a liturgical pattern that would remain intact for 400 years. The Tridentine Mass would become the hallmark of Roman Catholicism and its uniformity was accentuated by the fact that it had to be celebrated in Latin, even though that language was no longer anyone's mother tongue.

Rome moved quickly and with considerable success, given the challenges of the time. The Protestant Churches could not stabilise their liturgies as quickly as that, not least because those involved were translators, and even innovators. They had to find ways of expressing a new theological outlook that would not compromise their principles but, at the same time, that would not alienate congregations that had become accustomed to traditional ways. The Church of England managed to produce reasonably unified forms of service in only a decade (1549-59) but it would be a century more before that pattern settled down into what would become its classical form. Even then, the result was still called into question; and it would not be until the very end of the seventeenth century that the Book of Common Prayer as we know it would be accepted by the majority of English people and regarded as a heritage to be defended rather than as an innovation to be resisted or replaced.

The Sarum Rite

For most practical purposes, the pre-Reformation inheritance of the prayer book is contained in the Sarum rite, more than anywhere else. In some respects, like the use of the collects, Epistles and Gospels, the Book of Common Prayer is little more than a translation of Sarum. Elsewhere, it departs from its predecessor to a greater or lesser extent, but Thomas Cranmer and his colleagues were immersed in it, used it daily and had recourse to it on any number of occasions. That does not mean that the prayer book is just an English-language version of Sarum – in many important respects it is an entirely new liturgy. However, echoes of Sarum are never far away and, if we are to appreciate the prayer book properly, we must recognise the importance of its predecessor and understand both how it continues the ancient tradition and how it supersedes it.

The first thing that we must grasp is that the Sarum rite is essentially medieval, that is to say, pre-Reformation, in concept and in content. There was much in the medieval tradition that the Reformers found congenial and wished to preserve but their fundamental theological vision was something new, and simply translating the Latin liturgy into English was never an option for them.

The second thing we must realise is that the Sarum rite was not the composition of one man, as the 1549 prayer book was; rather, it was a collection of prayers and liturgical elements that came from a great variety of sources that had been put together for use in the cathedral church of Salisbury. There is very little in it that can be said to be original and it is possible, even probable, that parts of it were derived from sources that are no longer known to us. That does not diminish the status of Sarum as a use in its own right, because the pattern of composition is just as important as its content, but it puts the text in a wider context of interrelationships that were not carried over into the Book of Common Prayer.

The cathedral church of Salisbury, which was transferred from its original site at what is now known as Old Sarum to its present location around 1225, was singularly fortunate in the quality of its clergy and bishops and, in particular, Richard Poore, who is usually credited with having put the finishing touches on a rite that was already well advanced in formation.[21] Bishop Poore had an organised mind, which

---

21. See Pfaff, *Liturgy*, pp. 350-87, 412-44, for the history of the Sarum Use. Richard Poore was Dean of Salisbury (1197-1215) and then Bishop

gave his church a solid reputation for piety and efficiency among his contemporaries. The canons that he devised for the church were widely used as a benchmark for resolving controversial questions, and this reputation lasted into the sixteenth century. However, to what extent was Poore responsible for the use of Sarum as we now know it?

This question is extremely difficult to answer and matters have not been helped by the inadequacies of the main editions of the text. The first of these was by F.H. Dickinson and appeared in a series of fascicles between 1861 and 1885. It was based on the printed texts of the Sarum missal that appeared immediately before the Reformation and is therefore of little value for determining the earlier stages of the rite.[22] Even before Dickinson's work was complete, Henry Bradshaw approached J.W. Legg with the suggestion that Legg might produce an edition based on manuscript sources, which he eventually did.[23] However, the manuscripts Legg used were relatively late, having been written around 1300, or two generations after the move from Old to New Sarum, and so do not reflect the earliest stages of the rite, even if they undoubtedly contain much ancient material. W.H. Frere had rather better luck with his edition of the Sarum gradual, based on a manuscript that may go back to the early thirteenth century, but it is still not clear to what stage of the Sarum rite's evolution it really belongs.[24] More recently, the detailed research of R.W. Pfaff has shown that the Sarum rite has roots that go back at least as far as the mid-twelfth century, and possibly even to the founding of the see in 1075.[25] Nevertheless, why Sarum should have ousted its potential rivals remains unexplained. As Pfaff concluded:

> There seems to be no intrinsic reason why it is at Sarum, rather than Lincoln or London, that the most highly organized set of liturgical usages developed. ... But by the time of the close imitation, indeed almost adoption, of Sarum patterns at Exeter in 1337 something approaching a liturgical codification has

---

(1217-28). It was he who oversaw the move from Old to New Sarum. He was translated to Durham in 1228 and died there in 1237.

22. F.H. Dickinson, *Missale ad usum insignis et praeclarae ecclesiae Sarum* (Burntisland: Pitsligo Press, 1861-83).

23. J.W. Legg, *The Sarum Missal: Edited from Three Early Manuscripts* (Oxford: Oxford University Press, 1916).

24. W.H. Frere, *Graduale Sarisburiense: A Reproduction in Facsimile of a Manuscript of the Thirteenth Century*, 2 vols (London: Plainsong and Medieval Music Society, 1891-94).

25. Pfaff, *Liturgy*, pp. 363-64.

occurred, one for which the term 'Sarum Use' had for some time been widespread.[26]

If evidence for the antiquity of the Sarum missal is difficult to find, that for the breviary and other office books is virtually impossible. The extant texts are all late in date and have been so overlaid with additions made at various times that they are almost unreadable. The standard edition of the Sarum breviary is so complex that few people were able to use it profitably, and modern attempts to sort out the confusion are not much better.[27] In the absence of a reliable and readily comprehensible guide to the daily offices of Sarum, it is extremely difficult to decide how they were said or sung in practice, although Thomas Cranmer's remark that 'to turn the Book only was so hard and intricate a matter, that many times there was more business to find out what should be read, than to read it when it was found out' gives us some idea of the confusion that must have reigned in many places.[28]

The complexities of the service books was compounded by the way that they were constantly being added to, with new saints' days and other commemorations, the number of which mushroomed in the fifteenth century. By 1500 it was becoming apparent that the liturgy was in danger of sinking under its own weight. So problematic did this become that many clergy had recourse to the *directorium* (popularly known as the 'Pie'), which aimed to provide celebrants with some guidance in conducting services.[29] The simplification that the Reformation brought must have been greeted by many with a huge sigh of relief and, although there was some nostalgia for the old ways after they were abolished, few people showed the kind of attachment to the use of Sarum that the Book of Common Prayer would attract after it was abolished by the Puritans in 1645. To put it simply, if Sarum was a burden to the religious professionals who were the only ones who really used it, how

---

26. Ibid., p. 364.
27. See ibid., pp. 423-42. The classic edition is that of F. Procter and C. Wordsworth, *Breviarium ad usum insignis ecclesiae Sarum*, 3 vols (Cambridge: Cambridge University Press, 1879-86).
28. Cranmer's remark is in 'Concerning the Service of the Church', the preface to the 1549 prayer book. Modern students may well say much the same about the Alternative Service Book 1980 and *Common Worship* 2000, not to mention other similar liturgical books elsewhere, which offer so many options and alternatives that the human body lacks the fingers necessary to hold all the places required.
29. Pfaff, *Liturgy*, pp. 427-28.

much more cumbersome would it have been to lay people who had no special training in liturgy and who would have been lost almost before they had begun? If England was to have a common prayer, known to the laity as well as to the clergy, simplification was essential, and that would inevitably spell the death of the use of Sarum, along with the medieval complexity that it exemplified.

When we examine the contents of the Sarum rite, we soon discover that almost all of it can be traced to earlier sources. This should surprise nobody. Originality was not regarded as a virtue in medieval times, nor was borrowing from other sources thought of as plagiarism. Liturgists were free to adopt (and adapt) whatever they could find, and they did so. In the case of Sarum, the compilers were particularly indebted to sacramentaries that were mainly of Roman or Gallican origin. There was no hard and fast line drawn between these two sources and some elements turn up in each. Gallican collects tend to be more loosely structured than Roman ones, and closer to Eastern models, but this is a tendency rather than a rule and too much should not be made of it. The Gallican rites were in fact older than the Roman one, which infiltrated and eventually replaced them.

A key moment in the evolution of medieval Western liturgy came during the reign of Charlemagne (768-814). Charlemagne sponsored a revival of learning that included a wholesale revamping of public worship. He asked Pope Hadrian I (772-95) for a copy of the sacramentary then in use at Rome; and Hadrian responded by sending him a text that he claimed had been composed by Gregory I 'the Great'. This proved to be inadequate, so a supplement was added by Benedict of Aniane (747-821), after whom it is now named. Originally, this appendix was distinguished by a preface indicating its secondary nature but, over time, that preface disappeared and the two parts of the sacramentary merged into one. This is what we now know as the Gregorian sacramentary and it was a major source of material for the Sarum rite.[30] There were, however, earlier sacramentaries in existence which were also known to Charlemagne's scholars. One of these, which contains a number of Gallican features, was attributed to Pope Gelasius I (492-96), though much of the material

---

30. It has been comprehensively edited by J. Deshusses, *Le Sacramentaire grégorien: Ses Principales formes d'après les plus anciens manuscrits*, 3 vols (Fribourg: Presses Universitaires de Fribourg, 1971-82). See also an older edition, H.A. Wilson (ed.), *The Gregorian Sacramentary under Charles the Great* (London: Harrison & Son, 1915; repr. Forgotten Books, 2012).

in it comes from a later time.[31] Another was the so-called Leonine sacramentary, attributed to Pope Leo I (440-61) but for the most part coming from other fifth- or sixth-century sources.[32] Both of these can be found alongside the Gregorian sacramentary in the Sarum rite and so have entered into the inheritance of the Book of Common Prayer.

The Reformation Era

The Henrician Reformation

When Martin Luther (1483-1546) posted his *Ninety-five Theses* on the door of the university church at Wittenberg on 31 October 1517, he lit a spark that burst into flame all across Western Europe. His initial protest was against the sale of indulgences, which had recently increased to scandalous proportions in Germany, and he attracted considerable sympathy from people who sensed that something was seriously wrong with the Church. Before long, the revolt against the prevailing establishment touched on the sacramental system that undergirded the medieval Church, and it was that aspect that attracted the attention of King Henry VIII of England. In 1521 Henry wrote a rejoinder to Luther called the *Assertio septem sacramentorum* in which he defended what had become traditional Catholic practice. He dealt with all seven of the recognised sacraments but concentrated on the Lord's Supper, which he rightly saw as the centrepiece of the entire system. This inevitably led him to focus on public worship, though it would be some time before the logic of his argument – that theological change would revolutionise devotional practice – would have a serious effect in England.[33]

There were several reasons for this. One was that much of the previous century had been spent in trying to suppress the Lollards, followers of John Wyclif (1328-84) who in some respects were forerunners of the Reformation. They had had considerable influence in Bohemia, whence some of their ideas had filtered into Germany and influenced Luther,

---

31. H.A. Wilson (ed.), *The Gelasian Sacramentary: Liber sacramentorum Romanae ecclesiae* (Oxford: Clarendon Press, 1894; repr. Forgotten Books, 2018).

32. C.L. Feltoe (ed.), *Sacramentarium Leonianum* (Cambridge: Cambridge University Press, 1896).

33. Henry VIII Fid. Def., *His Defence of the Faith and Its Seven Sacraments* (Sevenoaks: Ducketts Booksellers/Fisher Press, 2008). This is a reprint of the 1523 Latin text with an English translation and modern introduction by R. Rex.

a point that Henry VIII recognised in his polemic. The result of anti-Lollard persecution was that it was made illegal to translate the Bible into the vernacular, as the Wycliffites had done, which meant that access to the Scriptures in English was one of the earliest and most insistent demands of would-be Reformers. William Tyndale (1494-1536) began his translation work around the same time that Henry VIII wrote his *Assertio*, but he was forced to flee the country and published his English New Testament in Germany (in 1525). It would be another ten years before the complete Bible appeared in English and it was not until 1538, after England had broken with the papacy, that official permission would be given to print and distribute it.

The work of Bible translation would go on until 1611, when the King James (Authorised) Version (KJV) was finally published, but from the start the English Bible was to play a major role in liturgical revision. It was not just that, once an English translation became widely available, it was inevitable that it would be used when reading the scriptural passages in the lectionary. The style of the text became the model for religious language generally and, when the liturgy was finally translated, it was that style that would predominate. This tendency was reinforced by the desire of the Reformers to make as much use of the Scriptures in worship as they could. Prayers were suffused with biblical references and imagery. The psalter, translated by Miles Coverdale in his Bible of 1535, became the standard text used in the prayer book, with only a few very minor alterations. So popular would Coverdale's version become that it survived every subsequent revision and was incorporated more or less as it stood into the 1662 service book. Even today, it retains its attraction for many, and modern versions of the liturgical psalter often try to incorporate as much of Coverdale as they can.

The break with Rome in 1534 encouraged this development but added another dimension to it – the possibility of doctrinal change. This had a limited effect on translations of the Bible, being largely confined to choices of translation – 'church' *versus* 'congregation', for example, or 'elder' *versus* 'priest' – though these choices would be important as it became clear that the Bible would be the ultimate and often the only source for the Church's professed beliefs. Traditional practices not attested in the New Testament might be retained if they did not contradict anything in it but, if the Bible was to be the standard of doctrine, it was inevitable that worship patterns would be expected to conform to it, not the other way round.

To some extent the way had already been prepared by the publication of English-language primers, which had made parts of the liturgy, including selected passages of Scripture, available to the public in their mother tongue for a century and a half before the Reformation. In the late 1520s the suspicion grew that some of these primers were being influenced by Lutheran ideas and on 24 May 1530 Archbishop William Warham and others issued a denunciation of one of them, citing examples of covert Lutheranism that it supposedly contained.[34] It is not known which primer was thus censured but it may have been the *Hortulus animae* of George Joye (*c.* 1495-1553), which also attracted the wrath of William Tyndale. This was because Joye had had the audacity to borrow Tyndale's translations for the lessons he included in it and he had not hesitated to alter them as he saw fit.[35] In 1534 William Marshall issued a primer which (as we now know) contained the entire text of the *Hortulus* along with a great deal of new matter. As Joye had done, Marshall omitted both the litany and the *Dirige* (prayers for the dead), which provoked an immediate reaction. Marshall then reissued his primer, reinstating the missing services but adding prefaces to them that made it clear what his true opinion of them was. To those who thought that it was necessary to ask the Virgin Mary and the saints to intercede for us with God, he had this to say:

> although it be nothing like nor true, as concerning the necessity, that we by commandment of Holy Scripture must of necessity pray to our blessed Lady and saints, or that otherwise we cannot be heard: yet it is true, as concerning that we must needs have a peacemaker and mediator to our heavenly Father, which is his only Son, and our only sufficient and eternal Mediator Jesu Christ.[36]

34. D. Wilkins (ed.), *Concilia Magnae Britannae et Hiberniae*, 4 vols (London: Various Printers, 1737), vol. 3, pp. 733-35. Taken from Warham's register, fo. 187r-v.

35. G.L. Bray, *Documents of the English Reformation*, 3rd edn (Cambridge: James Clarke, 2019), pp. 17-20. The *Hortulus* disappeared from view until a single copy of it was unearthed in 1949. On the subject of the primers, see Butterworth, *The English Primers*, which is still the standard work on the subject.

36. Burton, *Three Primers*, pp. 123-24.

Having rejected the intercession of Mary and the saints, Marshall went on to add:

> Wherefore for the contentation of such weak minds, and somewhat to bear their infirmities, I have now at this my second edition of the said Primer, caused the Litany to be printed and put into the same, trusting that they by their old untrue opinion before alleged, nor yet by any other like, will abuse the same. Right doubtful it is, as I think, to pray unto all those that be mentioned, named, and called saints in the common Primers in Latin. For although many of them (by what authority I cannot tell) have been canonised and made saints, by such as have been bishops of Rome: yet whether they be saints or no, I commit to the secret judgment of God.[37]

Marshall subjected the *Dirige* to similar treatment, making it quite clear that he regarded the service as an abuse of Scripture, even though it frequently quoted both the Psalms and the Book of Job.[38] The traditional forms of the litany and the *Dirige* survived in the primer issued by Bishop John Hilsey of Rochester in 1539, although the latter came in for particular criticism and the attention of the worshippers was directed to the triumph of the saints in heaven and away from excessive mourning for them on earth.[39]

These primers, some of which were revised and reissued on an almost annual basis, would all contribute to the Book of Common Prayer in due course but their real importance lies in the way in which they prepared the public to receive a liturgy in English. By 1539 it seemed that the Reformation was in full swing and Archbishop Cranmer began to draft a liturgy for the new Church order. Moves in that direction were already well advanced on the Continent and Cranmer borrowed freely from some of the Lutheran services that had been introduced in Germany. He was also aware of the reformed breviary produced by the Catholic Francisco de Quiñones (c. 1482-1540) in 1535 and reissued in a revised version the following year. It was becoming clear that any English rite would have to streamline the traditional pattern of worship, make its doctrine conform to that of the Reformed Church and make it accessible to the wider public.

---

37. Ibid., p. 124.
38. Ibid., pp. 232-34.
39. Ibid., pp. 381-87, 407-21.

Cranmer's draft made considerable progress on the first two of these requirements but was less ambitious on the third. He reduced the many daily offices to Morning and Evening Prayer and added many more readings from Holy Scripture but, when it came to translation, only the Lord's Prayer and the Scripture readings were in English – the rest remained in Latin. This may have been because Cranmer knew that the king was too conservative to be pushed easily into accepting a vernacular liturgy, or it may have been because the services were intended mainly for the clergy's private use and not for public worship. The continued use of Latin also made it easier for him to share his experiments with Protestant leaders in other countries, not least in Denmark, with which England was at that time concluding an alliance. Whatever the reason (or combination of reasons), the draft was never printed and remained in manuscript form until relatively recent times.[40]

Some progress was made, however, with the reform of the service books, a task made necessary because of the break with Rome, if for no other reason. At a session of the Canterbury convocation on 21 February 1543 Cranmer announced that it was the king's pleasure:

> that all mass books, antiphoners, portuises in the Church of England should be newly examined, corrected, reformed and castigat[ed] from all manner of mention of the bishop of Rome's name, from all apocryphas, feigned legends, superstitions, orations, collects, versicles and responses, and that the names and memories of all saints which be not mentioned in the Scripture or authentical doctors should be abolished and put out of the same books and calendars, and that the services should be made out of the Scriptures and other authentic doctors.[41]

The records go on to state that:

> It was ordered also that every Sunday and holy day throughout the year the curate of every parish church, after the *Te Deum*

---

40. British Library, Royal MS 7B IV. First edited by F.A. Gasquet and E. Bishop, *Edward VI and the Book of Common Prayer* (London: John Hodges, 1890; repr. Milton Keynes: Alpha Editions, 2020), pp. 311-96, and then again by J.W. Legg, *Cranmer's Liturgical Projects: A Complete Edition of British Museum MSS* (London: Harrison & Son, 1915).
41. G.L. Bray (ed.), *Records of Convocation*, 20 vols (Woodbridge: Boydell & Brewer, 2005-06), vol. VII, p. 271.

and *Magnificat*, should openly read unto the people one chapter of the New Testament in English without exposition and when the New Testament was read over, then to begin the Old.[42]

Cranmer attempted a second draft liturgy sometime around 1545 but this was more conservative, in line with the king's attempts to rein in the forces of change. In this second version the full array of medieval offices is restored, numerous saints' days are once more commemorated, the feast of Corpus Christi is given greater prominence than one might expect and the second edition of Quiñones' breviary is the dominant external influence. Only the inclusion of Old Testament iconoclast kings like Hezekiah and Josiah gives us a clue that the archbishop had not really changed his mind but was biding his time. Like the previous draft, this one never saw the light of day but, unlike it, when Cranmer was finally free to do what he wanted, it was disregarded.

By about 1542, it was clear that there would be no substantial change to the liturgy as long as Henry VIII was alive but circumstances intervened. On 20 August 1543 the king issued a proclamation asking that prayers should be offered because of the bad weather and military reversals that threatened the country at that time.[43] Unfortunately, the response was disappointing and some put that down to the fact that few people could follow the Latin services well enough to engage with them properly. As a result, on 11 June 1544 the king issued a decree authorising the printing of a litany in English for the same purpose, thereby making it the first official liturgical text of the post-Reformation era.[44]

Furthermore, the text was substantially altered, removing the invocation of particular saints and other elements that were not congenial to the Reformers. The principal source remained the Sarum litany, as we might expect, but there was a substantial admixture of Luther's litany

---

42. Ibid. The New Testament has 260 chapters, so it would have taken just over two years to get through it. The Old Testament (minus the Psalter and the Apocrypha) has 779 chapters, which would mean about six years of reading, assuming that two chapters would be read on each of the appointed days. This was repeated in the Edwardian Injunctions 1547, no. 21; see Bray, *Documents*, p. 222.

43. Wilkins, *Concilia*, vol. 3, pp. 868-69. Printed from Cranmer's Register, fo. 22r-v.

44. Ibid., pp. 869-70. Printed from Cranmer's Register, fos 48v-49r.

and hints of other sources as well.[45] This litany was then reproduced in King Henry VIII's primer, issued the following year and, with only a few minor alterations, entered the Book of Common Prayer in 1549, where it has remained ever since.[46] It seems that Cranmer was also planning to provide English-language versions of different processions, as he indicated in a letter to the king dated 7 October 1544, but nothing came of that and by the time the Edwardian Injunctions were issued, the project had been abandoned.[47]

At the same time, the convocation of Canterbury began to prepare a series of homilies that would expound basic Christian teaching in concise and accessible English-language sermons. The work was put on hold and not published until after Henry VIII's death in 1547, but momentum for change was building and once the king with his deep-seated conservatism had passed away, it surfaced and swept all before it.

Continental European Developments

It was not long after his challenge to Rome that Martin Luther began to question the traditional pattern of public worship and to suggest changes to it. He began attacking processions as early as 1519 and, a year or two later, he abolished the litany, only to restore it (in an amended version) in 1529. However, serious change appeared in 1523 and was to continue at periodic intervals until 1537 or even later, by which time the Lutheran states of Germany were developing their own orders. In his *Von ordenung gottis dienst yn der gemeyne* of 1523 Luther abolished the daily Mass and most of the saints' days. In their place he substituted Morning and Evening Prayer, complete with a systematic lectionary of Bible readings, followed by a Psalm, responses and a collect. The reading of the day was meant to be accompanied by a short exposition of the text, though this seems to have been distinct from a sermon, which was

---

45. F.E. Brightman, *The English Rite*, 2nd edn, 2 vols (London: Rivingtons, 1921), vol. 1, p. lxv. Brightman cites parallels in the Roman litany, the York litany, the liturgy of Constantinople and another unidentified litany, which he thought might have been that of Bressanone (Brixen).

46. Burton, *Three Primers*, pp. 480-87. The *Dirige* was also printed on pp. 487-92, though without Psalm 5:8, which gave the service its title, but it did not survive in the 1549 prayer book and has never been revived.

47. Brightman, *The English Rite*, vol. 1, pp. lxi-lxiii. See also Edwardian Injunctions 1547, no. 23, in Bray, *Documents*, p. 223.

prescribed for the Sunday services of Mass and Vespers, both of which were to be sung as before.[48]

A Reformed Latin missal (*Formula missae et communionis pro ecclesia Wittembergensi*) appeared almost at the same time. It retained the traditional pattern of the Mass as far as the sermon (after the creed) but, after that, the order was drastically reduced in scope, with any suggestion of an offering being repudiated. There were no intercessions and the consecration of the elements was effected by the words of institution, which immediately follow the *Sursum corda* and substitute for the proper preface of the medieval rites. A German version (*Deutsche Messe und ordnung Gottis diensts*) with further simplifications and some rearrangement was issued in 1526. Luther intended it for use alongside the Latin, not instead of it, which suggests that he did not think that the modifications he had made were particularly significant. However, one important addition was an exhortation, which may have been inspired by the example of Martin Bucer (see below), which the celebrant was to read before the words of institution. There was also a prayer of thanksgiving for the benefits of Communion at the end of the service.

Both of these features would later appear in the prayer book, although they were probably not derived directly from the *Deutsche Messe*. In other respects, the traditional Mass vestments, altar candles and the elevation of the host remained intact, which would not be the case in England when the time for reformation came. Lutherans have managed to avoid theological controversy over such things, with the result that their services appear to Anglicans to be quite 'high church' in style, even when they are not in substance.

The *Deutsche Messe* was quickly followed by a German baptismal order which was originally little more than a translation of a traditional Latin one, which Luther believed had been preserved relatively uncorrupted through the centuries. However, in 1526 he came out with a second edition that put much less emphasis on exorcism and removed most of the ancient ceremonial.

---

48. For this and the other German liturgical texts of the sixteenth century, see A.L. Richter, *Die evangelischen Kirchenordnungen des sechszehnten Jahrhunderts: Urkunden und Regesten zur Geschichte des Rechts und der Verfassung der evangelischen Kirche in Deutschland*, 2 vols (Weimar: Landes-Industriecomptoir, 1864); E. Sehling, *Die evangelischen Kirchenordnungen des sechszehnten Jahrhunderts*, 24 vols (Leipzig: O.R. Reisland, 1902-13); H. Lietzmann, *Liturgische Texte*, 8 vols (Bonn: A. Marcus und E. Weber, 1909-10).

In 1534, Luther issued a form for the solemnisation of matrimony (*Traubüchlein für die einfältigen Pfarrherrn*) followed by an ordinal (*Formula ordinandorum ministrorum verbi*) in Latin and German three years later. Luther wrote primarily for his own church at Wittenberg and did not attempt to impose a uniform order on other churches, though, of course, many of those who followed his teaching also accepted his liturgical outlook, with varying degrees of conformity to the Wittenberg pattern. Some copied him more or less faithfully, others retained a greater admixture of traditional elements, while those who lived closer to Switzerland often incorporated elements drawn from there. F.E. Brightman gives a fair sampling of these different kinds in *The English Rite*, pointing out that, for the study of the Book of Common Prayer, the Lutheran orders adopted in Ernestine Saxony (1528) and in Brandenburg-Nürnberg (1533) were the most influential on the development of later church orders, of which more than a hundred have survived.[49]

Independent of Luther, and with a different take on the sacraments, was Huldrych Zwingli (1484-1531), who undertook the reformation of the church in Zurich. Like Luther, and at more or less the same time, Zwingli produced a conservative revision of the Mass in 1523.[50] He retained the Latin, apart from the scriptural lessons, and even composed new prayers in the classical language. These replaced the traditional canon and are noteworthy for their emphasis on preaching the Word (second prayer) and worthy reception of the elements (fourth prayer). Communion follows immediately after the words of institution and there is no offertory or prayer of consecration. There is, however, a brief thanksgiving after Communion and the service ends with the *Nunc dimittis*. Like Luther, Zwingli followed this rite in 1525 with a more radical one, this time in German and intended for use only four times in the year – Christmas, Easter, Pentecost and sometime in the autumn. In this rite, the lessons were standardised as 1 Corinthians 11:20-29 and John 6:47-63, followed by the *Gloria* and the Apostles' Creed. After that, there was a short exhortation and a prayer for worthy reception that led

---

49. Brightman, *The English Rite*, vol. 1, pp. xxxviii-xxxix. See also Cuming, *A History of Anglican Liturgy*, pp. 21-25, for further details.

50. *De canone missae epicheiresis.* An English translation can be found in R.C.D. Jasper and G.J. Cuming, *Prayers of the Eucharist: Early and Reformed*, 4th edn, ed. P.F. Bradshaw and M.E. Johnson (Collegeville, MN: Liturgical Press, 2019), pp. 267-71.

straight to the words of institution and Communion. The service ends with Psalm 113, a thanksgiving and a blessing.[51]

There does not appear to have been any direct influence from Zurich on the prayer book but a link can be found by way of Strasbourg and the work of Martin Bucer. Bucer was the great networker of the early Reformation. He got on well with both the Lutherans and the Swiss; the young John Calvin spent three years with him in Strasbourg. Towards the end of his life, when he was forced out of his native city by a resurgent Catholicism, Bucer found refuge in England, where he played a leading role in the ongoing Reformation under Edward VI. It is extremely difficult to tell how far Bucer was the source of liturgical practice and how far he was merely a conduit for innovations that emerged elsewhere or that were inherent in the Reformed programme and would have been influential even without him. What we do know is that, wherever features like the post-Communion thanksgiving or the exhortation preceding the institution made their appearance, Bucer was never far away. It is fair to say that it is unlikely that this was entirely coincidental.

The first appearance of a Reformed liturgy in Strasbourg occurred on 16 February 1524, when Diebold Schwarz introduced what was in effect a German translation of the Roman rite, minus any reference to a eucharistic sacrifice and shorn of excess ceremonial. In the course of the next fifteen years, this rite went through no fewer than thirteen revisions, each one of them more radical than the last. One of the features that remained constant throughout was an emphasis on confession of sin and an appeal to the Holy Spirit, based on Romans 12:1, that the bodies of the communicants may be made a 'living sacrifice, holy and acceptable to God' (ESV), which can fairly be regarded as the ultimate expression of what would later be known as the 'receptionist' position. In the course of 1524 there were no fewer than five versions of this order that appeared, along with a theological justification for them written by Martin Bucer. In that work, Bucer described what happened at what he now called the Lord's Supper:

> [the celebrant] admonishes those who wish to observe the Lord's Supper with him that they are to do so in memory of Christ, to die to their sins, to bear their cross willingly, and be strengthened in faith for what must come to pass when we contemplate with believing hearts what measureless grace

---

51. *Aktion oder Brauch des Nachtmahls.* English translation in Jasper and Cuming, *Prayers of the Eucharist*, pp. 271-72.

and goodness Christ hath shown to us, in that for us he offered up to his Father his life and blood upon the cross. After this exhortation, he reads the Gospel concerning the Lord's Supper, as the three Evangelists and Paul in 1 Corinthians 11 have described it. Then the minister distributes the bread and cup of the Lord among them, having partaken of them also himself. The congregation then sing a hymn of praise, and afterwards the minister closes the Supper with a short prayer, blesses the people, and lets them go in the peace of the Lord.[52]

It does not take much imagination to see that this description could fit the Book of Common Prayer almost equally well, and the similarities are striking. One of the confessions used in the Strasbourg rite found its way into the prayer book, as did the concept of 'comfortable words', quoted from Scripture as an encouragement to worshippers to trust in Christ for their salvation.

Bucer's hand can also be seen at work in the church order that he was asked to prepare for Cologne in 1542. Archbishop-Elector Hermann von Wied (1515-46) was slowly being converted to Protestantism and he wanted a Reformed liturgy for his archdiocese. The Reformation was not to take root in Cologne but the church order survived and became highly influential elsewhere. Archbishop von Wied ordered that the Cologne liturgy should be based on that of Brandenburg-Nürnberg, but Bucer did not hesitate to add material from a number of other sources. As in other similar cases, an initial text was produced in 1544 and then thoroughly revised. The final product appeared in 1545 as the *Simplex ac pia deliberatio*. It was radical enough to ensure that von Wied would be deposed from his see; it circulated widely across Europe and was highly regarded, not least by Thomas Cranmer, although Martin Luther criticised it as 'Zwinglian'.[53]

Bucer did in fact have leanings towards Zwingli that became clearer as time went on, but neither he nor the Cologne order went so far as to

52. M. Bucer, *Grund und Ursach ... der Neuerungen an dem Nachtmahl des Herrn*, in *Martin Bucers Deutsche Schriften*, 19 vols, ed. R. Stupperich (Gütersloh: Gerd Mohn, 1960-2016), vol. 1, pp. 185-278. English translation by W.D. Maxwell, *An Outline of Christian Worship: Its Development and Forms*, 9th edn (London: Oxford University Press, 1963), pp. 87-111. This extract is also found in Cuming, *A History of Anglican Liturgy*, p. 278.
53. Brightman, *The English Rite*, vol. 1, pp. xlv-xlix. See also Cuming, *A History of Anglican Liturgy*, pp. 25-27.

regard the Lord's Supper as no more than a symbolic re-enactment of Christ's atoning death.[54] His position was much closer to that of John Calvin, a pupil of Bucer. Calvin believed that in the Supper Christ made himself present to those who believed in him by the inner witness of his Holy Spirit. The worthy receivers were those who were enlightened by the Spirit to perceive the presence of Christ in the means that he himself had ordained, and they benefited accordingly. This was essentially what Cranmer came to believe and what he wanted to enshrine in the Book of Common Prayer. Labels like 'Zwinglian' or 'Calvinist' do not do Cranmer justice and should be avoided when discussing his position or that of the prayer book. Cranmer moved in the world of Bucer; but that world included Calvin and drew on both Luther and Heinrich Bullinger (1504-75), Zwingli's successor at Zurich, without identifying completely with either. It was to some extent a *via media* between Wittenberg and the Swiss and it was that *via media* that would characterise the reformed liturgy of the Church of England.[55]

A rather different influence on Cranmer was the breviary of Francisco de Quiñones, commissioned by Pope Clement VII (1523-34) and issued under the authority of his successor, Paul III (1534-49). Quiñones removed many of the accretions that had crept into the services over time and he greatly increased the use of the psalter and the readings from

---

54. This is a popular misunderstanding of Zwingli's true position. As W.D. Maxwell states: 'Zwingli's doctrine of the Lord's Supper is not to be simply branded as memorialism and so dismissed; it was more complex than that. … The striking difference between Zwingli and his two fellow Reformers lay in early training and consequent approach to theological doctrine. Calvin and Luther were scholastics, while Zwingli was a humanist. Consequently, Zwingli was more rationalistic in his theological outlook, less mystical, and more subjective and analytical.' Cf. *An Outline of Christian Worship: Its Development and Forms*, p. 81. See also B. Gordon, *Zwingli: God's Armed Prophet* (New Haven, CT: Yale University Press, 2021), pp. 147-81.

55. One of the major offenders in this respect is G. Dix, *The Shape of the Liturgy* (London: Dacre Press, 1946), who argues that Cranmer is pure Zwingli (p. 659). This was ably refuted by G.B. Timms, *Dixit Cranmer: A Reply to Dom Gregory Dix* (London: Mowbray & Co., 1946), but the misunderstanding has persisted at the popular level. In later times the *via media* would be explained as the middle way between Wittenberg and Geneva, because by the end of the sixteenth century Geneva had come to represent the Swiss churches more generally, at least in English eyes. The popular modern notion that the *via media* was a mediating position between Rome and Wittenberg is historically false.

both the Old and New Testaments. The daily offices were reorganised and made much more regular than they had been before, with the *Venite* (Psalm 95) and the *Te Deum* both appointed for daily Matins, except that the latter was replaced by Psalm 51 in Advent and Lent. The penitential Psalms were confined to Ash Wednesday and to Fridays in Lent, as was the litany. As for the creed, the Athanasian Creed was limited to Sundays and replaced by the Apostles' Creed on other days. Thomas Cranmer did not follow Quiñones in every respect, but there is a clear resemblance between what the latter did and what is found in the 1549 prayer book. Quiñones' breviary of 1535 was greeted with strenuous opposition from Catholic theologians and he had to modify a number of his innovations in a revision that appeared the following year. It is instructive to note that, for the most part, Cranmer relied on the original text, though he made some use of the revision as well. Meanwhile, Quiñones' work fell out of favour at Rome. Pope Paul IV (1555-59) condemned it in 1558 and it was finally suppressed ten years later, in the run up to the introduction of the Tridentine reforms that were to define Roman Catholicism for the next four centuries.[56]

The 1548 Order for Communion

When Henry VIII died on 28 January 1547, the throne passed to his nine-year-old son Edward VI (1547-53). Edward VI was too young to govern on his own and so a regency council was set up and Archbishop Cranmer was entrusted with church affairs. This enabled him to enact the far-reaching reforms that he had been planning for some time, though he himself was still moving towards a clearly Protestant theological position, which he had not yet fully embraced. Even so, he was quite convinced about the supremacy of Holy Scripture as the only legitimate source for Christian doctrine and he was fully persuaded of the doctrine of justification by faith alone. This is attested most obviously in the rapid publication of *Certayne Sermons, or Homilies* (the first book of Homilies) in 1547, which had been prepared about five years earlier but had not been published, probably for fear that the old king would not have accepted it. Where Cranmer remained to be convinced was in his understanding of the sacraments and, in particular, of the Lord's Supper. That he moved

---

56. The reforms were decreed at the Council of Trent (1545-63) but not fully implemented until 1570. Modern Roman Catholics who object to the reforms of the Second Vatican Council (1962-65) are advocates of the Tridentine Rite, which they regard as 'traditional' Catholicism.

from an 'objective' position, according to which the elements of bread and wine were consecrated to become the body and blood of Christ, whether they were worthily received as such by the communicant or not, to a more 'subjective' (or 'receptionist') view, which was that it was (and could only be) by faith that the believer had communion with Christ in and through the species of bread and wine, is certain and was clearly attested at his trial in 1555. What is disputed by modern historians is whether he moved straight from one to the other or whether there was a gradual transition, and, if so, when that transition occurred.

At Cranmer's trial, his accusers claimed that he had held three different positions over the course of the preceding decade. They believed that he had moved from a belief in transubstantiation (which they naturally regarded as 'orthodox') to a Lutheran perspective, according to which Christ was 'really present' in, with and under the species of bread and wine in a way that was objective but that did not entail transubstantiation, to the purely receptionist idea that he supposedly held at the time of his trial. Cranmer himself rejected this interpretation of his theological development and insisted that he moved straight from the traditional transubstantionist doctrine to the receptionist view, with no middle ground in between. Which of these two versions is closer to the truth?

If we look at the textual evidence provided by the liturgies that he composed in 1548, 1549 and 1552, it is relatively easy to assert that he moved gradually from one position to the other, though whether the intermediate stage(s) represented by 1548 and 1549 can properly be called 'Lutheran' is problematic. That there would be resemblances between Cranmer and the Lutherans is only to be expected, since Cranmer undoubtedly did draw on Lutheran material in the construction of his liturgies, but there is nothing that obliges us to accept that these borrowings reflected a 'Lutheran' view of the sacrament that is substantially different from the position of someone like Bucer. They may have been compatible with some form of Lutheranism but whether they were dependent on it must remain uncertain.

The other view of the matter is that Cranmer was persuaded, probably by Nicholas Ridley and possibly as early as 1546, that the receptionist position was the correct one and that his liturgical experimentation in the period 1548-52 must be interpreted in that light. According to this theory, Cranmer never wavered in his desire to restructure the liturgy in a way that made receptionism the only viable doctrinal interpretation of it, but that circumstances forced him to move cautiously. In fact, these two views are not mutually exclusive and they can be reconciled by saying that Cranmer's period of transition from the traditional to the receptionist position, though not sudden, did not take long. In the process he passed through a phase that might be described as 'Lutheran', especially in light of later theological decisions taken by Lutherans in Germany, but he never settled on it or sought to define his own doctrine in that light.[57] The year 1547 was one of rapid change in the liturgical sphere and it is impossible to say for sure how much of that was due to the sudden release of pent-up desires after the death of Henry VIII and how much must be attributed to fresh inspiration.

What we know for certain is that in 1547 someone translated Hermann von Wied's Cologne order into English.[58] It was quickly taken up by Archbishop Cranmer, who was probably unaware that much of it had been drafted by Martin Bucer, and so became the basis for the next stage of liturgical reform in England. On 17 December 1547 Parliament passed the Sacrament Act in which it outlawed any kind of disrespect for the Lord's Supper and decreed that henceforth Communion would be given and received in both kinds, by clergy and people alike.[59] The withdrawal of the cup from the laity had become a major controversy in the late fourteenth century. Nevertheless, it was affirmed by the Council of Constance in 1415 at which the Czech reformer Jan Hus was condemned for heresy (and later executed), partly because he refused to go along with it.[60] Restoration of Communion in both kinds was an attack on papal authority without necessarily touching on the doctrine of the Eucharist itself, so it could gain support from conservatives as well as reformers. In preparation for implementing the Act, Cranmer drew up an order for the Communion, which was designed to ensure

---

57. This is the view advanced by Colin Buchanan, 'What Did Cranmer Think He Was Doing?', in *An Evangelical among the Anglican Liturgists* (London: SPCK, 2009), pp. 71-113, reprinted from a Grove Liturgical Study originally published in 1976 and revised in 1982. Both D. MacCulloch, *Thomas Cranmer*, rev. edn (New Haven, CT: Yale University Press, 2016), pp. 507-13, and G.P. Jeanes, *Signs of God's Promise: Thomas Cranmer's Sacramental Theology and the Book of Common Prayer* (London: T. & T. Clark, 2008), pp. 237-40, have endorsed his position.

58. It was published anonymously as *A Simple and Religious Consultation*. The Communion service is reproduced in Cuming, *A History of Anglican Liturgy*, pp. 286-304, and in an abbreviated form in Jasper and Cuming, *Prayers of the Eucharist*, pp. 251-58.

59. Bray, *Documents*, pp. 227-31.

60. *Conciliorum Oecumenicorum Decreta* (Bologna: Istituto per le scienze religiose, 1973), pp. 420-31. English translation in N. Tanner (ed.), *Decrees of the Ecumenical Councils*, 2 vols (London: Sheed & Ward, 1990), vol. 1, pp. 420-31.

that there would be a uniform procedure across the country. Dated 8 March 1548, the new order was to be introduced on Easter Sunday (1 April) and the Act allowed a month's grace before there would be prosecutions for non-compliance.[61]

On paper, the order was designed to be a supplement to the Latin missal and not a replacement for it. In some ways it can be compared to the primers, which were a guide for people who knew no Latin, but it was different from them in that it was meant to be inserted into the Latin at key points, in order to guide worshippers as they presented themselves for Communion. The celebrant was provided with a form of exhortation, which he was free to modify if he wanted to do so, announcing when he was going to offer Communion to his parishioners and urging them to prepare themselves accordingly. This was then followed by forms of confession, absolution, 'comfortable words' taken from the Scriptures, a prayer before reception (to be said by the celebrant on behalf of the communicants), the administration and, finally, a benediction of the communicants after reception.

How much of the order was used must have varied from place to place but, as it generally follows the Sarum rite, there is no reason to suppose that it was resisted to any great extent. What is of interest to us is that some of it was inspired by the Lutheran form from Cologne and much of the language used was recycled in the 1549 prayer book and subsequent revisions, so that its contents are still familiar today. In a real sense therefore, the order marks the cautious but unmistakable beginning of what would become the standard for the Reformed Church of England.

One thing that can be said for certain about the order was that it was conceived as a temporary stopgap from the very beginning. The royal proclamation that accompanied it when it was issued stated quite clearly:

> We will our subjects ... also with such obedience and conformity to receive this our ordinance, and godly direction, that we may be encouraged from time to time, further to travail for the reformation and setting forth of such godly orders as may be most to God's glory, the edifying of our subjects, and for the advancement of true religion. Which thing we (by the help of God) most earnestly intend to bring into effect. ... We would not have our subjects, so much to

---

61. H.A. Wilson (ed.), *The Order of the Communion, 1548* (London: Harrison & Son, 1908; repr. Forgotten Books, 2012).

mislike our judgment, so much to mistrust our zeal, as though we either could not discern what were to be done, or would not do all things in due time.[62]

While this was going on, other changes were starting to appear as well. In November 1547 a revised version of the litany was issued in which the invocation of the saints was quietly dropped. In January 1548, before the order was ready, Candlemas, Ash Wednesday and Palm Sunday were shorn respectively of their candles, ashes and palms and the veneration of the cross on Good Friday was also prohibited. For the moment, although the words of the traditional services remained unaltered, the atmosphere in which they were conducted was starting to change and the way towards a genuine reformation was being prepared.

The 1549 Book of Common Prayer

The next stage in the process of reforming the liturgy was not long in coming. By 9 September 1548 a commission under the chairmanship of Thomas Cranmer had been put together and was beginning its deliberations.[63] Its members were:

Bishops		
George Day	Chichester	Conservative
Thomas Goodrich	Ely	Moderate
Henry Holbeach	Lincoln	Reformist
Nicholas Ridley	Rochester	Reformist
John Skip	Hereford	Conservative
Thomas Thirlby	Westminster	Moderate
Divines		
Richard Cox	Dean of Christ Church, Oxford	Reformist
Simon Haynes	Dean of Exeter	Reformist
William May	Dean of St Paul's	Reformist
John Redman	Master of Trinity College, Cambridge	Conservative
Thomas Robertson	Archdeacon of Exeter	Conservative
John Taylor	Dean of Lincoln	Reformist

---

62. Ibid., no pagination.
63. W. Page, 'The First Book of Common Prayer and the Windsor Commission', *Church Quarterly Review* 98, no. 195 (1924), pp. 51-64.

The balance tilted towards the Reformists, especially among the divines, and the inclusion of John Redman, the only member of the committee who was not also a member of the Canterbury convocation, may indicate that liturgical traditionalists were in short supply.[64] The discussions lasted only about three weeks, after which a finished draft was delivered to the king at Windsor, apparently with the unanimous assent of the committee. That the work could be accomplished so quickly shows that most of it had been done already. English-language texts of the daily offices were already available in the primers and Cranmer seems to have been at work on the occasional offices for some time before the committee met. It was the text of the Lord's Supper that occupied most of the meetings; and it came out in later debate that the bishops (at least) were not as unanimous as they had been made to appear. Among the eight who voted against the new rite in the House of Lords were Chichester, Hereford and Westminster, or half of those who had taken part in the discussions.[65]

On 21 January 1549 Parliament passed the Act of Uniformity authorising the new services and enjoining the use of an entirely English-language Book of Common Prayer from the following Whitsun (9 June). The prayer book was printed as early as 7 March and was soon available in multiple editions, in good time for implementing the provisions of the Act. It was meant to replace the breviary, the missal, the manual and the processional; the pontifical was held over for the time being, though not for long. Within a year it had been replaced by the Ordinal, which, although not officially part of the Book of Common Prayer, was printed with it, as it still is.[66]

As far as the breviary was concerned, the 1549 prayer book was strongly influenced by the reforms of Quiñones. The complexities of the medieval services were ironed out and their number was reduced to two – Matins and Evensong. One might even say that they were effectively a single service, with variations in the canticles and Scripture readings only. These were important, however, because one of the main purposes of the daily offices was to allow for systematic and extensive readings from the Bible. The psalter was also rearranged into a 30-day cycle, so that all the Psalms would be read in the course of a month. This pattern was to prove enduring and the daily offices in the 1662 prayer

---

64. Deans and archdeacons were members of convocation *ex officio*. Note that there were no representatives on the commission from the province of York, which was generally more traditionalist than Canterbury.

65. The vote in the upper house was taken on 15 January 1549.

66. See P.F. Bradshaw, *The Anglican Ordinal: Its History and Development from the Reformation to the Present Day* (London: SPCK, 1971), pp. 18-36.

book remain very close to those in 1549, with only minor alterations here and there. Furthermore, they show a creative distinctiveness that is not really paralleled elsewhere in Europe. It is possible to find Lutheran and Reformed orders of worship that are similar to the Anglican pattern, but they are not typical and were never in widespread use. The prayers and readings are often little more than translations of the Sarum rite, but their arrangement is quite different. Here, if anywhere, the Church of England can claim a genuine originality that has been preserved through the centuries.[67]

Turning to the manual, much of the 1549 prayer book is little more than a translation of Sarum. As elsewhere, the excess of ceremonial is severely pared down, the reading of Scripture is increased and exhortations are added at appropriate points. Cranmer was heavily dependent on Lutheran models for the arrangement of his material, and much of what he produced resembles the Cologne order in particular, though it is not clear why this is so. It seems unlikely that he waited until an English translation was produced in 1547 and it is probable that he was at work on various services for at least a decade before that. The resemblances to Cologne may therefore be due more to the outlook which Cranmer shared in common with Hermann von Wied than to any version of the latter's text.

The most noticeable changes occur in the services connected with illness and dying. In the Sarum rite the visitation of the sick and extreme unction were separate from each other, but the 1549 prayer book combines them under visitation. The burial service is greatly shortened and the graveside committal is rearranged, with elements taken from different parts of the Sarum rite and the expected Lutheran orders. The remaining services reflect traditional ceremonies that may have been retained because of popular devotion to them, more than anything else. Cranmer was certainly exercised by the need to defend why he retained some but not others, and his essay on the subject, printed as an appendix to the 1549 prayer book has survived as a second preface to the 1662 one.[68]

The main focus of attention in the 1549 rite has always been the Lord's Supper. It is now generally accepted that Cranmer conceived of it as the next stage in the progressive development of a truly reformed rite that would eventually establish itself in the Church of England and not his last word on the subject. For this reason, the service of Holy

---

67. For the details, see Cuming, *A History of Anglican Liturgy*, pp. 47-51.
68. See ibid., pp. 59-67, for the details.

Communion has caused more excitement and more enduring division in the Church than anything else in the prayer book. Seen from the standpoint of the Sarum rite, 1549 can be, and sometimes has been, defended as fully Reformed, even on occasion by Presbyterians.[69] The grounds for holding that view lie mainly in the way in which the canon of the Eucharist was altered to reflect non-Roman approaches. In the words of W.D. Maxwell:

> Although as much as possible of the old rite was retained, its character was fundamentally changed by the revision of the Canon: an epiclesis, based upon St Basil's, was inserted as part of the consecration preceding the Words of Institution, and the doctrine of sacrifice was expressed as a 'sacrifice of praise and thanksgiving' and the offering of 'ourselves, our souls and bodies, to be a reasonable, holy and lively sacrifice unto' God.[70]

That may well be true but, at the time, Stephen Gardiner (1483-1555), the bishop of Winchester, argued that it could be used in good conscience by traditionalists because it retained enough of the medieval Mass to make it compatible with a doctrine of transubstantiation, whether that was Cranmer's intention or not. Gardiner was making the classical mistake of starting with the position that he himself held and then trying to find it in the Reformed rite, which he could only do by a selective reading of the text. The fact of the matter is that the 1549 prayer book did not say what Gardiner wanted it to say, but neither did it go out of its way to exclude Gardiner's position entirely. By keeping as much of the traditional rite as possible, Cranmer was allowing for an ambiguity of interpretation that made it possible for his opponents to close their eyes to what they did not want to see. That is what Gardiner did, and what both Cranmer and his Reformed colleagues were to find so intolerable.

Our knowledge of this comes primarily from Thomas Cranmer himself, who objected to Gardiner's interpretation in his *Defence of the True and Catholic Doctrine of the Sacrament*, which must be regarded as the most accurate and complete exposition of Cranmer's intentions

---

69. See, for example, Maxwell, *An Outline of Christian Worship*, pp. 144-51.
70. Ibid., p. 146. This view is supported and amplified by Colin Buchanan, *An Evangelical among the Anglican Liturgists*, pp. 87-92.

in composing the 1549 rite.[71] Gardiner would later publish a book in response to Cranmer's *Defence*, which elicited a rejoinder from the archbishop, but by then the debate had moved on and Gardiner was much more firmly in the Roman camp than he had previously been.[72] In his reply to Cranmer, Gardiner singled out three main statements in the order for Holy Communion that he believed retained the traditional Catholic teaching:[73]

1. In the canon, before the institution: 'Hear us, O merciful Father, we beseech thee, and with thy Holy Spirit and Word vouchsafe to bless and *sanctify* these thy gifts and creatures that *they may be unto us the Body and Blood* of thy most dearly beloved Son.'

2. In the canon: 'humbly beseeching thee that whosoever shall be *partakers of this Holy Communion may worthily receive the most precious Body and Blood* of thy Son and be fulfilled with thy grace and heavenly benediction, and made one Body with thy Son Jesus Christ, that he may dwell in them and they in him.'

3. In the prayer of humble access: 'Grant us so to eat the flesh of thy dear Son Jesus Christ and to drink his blood *in these holy mysteries* that we may continually dwell in him.'

However, as Gregory Dix pointed out, to interpret these phrases as an expression of transubstantiation is directly contrary to what Cranmer said in his *Defence*:[74]

---

71. T. Cranmer, *A Defence of the True and Catholic Doctrine of the Sacrament of the Body and Blood of Our Saviour Christ* (London: R. Wolfe, 1550; repr. Eugene, OR: Wipf & Stock, 2004).

72. S. Gardiner, *An Explicatio and Assertion of the True Catholique Faythe* (Rouen: Robert Caly, 1551); T. Cranmer, *An Answer unto a Crafty and Sophisticall Cavillation, devised by Stephen Gardiner* (London: R. Wolfe, 1551).

73. As cited in Dix, *The Shape of the Liturgy*, pp. 657-58. See also Brightman, *The English Rite*, vol. 1, pp. cxlv-cxlvi. Gardiner's somewhat specious arguments are mentioned by MacCulloch, *Thomas Cranmer*, pp. 486-90. MacCulloch comments (p. 486): 'Gardiner's use of the 1549 BCP against Cranmer ... has proved of lasting importance, providing theological fools' gold for those Anglo-Catholics who have sought to reinterpret the first Prayer Book and Cranmer's intentions within it.'

74. Cranmer, *Defence*, 3.2.

[The papists] say that every man, good and evil, eateth the Body of Christ: We say, that both do eat the sacramental bread and drink the wine, but none do eat the very Body of Christ and drink his Blood, but only they that be lively members of his Body.

Or again:[75]

The eating of Christ's flesh and drinking of his blood is not to be understand[ed] simply and plainly as the words do properly signify, that we do eat and drink him with our mouths; but it is a figurative speech spiritually to be understand[ed].

And again:[76]

The true eating of Christ's very flesh and drinking of his blood [is] ... an inward, spiritual and pure eating with heart and mind. ... The same flesh and blood now sitteth at the right hand of the Father, making continual intercession for us, and to imprint and digest this in our minds, putting our whole affiance and trust in him as teaching our salvation and offering ourselves clearly unto him, to love and serve him all the days of our life. This is truly, sincerely and spiritually to eat his flesh and to drink his blood.

These and many other statements of a similar nature make it quite clear that Cranmer did not understand the 1549 Book of Common Prayer as conveying any sort of transubstantiation and that his intention in the rite of Holy Communion was to proclaim a memorial of Christ's atoning sacrifice, not to re-present it in any way that would be compatible with medieval Catholic teaching.[77]

Working from Cranmer's On the Lord's Supper, Colin Buchanan has pinpointed five assertions made by Gardiner that led to changes in the 1549 prayer book, though he leaves open the question as to whether it

75. Ibid.
76. Ibid., 3.15.
77. This is acknowledged by Dix, The Shape of the Liturgy, p. 647, who added that Cranmer believed that his rite of 1549 was 'essentially consistent with the doctrine of "justification by faith alone"'.

was Gardiner who provoked those changes or whether they would have occurred anyhow as a matter of course. They are as follows:[78]

Gardiner's claims	Cranmer's actions
1. The intercession is effective because it comes in the canon.	1. Intercession removed.
2. The 'petition for consecration' was our trust in God to make the body of Christ present.	2. Words 'that may be unto us' altered to 'that we receiving'.
3. The prayer of humble access was addressed to Christ as if he were present in the sacrament to be adored.	3. Prayer removed to a point well before the words of institution.
4. The words of administration teach that the body and blood of Christ are present under the forms of bread and wine.	4. Words of administration changed to remove any reference to Christ's body and blood.
5. Christ's whole body was present in every part of the consecrated bread.	5. Rubric deleted.

In his opposition to the traditionalists on the bench of bishops, Cranmer was supported by Continental Reformers who arrived in England just before the 1549 prayer book came into use and who were soon making comments of their own on it. Martin Bucer, Peter Martyr Vermigli and Jan Łaski all appreciated how far Cranmer had come from a traditionalist position. Bucer, in particular, was careful to express his admiration for that in his extensive and detailed critique of the 1549 liturgy, known as the *Censura*.[79] How far Bucer and the others actually influenced the composition of the 1552 version remains a subject of debate. Some of the suggestions that he made for improving the 1549 rite were incorporated into the 1552 revision, but it is impossible to be certain how much that was due to him and how much his opinions coincided with what Cranmer was already thinking. In a sense it hardly matters. Bucer and Cranmer approached the subject from different angles but were essentially on the same wavelength, and the 1552 revision served to make that clear. Without clinging to the coat-tails of any one person, Cranmer was moving into the orbit of Swiss ('Reformed') theology, which even then was reaching a common position in the so-called

78. Buchanan, *An Evangelical among the Anglican Liturgists*, p. 111.
79. E.C. Whitaker, *Martin Bucer and the Book of Common Prayer* (Great Wakering: Mayhew-McCrimmon, 1974), provides the original Latin text with a parallel English translation.

Consensus Tigurinus of 1549, which brought the Zwinglians of Zurich, led by Heinrich Bullinger, and John Calvin in Geneva to a common mind.[80] Cranmer was among them.

Colin Buchanan has supplied us with a list of fourteen items mentioned in Bucer's *Censura* that Cranmer altered in his revision, though once again, whether those alterations would have been made in any case must remain uncertain:[81]

Bucer's remarks	Cranmer's action
1. Vestments are a source of superstition.	1. Vestments reduced to the surplice.
2. Tables should not be at the east end.	2. Tables to stand in the body of the church.
3. Homilies should not be cut in pieces.	3. Mention of 'portion of homily' omitted from the rubric.
4. No provision should be made to limit the consecration of bread and wine to what was needed for Communion.	4. Rubric omitted; left over bread and wine to be given to the curate for his own use.
5. *Sanctus* and *Agnus Dei* should not be sung while the minister is praying.	5. *Sanctus* not to be sung and *Agnus Dei* omitted.
6. No prayers for the dead.	6. Prayers for the dead removed.
7. Prayer that God should bless and sanctify the gifts, black crosses and manual acts ill-advised.	7. Prayer changed; crosses and manual acts omitted.
8. Angels should not be asked to take our prayers to the tabernacle.	8. Omitted.
9. No 'half-Mass' or pretence at a Mass allowed.	9. Vestments abolished; surplices worn for all services. Ante-Communion developed into a service in its own right.
10. 'Chapels annexed' for the use of the rich should not be encouraged.	10. No mention of 'chapels annexed' in the rubrics.

80. For the *Consensus Tigurinus*, see H. Faulenbach and E. Busch (eds), *Reformierte Bekenntnisschriften*, 3 vols (Neukirchen-Vluyn: Neukirchener Verlag, 2002-16), vol. 1/2, pp. 467-90. English translation in J.T. Dennison Jr (ed.), *Reformed Confessions of the Sixteenth and Seventeenth Centuries in English Translation*, 4 vols (Grand Rapids, MI: Reformation Heritage Books, 2008-14), vol. 1, pp. 537-45.

81. Buchanan, *An Evangelical among the Anglican Liturgists*, pp. 111-12.

Bucer's remarks	Cranmer's action
11. Wafers undesirable.	11. Wafers abolished.
12. Frequent Communion should be restored, and **sending one member of the household to communicate** on behalf of the others should cease.	12. The minimum of one communicant is added, with an exhortation to others. Vicarious Communion no longer mentioned.
13. Minimum of once annual Communion should be removed.	13. Minimum raised to thrice a year.
14. Bread should be put in communicants' hands, not mouths.	14. Rubric provides that Communion should be given in the hands.

It will be seen from this list that Bucer's objections have to do with practices, rather than with doctrines as such. His concern was that too many traditional actions were retained in 1549 that might give rise to misunderstanding and ought to be removed for that reason. To put it another way, Bucer wanted the form of 1549 to be changed in order to conform with what he regarded as its substance, an aim that Cranmer shared and sought to implement in his revision.

One small but revealing detail is that the 1549 prayer book made no provision for a further consecration of bread and wine if supply ran out during the service, as had been done in the order the year before. What actually happened in that case is unknown but it would not be until 1662 that specific directions for a fresh consecration would be given. It is quite likely that Cranmer and his associates saw no need for that, surmising (as they probably did) that the words of consecration were intended for the worshippers, not for the elements, and that, since the worshippers had already heard them once, there was no need to repeat them.[82]

The revised Ordinal was not ready in time to be included in the 1549 prayer book but it appeared soon afterwards and, like the daily and occasional offices, the 1662 version is clearly descended from it. The main innovation is the deletion of the minor orders, leaving only the episcopate, the presbyterate and the diaconate, which Cranmer believed were all of apostolic origin. The forms of the different services reflect the influence of Martin Bucer and come particularly close to the Reformed

---

82. This is what Dix, *The Shape of the Liturgy*, pp. 664-65, thought and he was probably right.

(as opposed to the Lutheran or Catholic) tradition. As elsewhere, much of the material is translated from the Latin, but the Ordinal shows a greater freedom in altering and in abbreviating historical precedents. The finished product has served the Anglican Communion in good stead, though it was to become a bone of contention in dialogue with Roman Catholics, who were to claim that its structure and contents show that it suffers from what is called 'defect of intention', that is to say, the services do not *intend* to ordain ministers to the same functions as the traditional medieval ones did. Whether that is correct or not has been hotly debated in the past 150 years, with the ecumenical climate of our time tending to agree that the validity of the rite does not depend on so nebulous a concept as 'intention'.[83]

The 1552 Book of Common Prayer

That the 1549 prayer book was a first step in the process of reform and not a definitive expression of it becomes apparent when we look more carefully at what transpired in 1552. Most of the daily and occasional offices were left virtually unchanged, as there was little need to revise them. In contrast to that, the service of the Lord's Supper underwent substantial revision, which has been variously interpreted, either as an unfortunate defacing or as a necessary and welcome purification of 1549. The difference between the two rites is seen, above all, in the institution narrative, which in 1552 was designed to emphasise the reception of the elements as the high point of Communion. In the revised rite, the words of institution lead straight into the administration of the elements, with no hint of a consecration in the traditional sense. Some commentators have tried to find a consecration in the words of institution themselves, but that is to read into them something that is not there. In 1552 the focus throughout is on the spiritual state of the believer, not on the nature of the elements used to represent the body and blood of Christ. Traditionalist supporters of 1549 saw that immediately and refused to acquiesce in the new form of worship. To accept 1552 was to give wholehearted support to the Reformation and that is what its authors, and Cranmer, in particular, intended.

In more recent times, when there has been a marked shift away from Reformation principles in liturgical revision and towards a recovery of

---

83. See Bradshaw, *Anglican Ordinal*, pp. 123-208; R.W. Franklin (ed.), *Anglican Orders: Essays on the Centenary of* Apostolicae Curae *1896-1996* (London: Mowbray; and Harrisburg, PA: Morehouse Publishing, 1996).

more primitive and supposedly 'catholic' forms of order, the 1552 prayer book has suffered from a bad press. In the first half of the twentieth century, it was almost taken for granted in Anglican liturgical circles that it was an inferior product and it was slighted accordingly.[84] More recently, in what is otherwise an excellent edition of the classical prayer books, it has been omitted altogether, despite its obvious historical importance.[85]

Perhaps the best way to approach the 1552 revision is to start with the justification for it put forth in the Act of Uniformity by which it was introduced.[86] The Act opens with a reaffirmation of the 1549 Book of Common Prayer which is described as:

> a very godly order set forth by authority of Parliament for common prayer and administration of the sacraments, to be used in the mother tongue within the Church of England, agreeable to the Word of God and the primitive church, very comfortable to all good people desiring to live in Christian conversation and most profitable to the estate of this realm.[87]

This is followed in the next paragraph with a criticism of large numbers of people who have failed to appreciate the blessing they have received and have refused to attend worship according to the new rite. The Act was determined to put that right by making church attendance compulsory. However, a little further on in the Act a more serious problem is mentioned. It was not just that people were staying away, but also that 'there hath arisen in the use and exercise of this aforesaid common service in the church, heretofore set forth, divers doubts for the fashion and manner of the ministration of the same'.[88]

---

84. See, for example, F. Proctor and W.H. Frere, *A New History of the Book of Common Prayer with a Rationale of Its Offices*, 3rd edn (London: Macmillan, 1905). This was long the standard introduction to its subject and was regularly reprinted until 1961.

85. B. Cummings (ed.), *The Book of Common Prayer: The Texts of 1549, 1559 and 1662* (Oxford: Oxford University Press, 2011). However, even in J.R. Porter (ed.), *The First and Second Prayer Books of Edward VI* (London: J.M. Dent & Sons, 1910; repr. Prayer Book Society, 1999), where it is printed, the editor is not slow to insist on what he sees as its inferior quality.

86. Bray, *Documents*, pp. 250-52. The Act was passed on 14 April 1552 and came into force on 1 November.

87. Ibid., p. 250.

88. Ibid., p. 251.

The Act does not describe what these doubts were in any detail, nor does it say exactly where they have come from, but it does mention the 'curiosity' (i.e. 'eccentricity') of various ministers and 'mistakers', or people who have not understood what the 1549 prayer book was all about. This unfortunate circumstance, which the Act blames entirely on the clergy and people who have failed to respond properly, is to be compensated by 'the more plain and manifest explanation hereof, as for the more perfection of the said order of common service, in some places where it is necessary to make the same prayers and fashion of service more earnest and fit to stir Christian people to the true honouring of Almighty God'.[89] In other words, the 1552 prayer book was intended to clarify points of misunderstanding and remove any cause for the doubts that had arisen from the 1549 liturgy.

In pursuit of that aim, the daily offices of Matins and Evensong were definitively detached from any residue of the traditional monastic hours which had given rise to them and were reconstituted as independent services of Morning and Evening Prayer. This was achieved primarily by the addition of a number of exhortatory sentences and a general confession at the beginning. These had previously been omitted, perhaps because it was thought that they would occur later in the service for the Lord's Supper, which was expected to follow on from them. The 1552 rite recognised that frequent Communion was unlikely and that breaking off the Lord's Supper before the consecration – the so-called 'Ante-Communion' – was unsatisfactory. The solution was therefore to provide separate services in which the question of Communion did not arise. That in turn made it easier to dispense with the traditional Mass vestments which were no longer needed (and were not appropriate) for those services. Once that happened, the Lord's Supper could also be celebrated without the traditional vestments because people would no longer expect to see them as a matter of course.

The extent to which the daily offices are dependent on Continental sources is impossible to determine with any certainty. Undoubtedly, Cranmer was familiar with many contemporary Protestant liturgies, as he was with Quiñones' revised breviary, and felt free to borrow from them, but how much of this was deliberate is unknown and unknowable. The Reformers of the time generally thought alike and 'borrowing', if that is the right word for it, came naturally to them, so that we should not be surprised to discover similar phrases in orders of service prepared by men like Valérand Poullain (Strasbourg) and Jan Łaski (Emden). The

---

89. Ibid.

shadow of Martin Bucer is everywhere present but it is impossible to
know precisely what his impact was. We have no way of knowing for
sure; and in any case Bucer had been dead for more than a year before
the 1552 prayer book appeared and so was not available for comment in
the latter stages of revision.

The occasional offices and the Ordinal were scarcely revised at
all in 1552, the few changes that were made being for the most part
designed to avoid any occasion for superstition or abuse. An obvious
example of that was the abandonment of the reserved sacrament for
use at the visitation of the sick. Instead, and following the suggestion
of Peter Martyr Vermigli, the minister was obliged to consecrate the
bread and wine afresh each time he offered the sick Communion. The
most extensive changes occurred in the rite of public baptism, which
was to take place at the font in the church and shorn of superstitious
accretions like exorcism, the blessing of the font and so on. Godparents
were not asked to pledge their own faith as an assurance that it would
be transmitted to the child but they were expected to promise to bring
them up to profess that faith in due course. The traditional signing
with the cross was retained, but only after baptism, as a sign of reception
into the Church. The service concludes in a way that resembles the
Lord's Supper, with the congregation reciting the Lord's Prayer and
the officiant offering a prayer of thanksgiving. The services of private
baptism and confirmation are left virtually unchanged.[90]

It is, of course, the service of the Lord's Supper that was most seriously
affected by the 1552 revision and that has commanded almost all the
attention paid to the prayer book of that year. The first part of the service
was left more or less intact, though the *Gloria* was removed to the end.
Major changes start to appear after the sermon, which is followed
immediately by the offertory. On the surface, the offertory appears to
continue the traditional pattern but in fact it is quite different. Instead
of the customary presentation of bread and wine for consecration, it is
altered to a financial contribution, in line with contemporary Lutheran
practice. The 1552 prayer book makes no provision for the preparation
of the bread and wine, and Cranmer's intentions in this respect are
unclear. He may have expected the elements to be placed on the
Communion table before the beginning of the service. However, there is
evidence from later in the sixteenth century that they were prepared
immediately after the prayer of humble access and before the words of

---

90. For the details, see Cuming, *A History of Anglican Liturgy*, pp. 81-83.

institution, and this seems to have become quite common, though no special provision for it was made, either then or later.[91]

Between the offertory and the *Sursum corda* come a number of items, most of which were moved here from later on in the service. The main exception is the provision of three exhortations, following the prayer for the Church militant. Two of these had been present in 1549 but as options before the offertory. In 1552 the third exhortation became compulsory, with the other two still available at the discretion of the minister. The importance of this has been obscured in modern times because this exhortation is almost always left out, which leaves worshippers with a distorted view of what is expected of them.[92] Following that come the words of invitation, the general confession and absolution and, finally, the comfortable words of Scripture.

After the *Sursum corda* the service continues with the prayer of humble access, placed before the words of institution instead of immediately before the Communion, which follows the institution. The 1552 prayer book avoids any mention of 'consecration' but the question arises because in 1662 that term is introduced to describe exactly the same narrative. Was it intended to be a consecration? Here there has been a great difference of opinion but in recent years it has generally been accepted that 'consecration' is a misleading word to use to describe what was being done in the service. It is made perfectly clear that communicants were receiving 'creatures of bread and wine' which were meant to allow them to become 'partakers of his [Christ's] most blessed body and blood' – in other words, the elements were material means to a spiritual end and not the end in themselves. Following the institution came the actual Communion, with entirely new words of administration that made it clear that the communicants were receiving material substances that were intended to remind them of the atoning death of Christ. Any possibility of reading transubstantiation into the service was thus rigorously excluded.

This view of the matter is supported by Cranmer himself, who defined 'consecration' as follows:

---

91. In the 1662 liturgy, however, the celebrant is directed to provide 'sufficient' bread and wine at the time of the offertory and then to arrange them for consecration immediately after the prayer of humble access, so that both the traditional and what had become the customary practice are recognised.

92. Note that Dix, *The Shape of the Liturgy*, pp. 662-63, makes this point quite forcefully.

> Consecration is the separation of any thing from a profane
> and worldly use unto a spiritual and godly use. ... Even so
> when common bread and wine be taken and severed from
> other bread and wine, although it be of the same substance
> that the other is from which it is severed, yet it is now called
> 'consecrated' or 'holy' bread and holy wine. Not that the bread
> or wine have or can have any holiness in them, but that they
> be used to an holy work and represent holy and godly things.[93]

The service then concludes with the Lord's Prayer, a choice of either an oblation or a thanksgiving, the *Gloria* and the final blessing. Criticism of this portion of the service has usually focussed on the choice allowed between an oblation and a thanksgiving, both of which would seem to have a place in it. The slight awkwardness of this situation came about because the prayer of oblation no longer referred to the elements but to the communicants, who offer themselves as a living sacrifice, further undercutting any notion that the sacrifice lies in the consecrated bread and wine. The self-offering of the communicants only makes sense after the reception of the bread and wine, since it is by the atoning work of Christ that believers are strengthened to do the will of God in this way. Because of that, the oblation and the thanksgiving both belong after the Communion as slightly different responses to its benefits, making their availability as alternatives quite comprehensible. Once the communicants have rededicated themselves to the service of God, the *Gloria* sums up the renewed spirit of the congregation and the service comes to an end.

Perhaps the fairest judgement of the 1552 prayer book, from an essentially hostile witness, is the following assessment of it made by Gregory Dix:

> The rite of 1552 does in fact express with great accuracy
> the doctrine, which Cranmer once said that he had learned
> from Ridley. ... What had largely assisted the general
> misunderstanding of 1549 was its retention of the traditional
> Shape of the Liturgy. Cranmer realised that this was a mistake
> if he wanted the new belief to be adopted; and in 1552 he made
> radical changes in this in order to bring out the doctrinal
> implications of 1549. But the wording of the prayers of 1549

---

93. Cranmer, *Defence*, 3.15. See Dix, *The Shape of the Liturgy*, pp. 650-52, for further examples.

needed no such drastic treatment. Rearranged in their new order they served with remarkably few changes to express the full Zwinglian doctrine – in itself a reasonable vindication of Cranmer's claim that this had been their most obvious meaning all along.[94]

One of the most famous legacies of the 1552 rite is the so-called 'Black Rubric' added by Cranmer in order to reassure John Knox (and others who thought like him) that the practice of kneeling to receive Communion was not to be construed as an adoration of the sacrament. Knox, of course, would have preferred to abandon kneeling altogether, so the 'Black Rubric' must be seen as a compromise, not as a straightforward concession to him.[95]

Also worthy of mention is that the 1552 prayer book abolished the Mass vestments that had been worn hitherto and ordered that the Communion table should be placed lengthwise in the nave of the church, with the celebrant standing on the 'north' side. This meant that he would stand halfway down the table on the left-hand side (from the standpoint of the congregation), which presumably was intended to demystify the rite and give people the impression that the priest was standing in their midst as one of them. The rubric withstood the test of time and was retained, even after the table was put back in the chancel. In that case, the 'north side' came to be interpreted as the 'north end', a rather odd position that remained the norm until the nineteenth century and that still survives in some places, though modern liturgical revisions have (sensibly) encouraged the celebrant to stand behind the table, facing the congregation, which is the most obvious place for him to be.

Whether the 1552 revision was meant to be definitive, or whether it was just the next stage in a process that would eventually be taken further, is a question that cannot now be answered. There were certainly those who wanted to go beyond 1552 towards something more like the orders then in use in Geneva or Zurich. However, less than a year

---

94. Dix, *The Shape of the Liturgy*, p. 659. Apart from the mistaken definition of Cranmer's doctrine as 'Zwinglian', this is a good analysis of how 1552 differs from 1549.

95. It was left out of 1559 but reinstated (in an abridged form) in 1662. See C. Hefling, *The Book of Common Prayer: A Guide* (Oxford: Oxford University Press, 2021), pp. 121-24, 265-69, and P.W.M. Blayney, *The Printing and the Printers of the Book of Common Prayer, 1549-1561* (Cambridge: Cambridge University Press, 2022), pp. 209-12.

after the introduction of the 1552 prayer book, Cranmer was under arrest and unable to pursue his programme of further reformation. The 1552 liturgy continued in use only among the English exiles on the Continent, who were divided between those who (like John Knox) felt free to advance further reforms and those who (like Richard Cox) believed that, because the 1552 rite had been approved by Parliament, revisions to it should wait until Parliament was free to agree to them.[96] Knox and Cox famously disagreed over this and the exiles were split as a result. Nevertheless, it should be noted that neither side was wedded to the 1552 prayer book as such – what divided them was the procedure for revision, not the possibility or desirability of it, on which they appear to have been at one. This is made clear by a letter that Richard Cox wrote to John Calvin, dated 5 April 1555, in which he explained how he and his supporters had modified the use of the 1552 prayer book in order to accommodate the scruples of John Knox and those who sided with him:

> When the magistrates [of Frankfurt] lately gave us permission to adopt the rites of our native country, we freely relinquished all those ceremonies which were regarded by our brethren as offensive and inconvenient. For we gave up private baptisms, confirmation of children, saints' days, kneeling at the Holy Communion, the linen surplices of the ministers, crosses, and other things of like character. And we gave them up, not as being impure and papistical, which certain of our brethren often charged them with being; but whereas they were in their own nature indifferent, and either ordained or allowed by godly fathers for the edification of our people, we notwithstanding chose rather to lay them aside than to offend the minds or alienate the affections of the brethren. We retain however the remainder of the form of prayer and of the administration of the sacraments, which is prescribed in our book, and this with the consent of almost the whole church.[97]

---

96. It was also briefly adopted in Scotland by the Lords of the Congregation (the Reformist party in the Church of Scotland) in 1557 until it was replaced by a *Book of Common Order* in 1562 and finally made redundant two years later. See Maxwell, *An Outline of Christian Worship*, pp. 120-21. In England, the 1552 prayer book was formally abolished on 8 November 1553, with effect from 20 December.

97. H. Robinson (ed.), *Original Letters Relative to the English Reformation*, 2 vols (Cambridge: Cambridge University Press, 1846 and 47), vol. 2,

There the matter rested until the accession of Queen Elizabeth I (1558-1603), when the Church of England found itself once more looking for an agreed form for its public worship.

The Elizabethan Settlement

When Elizabeth I succeeded her sister Mary I, she found herself confronted with three different strands of thought in the Church. First, there were the bishops and supporters of the Catholic restoration under Mary. Many of these had suffered deprivation and imprisonment under Edward VI and had been hardened by their sufferings. They were also much more committed to the Roman cause than they had been before, not least because of the papal reforms that were being introduced by the Council of Trent (1545-63), which promised to do away with the most egregious abuses of the medieval Church even as it drew a clear line against Protestantism. Second, there were those churchmen and lay people who had suffered Mary's reign in silence but who had been alienated by her reactionary policies and wanted to return to the *status quo ante*, as it had been at the death of Edward VI, or something like it. Finally, there were the Marian exiles, who returned home with direct experience of Continental Protestantism and a determination to see the Church of England brought into line with what they regarded as the best examples of Reformed worship and practice.

Keeping all three of these happy would be impossible, but the queen knew that she could not afford to alienate any of them too much. Some kind of compromise would be necessary and it was not long before one began to emerge. The Catholic bishops would be the hardest to please and reconciling them proved to be a thankless task. Within a year they were all gone, deprived of their sees and sent into retirement or exile. In marked contrast to Mary I, Elizabeth I made no attempt to persecute them or to create new martyrs, so their disappearance was effected with minimal disturbance to the body politic. Nevertheless, the queen was aware that some of them might still be won over and she was prepared to make concessions – most of them symbolic and superficial – to their sensibilities, if that could be done without unduly upsetting the other two groups. The solution was to return to the situation as it had been in

---

pp. 753-54. See also H.J. Wotherspoon and G.W. Sprott, *The Second Prayer Book of King Edward the Sixth (1552) with Historical Introduction and Notes; and the Liturgy of Compromise Used in the English Congregation at Frankfort* (Edinburgh: William Blackwood & Sons, 1905).

1553 but with the proviso that some revision would be undertaken. Thus it was that the Articles of Religion were overhauled and a second book of Homilies was issued in 1563 (it was reissued in 1571 with an additional homily).

With respect to the prayer book, matters were somewhat more complicated. The 1552 liturgy had been the exiles' text, and they were familiar with it, but open to further revision. Few people in England would have remembered it though and, if they had any memory of an English-language liturgy, it would probably have been the 1549 Book of Common Prayer that came to mind. This is borne out by the fact that, before a new prayer book was issued, some people seem to have assumed that the 1549 version would be resurrected, and its text was used for musical compositions produced for the Chapel Royal at that time.[98] It was also the case that the Latin liturgy that appeared in 1560 reflected the Latin version of the 1549 prayer book to an unexpected degree, though it is not clear why that was so, and the new book was rejected by several of the colleges where it was supposed to be used. How much Queen Elizabeth I influenced this tendency can be no more than a matter of speculation, although, of course, she would have known the 1549 prayer book very well and may have preferred it to the less familiar 1552 version.

Whatever the case, the solution actually adopted was to begin with 1552 and to modify it to a limited extent. The exiles had to give up any hope of reform along the lines already proposed in Frankfurt, but there was no question of returning to 1549. All that was allowed was a modest revision that incorporated elements of 1549 without disturbing the substance of 1552. There were, in fact, only two changes of any significance. The first was the combination of the 1549 and 1552 words of administration in Holy Communion, which combined both the 'objectivity' of 1549 and the 'subjectivity' of 1552, but at the price of creating sentences that were far too long for ordinary use. The other potentially important change was the ornaments rubric (at the beginning of Morning Prayer) which again legalised the ministerial vestments worn in the second year of Edward VI's reign, which had been abolished in 1552. This followed a provision in the Act of Uniformity of 1559, but one that was seemingly contradicted by the royal injunctions issued somewhat later, which preferred the simpler vestments of 1552.[99]

---

98. See B.D. Spinks, *The Rise and Fall of the Incomparable Liturgy: The Book of Common Prayer, 1559-1906* (London: SPCK, 2017), p. 9.

99. See Bray, *Documents*, p. 299, for section 13 of the Act and, p. 307, for Elizabethan Injunctions 1559, no. 30. The other changes concerned the

This discrepancy led to what has become known as the Vestiarian Controversy, which was resolved by following the directions of the 1552 prayer book rather than those of 1549.[100] For the next three centuries that solution prevailed, until it was challenged by the ritualists of the late nineteenth century, who used the ornaments rubric to promote the restoration of vestments that had long been forgotten. The result is that, since then, the Anglican Communion has been bedevilled with a pseudo-theological controversy that should never have arisen, with high church clergy wearing vestments to which no theological significance can be attached.[101]

Whether the 1552 liturgy was ever meant to be the definitive expression of Reformed worship may be questioned, and there were certainly those who did not see it that way. Almost immediately there were voices calling for further changes, and they would be remarkably consistent (and persistent) until 1689 and even later. Nevertheless, whether by accident or by design, it is the 1552 prayer book that became the basis for the classical Anglican liturgy and all subsequent changes up to 1662 must be seen in that light. Not all of these modifications moved in a progressive direction, and some of the better-known ones harked back to 1549, but they were never enough to alter the basic shape of the rite. The 1662 Book of Common Prayer is the child of 1552, not of 1549. This was made perfectly clear by Gregory Dix, who was forced to recognise the fact, very much against his own preferences:

> [The year] 1552 still supplies the whole structure of the present liturgy and some ninety-five percent of its wording. We do not, of course, receive it because it is Cranmer's, but as twice revised (in 1559 and 1662) and as the rite of the Church of England. Yet the fact remains that our rite is as it is because Cranmer thought as he thought.[102]

---

place where Morning and Evening Prayer should be read, the omission of anti-papal statements in the litany and Ordinal, and the addition (in 1561) of 57 minor saints' days. The Black Rubric also disappeared, although, since it had not been officially authorised by Parliament in 1552, it could be argued that it was not really part of the prayer book at all.

100. See *The Advertisements for Due Order, 1566*, in G.L. Bray (ed.), *The Anglican Canons, 1529-1947* (Woodbridge: Boydell & Brewer, 1998), p. 166.
101. Of course, many of those who wear the vestments do attach theological significance to them, although this has no legal force and cannot formally be required of any minister.
102. Dix, *The Shape of the Liturgy*, pp. 669-70.

Parliament passed a new Act of Uniformity on 8 May 1559 and the slightly revised prayer book came into official use on 24 June.[103] There was the usual hesitancy on the part of some conservatives, who were slow to conform to it, and disappointed radicals made their views known throughout Elizabeth's reign, even going to the point of seeking to have Parliament adopt a more thorough-going 'Protestant' form of worship in 1584, and again in 1587, but they failed to gain any traction.[104] By the end of the sixteenth century, most people in England had reconciled themselves to the 1559 liturgy and many had grown attached to its spiritual outlook.[105] It was famously defended in great, even in excruciating, detail by Richard Hooker (1554-1600), whom some have even claimed was the true founder of 'Anglicanism'.[106] That is obviously going too far – Hooker was intent on justifying what already existed, not on producing something new – but his work shows that the 1559 prayer book was bedding down and that it would not be easily dislodged. It had the great advantage over its predecessors in that it survived far longer than they did. If we overlook the very minor alterations that were made in 1604, it survived for just over a century, by which time only a few specialists had any knowledge of what had gone before it.

Discontent with 1559, such as it was, was largely confined to the more radical Protestants, who were increasingly being called 'Puritans' by their opponents. There was not much they could do under Elizabeth I but, when she was succeeded by James VI of Scotland in 1603, they decided to ask him to reopen the question of prayer book revision. The result was the Hampton Court Conference held in early 1604, where it was agreed to make some alterations to the 1559 prayer book. Some of them were merely cosmetic, as for example, the change of the title 'Of them that be baptized in private houses' to 'The Ministration of Private Baptism'. The Catechism was enlarged by including sections on the two sacraments, four lessons from the Apocrypha were replaced by texts from the Old Testament, and a prayer for the royal family was added to the daily offices, along with six prayers of thanksgiving for particular

---

103. Very little is known about the process of approving the 1559 liturgy, other than what we can glean from parliamentary records relating to the passing of the Act of Uniformity. See J. Booty, *The Book of Common Prayer, 1559: The Elizabethan Prayer Book* (Washington, DC: Folger Shakespeare Library, 1978).
104. Spinks, *Incomparable Liturgy*, pp. 23-27.
105. See the evidence in J. Maltby, *Prayer Book and People in Elizabethan and Early Stuart England* (Cambridge: Cambridge University Press, 1998).
106. R. Hooker, *Laws of Ecclesiastical Polity*, 5.25.1.

things, which could be used as appropriate. The conference also initiated a new translation of the Bible which appeared in 1611.[107] Its readings were incorporated into the 1662 Book of Common Prayer as being the most up-to-date and accurate translation available. The calendar of saints' days was also considerably enlarged at this time, though with what effect is hard to say. Most of the names added were (and are) obscure and probably little attention was paid to them in practice.

The Pull of 1549

The 1549 prayer book has long enjoyed a certain prestige in the Anglican world as the first full-length English-language liturgy of the reformed Church of England but this is not its true historical significance. From at least the time of Archbishop William Laud (1633-45), if not before, the 1549 prayer book has been used by those of a high church disposition as a counterfoil to the official liturgy of the Church, which they have sought to revise in its direction. Until the revival of liturgical studies in modern times, most Anglicans recoiled at the thought of going back any further than 1549 because that would have entailed a clear repudiation of the Reformation. However, 1549 had the advantage (from their point of view) of containing much traditional material and of being open to a 'catholic' interpretation to a degree that later forms of worship were not. Anglo-Catholics of modern times have not found the 1549 prayer book altogether satisfactory and some have expressed disapproval of what they see as its 'Protestant' character. Nonetheless, more mainstream representatives of the high church tradition have been content to use it as a starting point for their own liturgical proposals. Both the Scottish prayer book of 1637 and the American prayer books of 1789 and later incorporated elements from the 1549 prayer book and created what some have regarded as a parallel liturgical tradition within the Anglican world, although their divergence from the mainstream should not be exaggerated.[108]

Discontent with the 1559 liturgy from the high church end of the spectrum was slow to emerge. For the most part, its earliest representatives concentrated on the externals of vestments and decoration. Whereas the Puritans preferred simplicity and regarded even such garments as the

---

107. This was the King James Bible, or Authorized Version, although in fact it was never officially authorised by anyone.

108. See W.J. Grisbrooke, *Anglican Liturgies of the Seventeenth and Eighteenth Centuries* (London: SPCK, 1958).

surplice as dangerously papist, those of a more, high church disposition appreciated beauty and even splendour in worship and did what they could to encourage it. By pre-Reformation and contemporary Roman Catholic standards even their best efforts must have appeared somewhat spartan but they were always open to further embellishments and introduced them when and where they could. The Chapel Royal was one focus of their attention, as were a number of cathedrals where there were special provisions for the wearing of traditional vestments.

Exactly when interest in external liturgical furnishings evolved into a desire to alter the prayer book is hard to say, but it seems that at some point in the reign of James VI and I (1603-25) men like John Overall (1559-1619), Lancelot Andrewes (1555-1626) and, above all, Richard Neile (1562-1640) began to move in that direction. Overall is said to have restored the prayer of oblation in the Lord's Supper to its 1549 position and Andrewes tinkered with a number of alterations that moved in the same direction. These appear to have been personal idiosyncrasies, and were tolerated as such, but Richard Neile went further. After his appointment to the see of Durham in 1617, he gathered around him a number of younger men whom he encouraged to take a serious interest in liturgical matters. Among them was William Laud (1573-1645), who became Archbishop of Canterbury in 1633 and did what he could to turn some of his ideas into actual liturgy. Another important figure in later years was John Cosin (1594-1672), who served as domestic chaplain to both Overall and Neile and who was consecrated as bishop of Durham in 1660. In that position he played an important part in the negotiations preceding the adoption of the 1662 Book of Common Prayer, which he tried to move in a conservative direction, though with limited success.

These men moved in a narrow circle close to the court and so were able to exercise patronage and influence out of all proportion to their numbers. James VI and I used them to encourage the Scottish bishops to conform to English norms and he even took Andrewes and Neile with him when he went to Scotland in 1617. However, James was wise enough not to push things too far, especially when his plans for anglicising the Church of Scotland came badly unstuck.[109] His son Charles I (1625-49) was much less cautious and was openly favourable to the high church agenda to a degree that James VI and I had never been. Almost immediately after his accession, he commissioned John Cosin to prepare a *Collection of Private Devotions*, intended mainly for the ladies of the court. It appeared in 1627, to a storm of protest when it

109. See Spinks, *Incomparable Liturgy*, pp. 37-48.

was realised that Cosin had embellished Morning and Evening Prayer with material drawn from the medieval hours, and had even restored the long defunct offices of Terce, Sext and None. In the Communion office, he added a prayer that was clearly taken from the canon of 1549, although it was meant to be said privately during the consecration.[110] One of the prayers Cosin included for the ordination of priests and deacons was incorporated into the liturgy in 1662 but, apart from that, no trace of this *Collection* has survived.[111]

The focus of liturgical innovation now turned to Scotland. Almost from the beginning of the English Reformation the impact of the various prayer books had been felt in Scotland. After the Reformation was enacted by the Scottish Parliament in 1560, the English 1559 prayer book could be found in use, sometimes with minor alterations. The main reason for that seems to have been that there was no readily available alternative. The Scottish Reformers were generally sympathetic to what was going on in England, though they were not as constrained as the English were by the demands of the state. From time to time, suggestions for a more purely Scottish liturgy were put forward, but there was no compelling theological reason to deviate from the English forms and so the latter continued to exert considerable influence north of the border. Following the union of the crowns in 1603, James VI and I tried to get the Scottish bishops to introduce a Book of Common Prayer that would be as close to the English one as possible, but without success.[112] Conformity with England was always James' goal, as part of his project to unite the kingdoms of Great Britain, but the political situation was too delicate to allow him to realise his aim. On the other hand, when he died there was a growing divide between conformist clerics, who were sympathetic to his project, if not totally on board with it, and an increasingly large and influential Presbyterian party that was showing every sign of aligning itself with the English Puritans, making the Scottish Church scene more like the English one than might have been thought possible at the beginning of James' English reign.

Charles I revived his father's project and in 1629 John Maxwell (1586-1647), a Scot who would later become bishop of Ross, brought a draft to London for the king's approval. Maxwell wanted a truly Scottish liturgy, similar in substance to the English one but tailored to Scottish

---

110. By this, Cosin meant the words of institution, since the Book of Common Prayer contained no consecration prayer in the true sense.

111. Cuming, *A History of Anglican Liturgy*, p. 107.

112. G. Donaldson, *The Making of the Scottish Prayer Book of 1637* (Edinburgh: Edinburgh University Press, 1954), pp. 27-59.

needs and sensibilities. The king and Bishop William Laud (as he then was) tried to insist on the English 1604 Book of Common Prayer with no alterations at all. This produced a stalemate and nothing happened for several years but, after Charles I visited Scotland in 1633 for his coronation, developments came quickly. Charles took Laud and another up-and-coming English divine, Matthew Wren (1585-1667), with him. Together, they created a new diocese of Edinburgh and installed a bishop to their liking (though he died soon afterwards). The 1604 prayer book was widely used during the king's visit but this gave a misleading impression. The desire for a distinctive Scottish liturgy remained strong and a compromise gradually emerged. In 1634 Maxwell, now a bishop, went back to London and returned the following year with a new service book in hand. It was the first to use the King James Bible for the Scripture readings and Maxwell was given considerable freedom in the observance of saints' days. The reading of the Apocrypha was dropped from the lectionary and the word 'presbyter' was substituted for 'priest'. The Scots seem to have used the permission to diverge from the 1604 prayer book to maximum effect but there was no sign of any doctrinal deviation from it. At most there was greater tolerance for divergent customs (like allowing people to sit to receive communion rather than kneel) that assuaged Scottish prejudices without unduly alienating the king or Laud, who was now archbishop of Canterbury.

The printing of this new book began almost immediately but was halted because of an intervention by another Scot, James Wedderburn (1585-1639), who would soon become bishop of Dunblane. Wedderburn introduced some radical changes to the Communion office which reflected the influence of the 1549 prayer book. The 1549 prayer of consecration was reinstated, as was the oblation following immediately on it. In particular, the prayer contained an invocation of the Holy Spirit on the elements of bread and wine that was to all intents and purposes an *epiclesis* that the 1552 revision deliberately omitted and that was not to be restored in any subsequent revision up to and including that of 1662. In the context of the 1630s, the reintroduction of an *epiclesis* was a clear sign that those who supported it were leaning in the direction of Rome and, especially, of the ancient Churches of the East, where such an invocation of the Spirit had a very ancient pedigree.

Just as tellingly, the 1552 words of administration were dropped and only the 1549 ones retained, reopening the ambiguity that had allowed traditionalist Catholics to come to terms with the first prayer book of Edward VI.[113] Here, more than anywhere, Wedderburn's proposals

---

113. Cuming, *A History of Anglican Liturgy*, pp. 108-9.

received the specific approbation of Archbishop Laud, who thought that the 1552 words 'seem to relish somewhat of the Zwinglian tenet, that the sacrament is a bare sign taken in remembrance of Christ's passion'.[114] The prayer of humble access was restored to its original 1549 place immediately before the administration, allowing for the impression that communicants were being given access to the already consecrated elements, rather than being invited to participate in the celebrant's work of institution. Finally, the somewhat obscure rubric that encouraged the celebrant to 'use both his hands' during the consecration hinted at the restoration of the medieval elevation of the host, as did the allowance of unleavened wafers (mentioned in the closing rubrics), though that was not recommended. Subtleties of this kind could easily be ignored but their presence pointed to a return to 1549 and, therefore, in the eyes of many contemporaries, to 'popery' – a direction of travel that did not escape the notice of those who regarded it with horror.

For a very long time it was generally maintained that there was no essential difference in the Communion office between the English prayer books from 1552 onwards and the Scottish prayer book of 1637 but, by the late nineteenth century, it was becoming increasingly recognised that this was a form of special pleading. In the words of John Dowden (1840-1910), bishop of Edinburgh from 1886 onwards:

> It may be admitted that between the distinctive Liturgies of the two Churches there is no *essential* disagreement, but it is both untrue and unwise to pretend that the differences that exist are not *grave and important*. Grave and important differences most certainly there are; and in my judgement, in almost every instance in which these differences exist, the superiority is distinctly on the side of the Scottish Office.[115]

---

114. William Laud, *The Works of the Most Reverend Father in God, William Laud, D.D.*, ed. W. Scott and J. Bliss, 7 vols (Oxford: John Henry Parker, 1847-60), vol. 3, p. 357. It should be noted that Laud's assessment of Zwingli was mistaken, although it became and has remained very common in Anglican circles.

115. J. Dowden, *The Scottish Communion Office, 1764* (Oxford: Clarendon Press, 1922), p. 6. As an Irishman ordained in the Church of Ireland in 1864, Dowden had acquired a deep acquaintance with both the English and the Scottish liturgies by the time he came to write these words.

It is not necessary to share Dowden's preference for the Scottish office to see that his judgement of the importance of the differences between the liturgies of England and Scotland would have been shared by most people in 1637, when the majority of Scots (in particular) would have taken the opposite view to his regarding their relative merits. When it was introduced, the 1637 prayer book caused a riot in Edinburgh that may fairly be regarded as the opening salvo in what was to become the Civil War. It got nowhere in Scotland and, to the extent that it was known in England, it raised suspicions that members of the church hierarchy were pedalling back on the Reformation. The book came to be called 'Laud's Liturgy', which is unfair in terms of its original composition, since Archbishop Laud was not directly involved in preparing it and even resisted restoring the preface and the *Sanctus* in Holy Communion to their 1549 position, thereby frustrating Wedderburn's desire to restore the complete form of 1549.[116] However true that may be, once the book was in print Laud defended it in the following terms:

> I shall not find fault with the order of the prayers, as they stand in the Communion-book of England, (for, God be thanked, 'tis well;) yet, if a comparison must be made, I do think the order of the prayers, as they now stand in the Scottish Liturgy, to be the better, and more agreeable to use in the primitive church; and I believe, they which are learned will acknowledge it.[117]

Later generations of high churchmen were, therefore, not entirely wrong to associate Laud with a desire to return to the liturgical shape of the 1549 prayer book and for a long time the two things went together. It would not be until the twentieth century, with the revival of liturgical study more generally, that the connection would be transcended as new approaches to the worship of the Early Church and the emergence of an ecumenical dimension to the whole project of liturgical revision brought a fresh perspective to bear on traditional Anglican positions. At the time, the main result of Laud's efforts was the complete disintegration of everything that he stood for. In England, the 1604 Book of Common Prayer was banned by Parliament on 3 January 1645 (with effect from 13 March) and replaced by an order for public worship that was not

---

116. Donaldson, *The Making of the Scottish Prayer Book*, pp. 51-53; Grisbrooke, *Anglican Liturgies*, p. 3.
117. Laud, *Works of William Laud*, vol. 3, p. 343.

unlike that used by the Church of Scotland. The prayer book continued in clandestine or semi-clandestine use here and there, not least because in the two or three generations that it had had time to implant itself, a significant body of loyalists had grown up in England. These were not Laudians, by any means, and most of them were essentially Puritans, certainly as far as doctrine was concerned. In throwing out the 1604 liturgy, it is fair to say that Parliament overreacted to a greatly exaggerated threat but it also created a situation in which defenders of the old order were susceptible to Laudian tendencies, whether they recognised them as such or not.

In the fifteen years during which the prayer book was banned there was limited opportunity for anyone to express an opinion about it. However, one man who managed to do so was Jeremy Taylor (1613-67), who began his career as a protégé of Archbishop Laud and was forced to serve as a private chaplain to Lord Carbery during the Commonwealth. It was not an easy existence but, compared to what happened to many others, Taylor was well-off. In 1658 he published *A Collection of Offices, or Forms of Prayer in Cases Ordinary and Extraordinary*, which purported to be a supplement to the prayer book but which went beyond it in many important respects. The Communion rite, in particular, was very different from that of 1604 and had affinities with 1549, even though it was far from being a simple reproduction of it. W.J. Grisbrooke had this to say about it:

> it is clear that, despite the sturdy defence of the Book of Common Prayer to which a considerable part of it [the preface] is devoted, Taylor considers his own book to be in some ways superior, and to accord better with the ancient liturgical tradition of the church. This is certainly true, but it must be admitted from the outset that, considered purely as a specimen of liturgical craftsmanship, and ignoring issues of doctrine, it is immeasurably inferior to the Prayer Book. ... Nevertheless, Taylor's eucharistic rite is more satisfactory than Cranmer's, precisely because Taylor's eucharistic theology was, broadly speaking, in the common tradition of the church, whereas Cranmer's was not. What Taylor's liturgy loses in the matter of liturgical artistry, when compared with Cranmer's, it more than gains by its reverence for ancient and traditional models, and its adherence to a more normal – and incidentally, more typically Anglican – theology of the eucharistic action.[118]

118. Grisbrooke, *Anglican Liturgies*, pp. 20-21.

Quite how a rite that differed so substantially from Cranmer's can be regarded as 'more typically Anglican' is a question that must surely puzzle historians of English liturgy. That Taylor was moving away from the Reformation tradition can scarcely be doubted; what is equally certain is that his liturgical experiments had no influence on the revision of the 1604 Book of Common Prayer that was undertaken at the Restoration, and to which we must now turn.

The 1662 Revision

The restoration of the Church of England between 1660 and 1662 focussed on the reintroduction of the 1604 prayer book, but there were three competing visions of what that would entail. Generally speaking, Parliament was content to revive the old book without any substantial change and in this it probably reflected the broad mass of moderate opinion. The 1604 prayer book reappeared early in 1660 and was used in many places without specific authorisation, and nobody seems to have complained about that. It was, however, obvious that certain improvements to it could be made without altering it in any significant way. Obsolete or unclear words could be replaced, the rubrics could be adjusted here and there to make them conform more closely to the canons of the Church of 1604, and the King James Bible, which had not appeared until 1611, could be used for the Scripture readings. There was scope for additional prayers and thanksgivings, and even for a few new collects, such as one for Easter Eve (Holy Saturday), which had not been commemorated in 1604. A certain amount of editorial tidying-up was also desirable, if not very significant in doctrinal or liturgical terms. For example, when a Bible passage from the Old Testament or the Acts of the Apostles was read instead of the usual Epistle, that could be indicated as such, without introducing any substantial change. On matters such as these all parties involved could (and did) agree.

There were, however, two groups that were not satisfied with this. To the 'left', as we would say today, were the so-called Puritans, who wanted a more thoroughgoing revision, consonant with the proposals that they had been making ever since the Hampton Court Conference in 1604.[119]

---

119. The term 'Puritan' is unsatisfactory in some respects, because it included both Presbyterians and Independents. The Independents wanted nothing to do with the prayer book, so it was only the Presbyterians who were represented in the discussions concerning revision. However, to call them 'Presbyterians' at this juncture is to ignore the fact that they were prepared

Many of their objections to the 1604 liturgy were extremely trivial and their opponents often wondered why they bothered making them. They concluded that in reality the Puritans were not objecting to the points they raised so much as scheming for the virtual abandonment of set prayers altogether. This suspicion was reinforced by persistent Puritan attempts to make many of the rubrics, especially those that prescribed the dress and actions of the ministers, optional. They wanted the clergy to have the freedom to shorten or drop portions of the services that they found burdensome, and the laity to be able to receive Communion sitting or standing, instead of kneeling (as the liturgy prescribed). They claimed that what they were advocating was freedom for tender consciences, but others saw this as a ploy to deconstruct the services and even to introduce heretical doctrines if the minister found them appealing.

To the 'right' was (what we would now call) the high church party, represented by bishops like Matthew Wren and John Cosin, that wanted a more 'Laudian' reform in tune with the Scottish liturgy of 1637 and harking back to the 1549 prayer book. They were few in number and had little support in the country; but they were tightly knit and close to the king and the court. They were, therefore, able to exert a disproportionately greater influence on the outcome of the debates concerning revision. In the end, however, they proved to be just as ineffective as the Puritans. The main reason for that is that both sides had to agree that there was fundamentally nothing wrong with the 1604 prayer book, a position that the high churchmen could not honestly adopt. As a result, while they were able to make a few changes, like reintroducing the word 'priest' instead of 'minister' in the rubric preceding the prayer of absolution in the daily offices, nothing of substance was affected. The end result was an edited version of 1604 with a few concessions to high church sentiment – but nothing more than that.

The circumstances in which the revisers worked were far from ideal. The wounds of the civil war were still fresh and the time allowed for debate was extremely short – only four months in all. A conference was summoned to meet at 'the Master's lodging in the Savoy in the Strand' on 25 March 1661 and it was to consist of twelve bishops and

---

to accept episcopacy, even if they disliked such things as compulsory ordination by a bishop. In what follows here, the word 'Puritan' must therefore be taken to mean those who were prepared in principle to accept a revised Book of Common Prayer and be part of the Establishment.

twelve Puritans, with alternates provided for each of them. Those summoned were:

Bishops	Alternates	Puritans	Alternates
Accepted Frewen (York)	John Earle	Edward Reynolds	Thomas Horton
Gilbert Sheldon (London)	Peter Heylin	Anthony Tuckney	Thomas Jacomb
John Cosin (Durham)	John Hacket	John Conant	William Bates
John Warner (Rochester)	John Barwick	William Spurstow	John Rawlinson
Henry King (Chichester)	Peter Gunning	John Wallis	William Cooper
Humphrey Henchman (Salisbury)	John Pearson	Thomas Manton	John Lightfoot
George Morley (Worcester)	Thomas Pierce	Edmund Calamy	John Collins
Robert Sanderson (Lincoln)	Anthony Sparrow	Richard Baxter	Ben. Woodbridge
Benjamin Laney (Peterborough)	Herbert Thorndike	Arthur Jackson	William Drake
Bryan Walton (Chester)		Thomas Case	
Richard Sterne (Carlisle)		Samuel Clark	
John Gauden (Exeter)		Matthew Newcomen	

The bishops of the northern province of York were almost all summoned and one of the Puritans, Edward Reynolds, was already bishop of Norwich.[120] The conference did not meet until 15 April, when the bishops (not unreasonably) wanted to know what the Puritans were proposing. They asked them to present their demands in writing, which the Puritans did on 4 May, in a document known as *The Exceptions*.[121] Unfortunately, many of the things they wanted were trivial in nature,

---

120. The only northern bishop not to be summoned was Samuel Rutter, the bishop of Sodor and Man, who was not consecrated until the day before the conference assembled.
121. For a point-by-point analysis of these, see C.O. Buchanan, *The Savoy Conference Revisited*, Alcuin/GROW Joint Liturgical Studies 54 (Cambridge: Grove Books Limited, 2002).

even if perhaps desirable, and it is not surprising that some of the bishops came to think that their time was being wasted. There were some more important questions at stake, however, mostly to do with the degree of freedom that would be allowed to the minister. A particular bone of contention was the extent to which *ex tempore* prayer would be permitted. Another problem was the place of the Apocrypha, which the Puritans wanted to exclude from the Scripture readings and canticles. Today we find it hard to believe that compromise on questions like these proved to be so difficult and we are inclined to think that, if there had been good will on both sides, a mutually satisfactory agreement could almost certainly have been achieved. However, goodwill is precisely what was lacking and the discussions ended in stalemate.

The first thing that must be said is that the revisers of 1662 made more changes to the prayer book than anyone since 1552. Every aspect of the book was examined and over 600 alterations were approved, the most significant perhaps being the introduction of readings from the King James Version of the Bible on the grounds that it was the most recent and most reliable translation. This did not affect the psalter, however, which remained in its earlier ('Coverdale') form, nor did it influence the scriptural allusions found throughout the orders of worship. The Black Rubric, abandoned in 1559, was also restored. On the other hand, the words of institution in Holy Communion were officially renamed as the prayer of consecration, thereby introducing a term that had been used in an English-language liturgy for the first time in 1637. Whether changes of this kind were made to annoy the Puritans or to appease the more extreme high churchmen is hard to say – it may have been a bit of both.[122] Of the 96 requests for revision made by the Puritans, only seventeen were adopted, and few of them made any real difference in practice. Of those that did, the most important would appear to be the one that introduces a new rubric into the words of institution in the Communion office, directing the celebrant to break the bread and to put his hand on the cup at the moment of consecration. It seems somewhat strange to us that the Puritans would insist on that, but the manual acts were important to them because they reinforced the view that the

---

122. It is sometimes claimed that the reintroduction of the word 'consecration' was due to the influence of the Scottish liturgy of 1637, which also used it (following the 1549 prayer book), but the text itself was unaltered from the 1604 rite and, therefore, cannot be regarded as a consecration in the true sense of the word.

consecration of the elements was effected by the words of Jesus, not by any oblation made by the celebrant.

Another change of particular interest was the alteration of the rubric originally attached to the Catechism, saying that baptised (but unconfirmed) children were undoubtedly saved. Instead of that, a new rubric was inserted at the end of the order of public baptism stating only that a baptised child who dies before committing actual sin is 'undoubtedly saved'. This has often been misunderstood as an affirmation of baptismal regeneration but it is not, because the child would certainly have committed further sins had it lived. Baptism is not a kind of vaccination against sin but, in the case of infants dying before they come to the age of discretion, it is a reassurance that the faith of the parents and godparents will be honoured by God in His grace and says nothing about the effect of baptism on the spiritual condition of the child.

A complete list of the seventeen concessions agreed to by the bishops is as follows:

1. The Epistles and Gospels will follow the King James Version. (A desirable updating.)
2. 'For the Epistle' will be used when the first lesson is not from an Epistle. (Editorial adjustment.)
3. The Psalms will be corrected by the Great Bible of 1538. (Editorial adjustment.)
4. 'This day' will be used in collects and prefaces only on the day itself; otherwise 'as about this time' will be used instead. (Editorial adjustment.)
5. Communicants will be required to give notice 'at least sometime the day before'. (Allows slightly longer time, but hard to implement in practice.)
6. On repelling scandalous persons from Communion, [1603 (1604)] Canons 27-28 will be observed. (Clarification of existing practice. The minister's power to excommunicate was affirmed but he would have to report the matter to the bishop within fourteen days.)
7. The whole preface (Exodus 20:2) will be prefixed to the Ten Commandments. (Minor improvement.)
8. The second exhortation will be read before Communion. (Well meant, but generally ignored in practice.)
9. Confession before Communion will be read by one of the ministers, the people saying it after him. (Mandates congregational participation.)

10. The manual acts will be used in consecration. (Instead of in the prayer of oblation.)

11. The position of the baptismal font may be adjusted at the bishop's discretion, if people cannot hear what is being said there. (A practical improvement.)

12. In the Catechism, the words 'Yes, they do perform them' will be changed to 'because they promise them both by their sureties'. (A realistic alteration.)

13. The rubric about baptised children dying unconfirmed will be amended. (Reference to confirmation was dropped.)

14. The words 'or be ready and desirous to be confirmed' will be added to the rubric after confirmation. (A potentially important concession.)

15. In matrimony, 'I thee honour' will replace 'I thee worship'. (Not adopted.)

16. In matrimony, 'till death us do part' will replace 'till death us depart'. (Editorial adjustment.)

17. In the burial service, the words 'sure and certain' will be omitted before 'hope of the resurrection'. (Not adopted.)

In fairness to the Puritans, it must be said that they were prepared to compose a liturgy of their own in which their principles would be given clear expression. Richard Baxter undertook this task; and in recent times some liturgical scholars have looked favourably on what he produced.[123] Unfortunately, his liturgy evoked little sympathy at the time and was not taken seriously in the debates, although modern critics have described it as 'an admirable and dignified liturgy' and wondered whether the real problem was that 'it was too much ahead of its time' to be accepted.[124]

On the high church side, there had been some considerable activity going back several years. Matthew Wren had spent most of his enforced leisure during the Commonwealth making annotations on the 1604 prayer book and, after his release in 1660, he sent them to John Cosin. Cosin had already been collecting a number of observations, some of

---

123. The text of Baxter's liturgy is in B. Thompson, *Liturgies of the Western Church* (Philadelphia, PA: Fortress Press, 1980), pp. 385-93. An abbreviated Communion service can be found in Jasper and Cuming, *Prayers of the Eucharist*, pp. 334-41. The most detailed study, including the text, is G.J. Segger, *Richard Baxter's Reformed Liturgy: A Puritan Alternative to the Book of Common Prayer* (London: Taylor & Francis, 2016).

124. Jasper and Cuming, *Prayers of the Eucharist*, p. 341.

them attributable to his erstwhile mentor John Overall, but combined with (and modified by) a number of other sources. These he collected as notes written into a 1619 printing of the 1604 prayer book, which was itself full of typographical errors, which he corrected. The end result was what is now known as the 'Durham Book', after the see to which he was appointed in 1661.[125] Cosin showed great partiality for the 1549 prayer book, though it was consistently mediated through the Scottish liturgy of 1637. There are also similarities to the forms of service drawn up by Jeremy Taylor and by Robert Sanderson, bishop of Lincoln, though these appear to have been coincidental rather than deliberate.[126]

The Durham Book was in a constant state of flux during the Savoy Conference, as Cosin made additions and amendments to it. The end result was an almost unreadable manuscript that needed serious editing, a task that was assigned to William Sancroft (1617-93), a future archbishop of Canterbury. Sancroft not only put the assorted array of notes into a manageable order but also introduced a number of changes to Cosin's text. Many of these are of a purely editorial nature, though not all. He eventually produced what is known as a 'fair copy', based on a 1634 folio edition of the 1604 liturgy, which revealed a strong tendency to eliminate the more radical suggestions of the Durham Book. Almost all the avoidable alterations were taken out, possibly in the hope of maintaining the ones that really mattered to Cosin and his companions – those of the Communion office. However, even there, Sancroft left the canon of 1604 as it was and printed Cosin's revision of it as a 'Paper B', which he offered for debate in the convocation of Canterbury that was to meet on 21 November.

If Sancroft's strategy was to persuade the convocation to accept Cosin's reordering of the Communion office, it failed. The book that was finally approved by the two convocations and submitted to Parliament was one that conformed in all essentials to what the legislature had wanted from the beginning. In the words of Geoffrey Cuming:

> most of the alterations that give the Durham Book its special character ... are suppressed, and what emerges, after a general tidying-up and modernization, is still recognizably the book of 1604. Although Cosin and Wren must have been glad of the numerous minor improvements, to Cosin at least

125. G.J. Cuming, *The Durham Book: Being the First Draft of Revision of the Book of Common Prayer in 1661* (London: Oxford University Press, 1975).
126. Ibid., p. xx.

the rejection of the most important changes must have been a severe disappointment after a lifetime of work upon the Prayer Book and the labour spent on compiling the Durham Book.'[127]

Parliament duly annexed this revised book to its new Act of Uniformity, passed on 19 May 1662 and set to come into force on 24 August.[128] Much attention has focussed on its Communion office. However, there were a number of other features that distinguished the 1662 prayer book from what had been customary since 1552. A new preface was added, with the original 1549 one following on and renamed 'Concerning the Service of the Church'. Four prayers were extracted from the litany and placed at the end of both Morning and Evening Prayer, along with the addition of an extra prayer for the royal family. There were several occasional prayers added as options to be used when appropriate, as well as two thanksgiving prayers, one general and the other for the restoration of peace. New collects were provided for the third Sunday in Advent and for St Stephen's Day (26 December), and a set of collect, Epistle and Gospel was composed for the (very rare) sixth Sunday after Epiphany.

In the Communion office, a commemoration of the departed was added to the prayer for the Church militant, although the claim (made by some high churchmen) that this amounted to a reintroduction of a prayer for the dead cannot be sustained. It does, however, testify to a rare influence of the Scottish 1637 prayer book on the revision; and the rubric directing the presentation of the alms and the placing of the bread and wine on the holy Table comes straight out of the 1549 Prayer Book. At the same time, the Black Rubric of 1552, omitted in 1559, was restored, with the words 'real and essential presence' (of Christ) being replaced by 'corporal presence', so as to exclude transubstantiation without denying that Jesus promised to meet his faithful people in the breaking of bread.

As far as baptism was concerned, care was taken to explain the meaning of the signing with the cross, which had been controversial among the Puritans, and greater attention was given to the examination of the godparents. Public baptism was given clear preference over the private service, though the latter was not eliminated, as many Puritans had wished. Also significant, especially for later times, was the inclusion of a service of adult baptism which had previously not been thought to be necessary. It was added because the universality of infant baptism

127. Ibid., pp. xxv-xxvi.
128. For the text of the Act, see Bray, *Documents*, pp. 492-504.

had broken down under the Commonwealth and because native people in the newly established colonies were being converted to Christianity and had to be baptised. In this somewhat curious way, the primitive practice of baptism was restored, though it would be some centuries before the true significance of this would be appreciated.

Various other changes were introduced to the occasional offices, most of them cosmetic in nature, and the commination was specifically tied to Ash Wednesday for the first time. The Ordinal was thoroughly overhauled, with the forms used for deacons, priests and bishops being more clearly distinguished from one another than had previously been the case. There was also a form of prayer to be used at sea, in recognition of the importance of maritime trade and overseas expansion, which had grown exponentially since 1604. The state prayers for 30 January (death of King Charles I), 29 May (restoration of King Charles II) and 5 November (the foiling of the Gunpowder Plot) were included at the end, with the last of these undergoing some revision. There might have been a service for the consecration of churches and chapels, but for some reason that seems to have been lost and was not included in the final draft. Provision was also made for translating the prayer book into Latin, but that could not be finished in time for 24 August, and it was not completed until 1670. Meanwhile, editions in French (for the Channel Islands), Welsh and even Greek were produced and used when occasion demanded. The Church of Ireland also welcomed the 1662 prayer book, although it was not until four years later that its use became mandatory in that country and it was not translated into Irish until 1712. The Irish liturgy contained an additional set of state prayers on 23 October to commemorate the foiling of the Ulster rebellion in 1641 but was otherwise identical to the English book. As for the Irish-language edition, it did nothing to win the native population over to Protestantism and it is doubtful whether it was ever used at all in a Church that had by then become almost exclusively associated with the English Protestant Ascendancy.

Since the Reformation

The Reception of the 1662 Liturgy

The imposition of the 1662 Book of Common Prayer led immediately to the exodus of a significant number of Puritan ministers who could not bring themselves to use it with a clear conscience. A case can certainly be made for saying that greater flexibility towards the Puritan position would have kept more of them on side with minimal cost, and most modern observers, including many who are not naturally sympathetic to them, would agree with that.[129] The sense that, with a little goodwill on all sides, a viable solution could be found, remained powerful and the possibility that, as the emotions of the civil war started to cool, something along those lines would eventually emerge continued to fuel the hopes of moderate Puritans like Richard Baxter. Those hopes came to nothing in the end but they were not doomed to failure from the start. The 1662 prayer book had been accepted in the House of Commons by a majority of only six votes, which showed that there was considerable sympathy for the dissenters and proposals for embracing them within the Establishment were soon circulating.[130] Among them were suggestions for reforming the liturgy by abolishing the use of the Apocrypha, by removing language that could be interpreted as supporting the idea of baptismal regeneration and so on.

A desire for toleration and for the comprehension of all Protestants within the Church of England continued to manifest itself, despite many setbacks, during the reign of Charles II (1660-85). One of the problems was that it seemed difficult to grant toleration to Protestant dissenters but not to Roman Catholics, for whom there was much less sympathy in Parliament. Quakers and Anabaptists were another headache, since their beliefs fell outside the Protestant norm and they could not be comprehended within it. Matters came to a head in the reign of James II (1685-88). He had converted to Roman Catholicism as far back as 1673 and there had been a serious, but unsuccessful, attempt to exclude him from the succession. When he became king, he naturally wanted to grant toleration to his fellow Catholics, but he could not reasonably do that without including the Protestant dissenters as well. This policy was strongly resisted within the Church of England. Nevertheless, James pressed ahead and issued a Declaration of Indulgence in 1687, granting liberty of conscience all round.

The practical effect of this was to increase fears of Roman Catholic ascendancy, which were confirmed when the queen gave birth to a son in 1688. Parliament had to act and the upshot was the invasion of

---

129. See, for example, R.S. Bosher, *The Making of the Restoration Settlement: The Influence of the Laudians, 1649-1662* (London: Dacre Press, 1951), p. 276.
130. For a survey of these, see T.J. Fawcett, *The Liturgy of Comprehension 1689: An Abortive Attempt to Revise the Book of Common Prayer* (Southend-on-Sea: Mayhew-McCrimmon, 1973), pp. 6-10.

England by William of Orange, who claimed the crown for himself and his wife Mary, the Protestant daughter of James II. The political crisis produced a new incentive for a reconciliation between the Church and the Protestant dissenters and moves were set on foot to achieve this by reopening issues than had lain dormant since 1662. Opposition to this was greatly diminished when a number of high church bishops refused to take the oath of allegiance to William and Mary and were deprived of their sees as 'Non-jurors'. Their removal paved the way for the so-called Latitudinarians within the Establishment to make suggestions for a revision of the liturgy that would be acceptable to the majority of dissenters. The Latitudinarians had been at work even before James II was deposed. Their efforts came into the open in 1689, when a commission to reform the prayer book was established.[131] Membership of this commission was large and broadly based, but it soon became apparent that there was a high church element, strong in the lower house of the convocation of Canterbury, that did not want accommodation with the dissenters.

The result was a pamphlet war in which the high church party did its best to discredit the dissenters by claiming that their willingness to conform to the Establishment was insincere and that, in any case, for the Church to act when so many of its bishops were under sequestration as Non-jurors would call into question the legitimacy of the whole proceedings. Against this opposition, those who favoured toleration found themselves waging an uphill battle. They argued that including the erstwhile dissenters would strengthen the Church by establishing a solid phalanx of opposition to Rome. However, that argument was countered by the claim that the price for such agreement was too high, since it would have diluted the doctrinal and disciplinary integrity of the existing Church. The willingness of the Latitudinarians to revisit the *Exceptions* of 1661 and accept about 60 per cent of them was further presented as a compromise without any corresponding benefit, since the dissenters would never be satisfied with half a loaf – they wanted the whole thing. In the end, the proposal to open discussions with them was defeated in the convocation of Canterbury and the suggested revisions were never discussed at all. In fact, the proposed revisions to the prayer book of 1689 (the so-called 'Liturgy of Comprehension') were kept secret and not made public until 1854, long after the original controversy had faded into history. As a result, the proposed liturgy has never been more

---

131. On 17 September; see ibid., pp. 26-45.

than a historical curiosity, a text that nobody has ever used or even examined seriously.

The high churchmen who wrecked the comprehension scheme in 1689 did not do so out of any special love for the 1662 rite. To them, the 1662 prayer book was merely one element in a wider structure of Church Establishment, but they defended it because, to their minds, altering one part of the edifice would bring the rest crashing down with it. They were thus in no position to propose any alternative prayer book and clung to the one they had inherited, whether they liked it or not. The Non-jurors were initially determined to stick to the 1662 liturgy as part of their claim to be the only legitimate members of the Church of England, but they were not constrained by its Establishment and over time some of them became more open to change. Theologically speaking, they and the conforming high churchmen were on the same page, and indeed the latter were often under suspicion because of it. It would not be until well into the eighteenth century that there would be any attempt to produce a high church prayer book that could rival the 1662 liturgy and political circumstances would ensure that, even when that happened, the results would remain virtually unknown outside Non-juring circles. Indeed, had it not been for the activities of high churchmen of a later generation, these efforts would probably never have seen the light of day and might now be entirely forgotten. Their importance, such as it is, does not derive from their origins but from the claims made on their behalf long afterwards.

The first stirrings of discontent came in the writings of Edward Stephens (1633-1706), an eccentric lawyer who developed an animosity towards Thomas Cranmer that bordered on hatred. However, unlike some of his contemporaries who returned to the Church of Rome, Stephens had an almost equal dislike of contemporary Catholicism. Instead of that, he came increasingly to believe that it was in the liturgies of the Eastern Orthodox Church that the true eucharistic doctrine could be found and he directed his energies towards reconstructing the Anglican rites in a way that would conform to them. He did not stray beyond the existing prayer books but rearranged them in a way that would fulfil his desires. Not surprisingly, what emerged was very similar to the 1549 Book of Common Prayer, although with elements of the Scottish liturgy of 1637 as well. He published his conclusions and his proposed liturgy in 1702 and again in 1705. However, there is little sign that anyone took him seriously and his work has generally been neglected ever since.[132]

Stephens' importance lies in the fact that his work is a bridge between the high church tradition of the seventeenth century and what some of the Non-jurors would produce in the eighteenth. It is rooted in an elevation of form over substance – what mattered to him was the (supposed) antiquity of a rite, not its theological content, and in fact it is hard to know what Stephens himself believed about the sacrament.[133] It is particularly unfortunate that he accepted the so-called *Apostolic Constitutions*, a late fourth- or fifth-century compilation of distinctly Arian sympathies, as authentic, which led him to believe that the Clementine liturgy in Book Eight was the work of Clement of Rome and therefore as close to the apostles as we can get. That erroneous belief was to have a major impact on eighteenth-century developments and is one of several reasons why those developments are generally neglected today.

The pathways pioneered by Stephens were followed in two very different directions. On the one hand, there were men like William Whiston (1667-1752) and John Henley (1692-1756), who were Arian in theology and who wanted to revise the 1662 liturgy in order to remove all reference to the Trinity and the deity of Christ.[134] Belief in the antiquity of the Arian *Apostolic Constitutions* naturally aided this but the obviously heretical intentions of the revisers alerted the more orthodox theologians of the Church to the danger that was presenting itself in the guise of 'authenticity'. The 1662 prayer book now came to be seen as a standard of doctrine in a way that had not been true before, and resistance to any change in it hardened accordingly.

Very different from this was the approach of certain Non-jurors who were impeccably orthodox in trinitarian terms but dissatisfied with the 1662 prayer book because it did not reflect the earliest liturgies

---

132. For an account of Stephens, see Grisbrooke, *Anglican Liturgies*, pp. 37-55. Grisbrooke prints Stephens' two liturgies on pp. 201-19 and 233-45.
133. Grisbrooke, ibid., p. 53, writes: 'It is unfortunate that Stephens has not left us a more detailed account of his doctrine of the Eucharist. Nevertheless, the evidence which we have considered suffices to create a picture of a eucharistic theology at once more "advanced" than that of the great majority of the Caroline divines, and less so – if only in so far as it is less precise – than that of the later Nonjurors, whose characteristic modes of thought and expression Stephens to some extent anticipates.'
134. See Grisbrooke, *Anglican Liturgies*, pp. 56-70, for a detailed exposition of their position and, pp. 247-71, for the texts of their liturgies.

known to them. In particular, it did not allow for any interpretation of the Eucharist as a sacrifice, in the way that they supposed the ancient liturgies did. Their inspiration came from John Johnson (1662-1725), who was instituted as rector of Cranbrook, Kent in 1707. Johnson soon produced *The Propitiatory Oblation in the Holy Eucharist* (1710) and his most important work, *The Unbloody Sacrifice and Altar Unvailed and Supported* (1714). In them he advocated a view of the Eucharist that seemed to many of his contemporaries to be perilously close to Roman Catholicism, although he himself believed that it was fully compatible with the 1662 rite. As analysed by W.J. Grisbrooke, Johnson argued that: 'the Eucharist is offered for the same ends as the sacrifices of the ancients, *viz.*, to render prayer acceptable, to express thanks, to expiate guilt, to own God's dominion, to procure the divine favour, and to preserve covenant and communion with God'.[135]

Johnson also concluded that, because the Eucharist is a true representation of the one sacrifice of Christ, which was both propitiatory and expiatory, it followed that the Eucharist was not only propitiatory, as all sacrifices are, but also expiatory, since otherwise it could not be a true representation.[136] Johnson went out of his way to deny any notion of transubstantiation and claimed that the Church Fathers, on whose testimony he relied so much, believed that the eucharistic bread and wine were types, figures or symbols of the body and blood of Christ, and not the body and blood themselves. Nonetheless, in the eyes of his opponents he protested too much and it is indeed difficult to see how he could reconcile his affirmative statements about the efficacy of the Eucharist with his insistence that, in the end, it was just a symbolic ritual.

The Non-jurors who succumbed to his line of argument did not feel constrained to respect the 1662 Book of Common Prayer in the way that Johnson did and they were quick to adopt his teaching and adapt it to their own purposes. In 1718 a number of them produced a liturgy in which they advocated what became known as the four 'usages'.[137] These were as follows:

1. the express invocation (*epiclesis*) of the Holy Spirit in the consecration of the elements

---

135. Ibid., p. 73, summarising Johnson, *Unbloody Sacrifice*, Part 2, Chapter 1, section 2.
136. Ibid., p. 73, paraphrasing Johnson, *Propitiatory Oblation*, p. 32.
137. For a commentary, see Grisbrooke, *Anglican Liturgies*, pp. 71-112, and for the text, pp. 275-96.

2. the removal of the prayer of oblation from its position after the Communion in the 1552/1662 rites to its original place before it in 1549
3. the commemoration of the faithful departed by praying for them
4. the addition of water to the wine in the chalice.

None of these things was present or authorised in the 1662 prayer book, which was therefore regarded as deficient. To those who advocated them (the Usagers), the four usages were essential for a true Eucharist and they were not prepared to compromise. Unfortunately for them, a great many Non-jurors dissented from their opinion and refused to go along with what they saw as innovations. The result was a schism that was to persist until the Non-jurors finally disappeared in the early years of the nineteenth century.

An examination of the usages will show that the 1549 rite could be cited in support of the first two of them. The third could be accommodated by removing the words 'militant here in earth' from the prayer for the Church in the Lord's Supper and the fourth could be introduced merely by adding an appropriate rubric. It is the last of these usages which is the most curious. Research into the practices of the synagogue and the Early Church suggest that at the Last Supper Jesus may well have mixed water with the wine that he gave his disciples but that is not stated in the New Testament and does not appear to have had any doctrinal significance. If it happened, it was just a widespread ancient habit, possibly designed to dilute the acerbic taste of so much wine at that time, and the Roman Catholic Church attached no particular significance to it. However, in the eyes of the Non-jurors, that indifference on the part of Rome was merely one more indication of how corrupt a Church it was – prepared to deviate from Jesus' own practice and denying its importance.[138]

The Re-emergence of a Scottish Prayer Book

The Non-jurors lived in an ecclesiastical fantasy world but the Usagers among them became increasingly convinced that they stood for practices that went back to the Early Church and were therefore essential. They were ignored in England but believed that they might have more success in Scotland, where Episcopalianism had been disestablished in 1690. Most erstwhile Episcopalians conformed to the Presbyterian settlement

---

138. See Dowden, *Scottish Communion Office*, p. 56.

that was then introduced there, but a small number did not. The Scottish Episcopal Church, as it subsequently constituted itself, was particularly susceptible to the argument that it represented ancient tradition, though most of its members were more inclined to see that embodied in the 1662 Book of Common Prayer than in the Non-jurors' new liturgy. That led to a campaign to promote the usages in Scotland, which gradually gained traction, thanks to the sheer persistence of its advocates, who were able to point out that much of what was in the Usagers' 1718 liturgy had been taken from the Scottish liturgy of 1637.

Elements of the 1637 prayer book had survived here and there among some Scottish Episcopalians and in 1722 there was a reprint of its Communion office that omitted the exhortations and both the rubrics and the collects after the blessing. This reprint and those that followed came to be called the 'wee bookies' and they slowly began to spread across the Episcopal Church. In 1731 the Scottish bishops gave this revised 1637 liturgy their blessing, without making it compulsory, and after that the way to further change was opened up, though it would take a generation for it to produce lasting results.[139] The most significant figure in this development was Thomas Rattray (1684-1743).[140] Rattray claimed to have rediscovered the primitive liturgy of the Church of Jerusalem, which he equated with the earliest version of the Eastern Orthodox liturgy of St James.[141] Rattray found what he thought was this version in the so-called Clementine liturgy, preserved in the *Apostolic Constitutions*. His learning was very great and carried conviction, although we now know that he was fundamentally mistaken. In 1755 Bishop William Falconer (or Falconar) (1707-84) produced a Communion office that clearly reflected Rattray's work, which then became foundational for subsequent liturgical revision in Scotland.[142] By that time the Scottish Episcopal Church had been officially proscribed following the 1745 rebellion, which many Episcopalians had supported. In 1789 the bishops and clergy agreed to pray for the king and petitioned Parliament for a relaxation of the penal laws, which was granted on the second attempt in 1792.

---

139. Ibid., pp. 63-77.
140. Bishop of Brechin (1727) and then Dunkeld (1731), and primus of the Scottish Episcopal Church from 1738 until his death.
141. T. Rattray, *The Ancient Liturgy of the Church of Jerusalem: Being the Liturgy of St. James* (London: James Bettenham, 1744).
142. Falconer was bishop of Moray (1742-1778) and Edinburgh (1776-1784), as well as primus of the Scottish Episcopal Church (1762-1782).

During these years, Falconer raised the question of composing a Communion office for the Scottish Episcopal Church when he became primus in 1762, and one was duly produced two years later.[143] He could not have known it at the time, but it was to remain the recognised Scottish text until 1911, with only a few minor changes in the interval.[144] The 1764 Communion office was clearly indebted to the 1637 Scottish prayer book and through it to its 1549 predecessor. However, thanks to the efforts of Thomas Rattray, there was an important difference. The invocation (*epiclesis*) was moved to a position more in keeping with Rattray's discoveries in the Eastern liturgies and there it was to remain.

Despite some moves in its favour, the 1764 Communion office did not displace the 1662 liturgy in Scotland, which remained in general use throughout the nineteenth century, so much so, in fact, that, when the Scots adopted a new code of canons in 1863, the 1662 prayer book was granted precedence in all circumstances.[145] The 1764 Communion office might have faded into oblivion altogether had it not been for the fact that the Scottish bishops were asked to consecrate bishops for the Episcopal Church in the United States following the War of Independence. As part of their agreement to do so, the Scots implored Samuel Seabury, whom they consecrated as bishop of Connecticut on 14 November 1784, to adopt what they saw as a more primitive liturgy than that of 1662. On the following day Seabury and his Scottish consecrators signed seven articles of agreement that were designed 'to serve as a Concordate or Bond of Union between the Catholic remainder of the antient [*sic*] Church of Scotland and the now rising Church in the state of Connecticut'.[146]

Seabury's initial attempt to apply these articles at a convention of seven American states held in Philadelphia from 27 September to 7 October 1785 was too radical to receive general acceptance. Nonetheless, a year later, on 22 September 1786, he succeeded in getting a slightly revised version of the 1764 Scottish office approved by his own diocese of Connecticut.[147] That arrangement did not last long because in 1789

---

143. *The Communion Office for the Use of the Church of Scotland, as far as Concerneth the Ministration of that Holy Sacrament* (Edinburgh: Drummond, 1764).
144. See Dowden, *Scottish Communion Office*, p. 79, for a list of these.
145. Ibid., pp. 85-88.
146. Ibid., p. 99.
147. The seven states represented at Philadelphia were New York, New Jersey, Pennsylvania, Delaware, Maryland, Virginia and South Carolina; but

the surviving Episcopal churches in the newly formed United States met to hammer out a prayer book for use throughout what was to become the Protestant Episcopal Church. The form that it adopted included the 1764 prayer of consecration, followed by the oblation and invocation as it prescribed, giving the new prayer book something of the flavour of 1549 without following it exactly. In other respects, the influence of 1662 remained, notably in the positioning of the prayer of humble access before the prayer of consecration instead of after it, as had been the case in 1549, 1637 and 1764. The American Book of Common Prayer also preserved the 1552 words of administration alongside those of 1549, which neither the 1637 nor the 1764 offices had done. As a result, although the American prayer book tradition is in some respects distinct from the English one, it is not as independent of 1662 as Samuel Seabury and his Scottish supporters originally envisaged.[148]

One of the factors inhibiting more radical liturgical revision was the fear expressed in England and elsewhere that the Americans were in danger of abandoning doctrinal orthodoxy. There was considerable disquiet in Enlightenment circles at the *Quicunque Vult* (the Athanasian Creed) with its clauses that damned heretics to everlasting destruction, and that creed was duly excised from the American prayer book. A similar attempt to delete the Nicene Creed from the service of Holy Communion was resisted but the mere fact that it could be proposed was a warning of what liturgical change might entail. That fear has resurfaced whenever liturgical reform has been proposed, and it must be regarded as one of the factors that has ensured that the 1662 Book of Common Prayer would remain the norm for the Church of England, and by extension of the wider Anglican Communion, where matters of doctrine are concerned.

The Nineteenth Century

The Scottish and American prayer books represented a certain departure from 1662 but the effects of this on the wider Anglican world were negligible. As Anglican missionaries took the English tradition with them across the globe, it was the 1662 liturgy that formed the backbone of their worship. This was as true of the settler colonies of Canada, Australia and New Zealand as it was of outreach to the un-Christianised parts of Africa and Asia. In England itself, devotion to the 1662 rite remained unchallenged. The Wesleys remained personally attached to

---

Connecticut was not among them.
148. Dowden, *Scottish Communion Office*, pp. 99-105.

it, even as they introduced the greatest liturgical innovation of them all – congregational hymn singing. It is hard for us to believe, but the 1662 prayer book made no provision for that and for a long time singing hymns in church was technically illegal. Charles Simeon (1759-1836), a leader of the Evangelical movement, thought that the English liturgy was beyond compare, and said so. In November 1811 he gave a series of lectures on the subject in Cambridge (and published them the following year).[149] As he put it: 'A tender seriousness, a meek devotion and an humble joy, are the qualities which it was intended, and is calculated, to produce in all her members.'[150]

Like the Methodists, Anglican Evangelicals were driven to add additional forms of worship to their repertoire and seldom felt constrained by the prayer book, though they continued to use it and to honour it in the settings for which it was devised. The quality of services varied enormously from one place to another but this was not the fault of the liturgy itself. On the contrary, the Book of Common Prayer remained a treasured resource and to some extent it could compensate for substandard performances by clergy and others who led public worship.[151]

It might be expected that the rise of the Oxford Movement after 1833 would entail at least a degree of rejection of the prayer book but, although that was to happen over time, it was not characteristic of the earliest Tractarians, as the forerunners of the movement are known from the *Tracts for the Times* they produced in defence of their views. On the contrary, John Henry Newman (1801-90) argued in Tract 3 (*On Alterations in the Liturgy*, 9 September 1833) that he and his colleagues were the only true prayer book loyalists; and that theme was to recur in Tracts 38 and 41 (published the following year).[152] Their strategy was to follow the 1662 rubrics to the letter, in the hope that the bishops would then feel bound to enforce them, though they were to be disappointed. One of the problems was that some of the rubrics, and notably the one

---

149. C. Simeon, *The Excellency of the Liturgy: In Four Discourses, Preached before the University of Cambridge, in November, 1811* (Cambridge: J. Smith, 1812). See also A. Atherstone, *Charles Simeon on* The Excellency of the Liturgy, Alcuin/GROW Joint Liturgical Study 72 (Norwich: Hymns Ancient and Modern, 2011).
150. Simeon, *The Excellency of the Liturgy*, p. 54.
151. For an overview and examples of how the prayer book was used, see Spinks, *Incomparable Liturgy*, pp. 130-37.
152. Ibid., pp. 137-38.

that enjoined the wearing of liturgical vestments as they had been in 1548, the second year of Edward VI's reign, had long been ignored and had fallen into disuse. Reviving them, even if it could be argued that it was strictly legal, was bound to incur accusations of 'popery' and to lead Evangelicals and others to be more selective in their fulsome praise for the 1662 rite. The fact that some high churchmen (not all of them Tractarians by any means) could use ambiguous phrases in the prayer book to support such notions as baptismal regeneration and Eucharistic sacrifice reminded Evangelicals that they were not as wedded to the text as they might theoretically profess to be, and that a few modest changes would not go amiss. The difficulty was trying to decide which changes were desirable and which were not, since there were many liberal churchmen who agreed with them about the sacramental questions but who would have gone much further, for example, by dropping as many references to sin and to the Trinity as they could. Evangelicals could never be sure that revision would avoid such radicalism and so they often preferred to stick with what they had, even if some parts of the prayer book made them uncomfortable.

Rising interest in the 1662 liturgy and its origins led Francis Procter (1812-1905) to publish his textbook *A History of the Book of Common Prayer, with a Rationale of Its Offices* in 1855. For its time, it was a remarkable compendium of liturgical knowledge and the author updated it periodically as new information became available. In 1901, with Procter's permission, the work was revised and rewritten by W.H. Frere (see below) and, with a few corrections and alterations in 1902 and 1905, it remained a primary source book for more than half a century.[153]

Matters became more serious as Tractarianism morphed into full-blown Anglo-Catholicism. It was probably only a matter of time before people who were interested in reviving pre-Reformation liturgies and practices would find the prayer book inadequate and seek to 'enrich' it with borrowings from other sources – in this case, mostly from the Roman rite, although sometimes from Eastern Orthodox ones as well. After about 1860 this new kind of Catholic ritualism found its way into print and began to attract a following.[154] This led to differences of

---

153. The seventeenth and last printing of the 1905 impression was Procter and Frere, *A New History of the Book of Common Prayer with a Rationale of Its Offices* (London: Macmillan & Co., 1961).
154. Particularly notable were P. Medd, *The Priest to the Altar* (privately printed,1861) (2nd edn, London: Rivingtons, 1869) (5th edn, Oxford: Oxford University Press; London: Longmans, 1904), F.G. Lee, *The Altar*

opinion within the Anglo-Catholic movement which may be classified as follows. On one end were the 'conservatives', who insisted on maintaining complete fidelity to 1662, even while allowing additions to (and interpretations of) it that could be described as 'enrichment'. Somewhat more adventurous were those who wanted a return to the order of the 1549 prayer book (if not necessarily to the book itself) and who were prepared to supplement this with material taken from the Sarum rite in particular. Finally, there were the radicals, who argued that, if Cranmer and his colleagues had been prepared to 'borrow' from the Roman rite in the sixteenth century, there was no reason why their successors three hundred years later should not do the same. From that position, they went on to propose major reorderings of the prayer book to make worship conform to contemporary Roman practice as much as possible. There were, of course, gradations within these broad groupings, though books and tracts catering to one or other of them were soon making their appearance and contributing to further definition of these different perspectives.

It is often forgotten now but the first moves to amend the 1662 liturgy came from Evangelicals who wanted to remove anything that could be used by Anglo-Catholics in support of their position. Even before full-blown ritualism made its appearance, Thomas Spencer (1796-1853) published *The Reformed Prayer Book* (1842), in which he emended the Book of Common Prayer along those lines, and in 1859 Robert Grosvenor, Lord Ebury (1801-93) and his friends founded the Prayer Book Revision Society, which in 1873 published the *Book of Common Prayer Revised*, the text that came to be used by the Free Church of England, which emerged about the same time.[155] In the meantime, in 1859 the Church of England removed the services that had been introduced to commemorate the death of Charles I on 30 January, the restoration of Charles II on 29 May and the Gunpowder Plot on 5 November. Although these had never been an official part of the prayer book, their disappearance was taken as evidence that change to the prayer book was possible and encouraged

---

Service Book (London: Chiswick Press, 1867), O. Shipley, *The Ritual of the Altar* (London: Longmans, 1870). Somewhat later on came A.H. Stanton, *Catholic Prayers for Church of England People* (London: W. Knott, 1880). For a study of these books and others like them, see M. Dalby, *Anglican Missals and Their Canons: 1549, Interim Rite and Roman*, Alcuin/GROW Joint Liturgical Study 41 (Cambridge: Grove Books, 1998), pp. 3-15.

155. The exact date of its founding is unclear but its first bishop was consecrated in 1876.

those who wanted to see it happen. A Royal Commission on Ritual was appointed in 1867 and resulted in Acts of Parliament that allowed some changes to Morning and Evening Prayer (1872) and attempted to regulate ritualistic practices (1874). The prosecution of Anglo-Catholic clergy under the Public Worship Regulation Act 1874 brought the procedure into disrepute and led to an increasingly bitter feud between Anglo-Catholics and the rest of the Church of England.

Modern accounts of this period have mostly been written by Anglo-Catholics or their sympathisers, with the predictable result that Evangelicals and broad churchmen who opposed them are often portrayed as narrow-minded and un-Christian in their behaviour. There is some truth in that accusation but it must be remembered that their reaction was provoked by extremists on the other side who were just as bad, if not worse than they were. Whatever excuses are made for them, there can be no doubt that the ritualists were breaking the law and justifying themselves by appealing to what they claimed was 'higher authority', in this case including even the See of Rome. Modern observers find it hard to understand their mentality but one thing at least is crystal clear – their actions were far removed from anything that could be attributed to Jesus or to the New Testament Church, in whose name they claimed to be acting.[156]

One of the positive results of the late nineteenth-century controversies was the explosion of interest in liturgical studies, in which Anglicans played a notable part. Almost all of them were high churchmen of varying kinds, which gave them a certain bias, but there can be no denying their accomplishments. Texts that had long slumbered in archives were taken out and edited. Comparisons with liturgies used elsewhere were undertaken and the sources used to construct the Book of Common Prayer were rediscovered and catalogued for the first time. The range of books and studies produced was very wide and went far beyond the prayer book. However, some things stand out and many of those involved made a permanent contribution to our understanding of how the Anglican liturgical tradition developed: for example, the work of Henry Austin Wilson (1854-1927), who produced critical editions of the Gelasian sacramentary (1894) and of the Gregorian sacramentary (1915), both of which contributed to the prayer book; Walter Howard Frere (1863-1938), who edited the Sarum rite in two volumes (1898 and 1901); and John Wickham Legg (1843-1921), whose *Cranmer's Liturgical*

---

156. For a reasonably impartial account, see R.C.D. Jasper, *The Development of the Anglican Liturgy, 1662-1980* (London: SPCK, 1989), pp. 40-112.

Projects (1915) detailed the way in which the archbishop made use of the two editions of the Quiñones breviary, which he also edited. Pride of place, however, belongs to Frank Edward Brightman (1856-1932), whose exhaustive work *The English Rite* presents the different editions of the prayer book in parallel columns and tells us how each element in them was derived and from what source. Here and there Brightman's work has had to be updated as new evidence has come to light, but the modern liturgist still has to begin with him.

One important result of this activity was the founding of the Alcuin Club on 12 January 1897. This was a lay initiative that was guided by a desire to produce scholarly works of a high standard that would remain loyal to the Church of England and, in particular, to the 1662 liturgy. Dr Legg was among the founders and, before long, several clergymen were added, including Brightman, Frere and Wilson.[157] In the nature of the case, the Alcuin Club had a high church orientation from the beginning. However, it has always been open to broader influences and in recent years has co-operated with the originally Evangelical Group for the Renewal of Worship (GROW) to produce a highly valued Joint Liturgical Series. One of its earliest publications was *Liturgical Interpolations* by Thomas Alexander Lacey (1853-1931), who, despite his high church convictions and desire to work towards reunion with Rome, was highly critical of the way in which some Anglo-Catholics were introducing Roman elements into their reconstructions of the prayer book, a practice that he deplored.

Twentieth-Century Developments

It is generally agreed that the 1906 report of the Royal Commission on Ecclesiastical Discipline represents a turning point in the history of Anglican liturgy and, as a consequence, of the 1662 prayer book. For the first time it was officially recognised that change would have to come, though precisely what form that change would take was left undecided. It was fairly clear, though, that at the very least there would be an accommodation of ritualism and many were encouraged to hope that some movement in the direction of 1549, and perhaps even of the Sarum rite, would be permitted. By 1906 it was coming to the notice of English churchmen that moves in that direction had already been made in the United States, where the

---

157. See P.J. Jagger, *The Alcuin Club and Its Publications 1897-1987* (Norwich: Hymns Ancient and Modern,1986), for a history of the club and a catalogue of its publications up to 1987.

Episcopal Church had revised its liturgy as recently as 1892, and that other overseas Anglican churches were starting to move in the same direction. What sort of impact this would have on the Church of England or on the 1662 prayer book could not be predicted but one thing was clear – the age of uniformity in public worship was drawing to a close.

The emergence of a distinctively American prayer book tradition from 1892 onwards may be said to mark the beginning of the modern period in Anglican liturgical history. It is characterised by increasing variety, often motivated by the belief that what was being proposed represented a return to more primitive models. The advantages of that, it was argued, were that use of the earlier liturgies necessarily brought the modern Church closer to the time of the apostles and so made it less susceptible to subsequent 'corruption'. They also brought it closer to other great traditions of the Christian world, notably those of the Eastern Orthodox Churches. That neither of these assertions was necessarily true was barely suspected at first but, as liturgical study developed, the assumptions of the late eighteenth century were increasingly questioned. At the same time, the desirability of achieving a common text that was both primitive and universal also faded as liturgists realised that there was no golden age of uniformity to which they could hope to return. There was never any real hope of bringing the Eastern Orthodox into the discussion, since their liturgies were (and are) fixed and immutable, even if there are variations in the ways that they are celebrated. For their part, the Western Churches, including the Anglican, would certainly not be forsaking their liturgies for those of the East, however much some admired them.

There was also the fact that the great missionary expansion of the Western Churches, while it undoubtedly encouraged co-operation among them, challenged their inherited traditions by introducing new concepts of worship into the discussion of revision and by forcing Westerners to address the concerns of the present day, and not merely take refuge in the distant past. The Lambeth Conference of 1908 addressed liturgical questions with a degree of thoroughness previously unknown and concluded that a combination of 'adaptation and enrichment' was needed for the mission of the Anglican Church worldwide. 'Contextualisation' as this would later come to be called, became the order of the day, which inevitably meant greater diversity and a differentiation that often obscured whatever underlying unity there had once been within particular denominational traditions. Anglicans felt these pressures as much as anyone, and perhaps more than most, as they sought to give voice not only to different cultural contexts but also to different theological understandings that arose within individual provinces of the Communion as well as between them. Trying to balance culture and theology has been a major theme of modern Anglican liturgical revision, which has taken place not only within particular Churches but also in the ecumenical sphere in which Anglicans have been fully engaged.

Another influence at work was the growing belief that spiritual matters could not – and should not – be defined with the degree of precision that was common (and desirable) in other spheres of human thought. The words of Darwell Stone (1859-1941), yet another Anglo-Catholic liturgist, carried considerable weight, even among many who were not particularly sympathetic to his theology. He wrote:

> In the mystery of the Eucharist, where human thought is so apt to go astray, and human language is so inadequate to express even human thought, the interpreter will most likely be right who is patient of a wide latitude of interpretation and gentle to what seem to him offending expressions.[158]

That there were many who would agree that human thought is apt to go astray but drew the conclusion that greater precision in language was therefore required, does not seem to have registered with Stone. To put it another way, what motivated Thomas Cranmer to revise the 1549 prayer book in the direction of 1552, and what led subsequent generations to want to pursue the matter still further in the same overall direction, was rejected in favour of the exact opposite. Pseudo-mystical ambiguity was to be preferred over clarity, a formula that was to go far in the twentieth century but that inevitably ended up as an accommodation of conflicting views rather than a robust statement of the Church's official teaching. It was a recipe for chaos rather than clarity that over the next two generations would produce the theological incoherence with which we are all too familiar today.

One of the attractions of T.A. Lacey's proposals for liturgical reform was that he envisaged the retention of every syllable of the 1662 liturgy, subject only to a reordering of the material in the Communion office. His own view was that the prayer of oblation should be put immediately after the consecration prayer and that the prayer of humble access should precede the Communion itself. That would allow for the sanctification of the Eucharistic elements and prepare communicants to receive them as such without doing violence to the texts themselves. Various other

---

158. D. Stone, *A History of the Doctrine of the Holy Eucharist*, 2 vols (London: Longmans, Green & Co., 1909), vol. 2, p. 651.

possibilities were canvassed but a reform along these lines became increasingly popular, and not only in high church circles.[159] How these proposals would be drawn up and implemented was outlined by W.H. Frere, who did not believe that the convocations of Canterbury and York were competent to decide the questions involved without expert advice:

> The serious work [of revision] will only begin when the Convocations decide that it is at least as crucial a matter to revise the Prayer Book as to retranslate the Bible; and therefore are content to place the initial responsibility in the hands, not of a committee of Convocation, which, except in the Upper House, contains few of the scholars who are most competent for the work, but a body of revisers gathered and empowered for the purpose.[160]

It was obvious to Frere, and to many others, that any body of revisers constituted along these lines would be dominated by Anglo-Catholics, many of whom would be more interested in trying to recover 'primitive' forms of liturgy than in theology. However, many of the proposals that Frere made were unobjectionable, if occasionally somewhat utopian. For example, he wanted to reorder the calendar according to the ecclesiastical year, rather than the civil one, which certainly made sense, but he also advocated establishing a fixed date for Easter, which could only have been done by the State and would not have been accepted outside British Protestant circles.[161] For the most part, his suggestions involved allowing for greater variety and flexibility in the use of canticles and so on, and his Communion office was structured along Lacey's lines, although with the caution that further revision would be necessary in due course.

The biggest problem that the would-be revisers faced was general indifference in the Church. Many people saw no need for change at all and it was difficult to persuade the bishops, in particular, that revision was worth pursuing in a serious way. Nevertheless, the enthusiasts persevered and by 1912 the convocation of Canterbury had even appointed a committee of sixteen 'experts' to advise it on how to proceed.

---

159. Jasper, *Development*, pp. 83-85.
160. W.H. Frere, *Some Principles of Liturgical Reform: A Contribution to the Revision of the Book of Common Prayer* (London: John Murray, 1911), p. 8.
161. Frere could not have known it at the time but, within a decade, the Eastern Orthodox Churches would be torn apart by calendar reform along precisely these lines and the problems thus created remain unresolved to this day.

Anglo-Catholics dominated this, of course, and it is noticeable that the predominantly Evangelical convocation of York did not participate – and was apparently not asked to. Before long, the 'experts' were frustrated because they were largely confined to commenting on secondary details and could not advance the agendas that many of them had. The wider Church regarded them with suspicion, and understandably so. For example, many of them advocated the reintroduction of the reservation of the sacrament, not only for the convenience of offering Communion to the sick, who could not attend public worship, but also to facilitate adoration of the elements along lines that presupposed a doctrine of transubstantiation, although care was always taken not to say that openly. The fact that the 1662 rubrics said nothing about reservation was taken by some to imply that it was permitted, even though it had not been practised for over three hundred years and Article 28 expressly forbade it. The line between subtlety of this kind and subterfuge was an easy one to cross and it was not long before opposition to any sort of reform started to rear its head.

Another object of the revisers' zeal was their desire to legalise the wearing of liturgical vestments last seen in the reign of Edward VI. Once again, the rubrics appeared to favour this and it was recognised that the traditional vestments had disappeared without specific legal sanction. Whether that was justification for reintroducing them was another matter, of course, but, as Anglo-Catholics had for some time been doing so, the bishops eventually gave in and vestments were permitted, although it was stressed that they had no doctrinal significance.[162] Once again, Anglo-Catholicism was seen as worming its way into the mainstream of the Church of England by a combination of stealth, specious argument and cowardice on the part of those who might be expected to discipline offenders. The ritualists could not force people to wear them but over time that became the expectation in many places. Ordination candidates who refused to wear a stole, for example, had a hard time of it, as they still do in some places.[163] Gradually, the 'norm' shifted, so that what had been universal practice in 1850 came to be seen as anomalous less than a century later.

The events leading up to the preparation of the draft 1927 Book of Common Prayer and its slightly revised version a year later have been widely studied and, in a sense, form the starting point for modern liturgical

---

162. Jasper, *Development*, pp. 89-91.
163. See A. Atherstone, *Scarf or Stole at Ordination? A Plea for the Evangelical Conscience* (London: Latimer Trust, 2012).

revision in the Church of England. Similar revisions were taking place at
more or less the same time in several other countries, particularly in the
United States, Canada and South Africa, but they succeeded where that
in England failed. The main reason for the failure was the need to clear
Parliament, where a small majority defeated the proposals for reform,
even though they had received the approval of both convocations.[164]
Parliamentary opposition, buoyed by members of the House of Commons
from outside England, was rooted in the fear that the proposed changes
marked a move away from the Reformation and back to Rome. However,
there was also a strong sense that the whole process had been captured by
an elite group of liturgical scholars, most of whom were Anglo-Catholic
in sympathy. The rank and file of the Church of England had not been
consulted and the authorities refused to adopt a piecemeal, step-by-step
approach. Had they done so, there is every likelihood that the largely
uncontroversial changes they proposed to Morning and Evening Prayer,
for example, would have been accepted. Unfortunately for them, their 'all
or nothing' policy resulted in their obtaining nothing.[165]

Liturgical revision suffered a setback from which it would take a
generation to recover, although elements of the draft 1927/28 book
were approved for use here and there and became fairly common. On
the whole though, the 1662 prayer book continued to reign supreme,
albeit with a number of unofficial modifications to the rubrics which
had the general effect of shortening the services. Items like the litany,
the Athanasian Creed, the commination and the exhortations in the
Communion office were dropped more often than not, although extra
prayers might be added to the daily offices at the discretion of the officiant.
Hymn singing, for which there was no provision in the prayer book also
became all but universal, at least at the main services of public worship.
Growing pressure for liturgical development was met by the creation
of a permanent Liturgical Commission of the Church of England in
1955 but its activities were severely restricted and it did relatively little
for the first decade of its existence. Things began to change after 1964,
when Ronald Jasper (1917-90) became chairman of the commission, a
post that he was to occupy for the next sixteen years. Fortunately for us,
he has left a detailed account of his years of service, which culminated

---

164. D. Gray, *The 1927-28 Prayer Book Crisis*, Alcuin/GROW Joint Liturgical
Studies 60 and 61, 2 vols (Norwich: SCM/Canterbury Press, 2005 and
2006).

165. Cuming, *A History of Anglican Liturgy*, pp. 165-90; Jasper, *Development*,
pp. 113-46.

in the production of the Alternative Service Book in 1980.[166] Another prominent member of the commission in its early years was Geoffrey Cuming (1917-88), who has also left us an account of its proceedings.[167]

What we learn from them is that there were still relatively few competent Anglican liturgists in 1955, that they mostly knew one another before being appointed to the Commission and that they shared a broadly Anglo-Catholic outlook. It would not be until 1964 that a clear Evangelical, Colin Buchanan (1934-), would be appointed to the commission, an event that Jasper was to acknowledge as a difficult step towards a more comprehensive approach to liturgical questions. Buchanan was not alone – he was ably supported by a number of other Evangelicals, who also did what they could to resist Catholicising tendencies. Interestingly, these convinced Evangelicals were able to come to terms with some of the more conservative Anglo-Catholics and the agreements between them played a major part in securing liturgical texts that would be acceptable across the Church as a whole. Where the Evangelicals stood out, however, was in their robust defence of the 1662 rite, which they were sometimes prepared to modernise but which they did not want to abandon altogether. That was an unpopular view in the circles that had constituted the original Liturgical Commission, which was virtually united in its determination to have as little to do with the 1662 prayer book as possible. There was a general recognition that it could not simply be killed off but that, if a gradual process of change were to be initiated, it might in time die a natural death.[168]

It was after 1965 that major changes began to appear.[169] The lessons of the 1920s had been learned and this time there was a gradual introduction of experimental services which were labelled Series 1, Series 2 and Series 3. Series 1 was little more than a reissue of the draft

---

166. Jasper, *Development*, pp. 211-369.
167. Cuming, *A History of Anglican Liturgy*, pp. 208-29.
168. Jasper, *Development*, p. 241.
169. These are found chiefly in the Prayer Book (Miscellaneous Provisions) Measure 1965 (no. 3) (5 August 1965), in *The Public General Acts and Church Assembly Measures 1965* (London: HMSO, 1966), and the Prayer Book (Further Provisions) Measure 1968 (no. 2) (18 December 1968), in *The Public General Acts and Church Assembly Measures 1968* (London: HMSO, 1969). Both measures were repealed by the Church of England (Worship and Doctrine) Measure 1974 (no. 3) (12 December 1974), in *The Public General Acts and Church Assembly Measures 1974* (London: HMSO, 1975), but schedule 3.4 of that measure excepted the modifications made to the prayer book rubrics in 1965 and 1968.

revised 1928 book and could be seen as a revision of 1662 as much as anything else. Series 2 was more adventurous, using material from 1662 but reordering it in such a way as to break with the inherited tradition. However, it was to be Series 3 that would strike most churchgoers as genuinely new, because for the first time the language of the services was modernised. The 'thees' and 'thous' of seventeenth-century English were dropped, to the chagrin of traditionalists and lovers of classical English prose, but to the delight of many younger people. Series 3 also coincided with the widespread adoption of new translations of the Bible, in which corresponding linguistic changes were made, adding a sense of coherence to the process. It was this modernisation that won over the bulk of Evangelicals, who had resisted earlier changes for doctrinal reasons but who were attracted by the more contemporary feel of the language. There was some initial resistance from conservatives but, after 1971, the Liturgical Commission went over to modern language exclusively and, despite protests, there was no going back. Only very occasionally did tradition win out, as in the Lord's Prayer; the petition 'Lead us not into temptation' survived every attempt to alter it to something like 'Do not put us to the test' or 'Save us from the time of trial'.

Once the linguistic hurdle had been overcome, it was a relatively easy process that led to the Alternative Service Book (ASB) in 1980 and eventually to *Common Worship* in 2000. The appearance of the ASB was greeted as a major triumph by those members of the Liturgical Commission that had worked hard to achieve that result for a quarter of a century or more. However, its reception in the wider Church was less enthusiastic. Many found it too long (1,279 pages) and too complicated to use in its pure form, and fears were expressed that few people would buy a copy and use it for their own private devotions. Instead, most parishes acquired booklets of individual services, which they could then adapt to their own requirements. This strategy had already been adopted for Series 2 and 3, and it proved to be popular. At the same time, the provision for a wide range of alternatives that people could choose according to their churchmanship and preferences ensured that 'common prayer' would rapidly become a thing of the past. Even the clergy had to learn different versions of the new rites as they moved from one parish to another, a phenomenon that became more common as parishes were amalgamated into team and group ministries.

It was also admitted, even by Ronald Jasper, that the ASB was unimpressive as a literary product. In his words: 'A criticism often heard of the ASB is that its language is flat, that it lacks the sense of the numinous, and that it bears no comparison with 1662.'[170] Nevertheless, having conceded that, he went on to add: 'Use the ASB with love and imagination, work hard at it, and it can still attain great heights.'[171]

Geoffrey Cuming, for his part, could claim that the history of the 1662 prayer book 'ended with the authorization of Series One' and that: 'Elements of the Prayer Book are still to be found in the 1980 Book, but they have taken on the character of family heirlooms in a not wholly congenial setting. Other sources, other theologies have inspired the liturgies produced since 1965.'[172]

Outside England, similar processes were at work and the last decades of the twentieth century saw the emergence of a range of prayer books across the Anglican Communion. On the whole, they revealed a shift away from the pattern of 1662, sometimes in favour of 1549 but often ranging much further afield. Developments in the Roman Catholic Church after the Second Vatican Council (1962-65) led to a blossoming of liturgical revision there; and other Protestant Churches were also involved in what soon became an ecumenical renewal movement. There was a growing sense that the mainstream Churches of Western Christendom should try to harmonise their liturgies as far as possible, so that worshippers would sense relatively little difference if they moved from one denomination to another. This was most successful in the production of a common lectionary. However, there were also moves to standardise texts, particularly in the English-speaking world, where modern forms of language were now accepted as the norm.

Nevertheless, if there was increasing uniformity in some respects, it was counterbalanced by growing diversity in others. As always, this was felt most keenly at Holy Communion, which was rapidly becoming the main Sunday service in many churches. Liturgists had come to recognise that it would be impossible to impose a single canon that everyone would be happy to use, so different options were provided, sometimes as many as eight. This forced parishes to pick and choose which one(s) they would prefer and in practice many were led to produce services of their own, cobbled together from the available liturgical material perhaps, but not necessarily following a particular pattern. In many Evangelical churches formal liturgy was dropped altogether or else reduced to a minimum that might bear little relation to what was officially approved.

---

170. Jasper, *Development*, p. 366.
171. Ibid.
172. Cuming, *A History of Anglican Liturgy*, p. 230.

Outside the Church of England, variety was less marked within individual provinces, but they diverged increasingly from one another as each one tried to adapt to its particular circumstances. There was also less tolerance for more traditional forms of the liturgy, the use of which was discouraged and sometimes even officially abolished. In the United States, the Episcopal Church's new 1979 Book of Common Prayer was given a mixed reception, leading in some cases to open schism.[173] The result was that by the year 2000 'common worship' had practically disappeared, leaving little more than a skeleton pattern that could be fleshed out in many different ways. By then a generation had matured that had never known the 1662 prayer book, despite the fact that it remained the Church's official liturgy. In an effort to bring some sense of order to the increasingly divergent Anglican Communion, the 1662 rite came to be appealed to as the common Anglican standard, even though many people realised that it required some adaptation if it were to be used outside the Church of England. New state prayers would have to be produced for countries that did not recognise the British monarch as head of state, a number of rubrics would have to be updated and new prayers and thanksgivings would have to be added to meet needs that in many cases would have been unknown in 1662 – like prayers for air travel, for example. None of these things was (or is) particularly controversial; the problem was (and is) finding a way to implement these necessary alterations without sacrificing the substance of the 1662 book.

Looming over everything, of course, was the question of language, at least in the English-speaking world. To what extent should the 1662 prayer book be divested of its seventeenth-century flavour? This is a major issue for many, partly because the traditional forms have become hallowed over time and partly because it is not just a matter of changing 'thou' to 'you'; the cadences and sentence structures of the language have changed and most people would say that they have become less poetic, though that may be as much a matter of taste as anything else. In any case, it

---

173. American traditionalists usually preferred their own 1928 prayer book. The subsequent emergence of Anglican Churches outside the Episcopal Church has resulted in the composition of new liturgies, most notably the 2019 prayer book authorised by the Anglican Church in North America (ACNA) which is markedly more traditional than the 1979 book, even introducing features, like the Athanasian Creed, that have never been present in any American Episcopal liturgy. How widely it will be accepted remains to be seen.

continues to provoke controversy, and one that is more widespread than differences of theology that non-specialists find hard to detect.

The drift of liturgical revision away from the 1662 prayer book was not slow to provoke alarm in circles that feared the loss of one of the great treasures of English literature and spirituality. In 1975 some concerned individuals founded the Prayer Book Society, whose aim was to ensure that the 1662 liturgy would continue to play a central role in the life of the Church of England. Men like Ronald Jasper and Geoffrey Cuming were cool towards it, if not openly hostile, and, despite reassurances from highly placed people in the Church, there was little prospect of an authoritative source doing anything to promote it or ensure its preservation. Many parishes continued to offer 1662 services now and then, but often at inconvenient times (like 8 a.m.) and perhaps no more than once a month. Others simply disposed of their copies of 1662, making it impossible for them to hold any traditional service at all. In some churches it was possible to see the 1662 prayer books stacked up in a cupboard gathering dust – not being thrown out, but not being used either.

It is now unusual to find a church in England that uses 1662 as its main liturgical form of worship but it is too soon to write it off completely. Theological colleges have to teach liturgy to their students and, now that almost none of them knows anything about 1662, courses in it are supposed to be given. To those who know nothing, the controversies of the past are liable to seem arcane and irrelevant but that may make them more open to the services as they are. It is not 1662 that they find off-putting, rather the kinds of arguments for and against it that were common in the late nineteenth and early twentieth centuries. How many people who approach the Church's classical liturgy in this way will be won over to it is impossible to say but there is at least a chance that some will be and, if some are, there is hope for the future.

What does seem to be clear is that modern replacements for the prayer book have not taken hold in the way that their authors and chief supporters hoped they would. Variations of the ASB were certainly used between 1980 and 2000 but, when it was superseded by *Common Worship*, it vanished without trace. Certainly, there is no lobby for preserving it as there is for 1662 or as there was even for Series 2 and 3. *Common Worship* has now been in use for longer than the ASB but there is no sign that anybody is particularly attached to it either, or that they are ever likely to be. There is a vacuum in public worship that is filled by what people see as expedients, a situation that is unstable and unlikely to last very long.

On a different front, there has been a revival of interest in Thomas Cranmer and a fresh appreciation of his contribution to the Church of England. Nobody who is aware of the research that has been done in this field now believes that Cranmer preferred 1549 over 1552 – his intention to move on from the former even as it was rolling off the printing presses is now almost universally acknowledged. The generation of liturgists that produced the ASB has now passed away and has left few successors, the only ones of note being Paul Bradshaw (1945-) and Bryan Spinks (1948-), both of whom have moved to the United States and are nearing the end of their productive academic lives. Anglo-Catholicism is now much weaker than it was, removing what was long the chief source of antagonism to the 1662 prayer book. Perhaps most of all, churches in the developing world, where 1662 is still widely used and does not sound archaic in translation, are growing rapidly and seeking to affirm their Anglican identity. For many of them, the 1662 Book of Common Prayer has considerable appeal and the emergence of networks like GAFCON (Global Anglican Futures Conference) and the Global South has reinforced this. Many people think that spiritual renewal will come to the Anglican Communion from that direction and, if so, then it is not at all unlikely that the 1662 liturgy, or a slightly modified form of it, will return with it.

Most importantly of all, voices are now being heard that insist that it is neither the language nor the antiquity of the 1662 prayer book that is its most attractive feature, but its theology, which is a clear statement of the supreme authority of Holy Scripture and the doctrine of justification by faith alone. The eclipse of theology in liturgical studies cannot be sustained, as people come to realise that our patterns of worship reflect what we believe. Two generations have grown up with the understanding that liturgy shapes belief, and this has been a major motivating factor for those who wanted to replace 1662 with something of a different theological colour. However, that in turn has reminded the Church that its doctrinal foundations hang together – the Articles of Religion, the Homilies and the Book of Common Prayer are all of a piece. As the Anglican Communion flounders in liberal compromise and uncertainty, reaffirming those foundations becomes ever more important. Where this will lead is still unclear but the expectation that the 1662 prayer book would die a death of its own accord may turn out not to be the case.

The appearance in 2021 of an 'international version' of the 1662 prayer book is a sign of how this new interest in the classical Anglican liturgy may develop in the years ahead.[174] It makes the necessary changes with

---

174. Bray and Keane's *The Book of Common Prayer: International Edition.*

respect to the state prayers and obsolete words and it adds a number of prayers for special occasions and so on. It is, however, very conservative linguistically, even preserving such archaisms as 'holpen' instead of 'helped' (in the *Magnificat*), which may limit its acceptability in some circles. Nevertheless, it is an important publication in its own right and may well point the way ahead for further adaptations of 1662 in the years to come. Whatever the case, it is a reminder to us of the ongoing importance of the 1662 prayer book for the Anglican Communion and of the need for a modern *Companion* to it.

The Abiding Relevance of the 1662 Book of Common Prayer

The reasons for the virtual eclipse of the 1662 prayer book in the past generation are obvious and many of them are beyond dispute. The language is archaic, the social situation in which it was composed has changed almost beyond recognition, new understandings of the historical development of liturgy have emerged and there are demands for new kinds of service, not least in countries outside England, that make the case for a thorough overhaul of the 1662 text irrefutable. Even at the time there were many who were dissatisfied with it; and some of its 'emendations' of the 1552 liturgy were needlessly provocative. The baptismal services reflect a society that has disappeared and an understanding of baptism that nobody today would accept. Other parts of it, like the litany or the commination, are seldom used nowadays and the visitation of the sick, while still important in principle, cannot reasonably be carried out using the framework provided in the text.

With the virtue of hindsight, it might have been better if the liturgy had been progressively modernised and updated over time but that proved to be impossible and we cannot go back now. There have been some necessary changes to the rubrics since 1965, at least in England, but, welcome as those changes are, they merely scratch the surface.[175] Partisans of the 1662 prayer book do not always distinguish clearly between the traditional language that they love and the underlying message that needs to be communicated in a modern idiom. At the same time, the interplay between the traditional and the modern does not always favour the latter, and a dialogue between the past and the

---

175. Changes to the rubrics in the Ordinal were made in 1964. See Clergy (Ordination and Miscellaneous Provisions) Measure 1964 (no. 6) (10 June 1964), in *The Public General Acts and Church Assembly Measures 1964* (London: HMSO, 1965).

(imagined) present and future is bound to continue as we move through time while keeping our eyes firmly fixed on eternity.

So, what can be said in favour of the 1662 prayer book? Whether we like it or not, it remains one of the foundational documents of the Anglican Communion. It may not be recognised as such in every province, but it is true of the Church of England and, as long as the Communion is (at least partly) defined by being in communion with the See of Canterbury, the 1662 prayer book will retain its place within the firmament of Anglicanism. However, there is more to it than that. The enduring greatness of the 1662 liturgy is that it is one of the best attempts ever made to turn the Word of God as revealed in Holy Scripture into the words of the Church as we absorb the divine teaching and return it to God in wonder, love and praise. Its faults are mainly those of archaic language and outdated rubrics. Those blemishes are real but they are mostly few and superficial. The prayer book is focussed on the Gospel of Jesus Christ, foretold in the Old Testament and realised in the New. It takes the biblical framework of God's covenant with His people and teaches us how to shape our minds and prayers in ways that reflect our trust in His promises. It is a life-changing message, which penetrates more deeply into our hearts as we learn it and as it becomes part of our natural way of thinking. Its fixed expressions are not vain repetitions of the obvious but windows of light into the world of the Spirit, challenging us to grow in our relationship with God as we meditate on them and explore their application to our lives.

These basic principles can be expressed in different languages and in other ways – indeed, they must be if the message they contain is to go out into all the world and if God's Word is to do the work for which it was given. None of that, however, diminishes the value of the 1662 prayer book. As the Psalmist sang so long ago: 'Thy words have I hid within my heart: that I should not sin against thee.'[176] This is what the prayer book aims to do – to put God's Word in our hearts, so that we may follow His commandments and not sin against Him. As long as our worship retains that focus, it will be faithful to the prayer book and its message will continue to bring light and life to those who read and study it in the power of the Holy Spirit who has revealed God's Word to us.[177]

---

176. Psalm 119:11.
177. For a fuller exposition of these principles, see P. Adam, *The 'Very Pure Word of God': The Book of Common Prayer as a Model of Biblical Liturgy* (London: Latimer Trust, 2012).

Chapter 2

Introductory Material

The Preface

This was written for the 1662 prayer book and must be read in the light of the political events that led to its composition. The full text is reproduced here, with notes to explain the various allusions which it contains.

First Paragraph

> It hath been the wisdom of the Church of England, ever since the first compiling of her public liturgy, to keep the mean between the two extremes of too much stiffness in refusing and of too much easiness in admitting any variation from it.

This refers primarily to the first Edwardian prayer book of 1549 and then to the subsequent revisions in 1552, 1559 and 1604. Whether Thomas Cranmer was thinking along the lines claimed here is doubtful. His main purpose was not to achieve a golden mean between rigidity and laxity, but to give a clear statement of theological principles derived from his understanding of the Reformation. Some variety within the different rites was permitted, but this cannot reasonably be described as admitting 'variation from it'.

> For, as on the one side common experience showeth that where a change hath been made of things advisedly established (no evident necessity so requiring) sundry inconveniences have

thereupon ensued, and those many times more and greater
than the evils that were intended to be remedied by such
change; so on the other side, the particular forms of divine
worship, and the rites and ceremonies appointed to be used
therein, being things in their own nature indifferent and
alterable, and so acknowledged, it is but reasonable that
upon weighty and important considerations, according to
the various exigency of times and occasions, such changes
and alterations should be made therein as to those that are
in place of authority should from time to time seem either
necessary or expedient.

The first claim here is that unnecessary changes to the liturgy are
liable to be more trouble than they are worth, and that this has proved
to be the case in the past. However, that is hard to demonstrate from the
history of the prayer book. Were there any changes made in 1552, 1559 or
1604 that were unnecessary? Perhaps; but did they cause problems that
made matters worse than they had been before? That seems unlikely. It is
probably best to conclude that this is a statement of principle, outlining
what the authors of the preface feared, rather than a reference to past
actions for which there is little evidence.

The second claim is that the forms of the rites and ceremonies are
in their nature indifferent. This is reminiscent of Article 34, which
admits that traditions are alterable. The message seems to be that
changes should be approached cautiously and introduced only when
necessary, but that this can happen and, when it does, those in authority
have the power to decide what to do. It is understood that 'those in
authority' are, in the first instance, the members of the convocations
of Canterbury and York (the clergy) and, in the second instance, the
Members of Parliament (the bishops in the House of Lords and the laity
in both Houses). In reality, Parliament is superior to the convocations
and can overrule them if it sees fit to do so.

Accordingly we find that in the reigns of several princes of
blessed memory since the Reformation, the Church, upon
just and weighty considerations her thereunto moving, hath
yielded to make such alterations in some particulars as in
their respective times were thought convenient.

This sentence reads strangely. The 'several princes' were in fact only
two (Elizabeth I and James VI and I), and the revisions made – in 1559

and again in 1604 – were slight. The 1559 book altered the 1552 text in only three places, of which the most significant (and noticeable) was the inclusion of the 1549 words of administration in Holy Communion in addition those of 1552. It also dropped the so-called 'Black Rubric', which denied any significance in kneeling to receive Holy Communion, which was not technically part of the 1552 prayer book. Whether it can truly be said that the Church was moved to make these changes by 'just and weighty considerations' may be questioned. There was undoubtedly a desire to keep as many people happy as possible, but the claim made here seems to be taking things too far. In both 1559 and 1604 the modifications were so minimal as to make it a matter of debate as to whether there was really a revision at all.

> Yet so as that the main body and essentials of it (as well in the chiefest materials, as in the frame and order thereof) have still continued the same unto this day, and do yet stand firm and unshaken, notwithstanding all the vain attempts and impetuous assaults made against it by such men as are given to change and have always discovered a greater regard to their own private fantasies and interests than to the duty they owe to the public.

This sentence is a more honest description of what happened in 1559 and in 1604 than the previous one. Few changes were made, and the writers of the preface make it clear that they did not have a high opinion of those who wanted more. That their assessment of the motives of those who wanted further reform is tendentious is obvious and, in many cases, inaccurate, although it is possible to find some examples of the things that they criticise. Most of the would-be reformers were motivated by pastoral concerns, not by 'private fantasies and interests', even if some of their suggested alterations were of little significance. What we read here tells us more about the atmosphere of hostility to proposals for further change in which the revision of 1662 was conducted than anything else.

Second Paragraph

> By what undue means and for what mischievous purposes the use of the liturgy (though enjoined by the laws of the land, and those laws never yet repealed) came, during the late unhappy confusions, to be discontinued is too well known to the world, and we are not willing here to remember.

This is a reference to the abolition of the 1604 prayer book in January 1645, with no attention being paid to the legality of the action taken at the time. However, it must also be acknowledged that it was not in the interest of the restorers in 1662 to go into detail about what had transpired, because a balanced consideration of the facts would have weakened their case.

> But when, upon His Majesty's happy Restoration, it seemed probable that, amongst other things, the liturgy also would return of course (the same having never been legally abolished), unless some timely means were used to prevent it, those men who under the late usurped powers had made it a great part of their business to render the people disaffected thereunto saw themselves in point of reputation and interest concerned (unless they would freely acknowledge themselves to have erred, which such men are very hardly brought to do) with their utmost endeavours to hinder the restitution thereof.

Here again, the assumption is that the Restoration would see an automatic return to the conditions prevailing before 1645, and that those objecting to that (for whatever reason) must be regarded as arrogant usurpers with whom rational dialogue was impossible. As with everything that has gone before, this is propaganda rather than the disinterested statement of fact that it purports to be.

> In order whereunto divers pamphlets were published against the Book of Common Prayer, the old objections mustered up, with the addition of some new ones, more than formerly had been made, to make the number swell.

It is true that the objections made to the prayer book of 1559 (and of 1604) were not the only ones that were presented in 1662, nonetheless, the implication that this was a bad thing is tendentious. It could equally well be argued that the passage of time had allowed for a more profound examination of the inherited texts, with the result that a more detailed critique of them had emerged.

> In fine, great importunities were used to His Sacred Majesty that the said book might be revised, and such alterations therein, and additions thereunto made, as should be thought

requisite for the ease of tender consciences; whereunto His Majesty, out of his pious inclination to give satisfaction (so far as could be reasonably expected) to all his subjects of what persuasion soever, did graciously condescend.

In fact, shortly before his return to England, the king had issued the so-called Declaration of Breda in which he had promised to deal fairly with all those who genuinely sought a reform of the liturgy.[1] The compilers of the preface make it clear that the project of revision that was undertaken was the initiative of Charles II to which they were obliged to assent, even though they did not like it. Needless to say, the flattery shown to the king is wide of the mark – whatever motivated him, we can be certain that there was nothing pious about his 'inclination to give satisfaction … to all his subjects'. For him, it was politically the safest course and not much more than that.

Third Paragraph

In which review we have endeavoured to observe the like moderation as we find to have been used in the like case in former times.
In other words, the tradition of resisting change will be continued.

And therefore of the sundry alterations proposed unto us, we have rejected all such as were either of dangerous consequence (as secretly striking at some established doctrine or laudable practice of the Church of England, or indeed of the whole Catholic Church of Christ) or else of no consequence at all, but utterly frivolous and vain.

Of the 95 proposals for change that were advanced by the Puritans, only seventeen were accepted. Some of the others were undoubtedly of little importance but there is no evidence that any of them was 'of dangerous consequence' leading to potential heresy.

But such alterations as were tendered to us (by what persons, under what pretences, or to what purpose soever so tendered) as seemed to us in any degree requisite or expedient, we have

---

1. The Declaration was issued at Breda on 1 April 1660, shortly before Charles II returned to England on 29 May. It was read in both Houses of Parliament on 1 May. For the text, see Bray, Documents, pp. 490-91.

willingly and of our own accord assented unto, not enforced so to do by any strength of argument convincing us of the necessity of making the said alterations.

The changes that were adopted were ones that even the conservative bishops believed were desirable. Their concern was to emphasise that they had not had their arms twisted by their opponents and that they might well have made the same alterations without any prompting, unlikely as that must sound. Some of the changes, like the adoption of the King James Version for the readings from Scripture, were almost inevitable in any case.

> For we are fully persuaded in our judgements (and we here profess it to the world) that the book, as it stood before established by law, doth not contain in it anything contrary to the Word of God, or to sound doctrine, or which a godly man may not with a good conscience use and submit unto, or which is not fairly defensible against any that shall oppose the same, if it shall be allowed such just and favourable construction as in common equity ought to be allowed to all human writings, especially such as are set forth by authority, and even to the very best translations of the holy Scripture itself.

The claim here is that the 1604 prayer book was fully consonant with the Word of God and that no right-minded person could have objected to it. To the bishops, this assertion seemed right and necessary, because to admit that their previous practice had been wrong would have undermined their authority. They were, however, willing to admit that a new and more accurate translation of the Bible (the King James Version of 1611) had appeared since 1604, that the meaning of certain words and expressions had changed over time, and that some obscure or infelicitous phrasing could be brushed up. The Puritan reformers were their obvious targets, but it should be noted that their logic also worked against the high church party represented by men like John Cosin, who wanted to adopt features that had appeared in the abortive 1637 Scottish prayer book and in many cases went back to 1549. The unwillingness to make any major change to the 1604 text thus had the effect of preventing a return to the less Reformed liturgies of the past and guaranteed that it would be the tradition established by the 1552 version that would prevail in the Church.

Fourth Paragraph

> Our general aim therefore in this undertaking was not to gratify this or that party in any their unreasonable demands, but to do that which to our best understandings we conceived might most tend to the preservation of peace and unity in the Church, the procuring of reverence and exciting of piety and devotion in the public worship of God, and the cutting off occasion from them that seek occasion of cavil or quarrel against the liturgy of the Church.

This sentence is clearly aimed at the Puritan reformers, whose demands were thought to be unreasonable (as some of them probably were), and to promote peace and godliness in public worship. The principal effect of their efforts was to force about a thousand ministers out of their pulpits, procuring 'peace' at the cost of stifling the opposition. It was a high price to pay for securing what they wanted and the result was not unity but the emergence of organised dissent, which (in one form or another) has continued ever since.

> And as to the several variations from the former book, whether by alteration, addition, or otherwise, it shall suffice to give this general account, that most of the alterations were made, either first, for the better direction of them that are to officiate in any part of divine service, which is chiefly done in the calendars and rubrics; or secondly, for the more proper expressing of some words or phrases of ancient usage in terms more suitable to the language of the present times, and the clearer explanation of some other words and phrases that were either of doubtful signification or otherwise liable to misconstruction; or thirdly, for a more perfect rendering of such portions of holy Scripture as are inserted into the liturgy, which in the Epistles and Gospels especially and in sundry other places are now ordered to be read according to the last translation; and that it was thought convenient that some prayers and thanksgivings fitted to special occasions should be added in their due places, particularly for those at sea, together with an office for the baptism of such as are of riper years, which although not so necessary when the former book was compiled, yet by the growth of Anabaptism, through the licentiousness of the late times crept in amongst us, is now

become necessary, and may be always useful for the baptizing
of natives in our plantations and other converted to the faith.

This lengthy sentence gives us a summary of the kinds of alterations
made to the prayer book. Many of them were contained in the rubrics and
were therefore hardly noticed by most worshippers. A good number of
the changes involved the updating of archaic language, the clarification
of obscure words and the adoption of the most recent translation of
the Bible. In addition, some prayers and services were added for special
occasions, one of which was the baptism of adults. The need for that was
perceived to be twofold. First, there was the influence of the so-called
'Anabaptists', who rejected infant baptism, and, second, there was the
expansion of the Church overseas and the conversion of a number of
foreigners to Christianity. In the first case, the 'Anabaptists' mentioned
here were what we would now call simply 'Baptists', along with others
who had no strong feelings about baptism but who had neglected to
baptise their children during the Commonwealth period. In the second
case, we have here the first official recognition of the spread of the
Church of England to other countries. Later generations saw in these
words the first flickering of a missionary vocation for the Church, but
it has to be said that that was not a major concern of the compilers of
the preface, who seem to have regarded the conversion of 'natives' as
accidental rather than deliberate.

Fifth Paragraph

If any man who shall desire a more particular account of the
several alterations in any part of the liturgy shall take the
pains to compare the present book with the former, we doubt
not but the reason of the change may easily appear.

Comparison of the 1662 prayer book with that of 1604 would supposedly
make it obvious why the changes had been made, a statement that
reinforces the belief that the modifications in question were superficial
rather than substantial.

Sixth Paragraph

And having thus endeavoured to discharge our duties in
this weighty affair as in the sight of God, and to approve our
sincerity therein (so far as lay in us) to the consciences of
all men, although we know it impossible (in such variety of

apprehensions, humours, and interests as are in the world) to please all, nor can expect that men of factious, peevish, and perverse spirits should be satisfied with anything that can be done in this kind by any other than themselves, yet we have good hope that what is here presented, and hath been by the convocations of both provinces with great diligence examined and approved, will be also well accepted and approved by all sober, peaceable, and truly conscientious sons of the Church of England.

The assumption was that reasonable people would accept the changes as the work of competent authorities (the convocations of the clergy of the two provinces of Canterbury and York). Anyone who disagreed with them could be dismissed as 'men of factious, peevish, and perverse spirits', which most of them were not.

In sum, the preface to the 1662 prayer book is best regarded as an exercise of self-justification on the part of men who did not want to change anything of importance that they had inherited from the earlier Reformers and who were intent on presenting those who disagreed with them in the worst possible light. It is interesting and important mainly for the way in which it reveals the spirit that animated the revisers, who misrepresented their critics and did much to ensure that the Church of England would be split over secondary matters. That does not justify the opposition of the Puritans, which was often petty, but it does help us to understand why reconciliation, which ought to have been relatively straightforward, proved to be impossible.

Modern readers, for whom the questions involved are often obscure and even incomprehensible, must regret this development and be grateful that our own more ecumenical times have removed many of the causes for complaint that were advanced in 1662. Restoring the unity of the Church is a more complicated process than merely coming to terms with the decisions taken at that time, but it ought at least to be possible for us to view the erstwhile bones of contention with more objective eyes and to avoid falling back into the divisions that were then tearing the Church apart. The worth of the 1662 liturgy does not depend on defences like the ones advanced in this preface, but on the solid core of biblical doctrine that it contains and the disciplined structure that it exhibits. With a little flexibility and good will – qualities in painfully short supply back in 1662 – we should be able to overcome the unhappy differences of the past and worship the Lord together, in spirit and in truth, as the Father wants us to do (John 4:24).

Concerning the Service of the Church

This was the original preface in 1549 and was almost certainly written by Thomas Cranmer, who based his words on the preface to the reformed breviary of Cardinal Quiñones. Cranmer apparently wrote it first in Latin, the text of which survives and is more radical in its innovations than the translation that eventually appeared in 1549.[2]

It remained in place until a new preface was added in 1662 (see above), when it was slightly revised and placed immediately after it. Omissions in 1662 are indicated in grey, while additions made at that time are in **bold** type. It can be analysed as follows:

The Godly Order of the Early Church

> There was never anything by the wit of man so well devised or so sure[ly] established which in continuance of time hath not been corrupted, as among other things it may plainly appear by the common prayers in the Church, commonly called divine service.
>
> The first original and ground whereof, if a man would search out by the ancient Fathers, he shall find that the same was not ordained but of a good purpose and for a great advancement of godliness.
>
> For they so ordered the matter that all the whole Bible (or the greatest part thereof) should be read over once every year, intending thereby that the clergy, and especially such as were ministers in the congregation, should (by often reading and meditation in God's word) be stirred up to godliness themselves, and be more able to exhort others by wholesome doctrine and to confute them that were adversaries to the truth; and further, that the people (by daily hearing of holy Scripture read in the church) might continually profit more and more in the knowledge of God and be the more inflamed with the love of his true religion.[3]

---

2. The Latin text is in the British Library, MS Royal 7B.IV, and was printed by Legg, *Cranmer's Liturgical Projects*, pp. 15-17.

3. Cranmer's Latin draft for the prayer book provided for the reading of the whole Scripture at Morning and Evening Prayer in the course of a year. He also provided for the complete psalter to be read every month, as it still is.

The Corruption of the Traditional Services[4]

1. By undesirable interpolations and abbreviations to the reading to the Scriptures.

> But these many years passed this godly and decent order of the ancient Fathers hath been so altered, broken, and neglected by planting in uncertain stories **and** legends, **with multitude of** responds, verses, vain repetitions, commemorations, and synodals, that commonly when any book of the Bible was begun, before **after** three or four chapters were read out, all the rest were unread. And in this sort the Book of Isaiah was begun in Advent, and the Book of Genesis in Septuagesima, but they were only begun and never read through. After a like sort were other books of holy Scripture used.

2. By the use of an unknown language in worship.

> And moreover, whereas Saint Paul would have such language spoken to the people in the church as they might understand,[5] and have profit by hearing the same, the service in this Church of England these many years hath been read in Latin to the people, which they understood **understand** not, so that they have heard with their ears only, and their heart, spirit, and mind have not been edified thereby.

3. By ignoring most of the Psalms.

> And furthermore, notwithstanding that the ancient Fathers have divided the Psalms into seven portions, whereof every one was called a nocturn, now of late time a few of them have been daily said and the rest utterly omitted.

---

4. Cranmer here alters the meaning of Quiñones, who wanted to defend the Church's liturgical tradition as well as revise it. The attack on uncertain stories, legends etc. is new to him and is not found in Quiñones.

5. 1 Corinthians 14:1-19.

4. By over-complicated rules governing the service.

> Moreover, the number and hardness of the rules called the Pie,[6] and the manifold changings of the service, was the cause that to turn the book only was so hard and intricate a matter that many times there was more business to find out what should be read, than to read it when it was found out.

The Remedies Adopted

> These inconveniences therefore considered, here is set forth such an order whereby the same shall be redressed.

1. The introduction of a calendar of lessons.[7]

> And for a readiness in this matter, here is drawn out a calendar for that purpose, which is plain and easy to be understood, wherein (so much as may be) the reading of holy Scripture is so set forth that all things shall be done in order, without breaking one piece [thereof] from another.

2. The omission of all interpolations.

> For this cause be cut off anthems, responds, invitatories, and such like things as did break the continual course of the reading of the Scripture.

The New Regulations Justified

1. They are few and intelligible.

> Yet, because there is no remedy but that of necessity there must be some rules, therefore certain rules are here set forth, which as they are few in number, so they are plain and easy to be understanded **understood**.

---

6. Because they were printed in black and white (the colours of the magpie) and not in the customary red.
7. We now call this the lectionary, to distinguish it from the calendar, which details festivals, saints' days and the like.

2. They are more useful and convenient.

So that here you have an order for prayer and for the reading of the holy Scripture much agreeable to the mind and purpose of the old Fathers, and a great deal more profitable and commodious than that which of late was used.

It is more profitable, because here are left out many things, whereof some are untrue, some uncertain, some vain and superstitious; and **nothing** is ordained nothing to be read but the very pure word of God, the holy Scriptures, or that which is evidently grounded upon **agreeable to** the same, and that in such a language and order as is most easy and plain for the understanding both of the readers and hearers.

It is also more commodious, both for the shortness thereof and for the plainness of the order, and for that the rules be few and easy. Furthermore, by this order, the curates shall need none other books for their public service, but this book and the Bible: by the means whereof, the people shall not be at so great charge for books, as in time past they have been.

The Uniformity of Public Worship

And whereas heretofore there hath been great diversity in saying and singing in churches within this realm – some following Salisbury Use, some Hereford Use, and some the Use of Bangor, some of York, and some of Lincoln – now from henceforth all the whole realm shall have but one Use. And if any would judge this way more painful, because that all things must be read upon the book, whereas before by the reason of so often repetition, they could say many things by heart: if those men will weigh their labour with the profit in knowledge, which daily they shall obtain by reading upon the book, they will not refuse the pain, in consideration of the great profit that shall ensue thereof.

The Resolution of Doubts and Disagreements

And forasmuch as nothing can almost be so plainly set forth but doubts may arise in the use and practising **practice** of the same, to appease all such diversity (if any arise) and for the resolution of all doubts concerning the manner how to understand, do, and execute the things contained in this book, the parties that so doubt or diversely take anything shall alway resort to the bishop of the diocese, who by his discretion shall take order for the quieting and appeasing of the same, so that the same order be not contrary to anything contained in this book. **And if the bishop of the diocese be in doubt, then he may send for the resolution thereof to the archbishop**.

Appendix: *The Daily Offices*[8]

1. When used in public and in private.

> Though it be appointed in the afore written preface that all things shall be read and sung in the church in the English tongue, to the end that the congregation may be thereby edified, yet it is not meant but **that** when men say Morning and Evening Prayer privately they may say the same in any language that they themselves do understand.

2. When used by the clergy.

> Neither that any man shall be bound to the saying of them, but such as from time to time, in cathedral and collegiate churches, parish churches and chapels to the same annexed, shall serve the congregation. **And all priests and deacons are to say daily the Morning and Evening Prayer either privately or openly, not being let by sickness or some other urgent cause**.
>
> And the curate that ministereth in every parish church or chapel, being at home, and not being otherwise reasonably hindered, shall say the same in the parish church or chapel where he ministereth, and shall cause a bell to be tolled thereunto a convenient time before he begin, that the people may come to hear God's word and to pray with him.

The only alteration of any significance that was made in 1662 is this one in the last paragraph, which obliges the clergy to say the daily offices

---

8. This appeared as a concluding rubric in 1549 but was rewritten and integrated into the main text in 1662.

wherever they may be. Parish priests are meant to do so in church and to toll a bell, inviting parishioners to join them. There are some parishes in the Church of England where something like this still occurs, though it is rare nowadays.

Of Ceremonies

This was probably composed by Archbishop Cranmer and was placed immediately after the preface in the 1549 liturgy. It has remained unchanged in all subsequent editions of the prayer book.

Pre-Reformation Ceremonies

> Of such ceremonies as be used in the Church, and have had their beginning by the institution of man,

The Reformers were very conscious of the distinction between ceremonies instituted by God in His Word (for example, the use of water in baptism and of bread and wine in Holy Communion) and those that were of purely human origin, like making the sign of the cross in baptism or kneeling to receive Communion. The former could not be altered but the latter could be, depending on circumstances.

> some at first were of godly intent and purpose devised and yet at length turned to vanity and superstition.[9]
>
> Some entered into the Church by undiscreet devotion and such a zeal as was without knowledge, and for because they were winked at in the beginning, they grew daily to more and more abuses, which not only for their unprofitableness, but also because they have much blinded the people and obscured the glory of God, are worthy to be cut away and clean rejected.[10]
>
> Other there be which, although they have been devised by man, yet it is thought good to reserve them still, as well for a decent order in the Church (for the which they were first devised) as because they pertain to edification, whereunto all

---

9. Like the kiss of peace, for example.
10. This would include the veneration of saints and their relics, private masses and many devotional practices associated with the cult of the Virgin Mary.

things done in the Church (as the Apostle teacheth) ought to be referred.[11]

There was a considerable evolution on these matters from 1549 to 1552 and later editions of the prayer book. The 1549 liturgy retained the exorcism and anointing in baptism, the giving of tokens of gold and silver in holy matrimony, the anointing and making of the sign of the cross in the visitation of the sick and so on. The Puritans regarded the process as incomplete and pressed for further changes, but largely without success.

Authority to Omit or Alter Ceremonies

And although the keeping or omitting of a ceremony, in itself considered, is but a small thing, yet the wilful and contemptuous transgression and breaking of a common order and discipline is no small offence before God.
'Let all things be done among you,' saith Saint Paul, 'in a seemly and due order.'[12] The appointment of the which order pertaineth not to private men. Therefore no man ought to take in hand, nor presume to appoint or alter, any public or common order in Christ's Church, except he be lawfully called and authorized thereunto.

This is the gist of Article 34 and the principles behind it are defended at great length by Richard Hooker in *The Laws of Ecclesiastical Polity* (5.6-10).

The Approach of this Prayer Book to Ceremonies

And whereas in this our time, the minds of men are so diverse that some think it a great matter of conscience to depart from a piece of the least of their ceremonies, they be so addicted to their old customs; and again on the other side, some be so newfangled that they would innovate all things, and so despise the old that nothing can like them but that is new; it was thought expedient not so much to have respect how

---

11. 1 Corinthians 14:19.
12. 1 Corinthians 14:40. The verse appears to have been translated directly from the Greek.

to please and satisfy either of these parties, as how to please God and profit them both. And yet lest any man should be offended whom good reason might satisfy, here be certain causes rendered why some of the accustomed ceremonies be put away and some retained and kept still.

Why Some Ceremonies Have Been Abolished

1. They were too numerous and unbearable.

> Some are put away because the great excess and multitude of them hath so increased in these latter days that the burden of them was intolerable, whereof Saint Augustine in his time complained that they were grown to such a number that the estate of Christian people was in worse case concerning that matter than were the Jews. And he counselled that such yoke and burden should be taken away as time would serve quietly to do it.

Augustine of Hippo, *Epistula 65 ad Ianuarium* (19.35), states:

> I cannot, however, give my approval to those ceremonies that are departures from the custom of the Church, and that have been instituted on the pretext that they symbolise some holy mystery, although in order not to offend the piety of some or excite the pugnacity of others, I refrain from condemning too severely many things of this kind. What I deplore, and must often do so, is that relatively little attention is paid to many of the most wholesome rites that Scripture has enjoined, and that so many false notions have everywhere become more important. For example, a man who touches the ground with his bare feet during the octaves before his baptism will be rebuked more severely that someone who drowns his mind in alcohol. My opinion therefore is that wherever possible, all customs that are without Scriptural warrant, that have not been authorised by any council of bishops, and that are not attested by the practice of the universal Church, but that display so many variations in different places that it is virtually impossible to figure out why they were ever introduced in the first place, should be abolished without hesitation. Even if there is nothing in them that is

unorthodox, the Christian faith, which God in His mercy has made free, appointing only a few simple rites that must be observed, is so oppressed by these burdensome ceremonies that even Judaism is preferable, because although they have not been set free, the burdens to which they are subject have been imposed by the law of God and not by the vain conceits of men. The Church of God, which contains much chaff and many tares, puts up with many things, but even so, she does not approve, either by silence or by practice, anything that is contrary to faith or to the life of holiness.

But what would Saint Augustine have said if he had seen the ceremonies of late days used among us, whereunto the multitude used in his time was not to be compared? This our excessive multitude of ceremonies was so great, and many of them so dark, that they did more confound and darken than declare and set forth Christ's benefits unto us.

2. They were not in harmony with the Gospel.

And besides this, Christ's Gospel is not a ceremonial law (as much of Moses' law was),[13] but it is a religion to serve God, not in bondage of the figure or shadow, but in the freedom of the Spirit, being content only with those ceremonies which do serve to a decent order and godly discipline, and such as be apt to stir up the dull mind of man to the remembrance of his duty to God by some notable and special signification whereby he might be edified.

3. They were abused by ignorant lay people and greedy clergy.

Furthermore, the most weighty cause of the abolishment of certain ceremonies was that they were so far abused, partly by the superstitious blindness of the rude and unlearned and partly by the unsatiable avarice of such as sought more of their own lucre than the glory of God, that the abuses could not well be taken away, the thing remaining still.

---

13. See Galatians 4:9; Hebrews 6:5.

Why Some Ceremonies Have Been Retained

1. Some have been kept out of necessity.

> But now as concerning those persons which peradventure
> will be offended for that some of the old ceremonies are
> retained still: If they consider that without some ceremonies
> it is not possible to keep any order or quiet discipline in the
> Church, they shall easily perceive just cause to reform their
> judgements.

2. Some are ancient and deserving of respect.

> And if they think much that any of the old do remain, and
> would rather have all devised anew, then such men granting
> some ceremonies convenient to be had, surely where the old
> may be well used, there they cannot reasonably reprove the
> old only for their age without bewraying of their own folly.
> For in such a case they ought rather to have reverence unto
> them for their antiquity, if they will declare themselves to
> be more studious of unity and concord than of innovations
> and newfangledness, which (as much as may be with
> the true setting forth of Christ's religion) is always to be
> eschewed.

3. Some must be retained for the sake of discipline and order.

> Furthermore, such shall have no just cause with the
> ceremonies reserved to be offended. For as those be taken away
> which were most abused and did burden men's consciences
> without any cause, so the other that remain are retained for a
> discipline and order, which (upon just causes) may be altered
> and changed, and therefore are not to be esteemed equal with
> God's law.

4. Some are too simple and obvious to be abused.

> And moreover, they be neither dark nor dumb ceremonies,
> but are so set forth that every man may understand what
> they do mean and to what use they do serve. So that it is not

like that they in time to come should be abused as other have been.

5. National Churches are free to choose their own ceremonies.

> And in these our doings we condemn no other nations, nor prescribe anything but to our own people only. For we think it convenient that every country should use such ceremonies as they shall think best to the setting forth of God's honour and glory, and to the reducing of the people to a most perfect and godly living, without error or superstition; and that they should put away other things which from time to time they perceive to be most abused, as in men's ordinances it often chanceth diversely in divers countries.

This statement shows remarkable tolerance of the practice of other Churches, which at times would even extend to accepting non-Episcopal ordinations as valid. However, it must be remembered that this openness was for international consumption only. Within England, uniformity of practice was imposed and those who wanted to introduce foreign customs were strongly resisted.

The Order How the Psalter Is Appointed to Be Read

In the 1549 prayer book this section was introduced by the following words: 'The Table and Kalendar, expressing the Order of the Psalms and Lessons to be said at Matins and Evensong throughout the year, except certain proper feasts, as the rules following more plainly declare'. The words 'Matins and Evensong' were altered to 'Morning and Evening Prayer' in 1552 and retained in subsequent revisions, until the entire sentence was dropped in 1662.

> *The Psalter shall be read through once every month, as it is there appointed both for Morning and Evening Prayer. But in February it shall be read only to the twenty-eight or twenty-ninth day of the month.*

The 1549 text solved the problem of February by treating January to March as a 90-day unit, subdivided into three equal 30-day sections: 1-30 January, 31 January-1 March and 2-31 March. In leap years, the

Psalms appointed for the 23rd day of February were to be repeated on the 24th. This awkward pattern was abandoned in 1662.[14]

> *And whereas January, March, May, July, August, October and December have one and thirty days apiece, it is ordered that the same Psalms shall be read the last day of the said months which were read the day before, so that the Psalter may begin again the first day of the next month ensuing.*

Before 1662 the following clause stood at the end of this paragraph: 'Now to know what Psalms shall be read every day, look in the calendar the number that is appointed for the Psalms, and then find the same number in this Table, and upon that number shall you see what psalms shall be said at [1549: Matins and Evensong; 1552 and later: Morning and Evening Prayer].'

> *And whereas the 119th Psalm is divided into twenty-two portions and is overlong to be read at one time, it is so ordered that at one time shall not be read above four or five of the said portions.*

Before 1662 this paragraph ended with the following clause: 'As you shall perceive to be noted in this Table [1552 and later: following].' The rest was added in 1662.

> *And at the end of every psalm, and of every such part of the 119th Psalm, shall be repeated this hymn,*

Glory be to the Father, and to the Son, and to the Holy Ghost; As it was in the beginning, is now, and ever shall be, world without end. Amen.

> *Note that the Psalter followeth the division of the Hebrews and the translation of the Great English Bible set forth and used in the time of King Henry the Eighth and Edward the Sixth.*

Before 1662, this note was expressed more fully as: 'And here is also to be noted, that in this Table, and in all other parts of the Service,

---

14. See B. Sargent, *Day by Day: The Rhythm of the Bible in the Book of Common Prayer* (London: Latimer Trust, 2012), pp. 40-45.

where any Psalms are appointed, the number is expressed after the Great English Bible, which from the ninth Psalm unto the 148th Psalm (following the division of the Hebrews) doth vary in numbers from the common Latin translation.'

The adoption of the Hebrew Masoretic Text (MT) numbering of the Psalms reflects the sixteenth-century penchant for authenticity and the rediscovery of the Hebrew and Greek manuscripts that underlay the Latin Vulgate Bible. The basic text of the Psalms was essentially the same; but both the Greek Old Testament, or Septuagint (LXX), and the Latin had a slightly different numbering.[15] The MT Psalms 9 and 10 were combined into one, as were the MT Psalms 114 and 115. On the other hand, MT Psalm 116 was split in two, as was MT Psalm 147, so the overall number of 150 was preserved.

Today, scholars of all persuasions generally prefer the MT numbering, in line with the prayer book. However, the discovery of the Dead Sea Scrolls and the general advance of modern biblical studies have made it plain that the MT is only one possible recension of the psalter, and many are now persuaded that MT 9-10 and MT 114-115 were originally single compositions, as the LXX testifies. This has not altered the preference for the MT numbering but it can no longer be argued that the LXX version is corrupt or secondary.[16]

The text of the Great Bible is another matter. In its current form it appeared in 1539 and was a light revision of the translation originally produced by Miles Coverdale in 1535. As a translation, everyone agrees that it is inferior to that of the King James Version of 1611, which ought to have replaced it in 1662, and (of course) even more inferior to modern translations. In spite of this obvious objection, the revised Coverdale version was retained in 1662, partly because congregations had grown used to singing it and partly because it is rhythmically superior to the KJV. Coverdale wrote with singing in mind, in a way that the KJV translators did not. In modern times, various attempts have been made to improve the Coverdale Psalms without abandoning them completely but there is no reason why a modern, more accurate version

---

15. It should, however, be said that the Greek translation of the psalter often differs from the Hebrew original.

16. See R.D. Anderson, Jr, 'The Division and Order of the Psalms', *Westminster Theological Journal* 56 (1994), pp. 219-41, for a detailed exposition of the question.

should not replace them, as long as it is sensitive to the need to use the Psalms for chanting.

In the sixteenth century there was a debate among the Reformers as to whether the Psalms should be rendered into English metre and sung more or less like hymns. Various attempts to do that were made, with the one by Francis Rous, which appeared in 1650, being the most successful. Metrical versions of Psalm 23 ('The Lord's my shepherd, I'll not want') and Psalm 90 ('O God, our help in ages past') are frequently sung today but as hymns, and not in the course of Morning and Evening Prayer as prescribed in the prayer book.

The Current Division of the Psalter

The following list shows which Psalms are sung or said on which days, and the total number of verses that the appointed Psalms contain, which gives a better picture of how much Psalm singing is involved at any particular service.

Day	Morning Prayer	Total Verses	Evening Prayer	Total Verses
1	1-5	49	6-8	37
2	9-11	48	12-14	26
3	15-17	35	18	51
4	19-21	37	22-23	38
5	24-26	43	27-29	36
6	30-31	40	32-34	55
7	35-36	40	37	41
8	38-40	58	41-43	34
9	44-46	55	47-49	42
10	50-52	52	53-55	40
11	56-58	25	59-61	37
12	62-64	34	65-67	39
13	68	35	69-70	43
14	71-72	41	73-74	51
15	75-77	44	78	73
16	79-81	50	82-85	52
17	86-88	42	89	50
18	90-92	47	93-94	29
19	95-97	36	98-101	34
20	102-103	50	104	35
21	105	44	106	46
22	107	43	108-109	43
23	110-113	35	114-115	26

Day	Morning Prayer	Total Verses	Evening Prayer	Total Verses
24	116-118	47	119:1-32	32
25	119:33-72	40	119:73-104	32
26	119:105-144	40	119:145-176	32
27	120-125	39	126-131	40
28	132-135	48	136-138	44
29	139-141	48	142-143	21
30	144-146	46	147-50	48

The 60 daily selections range in length from 21 to 73 verses, as follows:

21-30 verses: 4 times
31-40 verses: 25 times
41-50 verses: 23 times
51-60 verses: 7 times
61-70 verses: 0 times
71-73 verses: 1 time

As for the number of Psalms read at any one time, the spread is as follows:

Less than 1: 5
1: 8
2: 10
3: 29
4: 5
5: 1
6: 2

The Order How the Rest of Holy Scripture Is Appointed to be Read

In the 1549 text, after 'Scripture' in the above title came the words 'beside the Psalter' which were omitted in 1662. Substantial additions to these instructions were made in 1552 and in 1604 (see below) but were deleted when a new lectionary was introduced and new instructions were added by the Prayer Book (Tables of Lessons) Act 1871 (34-35 Vict., c. 37). Revised tables of lessons were added by the National Assembly of the Church of England under the measure of 4 August 1922 (13 Geo. V, no. 3) and both lectionaries are still printed in modern editions of the 1662 prayer book.[17]

> The Old Testament is appointed for the first lessons at Morning and Evening Prayer, so that the most part thereof will be read every year once, as in the calendar is appointed.[18]
>
> The New Testament is appointed for the second lessons at Morning and Evening Prayer and shall be read over orderly every year thrice,[19] besides the Epistles and Gospels, except the Apocalypse, out of which there are only certain lessons appointed at the end of the year and certain proper lessons appointed upon divers feasts.
>
> And to know what lessons shall be read every day, look for the day of the month in the calendar following, and there ye shall find the chapters and portions of chapters that shall be read for the lessons both at Morning and Evening Prayer, **except only the moveable feasts, which are not in the calendar; and the immoveable, where there is a blank left in the column of lessons, the proper lessons for all which days are to be found in the Table of Proper Lessons.**[20]
>
> [1871] **If Evening Prayer is said at two different times in the same place of worship on any Sunday (except a Sunday for which alternative Second Lessons are specially appointed in the Table,) the Second Lesson at the second time may, at the discretion of the minister, be any chapter from the four Gospels, or any Lesson appointed in the Table of Lessons from the four Gospels. ...**
>
> And note that whensoever proper Psalms or lessons are appointed, then the Psalms and lessons of ordinary course

---

17. See Sargent, *Day by Day*, pp. 34-39.
18. In 1549 this read: 'The Old Testament is appointed for the first lessons, at Matins and Evensong, and shall be read through every year once, except certain Books and Chapters, which be least edifying, and might best be spared, and therefore are left unread.' The words 'Matins and Evensong' were altered to 'Morning and Evening Prayer' in 1552 and later, until the present wording was adopted in 1662.
19. Altered to 'twice, once in the morning and once in the evening' in 1871.
20. The words in bold were added in 1662.

appointed in the Psalter and calendar (if they be different) shall be omitted for that time.

[1871] **Note also, that upon occasions to be appointed by the Ordinary, other Psalms may, with his consent, be substituted for those appointed in the Psalter.**

[1871] **If any of the Holy-days for which Proper Lessons are appointed in the Table fall upon a Sunday which is the first Sunday in Advent, Easter Day, Whitsunday (Pentecost) or Trinity Sunday, the Lessons appointed for such Sunday shall be read, but if it fall upon any other Sunday, the Lessons appointed either for the Sunday or for the Holy-day may be read at the discretion of the minister.**

Note also that the Collect, Epistle, and Gospel appointed for the Sunday shall serve all the week after where it is not in this book otherwise ordered.[21]

Pre-1662 editions of the prayer book contained additional instructions that were added to cumulatively, as follows:

[1549] This is also to be noted, concerning the leap years, that the twenty-fifth day of February, which in Leap year is counted for two days, shall in those two days alter neither Psalm nor lesson, but the same Psalms and Lessons which be said the first day, shall also serve for the second day.[22]

And wheresoever the beginning of any Lesson, Epistle or Gospel, is not expressed, there ye must begin at the beginning of the Chapter.

[1552] **And wheresoever is not expressed how far shall be read, then shall you read to the end of the Chapter.**

---

21. From 1549 onwards this read: 'Ye must note also, that the Collect, Epistle and Gospel appointed for the Sunday, shall serve all the week after, except there fall some feast that has his proper.' The present wording was adopted in 1662.

22. This was altered in 1604 to read: 'When the years of our Lord may be divided into four even parts, which is every fourth year, then the Sunday letter leapeth, and that year the Psalms and Lessons which serve for the twenty-third day of February, shall be read again the day following, except it be Sunday, which hath proper Lessons of the Old Testament, appointed in the Table serving to that purpose.'

[1604] **Item, so oft as the first Chapter of Saint Matthew is read either for Lesson or Gospel, ye shall begin the same at 'The birth of Jesus Christ was on this wise'. And the third Chapter of Saint Luke's Gospel shall be read unto 'so that he was supposed to be the son of Joseph, etc.'**

These additions were deleted in 1662.

The Lectionary

The 1549 lectionary attempted to include as many chapters from both the Old and the New Testaments as possible. The New Testament was covered in its entirety, apart from the Book of Revelation, of which only three chapters were read.[23] Of the 950 chapters contained in the Old Testament and Apocrypha, only 729 were selected and not all of these were actually read because of interference from holy days, when special lessons were set, and the moveable Sundays after Epiphany and Trinity, which varied from year to year. The increase in the number of moveable feasts in 1559 reduced the range of Old Testament lessons considerably, and a thorough revision of the lectionary in 1561 resulted in only 610 chapters being read – 123 of them twice and four more three times.[24] That was the pattern that carried over into the 1662 liturgy. In general, the readings followed one another in biblical order, the big exception being Isaiah, which was detached from the normal sequence and read at the end of the year, beginning with the evening of 18 November. The reason for that was that Isaiah contains many prophecies of the coming of the Messiah (Christ) and was therefore thought to be especially appropriate to the Advent and Christmas seasons.

The purpose of the lectionary is to give churchgoers the opportunity to hear most of the Old and New Testaments read through on a continuous basis. The most controversial feature was the inclusion of readings from the Apocrypha, though only from the Wisdom of Solomon, Ecclesiasticus (Sirach) and Baruch. This difficulty was mitigated in 1922, when alternative readings from the canonical Scriptures were provided alongside those from the Apocrypha.

---

23. Revelation 1 and 22 (the last chapter) were read on the morning and evening of 27 December (Holy Innocents' Day), respectively. Chapter 19 was read on the evening of 1 November (All Saints' Day).
24. For the details, see Blayney, *Printing and Printers*, pp. 164-71.

All the lectionaries, up to and including that of 1871, provided readings for Sundays according to the ecclesiastical calendar, beginning at Advent, but otherwise followed the months of the civil calendar. The revised lectionary of 1922 is more consistent in this regard, using the ecclesiastical calendar throughout.

The 1871 lectionary uses the terms Matins and Evensong for Sundays and holy days, but Morning and Evening Prayer for the days of the civil calendar. The 1922 lectionary follows the latter practice, except for holy days, for which three lessons are provided – the first for Evensong on the eve of the feast day, and the other two for Matins and Evensong on the day itself.

The International Edition of the 1662 prayer book prints both the 1662 lectionary and a lectionary authorised for use in the Church of England in 1961 (but not printed in the English version of 1662). Both of these contain extensive readings from the Apocrypha, with no alternative provided.

Although these lectionaries are still theoretically current, they are seldom if ever used. In England, most churches follow the lectionary in *Common Worship* (2000), which is shared by many denominations around the world and provides an ecumenical dimension to services.

How useful the lectionaries are is hard to say because for the most part they are used only on Sundays. Some clergy will make use of them for their daily devotions but what effect this might have is impossible to gauge. Many individuals follow independent Bible reading schemes, often with notes provided by Scripture Union and other missionary societies with a similar purpose. One of the most popular of these is Robert Murray McCheyne's Bible reading plan, which covers the entire Old Testament once and both the psalter and the New Testament twice in a calendar year.[25] It is readily available online and has the great advantage of covering the entire text (minus the Apocrypha). It comes with no commentary attached.

There is no obligation placed on anyone to preach on the lectionary, though some clergy do so, at least from time to time.

Proper Lessons and Psalms for Sundays and Holy Days

The provision of proper lessons and Psalms for Sundays and holy days evolved over time, as indicated below, and was completely overhauled in 1871:

---

25. McCheyne lived from 1813 to 1843 and was a minister of the Church of Scotland.

- 1549: There was no table of proper lessons, but they were attached to the relevant Sundays and holy days under the general heading 'The Introits, Collects, Epistles and Gospels'. Apart from Easter, Whitsun (Pentecost) and Trinity Sunday, for which special provision was made, the lessons followed a continuous order. There were no Psalms specially appointed, except for Christmas, Easter, Ascension and Whitsun (Pentecost), where they were placed among the introits.
- 1552: There was still no separate table of proper lessons but, with the exception of some holy days, they were included in the calendar. The proper Psalms appointed in 1549 were also attached to the proper lessons.
- 1559: For the first time, separate tables were appointed for both lessons and Psalms. A separate list for holy days was created, with readings from the Apocrypha.
- 1662: Proper Psalms were provided for Ash Wednesday and Good Friday. There were also some minor alterations to the 1559 table of lessons.

The proper Psalms underwent some changes over this period, as follows:

- 1549: The third Psalm for the Evensong of Ascension was 148; and for Matins on Whitsun (Pentecost) the Psalms appointed were 48, 67 and 145.
- 1552: The third Psalm for Evening Prayer was changed to 108, which it has remained. Psalm 145 was dropped from Morning Prayer at Whitsun (Pentecost).
- 1604: The Psalms for Morning Prayer at Whitsun (Pentecost) were 45 and 47, the latter believed to have been a misprint for 67 (xlvii instead of lxvii).
- 1662: The Psalms for Morning Prayer at Whitsun (Pentecost) were altered to 48 and 68.

Rules Governing the Moveable and Immoveable Feasts

The most important of the moveable feasts is Easter, the rules governing which are the same for the entire Western Church (Roman Catholic and Protestant). The Eastern Orthodox Churches follow the old, or Julian calendar, and have slightly different rules for calculating the date of Easter. This calendar was formally adopted at the first Council of Nicaea

(325) and used in the West until 1582, when the current calendar was introduced by Pope Gregory XIII (1572-85). The Gregorian calendar was soon adopted by the Catholic countries of Europe; the Protestant and Eastern Orthodox ones lagged behind. The United Kingdom, Ireland and the British colonies made the change in 1752.[26]

The main effects of this change were as follows:

1. Ten days were dropped from the Julian calendar, initially 5-14 October 1582 inclusive. The year was considered to begin on 1 January. Century years not divisible by 400 were no longer counted as leap years.
2. Scotland adopted a new year beginning on 1 January in 1600, instead of on the following 25 March as remained the case in England and Ireland, but otherwise maintained the Julian calendar until 1752.
3. England, Ireland, the British colonies and Scotland dropped eleven days in 1752 (3-13 September inclusive) and the year 1752 was held to begin on 1 January instead of 25 March. In effect, this meant that 1751 was only just over nine months' long, and 1752 had only 354 days.
4. Russia adopted the Gregorian calendar for civil use in 1918 (losing thirteen days from 1-13 February inclusive) but, as that was the decision of a Bolshevik government, the Church did not follow suit. Many other Orthodox countries (including Greece in 1923) switched to the Gregorian calendar, their Churches included but, in spite of that, the entire Orthodox world continues to celebrate Easter according to the Julian calendar.

The Early Church did not have a fixed day for celebrating Easter and various systems of calculation were used. In Asia Minor, most Churches followed the Jewish Passover and celebrated it according to the Jewish calendar on 14 Nisan, whatever day of the week that might happen to be. Rome, on the other hand, always commemorated the Crucifixion on a Friday and kept the following Sunday as the day of Resurrection. That pattern was affirmed at the first Council of Nicaea in 325, but it would be another two centuries before it was finally adopted throughout the

---

26. For a detailed discussion of the way feasts and seasons of the Church developed, see P.F. Bradshaw and M.E. Johnson, *The Origins of Feasts, Fasts and Seasons in Early Christianity* (London: SPCK; Collegeville, MN: Liturgical Press, 2011).

Roman world (in 525) and longer still before the Celtic Churches of the British Isles accepted it.[27]

According to the Julian calendar, there is a cycle of 532 years, after which the date of Easter is repeated. This means that Easter in the year 526 recurred in 1058 and in 1590, by which time the Gregorian calendar had been introduced at Rome. It will recur again in 2122. The Gregorian calendar is more complex and does not repeat itself with the same regularity.

The rules governing the date of Easter are:

1. It must be kept on a Sunday.
2. It falls on the Sunday following the paschal moon, which reaches its fullness on the fourteenth day of its cycle, as long as that day comes after the spring equinox.
3. The spring equinox is held to occur on 21 March.
4. If the full paschal moon falls on a Sunday, Easter is celebrated a week later.
5. To these rules, the Eastern Churches add the proviso that Easter must fall after the Jewish Passover.

The result of this is that Western Easter can fall on any day between 22 March and 25 April inclusive and Eastern Orthodox Easter can fall on any day between 4 April and 8 May, by the Gregorian reckoning. Occasionally, when the Western Easter is late, the two Easters coincide but they can be up to five weeks apart. (The Eastern Orthodox Easter never comes before the Western one, however.)

In practice, Easter tends to fall in the second half of the period allotted to it, as can be seen from the following calculations, which give the number of times in three centuries when Easter falls in a particular week:

Century	20th	21st	22nd	Total
Week Containing Easter				
22-28 March	11	11	12	34
29 March-4 April	25	25	22	72
5-11 April	23	22	25	70
12-18 April	24	24	25	73
19-25 April	17	18	16	51

27. The decision to change in principle was taken at the Synod of Whitby in 664 but it was not until 768 (or even later) that the last Celtic Churches finally conformed to it.

The 1662 prayer book contains detailed tables and instructions for finding the date of Easter in any given year but, now that these have been computerised and made readily available online, they are redundant for practical purposes.

What has not changed is the Easter cycle, which begins nine weeks before and ends eight weeks after the day itself. The most important pre-Easter period is Lent, the 40 days of fasting that begin on Ash Wednesday. It is known in Latin as Quadragesima ('fortieth'), which has given its name to the first Sunday of the fasting season. By extension, the previous three Sundays are called Quinquagesima ('fiftieth'), Sexagesima ('sixtieth') and Septuagesima ('seventieth'), though in fact they are only 42, 49 and 56 days before Easter.

The cycle begins on Septuagesima Sunday, which can be any day between 18 January and 21 February (22 February in a leap year) inclusive.

Ash Wednesday can fall on any day from 4 February to 10 March.

There are always six Sundays in Lent, of which the fourth is commonly known as Mothering Sunday (Mother's Day), the fifth as Passion Sunday and the sixth as Palm Sunday.

There are five Sundays after Easter, of which the first is popularly known as 'Low' Sunday, so called because it comes immediately after the 'high' feast days of Easter itself and the last is often (unofficially) called Rogation Sunday, because of the three Rogation Days that follow it and lead up to the Ascension.[28]

Ascension Day is the Thursday after the fifth Sunday and can fall on any day from 30 April to 3 June. Whitsun (Pentecost) comes ten days later and may fall on any day from 10 May to 13 June. It is not known when the popular term 'Whitsunday', short for 'White Sunday', was first used for Pentecost, nor why it was so called, but the term had established itself long before the Reformation and is still in use today. The 1662 prayer book uses it exclusively, though 'Pentecost' has made a significant comeback in recent years and is generally preferred by liturgists as being more in keeping with the usage of the universal Church. The word means 'fiftieth' in Greek and was originally given to a Jewish feast that occurred fifty days after the end of Passover. It was at that feast, following the resurrection of Jesus, that the Holy Spirit descended on the disciples of Jesus and that the Christian Church (as we know it) was born (Acts 2:1-41).

---

28. For the Rogation days, see below under 'Days of Fasting and Abstinence'.

Trinity Sunday, which marks the beginning of a new period in the ecclesiastical year, comes a week later (i.e. any day from 17 May to 20 June). It was introduced into the calendar by Thomas Becket, archbishop of Canterbury (1162-70), who was consecrated on the Sunday after Pentecost. He had a special personal devotion to the Trinity and decreed that the day of his consecration should henceforth be known as Trinity Sunday, which it still is.

The rest of the ecclesiastical year is relatively straightforward. After Trinity, there may be anywhere from 22 to 27 Sundays, depending on the date of Easter. If Easter falls on 22 to 26 March inclusive, there are 27 Sundays after Trinity and, if it falls on 27 March to 2 April, inclusive there are 26. The prayer book, however, provides for only 25 Sundays after Trinity. When there are more, the deficit is made up by employing the unused Sundays after the Epiphany.[29] When there are fewer, the collect, Epistle and Gospel appointed for the twenty-fifth Sunday after Trinity are always used on the Sunday immediately preceding Advent, popularly known as 'Stir up' Sunday, from the opening words of the collect for that day.

Trinity ends with Advent Sunday, which is always four Sundays before Christmas and can fall on any day from 27 November to 3 December. This is the official beginning of the ecclesiastical year. The second Sunday in Advent is known as Bible Sunday, because the collect for that day is devoted to the Scriptures.

The Christmas season continues until Epiphany (6 January), which is then followed by one to six Sundays, all of which are provided for in the prayer book, though the collect, Epistle and Gospel for the sixth Sunday is used only when Easter falls on or after 22 April.

Days of Fasting and Abstinence

Following ancient Christian custom, the 1662 liturgy provides a number of days for fasting and abstinence, although the practice of such disciplines has always been voluntary in Anglican churches.

Lent is the most widely observed of the fasts. The word itself means 'spring', as it still does in Dutch, and the fast is attested from the first

---

29. Normally, this would be the second and third Sundays after Epiphany if Easter falls on 22 to 24 March, the third and fourth Sundays after Epiphany if Easter falls on 25 to 26 March, the third Sunday after Epiphany if it falls on 27 to 31 March and the fourth Sunday after Epiphany if Easter falls on 1 to 2 April.

Council of Nicaea onwards (Canon 5). Originally the fast ended on Palm Sunday, which marked the beginning of a second, or paschal fast, which is attested from the second century, but that distinction was lost early on and the two fasts have long since merged into one.

The day before Lent begins is popularly known as Shrove Tuesday, from the old English verb 'to shrive' which means 'to do penance for sin'. The fast itself begins on Ash Wednesday, a term derived from the ancient custom of covering oneself in sackcloth and ashes to show the sincerity of one's repentance. In modern times this is occasionally symbolised by the practice of 'ashing', in which ashes derived from the burning of the palm crosses from the previous year are daubed on the foreheads of those who go to church on that day. There is no provision for such a ritual in the prayer book, though there is a service of commination, used for the formal denunciation of sinners, which is in the prayer book and is still occasionally used.

In addition to Lent, there are the **Ember Days**, which occur in each of the four seasons of the year, on the Wednesday, Friday and Saturday after the following days:

1. The first Sunday in Lent (Quadragesima)
2. Pentecost
3. 14 September (Holy Cross Day)
4. 13 December (St Lucy's Day).

The origin of the word 'ember' is disputed, though it seems clear that it has nothing to do with the smouldering wood in a dying fire, which is its common modern meaning. It may be a corruption of the Latin *quattuor tempora* ('four seasons') or derived from the Old English word *ymbren*, meaning a 'circuit'. The Dutch word *quatertemper* and the German *Quatember* suggest the former derivation; but it is probable that the two were confused in English usage, which shows no trace of the *quattuor*. They are spread throughout the year towards the end of each season. The first of them is effectively absorbed by Lent but the other three are more distinct.

The observance of the Ember days was originally a local Roman custom, apparently enjoined on the English Church by Pope Gregory the Great. It was first mentioned at the Council of Clovesho in 747, by which time it seems to have been well established.

For some unknown reason, the Ember days came to be associated with preparation for ordination, and Canon 31 of the 1604 Church Canons specifically states that ordinations can only take place on the Sunday immediately following one of them. This is no longer strictly observed, though it is still common for clergy to be ordained shortly after one of the last three. However, such ordinations are nowadays denoted by Petertide (St Peter's Day, 29 June), Michaelmas (29 September) and Advent, and not by the Ember days themselves.

Finally, there are the **Rogation Days**, which are the Monday, Tuesday and Wednesday preceding Ascension Day. These owe their origin to Mamertus, bishop of Vienne (Gaul), who apparently decreed a three-day fast in his diocese as a response to a series of disasters that occurred there around 470. The practice proved very popular and was enjoined on the whole of Gaul by Canon 27 of the Council of Orleans in 511. It was introduced into England at an early date and was approved by the Council of Clovesho in 747, half a century or more before it appeared at Rome in the time of Pope Leo III (795-816).

The Elizabethan Injunctions of 1559 tied the Rogation Days to the custom known as the beating of the bounds, when clergy and parishioners processed around the parish to determine and proclaim where its boundaries lay. Homily 17 in the second book of Homilies is described as 'An exhortation to be spoken to such parishes where they use their perambulation in Rogation Week for the oversight of the bounds and limits of their town'. There is no service corresponding to this in the Book of Common Prayer, although in 1661 John Cosin proposed that one should be added, for which he composed the following collect:

> Almighty God, Lord of heaven and earth, in whom we live, move, and have our being, who doest good unto all men, making thy sun to rise on the evil and on the good, and sending rain on the just and the unjust; favourably behold us thy people, who do call upon thy name, and send us thy blessing from heaven, in giving fruitful seasons, and filling our hearts with food and gladness; that both our hearts and mouths may be continually filled with thy praises, giving thanks to thee in thy holy church, through Jesus Christ our Lord. Amen.

The proposed Epistle was James 5:13-18 and the proposed Gospel was Luke 11:1-10. The beating of the bounds still occurs in some parishes but no provision has ever officially been made for the Rogation Days.

In the Early Church there was provision made for fasting on Wednesdays and Fridays, as can be seen from the *Didache*, which makes it clear that the days were chosen in order to avoid Jewish custom, which was to fast on Mondays and Thursdays.[30] The only trace of these fasts in the prayer book is the direction to read the litany on Wednesdays. The Friday fast is familiar to many because of Roman Catholic practice but it has never been enjoined as part of Anglican devotion.

The Calendar

Closely connected to the ecclesiastical year is the calendar that lists days of special commemorations and celebrations. In ancient times, each local church had its own calendar, giving the names of prominent people, most of them martyrs, and designating the days of their death as the ones on which they would be remembered. This was not macabre, because the day of death was regarded as the final triumph of the saint who had begun his or her new life in heaven on that day. As time went on, the names of prominent martyrs and others not connected to the particular church in question would be added to the list, with the result that on some days several different people would be commemorated.[31]

The English Church adopted the Roman calendar at the Council of Clovesho in 747, but with some additions of its own. Commemorations of Gregory the Great and Augustine of Canterbury were both added at that time, and others followed. The papacy did not get involved until 1161, when it canonised Edward the Confessor, king from 1042 to 1066, and his name was added to the calendar. Roman influence remained strong throughout the middle ages, but it was supplemented by many names from Gaul (France) and also by the names of local English saints. The Sarum calendar, which was the one most widely used at the time of the Reformation, was identical to that of the 1662 prayer book with the following exceptions:

1. Sarum did not commemorate Evurtius or Bede, who were added later.
2. The dates assigned to Alban, Mary Magdalene and Cyprian of Carthage were altered.
3. A number of commemorations found in Sarum were dropped altogether from 1662.

---

30. *Didache* 8:1: 'Let not your fasts be together with the hypocrites, for they fast on the second and fifth days of the week; but keep your fast on the fourth day and the Preparation (Friday).'
31. See Sargent, *Day by Day*, pp. 11-15.

The evolution of the calendar can be traced back to 1532, when a petition was sent from the House of Commons to King Henry VIII, complaining that there were too many holy days and asking for their number to be reduced. This demand was echoed by the convocation of Canterbury in 1536, when it was decreed that, apart from the feasts of the apostles and the Virgin Mary, no commemorations were to be held during the harvest, and the patron saints of particular parishes were all to be remembered on the same day – the first Sunday in October.

In 1549 the minor commemorations, celebrated on the so-called 'black-letter days' were all abolished, apart from the feast of Mary Magdalene (22 July), which was made into a major ('red-letter') feast and given its own collect, Epistle and Gospel.

In 1552 the feast of Mary Magdalene disappeared, but the names of George, Lawrence and Clement were added. There were also special commemorations for the so-called 'Dog Days' and for the university and law terms.[32]

In 1559, the feast of St Barnabas, which had been omitted by accident in 1552, reappeared.

In 1561, the Royal Commissioners for Ecclesiastical Causes prepared a new calendar at the command of Queen Elizabeth I. The restored black-letter days contained all but three (Bede, Alban, Evurtius) of the 1662 list. The calendar was prefaced with the injunction that 'these [are] to be observed for holy days, and none other'.

In 1604 the feast of St Evurtius (properly Eunurchus) was added on 7 September, the birthday of the late Queen Elizabeth I, who had died the previous year.

In 1661 the names of Bede (27 May) and Alban (17 June) were added, from the *Preces Privatae* (Private Prayers), a devotional manual that had been issued in 1564. This was a very modest addition, considering that the *Preces Privatae* were so full of commemorations that there were only six days in the entire year that did not have one.

Not specifically mentioned in the calendar are two sets of quarter days, the first of which corresponds to the beginning of each of the seasons and the second of which represents their halfway point. The first set is:

25 March: Annunciation to Mary; the old 'New Year' in
    England (until 1751)

---

32. The 'dog days' were those in late summer when the Dog Star, Sirius, rises and sets with the sun.

24 June: John the Baptist, born six months before Jesus[33]
29 September: St Michael and All Angels (Michaelmas)
25 December: Christmas.

The second set is:

2 February: Imbolc, now Candlemas
1 May: Beltane, now St Philip and St James
1 August: Lughnasa, now Lammas or St Peter *ad Vincula*
1 November: Samhain, now All Saints' Day.

The first set corresponds to the beginning of the seasons and is focussed on the life of Jesus Christ, with the exception of Michaelmas. The second one is a Christianisation of the pagan Celtic tradition of celebrating the halfway point through the seasons of the year.

Saints' Days

The criteria for deciding which days should be considered 'red-letter days' are that they must be associated either with the life of Jesus Christ, his mother Mary or John the Baptist, or else with one of the disciples/apostles. There is however, one exception to this – All Saints' Day (1 November).

Other commemorations are less prominent and often ignored or restricted to places that have a special connection to the person concerned. The black-letter days were not included in the early prayer books and appeared for the first time in 1604. In modern times a number of other figures have been added by different Anglican Churches, but it must be said that some of them are obscure, controversial or unrelated to the Anglican world. In many cases, the criteria for inclusion in (or exclusion from) the calendar are far from clear, which makes commemoration even more problematic.

The **red-letter** days are the following:

30 November: St Andrew
21 December: St Thomas
26 December: St Stephen

---

33. Note that the Roman Calendar counted backwards from the first day of the following month, which is why John the Baptist's birthday is celebrated on 24 June (and not 25 June).

27 December: St John the Evangelist
28 December: Holy Innocents
1 January: Circumcision of Christ
25 January: Conversion of St Paul
2 February: Presentation of Christ in the Temple[34]
24 February: St Matthias
25 March: Annunciation of the Blessed Virgin Mary
25 April: St Mark
1 May: St Philip and St James[35]
11 June: St Barnabas
24 June: St John the Baptist
29 June: St Peter
25 July: St James
24 August: St Bartholomew
21 September: St Matthew
29 September: St Michael and All Angels
18 October: St Luke
28 October: St Simon and St Jude
1 November: All Saints[36]

The **black-letter** days are harder to analyse because they are much more diverse in origin. In broad terms, they can be grouped as being Biblical, Roman, Gaulish/French, British/English or Eastern in origin, along with some that are miscellaneous, as follows:

A. Biblical

2 July: Visitation of the Blessed Virgin Mary. This commemorates the visit of Mary to her cousin Elizabeth before the birth of John the Baptist. It was instituted by Pope Urban VI in 1389, confirmed by the Council of Basel in 1441 and adopted in England in 1480.

22 July: St Mary Magdalene. Briefly (1549-52) a red-letter day.

6 August: Transfiguration. Locally observed from early times but not enjoined generally until 1457, when Pope

---

34. Also called the feast of the Purification of the Blessed Virgin Mary and popularly known as Candlemas. It is a Christianisation of the pagan Celtic feast of Imbolc, now known in North America as Groundhog Day.
35. The date is a Christianisation of the pagan Celtic feast of Beltane.
36. A Christianisation of the pagan Celtic feast of Samhain.

Calixtus III chose it to commemorate the victory of Christian troops over the Turks at Belgrade. It may be for that reason that it was not made a red-letter day in 1549, despite its obvious claim to be one.

29 August: Beheading of John the Baptist. Attested from early times. Unusually for a saint, John's birth was commemorated as a red-letter day (24 June) but his death was not.

B. Roman
1. Connected with the city of Rome itself

18 January: Prisca. Said to have been a child martyr in the time of the Emperor Claudius (41-54) but this was rejected by Pope Gelasius I in 494. She may have been confused with Priscilla, the wife of Aquila (Romans 16:3).

20 January: Fabian. Bishop of Rome (236-50), martyred in the persecution of the Emperor Decius (249-51).[37]

21 January: Agnes. A virgin martyred (304) in the great persecution under the Emperor Diocletian (284-305).

12 March: Gregory I Magnus ('the Great'). The apostle of the English and pope from 590-604, his name was added to the calendar as early as 747.

6 May: St John the Evangelist *ante Portam Latinam*. Commemorates the miraculous deliverance of John, who was supposedly thrown into a cauldron of boiling oil in front of the Latin Gate in the reign of the Emperor Domitian (81-96), but he escaped unharmed. The legend is of very ancient origin, being traceable to Tertullian (*c.* 200), *De praescriptione haereticorum*, 36.

1 June: Nicomede. Supposedly martyred under Domitian. The date is that of the dedication of a church to him at Rome.

10 August: Lawrence. Of Spanish birth, he was archdeacon to Pope Sixtus II and martyred three days after him in 258, when he was slowly roasted to death. His reputation rests on his administration of the charities of the Roman Church.

---

37. Fabian is one of four popes commemorated in the prayer book calendar. The others are Gregory I the Great, Clement I and Silvester.

23 November: Clement of Rome. Author of a letter to the church at Corinth. He died about AD 95, but it is not certain that he was a martyr.

31 December: Silvester. Bishop of Rome (314-35) and associated, somewhat dubiously, with the conversion of the Emperor Constantine.

2. Connected with Italy, North Africa or Spain

22 January: Vincent. A deacon of Zaragoza, martyred at Valencia in 304, the story of his martyrdom is mostly fictitious.

5 February: Agatha. Martyred at Catania (Sicily) in the time of Decius.

14 February: Valentine. Probably the bishop of Interamna (Terni), martyred about 273. Possibly confused with another Valentine, supposedly a priest and martyr under the Emperor Claudius (41-54). The link between him and physical love is fictitious.

7 March: Perpetua. Martyred along with her companion Felicitas in North Africa, around 202. The *Acts of Perpetua* are an unusually authentic account of her martyrdom.

4 April: Ambrose. Bishop of Milan (374-97).

28 August: Augustine. Bishop of Hippo (396-430).

26 September: Cyprian. Bishop of Carthage, martyred (258) under the Emperor Valerian (253-60). He was confused with Cyprian, the converted magician of Antioch by the revisers of 1661. The true date of his martyrdom was 14 September.

13 December: Lucy. Supposedly martyred at Syracuse under Diocletian.

C. Gaulish/French

1. Gaulish martyrs

7 September: Evurtius (Eunurchus). Evurtius was originally a typographical error for Eunurchus. Supposedly a bishop of Orleans from about 320 to about 340, he was included in the calendar in 1604 in order to perpetuate the commemoration of Queen Elizabeth I, who was born on 7 September 1533.

6 October: Faith. Martyred at Agen about 290. The crypt of
St Paul's Cathedral in London is dedicated to her.

9 October: Denis. Patron saint of France, martyred about
286; frequently confused with Dionysius the Areopagite.

25 October: Crispin. Martyred at Soissons with his
companion Crispinian in the Diocletian persecution.

2. Gaulish evangelists

13 January: Hilary. Bishop of Poitiers, who died in 367. The
winter term at Oxford University is named after his feast
day.

11 November: Martin. Bishop of Tours, who died in 397.
Martin Luther was named after him. The transfer of
his remains to a basilica dedicated to him in 473 is
commemorated on 4 July.

13 November: Britius. Martin's successor as bishop of Tours
(397-444).

3. Frankish evangelists

1 September: Giles. An abbot in Languedoc, who died about
725.

17 September: Lambert. Bishop of Maastricht, martyred at
Liège about 709.

1 October: Remigius. Bishop of Reims who died about 530.
He baptised Clovis, king of the Franks, in 496.

6 November: Leonard. A disciple of Remigius, who founded
the monastery of Noblat, near Limoges. He died about 560.

D. British/English

1 March: David. Patron saint of Wales, who died about 589.

2 March: Chad. Bishop of Lichfield, who died in 672.

18 March: Edward. King of Wessex. Murdered at Corfe
Castle by order of his stepmother Aelfthryth in 978.
His remains were transferred in 980 from Wareham to
Shaftesbury, an event that is commemorated on 20 June.

3 April: Richard. Bishop of Chichester (1245-53), canonised
in 1260. He is the most recent in date of the saints
commemorated in the calendar.

19 April: Alphege. Archbishop of Canterbury, martyred by
the Vikings in 1012.

19 May: Dunstan. Archbishop of Canterbury (960-88).

26 May: Augustine. First archbishop of Canterbury (597-604). The date is that of his arrival in England in 597.

27 May: Bede. Died in 735 but not commemorated in the Sarum calendar.

5 June: Boniface. Wynfrith of Crediton, apostle of Germany, martyred in Friesland in 775.

17 June: Alban. The first British martyr, who was buried at the site of the modern St Albans cathedral. The date is probably an error for 22 June, which is given in both the Hereford and York missals.

15 July: Swithun. Bishop of Winchester (852-862). The date commemorates the transfer of his remains to the cathedral in 971. His feast day is famous for its supposed ability to predict the weather for the rest of the summer.

13 October: Edward the Confessor. King of England (1042-66). The date commemorates the first transfer of his body, which took place in 1163. There was a further transfer in 1269. He was canonised in 1161.

17 October: Etheldreda. The first Englishwoman to be canonised. She was the founder of the great convent at Ely and died in 679.

15 November: Machutus. A Welshman who became bishop of Aleth in Brittany and died about 630.

17 November: Hugh. Bishop of Lincoln (1186-1200). He was canonised in 1220.

20 November: Edmund. King of East Anglia, who was murdered by the Vikings in 870. His body was transferred to Bury St Edmunds in 903.

E. Eastern

3 February: Blasius. Bishop of Sebaste in Armenia, martyred about 316.

23 April: George. Patron saint of England, adopted by King Richard I (1189-99) and appointed England's patron by King Edward III in 1349, replacing Edward the Confessor. He is supposed to have been martyred in the Diocletian persecution, but nothing is known about him and he may not have existed.

20 July: Margaret. Supposedly martyred at Antioch in Pisidia around 290. Commemorated in the Greek Orthodox Church as Marina on 17 July.

26 July: Anne. Mother of the Virgin Mary, her name appears
for the first time in the *Protevangelium Iacobi*. It seems
that her festival was popularised in England by Anne
of Bohemia, wife of Richard II (1377-99). The name
Anne is a corruption of Hannah and was attributed to
Mary's mother because Mary's song (the *Magnificat*) was
modelled on that of Hannah, the mother of Samuel.

25 November: Catherine. Supposedly martyred by being
broken on the wheel at Alexandria under the Emperor
Maxentius (306-12).

6 December: Nicholas. Bishop of Myra in Lycia (southern
Turkey) and martyred in the Diocletian persecution. In
later times he was confused with Father Frost and became
the semi-pagan symbol of Christmas – St Nicholas or
Santa Claus.

F. Miscellaneous

3 May: Invention (Discovery) of the Cross, which was
supposedly unearthed by the Empress Helena on a visit
to Palestine in 326. It was celebrated as early as the sixth
century.

1 August: Lammas Day. The name is a corruption of 'loaf-
mass' and commemorates the offering of bread made
from the newly harvested wheat. The day is also called
St Peter *ad Vincula*, commemorating the release of the
Apostle Peter (Acts 12). The date reflects the dedication
of a church at Rome where the chains in which Peter had
been bound were supposedly preserved. In reality, the day
is a Christianisation of the pagan Celtic feast of Lughnasa.

7 August: Name of Jesus. Of unknown origin, but it was
celebrated in England before it was officially proclaimed
by Pope Alexander VI (1493-1503).

8 September: Nativity of the Blessed Virgin Mary.
Supposedly established by Pope Sergius I in 695 but the
reason for the choice of date is unknown.

14 September: Holy Cross Day. The dedication festival of two
churches in Jerusalem, built by the Emperor Constantine
in 335, to commemorate the discovery of the True Cross
by his mother Helena. The festival was not introduced
in the West until after 629, when it commemorated the

restoration of the Cross (which had been seized by the Persians) by the Emperor Heraclius in 629.

8 December: Conception of the Blessed Virgin Mary. Nine months before her birth on 8 September. Since 1854 it has been celebrated by the Roman Catholic Church as the Immaculate Conception, on the ground that Mary was supposedly born without sin. That doctrine is not recognised by the Anglican Church.

16 December: *O Sapientia*. The opening words of a series of seven antiphons sung with the *Magnificat* from 16 to 22 December. The antiphons originated in the Spanish festival of the Annunciation.

Chapter 3

The Daily Offices

Morning and Evening Prayer

Origin

Both Morning and Evening Prayer owe their origin to the monastic hours that had been standardised in the Sarum breviary.[1] There were eight of them in all, but only five were retained by the 1549 prayer book, where they were combined into two. The traditional hours and their relationship to the modern offices are as follows:

Office	Time	Inclusion in BCP
Matins	before daybreak	in Morning Prayer
Lauds	at daybreak	in Morning Prayer
Prime	at the first hour (6 a.m.)	in Morning Prayer
Terce	at the third hour (9 a.m.)	discarded
Sext	at noon	discarded
None	at the ninth hour (3 p.m.)	discarded
Vespers	at sunset	in Evening Prayer
Compline	at bedtime	in Evening Prayer

As the above table indicates, Terce, Sext and None were discarded in 1549, while the first three were combined as Morning Prayer (something that was already being done in practice) and the last two as Evening

---

1. The Sarum breviary was reformed in 1516, with a second edition in 1531. It was further reformed in 1541.

Prayer. The prayer book services are sometimes called Matins and Evensong, as they were in 1549, but this can be misleading. Matins was only one of the three offices that went into Morning Prayer and Evensong implies that it will be sung rather than said. For these reasons, it is therefore better (and more accurate) to retain the designations of Morning and Evening Prayer that were first used in 1552, though both sets of terms describe the same services and there is no liturgical or theological distinction between them.

The prayer book instructs that Morning and Evening Prayer are 'daily to be said and used throughout the year' but this refers to the services themselves, not to those who pray them. The duty of the clergy in this respect is set out towards the end of the preface 'Concerning the Service of the Church', where it is specified that they must say the daily offices unless they are prevented 'by sickness, or some other urgent cause'. It has to be said that this injunction is honoured more in the breach than in the observance and that for many clergy the phrase 'some other urgent cause' has been extended well beyond its intended meaning. Many people are inclined to think of the daily offices as a form of 'vain repetition' but that is to misunderstand their didactic purpose. Those who absorb them and who can say them without having to rely on the book know how they come to mind and inform our understanding even when we are not consciously thinking about them. They become part of the furniture of our spiritual lives and stand us in good stead both in good and in difficult times. As food for the soul, they may sometimes seem to be routine and boring, just as food for the body can often be but they nourish us nevertheless and bring us to a balanced maturity that is the essential foundation, not only for ministry but for the Christian life in general.[2]

Prefatory Rubrics

The daily offices are prefaced by three general rubrics which give directions for the place where they are to be said, the vesture of the clergy called to say them, and the permission granted to others to lead the services when no clergyman is present. In the past, the meaning of these rubrics was hotly disputed, particularly during the ritualist controversies at the end of the nineteenth and beginning of the twentieth

---

2. For a good defence of Morning and Evening Prayer, see M. Burkill, *Dearly Beloved: Building God's People through Morning and Evening Prayer* (London: Latimer Trust, 2012).

centuries, but these have died down and are now of little more than historical interest.

The **first rubric** states that Morning and Evening Prayer shall be said in the accustomed place, whether in the church, the chapel or the chancel (of the church), unless the bishop has directed otherwise. The curious sentence directing that 'the chancels shall remain as they have done in times past' reminds us that at the Reformation there was considerable pressure from some of the more determined Reformers to abolish chancels altogether. However, Thomas Cranmer believed that there was some usefulness in retaining chancels as places where communicants could gather and partake of the Lord's Supper apart from the other members of the congregation. In 1549, the daily offices were mandated to be said in the chancels but, in 1552 (and later), the emphasis was on finding a convenient place where the service could be heard, whether that was in the chancel or not.

Today, there is really no controversy about this. Very few people turn up for the daily offices in church and the clergy often say them privately. Everybody agrees that, if a public service is held, it ought to be audible and that those who want to attend it should be able to find it without any difficulty. These are practical matters rather than theological issues and are generally treated accordingly by those involved.

The **second rubric** addresses the question of 'the ornaments of the Church and of the ministers thereof', which are described as those in use in the Church of England in the second year of Edward VI (1548).[3] This apparently means that the traditional medieval vestments were meant to be worn by the clergy, and the rubric was so interpreted by the nineteenth-century ritualists. However, as was pointed out in the course of controversy, those vestments were removed from churches in accordance with Injunction 47 of Queen Elizabeth I in 1559, making the rubric inapplicable in its literal sense. Canon 58 of the 1603 (1604) Canons stipulated that ministers reading divine service and administering the sacraments should wear surplices and (if graduates) the hoods of their degrees, as had already been specified in the Advertisements of 1566, drawn up by Matthew Parker, archbishop of Canterbury (1559-75), which were meant to put an end to the controversy over vestments. The canon also allowed that non-graduates might wear a 'tippet', or scarf, which also became standard for graduates.

---

3. Strictly speaking, Edward VI's second year ran from 28 January 1548 to 27 January 1549. The important point is that this was before the introduction of the 1549 BCP on 9 June 1549.

The combination of surplice, scarf and hood is still commonly found when Morning and Evening Prayer are said publicly, especially on Sundays, but, if the services are held on weekdays with few people present, many clergy 'dress down' and wear ordinary clothes. There is no provision made for anything more elaborate, although clergy will often wear a stole instead of a scarf and dispense with the academic hood. This has now become a matter of personal preference for the clergy, who may be expected to conform to the custom of the parish, but no theological principle is involved and the matter is not worth the arguments over it that have been generated in the past.

As far as the ornaments of the Church are concerned, Canon F9 (1969) specifies that a church must have at least a Bible and a Book of Common Prayer for the use of the minister.[4] For the most part, however, the ornaments specified relate to the service of Holy Communion (as is also the case with the vestments prescribed for the clergy) and are only incidentally concerned with the daily offices.

The **third rubric** makes provision for lay readers or other suitable people to take the services when no priest is available. The only restriction placed on them (as on deacons) is that they are not allowed to say the words of absolution but must use the collect for the twenty-first Sunday after Trinity instead.[5] This provision is a rather odd hold-over from the pre-Reformation Church, when it was believed that priests had special absolving powers conferred on them at their ordination. The words of the absolution itself make it clear that it is not the priest, but God himself, who absolves, so there is no theological reason why it should not be used by anyone authorised to conduct the service.

The Order for Morning Prayer

The following table lists the 32 elements of Morning Prayer, with their correspondences to Matins, Lauds and Prime in the Sarum rite.

---

4. This repeats Canon 80 (1603), which reflects a series of sixteenth-century royal injunctions (1536 no. 7, 1538 no. 2, 1547 no. 7, 1559 no. 6). The principle goes back much further – at least to Canon 9 of the Council of London in 1328 (1329), enshrined in William Lyndwood's *Provinciale* as 3.27.3.
5. This rubric was added by the Prayer Book (Further Provisions) Measure 1968 (no. 2) (18 December 1968), section 1.1, in *The Public General Acts and Church Assembly Measures 1968* (London: HMSO, 1969).

BCP	Matins	Lauds	Prime
1. Sentences			
2. Exhortation			
3. Confession			
4. Absolution			
5. Our Father	Our Father[6] Hail Mary		Our Father
6. O Lord, open thou	O Lord, open thou		
7. O God, make speed	O God, make speed	O God, make speed	O God, make speed
8. *Gloria*	*Gloria*	*Gloria*	*Gloria*
9. Praise ye	Alleluia, praise be Invitatory/ Response	Alleluia, praise be	Alleluia, praise be Hymn
10. The Lord's Name			
11. *Venite*	*Venite* Hymn		
12. Psalms	Psalms[7]	Psalms[8] *Jubilate*[9]	Psalms[10]
13. *Gloria*	Nine *Gloriae* Benedictions	Four *Gloriae* Canticle	*Gloria*
14. Old Testament lesson	Lessons[11] Homily Responsories		
15. *Te Deum*	*Te Deum*[12]		
16. *Benedicite*		*Benedicite*[13]	
17. New Testament lesson		Short chapter Hymn	

---

6. Intoned 'secretly' (inaudibly) by the priest.

7. There were twelve Psalms and six antiphons on weekdays, but eighteen Psalms and nine antiphons on Sundays.

8. There were five Psalms and antiphons.

9. On Sundays only.

10. There were three Psalms and one antiphon on weekdays, and nine Psalms and one antiphon on Sundays.

11. There were three or nine taken from both the Old Testament and the New Testament.

12. On Sundays only.

13. On Sundays only.

BCP	Matins	Lauds	Prime
18. *Benedictus* or 19. *Jubilate*		Benedictus	
20. Apostles' Creed or 21. Athanasian Creed[233]			Athanasian Creed Short chapter
22. The Lord be with you			
23. Lesser litany			Lesser litany
24. Our Father			Our Father Apostles' Creed[15]
25. Suffrages		Suffrages	Suffrages Confession[16] Absolution[17]
26. Collect of the day		Collect of the day	
27. Collect for peace		Collect for peace	
28. Collect for Grace			Collect for Grace
29. Anthem			
30. State and Church prayers			Prayers for the intercession of the Virgin Mary and the saints
31. The Prayer of St Chrysostom			
32. The Grace[18]			Benediction

14. Prescribed for thirteen days in the year, *viz.*, Christmas, Epiphany, St Matthias, Easter, Ascension, Whitsun, St John the Baptist, St James, St Bartholomew, St Matthew, St Simon and St Jude, St Andrew and Trinity Sunday.
15. Said privately.
16. Mutual.
17. Mutual.
18. 2 Corinthians 13:14. This was the ordinary Sunday lesson at Terce.

Analysis of BCP Morning Prayer[19]

    A. Penitential introduction: 1552[20] (items 1-4 above).

    B. The Lord's Prayer and versicles: 1549[21] (items 5-10 above).

    C. Psalms, lessons and canticles: 1549[22] (items 11-19 above).

    D. The Confession of Faith: 1549 (items 20-21 above).

    E. Concluding prayers and thanksgivings: various dates (items 22-32 above).

The last section can be subdivided as follows:

1. The suffrages	1549
2. Intercession for State and Church[23]	
a. for the monarch	1559
b. for the royal family	1604[24]
c. for the clergy and people	1559
3. Prayers for special occasions	
a. for rain	1549[25]
b. for fair weather	1549[26]
c. in time of dearth and famine	1552[27]
d. in time of war and tumults	1552
e. in time of plague or sickness	1552
f. in the Ember Weeks	1662[28]
g. after any of the former	1559
h. for Parliament	1662
i. for all conditions of men	1662
4. Thanksgivings for special occasions	
a. general thanksgiving	1662
b. for rain	1604
c. for fair weather	1604

---

19. Dates indicate the year in which the item in question was added to the Book of Common Prayer.
20. This replaced private confession, which was still present in 1549.
21. The doxology to the Lord's Prayer and the response 'The Lord's Name be praised' were both added in 1662.
22. The *Jubilate* was added in 1552.
23. Placed at the end of the litany until 1662.
24. There was no royal family under Queen Elizabeth I.
25. Printed at the end of Holy Communion until 1552.
26. Printed at the end of Holy Communion until 1552.
27. Two forms.
28. Two forms.

d. for plenty	1604
e. for peace and deliverance	1604
f. for restoring peace at home	1662
g. for deliverance from the plague	1604[29]
h. prayer of St Chrysostom	1549[30]
i. the Grace	1559[31]

A. Penitential Introduction (shared with Evening Prayer)

The rubric before the sentences of Scriptures specifies that the minister is to read them with a loud voice. This is because before the Reformation, priests habitually prayed '*secreto*', i.e. inaudibly.

There are eleven sentences, of which seven (all from the Old Testament) were taken from the old lenten *capitula* (chapter) and from the penitential Psalms that were read daily during Lent. No fewer than three of them come from Psalm 51. Daniel 9:9-10 and the New Testament verses were selected by Thomas Cranmer, and 1 John 1:9 was added to the last one in 1662. They are all penitential in character and are designed for different needs, as follows:

1. Support for the fearful: Psalm 6:1/Jeremiah 10:24; Psalm 51:9; Psalm 143:2
2. Comfort for the doubting: Psalm 51:17; Daniel 9:9-10; Luke 15:18-19
3. Instruction of the ignorant: Ezekiel 18:27; 1 John 1:8-9
4. Admonition of the negligent: Psalm 51:3; Matthew 3:2
5. Caution to the hypocritical: Joel 2:13.

The exhortation that follows the sentences builds on them and probably reflects the influence of Valérand Poullain, who published something similar in the Strasbourg liturgy that appeared in February 1552, just at the time the 1552 prayer book was in preparation. The spiritual principles on which it is based are the following:

1. It is addressed to 'beloved brethren'. The people being asked to confess their sins are not unbelievers, but members of the Church, and the exhortation is an act of love towards them.

---

29. Two forms.
30. Printed at the end of the litany until 1662.
31. Printed at the end of the litany until 1662.

2. The command to confess and repent of sin is found throughout the Scriptures and is fundamental biblical teaching.

3. Our sins are many and our wickedness is great. Note that the former are the natural (and inevitable) outcome of the latter. It is our inherent wickedness that leads us to many different kinds of sin.

4. We must not try to hide them or pretend that they do not exist. We cannot fool God.

5. Almighty God is our heavenly Father. Our Creator and Lord is also our closest relative.

6. Confession must be made in the right spirit. We are called to be humble in our approach, lowly (self-deprecating), repentant and willing to obey from the heart.

7. The purpose of confession is to obtain forgiveness, which is freely given to us by our heavenly Father.

8. God's goodness and mercy are infinite. There is no sin too great for Him to forgive.

9. Humble repentance ought to be a constant feature of our lives, but especially when we meet together in church.

10. The purposes of our common worship are:
    a. to thank God for the blessings we have received from Him;
    b. to praise Him;
    c. to hear His Word; and
    d. to ask for the things we need, both physically and spiritually.

11. The exhortation concludes with an invitation to accompany the minister:
    a. with a pure heart (internal attitude);
    b. with a humble voice (external expression);
    c. to the throne of heavenly grace (into the presence of God).

Note that the internal attitude of the worshipper must come first. It then receives external expression as we come into the presence of God.

The minister invites the congregation to pray kneeling (a sign of humility and repentance) and to say the words of the confession *after* him. The word 'after' should not be understood to mean 'afterwards' in time, as if the minister says them first and the congregation repeats them later. Rather, it is to be read as a translation of the Latin *secundum* (French: *selon*), meaning 'in the same [words]', or 'according to'. Minister and people are meant to say them together in unison.

The general confession is an expression of the spiritual state of the entire congregation. It may reflect different experiences at the individual level, but in the eyes of God we are all like sheep who have gone astray and we stand equally in need of His forgiveness and restoration. There are not two classes of Christians, the 'carnal' and the 'spiritual', with different degrees of need, and no member of the Church has any cause to feel superior to anyone else. The general (or common) confession reaches the sinful heart of everyone, or what theologians call the 'total depravity' of the human race. Just as there is no confession of sin without the promise of redemption, so there is no salvation without the conviction and confession of sin. To use a medical analogy, the correct diagnosis of what is wrong is a necessary prelude to putting it right.

The confession begins with a description of the lost sheep that we have become.

1. We have erred and strayed from God's ways. There is a standard that He expects of us and we have turned away from it.
2. We have followed the 'devices and desires' of our own hearts. In other words, we have invented fantasies and succumbed to lusts that proceed from our fundamental rebellion against God.
3. We have broken the laws of God. God has given us laws by which we should live and we have disobeyed them.
4. We have not done what we should. These are the sins of omission.
5. We have done what we should not. These are the sins of commission.
6. There is no health in us. We are incapable of recovering our proper spiritual state on our own.

Halfway through, the confession turns from repentance to supplication:

1. We plead for God to show mercy to us, who are 'miserable offenders'. This phrase has provoked much comment and it is often omitted from modern liturgies, presumably because it is felt to be excessive, and even offensive. However, in reality, it is nothing but the truth, and to fail to admit that is to fall short of the repentance that God expects from us. The meaning of 'miserable' is difficult to convey in modern

English, where the word tends to mean 'nasty'. In this context, it is more or less synonymous with 'pitiable' and means 'in need of mercy'. That we are offenders, and not just sinners by birth, is borne out by Romans 7:7-25, where the Apostle Paul analyses the relationship between the law and sin. Without the law sin is 'dead', that is to say, it can do nothing. However, as soon as the light of the law is revealed, sin springs to life, as it were, and begins to torture us. This is the state that we find ourselves in, and to confess it is to demonstrate that we are not merely aware, but also convicted of our sinfulness.

2. We ask God to spare those who confess their faults, as He has promised to do (1 John 1:9).

3. We ask God not only to spare, but also to restore, those who are repentant. In other words, we are not just delivered from the punishment we deserve, but we are brought back into the right relationship with God.

4. We confess that God has promised forgiveness and restoration to us, but only in and through Jesus Christ, who has made full atonement for us. When God the Father looks at our sin, He sees His Son pleading mercy for us on the basis that he has died to pay the price that the Father's justice demands.

5. We pray that God will grant us the grace to live a 'godly, righteous, and sober life' from now on, in order that we might glorify him by so doing. We ask for 'godliness' or participation in the character of God by sharing in the mind of Christ (1 Corinthians 2:16). We ask for 'righteousness', the quality by which our thoughts and actions will conform to, and fulfil, the will of God in and for us. Finally, we ask for 'sobriety', the attribute that translates the Greek word *sophrōsynē*, or good judgement and discernment in everything that we do.

Immediately after the confession comes the absolution. For reasons that appear to be governed by misguided traditionalism, the opening rubric states that the words of absolution are to be pronounced only by someone who is in priest's orders, even though there is no suggestion that the 'ministers' referred to in the text must be so ordained. In fact, as the words themselves testify, it is not the priest, but God who absolves, and there is no theological reason why this prayer should not be said by anyone taking the service. That the people should receive the absolution kneeling is a reminder that they are still in the state of penitence but, as with all such directives, it is the spirit of the heart and not the posture of the body that counts in the sight of God.

The absolution first describes:

1. Who God is. He is the Almighty and the Father of our Lord Jesus Christ. This means that He is sovereign over all things and that He is the power behind all that Christ has done for us and has promised to us.
2. What God wants. He does not want sinners to die, but to repent of their sinfulness and live eternally with Him.
3. What God has done. He has empowered and commanded His servants ('ministers') to declare forgiveness to His repentant people. Of course, the servants of God are called to make this declaration to all people everywhere, but it only takes effect in those who repent and believe the message (Gospel) without reservation ('unfeignedly'). That is the emphasis here. It is not just the promise of 'absolution and remission' but the fact that they have been obtained that God's ministers are commanded to convey.

The absolution next prays that:

1. God will grant us 'true repentance, and his Holy Spirit'. Repentance is required of us but it is a divine gift, brought to us by the Holy Spirit. Human beings are capable of remorse, but this does not lead to forgiveness and new life. On the contrary, as in the case of Judas Iscariot, it is more likely to lead to self-destruction and death. We cannot forgive ourselves.
2. The Holy Spirit given to us will make our actions acceptable and pleasing to God. We pray this in the first instance for what we are doing right now. God's promises are eternal, which means that they are always present, and not merely something to be hoped for in the future.
3. The rest of our life may be 'pure and holy'. This is a prayer for the future that begins now. Purity and holiness are practically synonymous, but they are not completely identical. Purity emphasises the quality of our life and deeds, whereas holiness focusses on the purpose and ends to which they are directed. We desire purity in order to be holy, that is to say, we want to be blameless so that we may please God and be acceptable to him.

4. At the end we may come into the eternal joy of God's presence. The Christian life here on earth is a preparation and a pilgrimage that will culminate in heaven. We must never lose sight of that goal, but keep our eyes always firmly fixed on the prize.

The absolution ends with the affirmation that what we receive from God and what we pray for is only possible in and through Jesus Christ, who is the Lord of our lives whom we serve. Jesus is both the means to the end and the end itself. In this respect, he is different from the law of Moses, which could be described as the means to an end (holiness, righteousness etc.) but not the end itself, because the law cannot save us or give us eternal fellowship with God. As for other religions and philosophies, they are neither the means nor the end. They often claim to be at least the former – ways of achieving a higher life, happiness and so on – but, because they start in the wrong place, they cannot lead us to the right destination. Christians start in the right place, with conviction of sin, recognition of our powerlessness to do anything about it and acceptance that what we cannot do for ourselves God has done for us by sending His Son into the world to make atonement for us (John 3:16). In doing this, however, God has also shown us that to know the Son is to know the Father also, because Father and Son are one (John 10:30). There is no higher stage or further step than that.

Since 1968, those who are not permitted to say the words of absolution are directed instead to use the collect for the twenty-first Sunday after Trinity, which reads: 'Grant, we beseech thee, merciful Lord, to thy faithful people pardon and peace, that they may be cleansed from all their sins, and serve thee with a quiet mind; through Jesus Christ our Lord. Amen.' It is a summary of the absolution, making the same request for those who are faithful believers and expecting the same results. In no sense can it be regarded as inferior to the absolution itself, and those who are absolved in this way must not think that they have been cheated or fobbed off with some inferior form of blessing.

B. The Lord's Prayer and Versicles (shared with Evening Prayer)

According to the rubric, at this point the minister kneels along with the people, who remain kneeling, and they both pray together. The important here is that minister and people are no longer distinguished at this point but come together into the presence of God.

The form of the Lord's Prayer used here is the longer one, including the doxology, which is found in some manuscripts of Matthew 6:9-13 and in the *Didache*, which is possibly a first-century source. Whether the doxology formed part of the 'original' prayer or not need not trouble us. The 1549 prayer book omitted it, as did all subsequent versions until 1662. In the context of worship, the Lord's Prayer was probably followed by the doxology from a very early date and its inclusion in 1662 rounds out the element of praise that its presence at this point in the service is meant to emphasise.[32]

The versicles and responses are taken from Matins in the Sarum breviary and were included in 1549, though in the singular (e.g. 'O Lord, open thou my lips' etc.). The plural was introduced in the 1552 prayer book. They correspond to Psalm 51:15 and Psalm 70:1. They were used for this purpose from early times and there is nothing surprising about their presence here.

In the 1549 text the words 'Praise ye the Lord' were followed by 'Hallelujah' from Easter to Trinity Sunday, but the 'Hallelujah' was dropped in 1552.

The rubric before the *Gloria* was adapted from the 1637 Scottish prayer book and must be regarded as a concession to liturgical formalism, rather than anything else. Neither the posture (standing), nor the restriction of the words to the priest, is of any theological significance.

The *Gloria* itself can be traced back at least to the fourth century and is probably older, although the second part ('As it was in the beginning etc.') seems to have been added in the sixth century. It should be remembered that written testimony to such things is usually considerably later in date to their origins in the oral worship of the Church and often represents a standardisation of an existing practice rather than the introduction of something new.

C. Psalms, Lessons and Canticles

In this section, there is a divergence in the canticles appointed for Morning and Evening Prayer. At Morning Prayer, the Psalms open with the *Venite* (Psalm 95), a practice inherited from the Early Church that is intended to be both an invitation and an admonition to prayer. The Psalms are divided according to a 30-day cycle in which they are read through in their entirety. There is a tendency to have longer selections in the morning, as can be seen from Psalm 119 which is divided into five sections, three in the evening and two in the morning. The evening portions consist of four stanzas (32 verses each) and the morning ones of five (40 verses each). The lessons are intended to cover most of the Bible, the Old Testament

---

32. For an exposition and analysis of the Lord's Prayer, see the section on the Catechism in Chapter 6.

once and the New Testament twice in the year (apart from the book of Revelation, which is read only once in the traditional lectionaries.)

It should be said that the Latin titles given to the canticles (and also, in a slightly different way, to the Psalms) represent the opening words of the text, which was the traditional Latin (and Hebrew) way of naming them.

It is the canticles that retain our attention, not least because neither of the ones appointed to be read after the Old Testament lesson at Morning Prayer comes from the canonical Scriptures. The *Benedicite* occurs in the Septuagint version of Daniel and is part of what we now recognise as the Apocrypha, but the *Te Deum Laudamus* is a much later composition. Nobody knows for sure who wrote it, but the most widely accepted possible author is Niceta of Remesiana (*c.* 370-414), who composed it in Latin. The translation in the Book of Common Prayer is somewhat free in places, but not in a way that seriously distorts the original meaning. The only point of possible divergence is in the line: 'Make them to be numbered with thy saints: in glory everlasting.' This assumes that the Latin original had *numerari* ('to be numbered') but there is a variant reading, *munerari* ('to be rewarded'), which may be the original.[33] It makes little difference in practice; and it has to be said that modern attempts to make a more 'accurate' translation tend to lose the measured dignity of Cranmer's version, even if they are technically more 'correct'.

The *Te Deum* may be analysed as follows:

1. The worship of God by the created order (verses 1-6). Earth and heaven worship the everlasting Father in the words of the angels, quoted from Isaiah 6:3.
2. The worship of God by the Church (verses 7-13). The Church is composed of the glorious apostles, the 'goodly' prophets and the noble martyrs, along with all the saints throughout the world. Christian worship of the one God is trinitarian and this is recognised by singling out the Father, the Son and the Holy Spirit in turn.
3. The praise of Christ (verses 14-19). He is the king of glory and the Father's everlasting Son. When he determined to save the human race, he became incarnate in the womb of the Virgin Mary. After overcoming the pain of death, he opened the

---

33. See J. Wordsworth, *The* Te Deum: *Its Structure and Meaning and Its Musical Setting and Rendering; Together with a Revised Latin Text, Notes and Translation*, rev. edn (London: SPCK, 1903).

kingdom of heaven to all believers. There he sits at the right hand of God (the Father) until the time when he will return in judgement.

4. A plea for salvation in general (verses 20-23). Because of what the Son has done for us, we pray that he will come to the aid of his servants and unite us with all the saints in his eternal glory. We ask him to save us, to bless us, to rule over us and to exalt us for ever.

5. A plea for salvation in particular (verses 24-29). We pray every day and never cease to do so. We ask God to protect us from sin and to have mercy on us because we trust in Him. In the last verse the collective prayer gives way to the cry of the individual – I have trusted in God and so ask Him to keep me safe. The words 'let me never be confounded' express a typical Old Testament way of referring to sin as confusion, a reminder to us that, although the hymn is not found in the Bible, it is saturated with biblical imagery.

It is possible that the hymn in its present form is a combination of earlier forms of praise but it is not certain what they were. Perhaps verses 1-13 constituted one canticle, to which the other sections were later added, either progressively or all at once. What is certain is that there is a change of gear after verse 13 and again after verse 24 which hints at the possibility of different origins, but the surviving evidence is too scanty to allow us to draw any firm conclusions.

Traditionally, the *Te Deum* was not sung in Lent, to which abstinence the Sarum breviary added Advent and the period from Septuagesima to Ash Wednesday. The 1549 prayer book continued that tradition up to a point, by prescribing that in Lent the *Benedicite* should be used instead. The 1552 text removed the specific directions concerning Lent, making the two canticles alternatives at any time of the year. If there was ever a liturgical or theological reason for the earlier distinction, it has long since been lost, although the practice often continues, if only to encourage variety and ensure that the *Benedicite* is not completely lost.

The *Benedicite* is also known as *The Song of the Three Holy Children* (Shadrach, Meshach and Abednego, or, to use their Hebrew names, Hananiah, Mishael and Azariah, respectively), who appear in the Old Testament Book of Daniel (1:6-7; 3:8-30). A shorter version of it is found in the LXX, interpolated between Daniel 3:23 and 3:24, where it is assumed to be their composition, though it is unlikely that it has anything to do with them. Most probably, the words were put in their mouths at a later stage and by someone working in the Greek-speaking diaspora. This must remain speculation, but it is certain that the hymn is of pre-Christian origin, whatever its true source may have been.

The *Benedicite* is highly repetitive, making it easier to learn by heart at a time when few people could read and write. It is a hymn of creation, and may be analysed as follows:

1. The praise of God by the heavenly order. This includes the angels and the heavenly powers, but also the sun, the moon, the stars and what we would now call the weather, including the three elements of water, wind and fire.
2. The praise of God by the earthly creation. The fourth element, earth, is singled out for special attention. It embraces the physical world (mountains, plants, ground water and the sea) and the animals, which are subdivided into those that live in the sea, those that fly in the air and those that walk on the ground.
3. The praise of God by human beings. Moving on naturally from the animals that move across the ground, the hymn turns to humans and, more specifically, to God's chosen people. First, it mentions Israel, in general, and then breaks this down into the priests, the 'servants' of God, the souls of the righteous, the 'holy and humble men of heart' and finally Hananiah, Azariah and Mishael, the three young men mentioned in Daniel, who are exalted as specific examples of heroism and devotion whom we are meant to honour – and, as far as we can, to emulate.

The canticles appointed after the New Testament lesson are more familiar to most people because they are drawn directly from the Bible. The first is the *Benedictus*, the song of Zacharias after the birth of his son, John the Baptist (Luke 1:68-79).[34] Although it is found in the New Testament, the *Benedictus* is in many respects a product of the Old Testament, coming straight from the world of the Temple priesthood and the expectation of the Messiah that animated so many Jews at the time when John was born. In that sense, it is a bridge between the Testaments, linking the promises of the Old to their fulfilment, not in

---

34. Note that the wording in the 1662 prayer book differs slightly from both the Great Bible of 1539 and from the KJV.

John, but in the one whose coming John was being called to proclaim. It can be analysed as follows:

1. The fulfilment of prophecy. God has visited and redeemed His people, having raised up salvation in the house of David, as the prophets of old promised that He would. In one sense, Zacharias was clearly 'jumping the gun' as we might say today, since when he uttered these words the fulfilment of the promises still lay in the future. However, although, strictly speaking, that was true, it was also the case that John's birth marked the beginning of the new era. Jesus Christ did not spring out of nowhere: his coming was not only prophesied; it was also prepared. Those to whom he came knew what to expect and their failure to receive him would be their great tragedy and undoing. It is the same message proclaimed by John in the prologue to his Gospel, and by the Apostle Paul in Romans. There was nothing fundamentally new or unexpected about the coming of Jesus – it was all known in advance. This remains true today. The world does not believe, but not because it has never heard the message of salvation; it has heard and rejected it.

2. The content of prophecy. This has two fundamental parts:
   a. We have been delivered from the power of our enemies.
   b. We have been set free to do God's will and live according to His covenant.

3. The nature of the covenant:
   a. From the time of Abraham onwards, God has sworn to deliver us from our enemies.
   b. We have been set free from fear, in order to live in holiness and righteousness.

4. The mission of John:
   a. He is to be the new prophet, called to prepare the way for Almighty God Himself.
   b. He is to preach the message of salvation, of forgiveness of sin.

5. The purpose of God:
   a. In His mercy, the light of God has come to earth.
   b. The light will remove our darkness, save us from death, and give us peace.

The second canticle, *Jubilate Deo*, is Psalm 100, which recurs at Evening Prayer on the nineteenth day of the month. Some have thought that it was to be read at Morning Prayer only when the *Benedictus* occurs in the lectionary or on 24 June, when it is read as the Gospel on St John the Baptist's day. That makes sense, as far as it goes, but the rubric should not be interpreted to mean that the *Jubilate* ought not to be used on any other occasion. In fact, there is no restriction on its use and often it alternates with the *Benedictus* in the same way as the *Benedicite* alternates with the *Te Deum*. All such arrangements are voluntary and have no liturgical or theological significance.

The *Jubilate* is less detailed than the *Benedictus* and is best regarded as a kind of summary of it, though (of course) it was not written as such. Its message is straightforward and can be set out as follows:

1. We are called to be joyful in our service to God.
2. The Lord has created us and we are His people.
3. We must be thankful to Him and speak well of Him.
4. He is gracious and merciful to us.
5. His truth is everlasting.

On those five pillars rests the entire worship of the people of God.

D. The Confession of Faith (Shared with Evening Prayer)
Immediately after the reading of the Scriptures comes the confession of faith, an order that reminds us that it is the Word of God which determines the content of our belief, and that the confession is a useful summary of what that belief is. Occasionally, objections have been raised to particular clauses in the various confessions that the Church uses, but these are usually due to misunderstandings on the part of ill-informed readers rather than to any false teaching.[35]

The confession normally used at this point is the Apostles' Creed, so called because it was once believed that the apostles themselves composed it. That view is untenable now and, even at the time of the Reformation, it was being called into question. However, although it does not go back as far as the New Testament, it can claim to be a fair digest of apostolic teaching and forms of it are attested in the second century. There may be a connection with baptism, which was administered in the name of the Trinity, but the evidence is inconclusive. What is certain is that doctrinal summaries known as the 'rule of faith' (*regula fidei*) appear

---

35. See, for examples, the exposition of the Apostles' Creed in the section on the Catechism in Chapter 6 and the exposition of the Athanasian Creed at the end of this chapter.

as early as Tertullian and possibly earlier.[36] There is a great variety of them, although they share a common trinitarian structure in which the life, death and resurrection of Christ are recounted in considerable detail. By contrast, the opening section on the Father consists of a single, short sentence and there is nothing about the Holy Spirit beyond the mere confession of his existence.

The Apostles' Creed, as we know it, is of Western (Latin) origin and is not used in the Eastern Orthodox Churches, though they have no objection to it. It is probable that similar regulae fidei were in use in the Greek-speaking world in early times, but they were superseded by the so-called Nicene Creed, which can claim the authority of the ancient ecumenical councils. By contrast, the Apostles' Creed was never officially sanctioned by any church body. In the form that we now have it, it can be traced back to Pirminius of Reichenau (early eighth century) and owes its prominence to the fact that Charlemagne picked it up and authorised its inclusion in the Church's liturgy.

Before the Reformation, the Apostles' Creed occurred in the office of Prime, where it was said inaudibly by the priest, immediately after the Lord's Prayer. This rather peculiar custom is thought to derive from a practice in the Early Church in which statements of doctrine were regarded as secrets that had to be kept from the prying ears of unbaptised observers. Whether that is true or not, by the sixteenth century it was regarded as an abuse and, more than a decade before 1549, Cardinal Quiñones had indicated in his breviary that it should be said aloud on all days except Sunday, when it was to be replaced by the Athanasian Creed.[37]

In the 1549 prayer book the Creed was said after the lesser litany, and apparently kneeling, but from 1552 onwards the rubrics have directed the congregation to stand, perhaps because that posture is supposed to indicate a readiness to defend the faith. There is no direction to turn east for the recitation of the creed, nor is there any suggestion that congregants should bow their heads when the name of Jesus is mentioned.[38] The

---

36. See Irenaeus of Lyons, Adversus omnes haereses, 1.2, which contains a statement resembling a proto-creed. For a detailed history of the Creed and many examples of its early forms, see J.N.D. Kelly, Early Christian Creeds, 3rd edn (Harlow: Longman, 1981).

37. F. de Quiñones, Breviarium Romanum a Francisco Cardinali Quignonio: Editum et Recognitum: Iuxta Editionem Venetiis A.D. 1535 Impressam, ed. J.W. Legg (Cambridge: Cambridge University Press, 1888).

38. Justification for this latter practice was sometimes sought in Canon 18 of the 1603 (1604) Canons, which encourages 'due and lowly reverence' whenever the name of Jesus is mentioned in divine service, but that canon

important thing is that the Creed should not be omitted but should be said with conviction by every member of the congregation, for whom it is a personal profession of faith.

The translation of the Creed is generally faithful to the original, with one curious exception. The words *resurrectio carnis* ('resurrection of the flesh') are translated as 'resurrection of the body', a practice that has been maintained in modern liturgies as well.[39] It is virtually certain that the translators thought that 'body' and 'flesh' were synonymous, so this does not represent an alteration of doctrine. In fact, if 'body' is taken to include what has traditionally been called the 'rational soul', it can be argued that the translation is theologically better than the original because it emphasises that the entire human being, and not just the material flesh, will rise again.

The Creed can be analysed in a logical and straightforward manner, as follows:

1. The clause relating to the Father, who is described as the Almighty and as the Maker (i.e. Creator) of heaven and earth. This is uncontroversial, but it should be noted that what is said of the Father can be applied equally well to the Son and to the Holy Spirit.
2. The clause relating to Jesus Christ, His only Son. Mention is made of his birth, death, resurrection, ascension, heavenly session at the Father's right hand, and future return to judge the living and the dead.
3. The clause affirming the Holy Spirit, to which are added five miscellaneous items, which appear to follow from one another in a more or less logical order, though this is not specifically stated:
   a. the 'holy Catholic' Church (the universal company of all the faithful)
   b. the communion of saints (the fellowship of all believers)
   c. the forgiveness of sins (the atoning work of Christ)
   d. the resurrection of the body
   e. everlasting life.

---

was abrogated in 1969 along with all the others and the current ones contain nothing similar.

39. Note, however, that in the offices of baptism, the questions posed to the candidates and their sponsors ask whether they believe in the 'resurrection of the flesh'.

For the Athanasian Creed, see the section below on the Appendices to the Daily Offices.

E. Concluding Prayers and Thanksgivings
(Mostly Shared with Evening Prayer)
The Versicles before the Lord's Prayer [40]
These are divided into two parts, separated by 'Let us pray':

>   a. the mutual salutation (added in 1552); see Ruth 2:4, 2 Timothy 4:22.
>   b. the lesser litany (from 1549); see Psalm 123:3, Luke 17:13.

The rubric states that the people should be kneeling throughout, although in practice it is the connecting line, 'Let us pray', that gives the signal for the congregation to kneel. The minister is directed to speak with a loud voice, so that he can be heard. As elsewhere, this was probably to counteract the tendency of the pre-Reformation clergy to speak inaudibly.

The Lord's Prayer
The Lord's Prayer is repeated here in the shorter version (without the doxology). This may be because of the context, which is one of supplication rather than of praise. However, both forms of the Lord's Prayer were known and in regular use, so it may be for that reason that the shorter form has been preferred here. Some have objected to what they see as the 'vain repetition' of a standard prayer, but that judgement is unduly negative. The Lord's Prayer is a reminder to us that Jesus taught his disciples how to pray and, before we do so ourselves, it is good to be reminded of the standard that he set for them.

The Versicles after the Lord's Prayer
These versicles are also called the suffrages, which distinguishes them from what has gone before. They are six in number and lead into the prayers that follow, for which they were originally intended to serve as private preparation. All except the fifth are found in the office of Prime in the Sarum breviary. The fifth does however occur in Henry VIII's primer (1545).

Each suffrage is subdivided into two parts, the first to be said by the priest and the second by the congregation in response. With one

---

40. These also occur at Evening Prayer, as was specified in the rubrics before 1662.

exception, they are taken from the Psalms, and correspond to the collects that follow, though not in the same order:

1. Psalm 85:7. Collect of the day
2. 1 Samuel 10:24. Collect for the monarch
3. Psalm 20:9. Collect for the clergy and people
4. Psalm 132:9. Collect for the clergy and people
5. Psalm 28:9. Collect for peace
6. Psalm 51:10-11. Collect for Grace.

The rubric states that the priest must stand, which is exceptional and is probably due to the persistence of a pre-Reformation habit. Note that the 1552 prayer book replaced 'priest' with 'minister', which accords with the previous rubrics, since there is no need for the minister to be in priest's orders, but 'priest' was restored in 1662, almost certainly for traditionalist reasons. Today nobody pays much attention to this and it is customary for whoever is leading the service to continue as before, whether he/she is a priest or not.

The Three Collects

This is the name given to the collects that follow immediately after the suffrages. The first one is the 'Collect of the day', which is the same as that appointed for Holy Communion that week, or on that feast day. The second and third collects are the same throughout the year, though they differ in Morning and Evening Prayer. In Morning Prayer, they are collects for peace and for grace, whereas in Evening Prayer they are for peace (but in different words) and for protection against the dangers of the night.

For an analysis of the different collects of the day, see Chapter 4 on Collects, Epistles and Gospels set for Holy Communion.

The collect for peace is taken from the Gelasian sacramentary (1496), the Gregorian sacramentary (1345)[41] and the Sarum breviary, where it occurs at the end of the office of Lauds. It is extremely compact and full of theology in the original Latin, making it difficult to translate into English, but Thomas Cranmer managed to compose a brilliant and faithful paraphrase of the original. It can be analysed as follows:

---

41. The numbers in parentheses following the sacramentaries are those assigned to them by the editors of the modern collections: the Gelasian, L.C. Mohlberg (ed.), *Liber Sacramentorum Romanae Aeclesiae Ordinis Anni Circuli* (Rome: Herder, 1968); and, the Gregorian, Deshusses (ed.), *Le Sacramentaire grégorien.*

Our relationship to God:

1. God is the author of peace and loves harmony (1 Corinthians 14:33).
2. To know God is to have eternal life (John 17:3).
3. To serve Him is perfect freedom (John 8:31-36, Romans 6:15-23).

Our petitions to God:

1. To defend us against our enemies (Psalm 27:1).
2. To deliver us from fear (Psalm 27:3).

The collect for Grace is taken from the Gelasian sacramentary (1576), the Gregorian sacramentary (1491) and the Sarum breviary, where it occurs in the office of Prime.[42] It can be analysed as follows:

Thanksgiving:

1. God has brought us safely to the start of this day (Psalm 30:5).

Petitions:

1. We ask God to defend us today with His power (Psalm 31:3-5).
2. We ask Him to keep us from falling into sin (Psalm 19:13).
3. We ask Him to protect us against danger (Psalm 54:4-5).
4. We ask Him to oversee everything we do (Psalm 119:33-35).
5. We ask that everything we do will please Him (Psalm 23:3).

Before 1662 Morning Prayer ended here.

The Anthem

Provision was made in 1662 for singing an anthem at this point in the service. Hard as it is for us to believe, this is the only time in the 1662 prayer book where hymnody of any kind is authorised, and then only in places where it was already customary. We may assume that

---

42. A similar prayer is also found in *The Bobbio Missal: A Gallican Mass Book*, 2 vols., ed. E.A. Lowe (London: Henry Bradshaw Society, 1920 and 1924), 569.

cathedrals, royal chapels and other prominent places had choirs and a regular pattern of musical offerings. The high quality of many of these is attested by the surviving compositions of men like William Byrd, Thomas Tallis and Henry Purcell. Hymn singing as we now understand it was possible in dissenting chapels, and it was fostered by writers like Isaac Watts, but it did not become common until the Evangelical Revival of the mid-eighteenth century, when the works of John and Charles Wesley, Augustus Toplady, John Newton, William Cowper and others transformed everything. The Church of England was slow to adapt to this and as late as 1819 an action was brought to the consistory court against the unauthorised singing of hymns during Morning and Evening Prayer. Eventually it was decided that hymns were no different from metrical psalms and the way was opened up for the spread of hymnody in Anglican worship, although it was not formally authorised until 1872.[43] Today, of course, hymns have taken over to the extent that, for many people, they are what worship is all about. As far as the 1662 prayer book is concerned, the effect has been to make this provision for an anthem seem somewhat peculiar. In many churches it is interpreted to mean that this is an appropriate place to sing a hymn, but there are many other points in the service where hymns are sung without any specific provision being made for music. On this subject it is safe to say that 1662 is out of date and widely disregarded, even by its staunchest defenders.[44]

The Five Concluding Prayers

These were all placed at the end of the service in 1662, though they are much older in origin. Most of them were originally attached to the litany and are supposed to be omitted when the litany is read. However, because the last two of them have been retained in the litany, they are read along with it and thus not omitted as the first three are.

A Prayer for the Sovereign

The earliest form of this prayer is found in a book called *Psalmes or Prayers taken out of Holye Scripture* (1545). In 1553 it was placed in the Reformed primer as the fourth collect for the king at Morning Prayer. At the same time, another, shorter version was added to the collects for

---

43. Act of Uniformity Amendment Act 1872 (35-36 Victoria, c. 35), ss. 3-4.
44. On the many vicissitudes of English church music, see A. Gant, *O Sing unto the Lord: A History of English Church Music* (London: Profile Books, 2015).

peace and for protection against danger at Evening Prayer. In its current form, it was placed in 1559 just before the prayer of St Chrysostom in the litany. It was moved to its present position in 1662.

The prayer is based on the exhortation in 1 Timothy 2:1-2 and may be analysed as follows:

1. The Lord our heavenly Father is our true king:
    a. He is high and mighty, King of kings and Lord of lords.[45]
    b. He sees everyone who lives on the earth.
2. We pray to Him to bestow His favour on our earthly sovereign:
    a. We ask that he/she will be filled with the Holy Spirit.
    b. We ask that he/she will always do God's will.
    c. We ask that he/she will be filled with heavenly gifts.
    d. We ask that he/she will be granted a long and healthy life.
    e. We ask that he/she will be granted victory over his/her enemies.
    f. We ask that he/she will be granted everlasting joy and happiness after this life.

This prayer must be understood in the context of a monarchy in which the Sovereign is both an individual and the representative of the people. To pray for him/her is also to pray for the state over which he/she reigns, because everything in that state is done in his/her name. In countries that have an elected head of state a prayer like this one will have to be reworded, but its basic thrust is the same. A head of state, whether hereditary or elected, is not simply a private individual, and to pray for him/her is to pray for all those who serve him/her as well.

The first and most basic requirement is that the Sovereign must be filled with the Holy Spirit, without whom none of the rest is possible or meaningful. The Sovereign must obey God's will and do what is pleasing to Him. In order to further that purpose, he/she must be filled with 'heavenly gifts' which are not specified but which may be assumed to coincide with the fruits of the Spirit listed in Galatians 5:22-23. These are meant for every Christian, but it is especially important for them to be manifested in those who are given authority over others. Good health and a long life are also desirable in a ruler, the first because it is

---

45. The phrase 'king of kings and lord of lords' is taken from Revelation 17:14 and 19:16, where it is applied to Christ the Son, not to the Father, though, of course, it is suitable for him as well. (See 1 Corinthians 15:28).

difficult to perform the necessary duties of office without a sound mind and body, and the second because long life conveys experience and the wisdom that it brings, as well as bringing stability to the realm and its people. Rulers are also meant to be successful, and opposition to them may be manifested both at home and abroad. Finally, the reward of eternal life awaits every faithful believer, and so it is only right that we should pray that our rulers will also be blessed with it.

A Prayer for the Royal Family

This was added to the litany in 1604 and may have been written by Archbishop John Whitgift. In its current form it was composed by Archbishop William Laud in 1633 and placed in its present position in 1662. Only the royal consorts and the heir to the throne are mentioned by name, though when Prince Charles married Lady Diana Spencer on 29 July 1981, the wording 'Charles Prince of Wales' was altered to 'the Prince and Princess of Wales'. Queen Elizabeth the Queen Mother was also mentioned by name until her death on 30 March 2002, as was Philip, duke of Edinburgh, until he passed away on 9 April 2021. When Queen Elizabeth II died on 8 September 2022, the whole prayer had to be altered, with King Charles III taking her place, accompanied by his Queen Consort and the new Prince of Wales. By its nature, this prayer changes more often than any other in the prayer book, and it is often possible to work out at what date any given edition was printed by referring to it.

The prayer is much shorter than the one for the Sovereign, but it contains the essentials. God is honoured as the source of all goodness and is petitioned to bless the royal family by:

a. filling them with the Holy Spirit;
b. enriching them with heavenly grace;
c. prospering them with all happiness; and
d. bringing them into his eternal kingdom.

The principles are much the same as in the prayer for the Sovereign. It is right to pray for his/her family since they are inevitably his/her chief supports in this life and what they do impacts the tone of government as a whole.

A Prayer for the Clergy and People

This prayer can be found in the Gelasian sacramentary (1429, 1552), the Gregorian sacramentary (1308) and the Sarum missal. It was inserted into the first English litany in 1544 and introduced into the 1559 liturgy, where it was placed at the end of the litany. As with the other prayers, it was placed here in 1662. It can be analysed as follows:

1. God is honoured as the only worker of 'great marvels', a phrase that seems to be based on Psalm 136:4.
2. God is asked to send down His Spirit on bishops, clergy and congregations, a reference to the Pentecostal outpouring (Acts 2:2-4).[46]
3. God is asked to bless His people so that they may please Him.
4. God is asked to do this so that Jesus Christ, our Advocate (1 John 2:1) and Mediator (1 Timothy 2:5), will be glorified.

This prayer emphasises the absolute necessity of divine grace for the well-being of his people. Nobody can please God of his own volition – for that, the blessing and power of his Holy Spirit, present in and among us, is essential. At the heart of this prayer is the conviction that the heavenly work of Christ, seated at the right hand of the Father, will be glorified when its fruits are seen in the lives of the people for whom he is interceding.

A Prayer of St Chrysostom
This prayer is so called because it is found in late manuscripts of the Byzantine liturgy of St Chrysostom, as well as in the liturgy of St Basil. The attribution to John Chrysostom (347-407) is wrong, but Thomas Cranmer probably took it from a copy of the liturgy ascribed to him and assumed that it was his. It was placed at the end of the English litany in 1544, where it is still found, and added here in 1662. The prayer is addressed to 'Almighty God' but it is apparent from the content that it is the Son, Jesus Christ, who is meant by this. It can be analysed as follows:

1. What God has done. He has given us grace to unite in common prayer to Him.
2. What Jesus has promised to do. He will fulfil the requests of two or three who are gathered together in his name (Matthew 18:19-20).
3. What we now ask him to do in us:
   a. fulfil our desires in the way that is best for us
   b. grant us knowledge of his truth in this world
   c. grant us everlasting life in the world to come.

---

46. The clergy are referred to as 'curates', meaning all who have the cure of souls, and not simply 'assistant curates', as the term is usually used today.

Note that, while we ask God to fulfil our desires, we do so with the proviso that it should be in the way that is best ('most expedient') for us. This means that we may not get exactly what we have asked for but that God will respond to our pleas in ways that we will come to see are for our benefit.

We pray for understanding of the truth in this life, which is the preparation for eternal life after death. Our physical beings will change but our spiritual minds will remain the same, anchored in the truth of God's Word.

The Grace

This is 2 Corinthians 13:14 and was placed at the end of the litany in 1559. It was added here in 1662. It is a Christological exposition of the Trinity, as its order demonstrates:

a. The grace of Christ. He is the one who opens the doorway into the presence of God.
b. The love of God [the Father], who sent His Son into the world (John 3:16).
c. The fellowship of the Holy Spirit, who gives us the mind of Christ (Galatians 4:6).

The Order for Evening Prayer

Evening Prayer follows the general order of Morning Prayer, with some differences in the canticles and collects. The parts of it that are identical with Morning Prayer are indicated below by an asterisk (*). The numbering follows that of Morning Prayer, with blanks to indicate what is omitted in the Evening. The table also shows what items were carried over from Vespers and Compline, which were combined to form Evening Prayer in 1549.

BCP	Vespers	Compline
1.* Sentences		
2.* Exhortation		
3.* Confession		
4.* Absolution		
5.* Our Father	Our Father	Our Father[47]
		Ave Maria[48]
6.* O Lord, open thou	Opening prayers	Opening prayers
7.* O God, make speed		
8.* Gloria		
9.* Praise ye		
10.* The Lord's Name		

BCP	Vespers	Compline
11. —		
12. Psalms	Psalms[49]	Psalms[50]
13.* *Gloria*	*Gloria*	*Gloria*
14. Old Testament lesson	Scripture verse	Scripture verse
	Responsory	Hymn
	Hymn	
15. *Magnificat* or	*Magnificat*[51]	
16. *Cantate Domino*		
17. New Testament lesson		
18. *Nunc dimittis*		*Nunc dimittis*[52]
or 19. *Deus misereatur*		*Kyrie*
		Our Father
20.* Apostles' Creed		Apostles' Creed[53]
21. —		
22.* The Lord be with you		
23.* Lesser litany	*Kyrie*	
24.* Our Father	Our Father	
25.* Suffrages	Prayers	Prayers
		Confession
		Prayers
26.* Collect of the day	Collect of the day	
	Marian antiphon	
27. Collect (for peace)[54]	Variable collect	
28. Collect (for aid)		Collect (for aid)
29.* Anthem30.* State		
and Church prayers		
31.* Prayer of St Chrysostom		
32.* The Grace		

Since Evening Prayer generally follows Morning Prayer quite faithfully, it is not necessary to repeat what was said about Morning

---

47. Silently.
48. Silently.
49. Psalms 110-147, with antiphons divided among the seven days of the week.
50. Psalms 4, 31:1-6, 91 and 134, with an antiphon.
51. With antiphon.
52. With antiphon.
53. Said privately. The choir joined in at the end and chanted the words '*et vitam aeternam*. Amen.'
54. The theme is similar to the second collect at Morning Prayer but the words are different.

Prayer here. Only the canticles and the last two of the three collects are different and require separate comment.

Canticles

The four canticles appointed at Evening Prayer are all taken from the canonical Scriptures. The most commonly used ones come from Luke's Gospel (*Magnificat* and *Nunc dimittis*), while the two alternatives are both Psalms (98 and 67). As with Morning Prayer, it is customary to use the alternates in Lent, but this is not required. It should, however, be noted that Psalm 67 naturally occurs on the twelfth evening and Psalm 98 on the nineteenth evening in the monthly course of the psalter.

The *Magnificat* and Psalm 98 were appointed after the Old Testament lesson; the *Nunc dimittis* and Psalm 67 after the New Testament one.

The Magnificat *(Luke 1:46-55)*

This is the song of the Virgin Mary recorded by Luke and modelled on the song of Hannah (1 Samuel 2:1-10), which explains why the name Hannah (or Anne) was later given to Mary's mother. It was included in the 1549 prayer book, having been sung at Vespers in the Sarum breviary, and it has survived every revision. Apparently, it was Benedict of Nursia (sixth century) who originally assigned it to Vespers, although in the Eastern Churches it is sung in the morning. In the middle ages it was accompanied by ornate ritual, an unfortunate circumstance that led the Puritans to press for its removal from the prayer book, even though it is canonical Scripture. The text may be analysed as follows:

1. Mary's relationship to God
   a. Mary magnifies God because He has blessed her in spite of her humble origins.
   b. God has magnified Mary, because all future generations will call her blessed.
   c. God's mercy is, was and always will be shown to those who fear Him.
2. God's relationship to humanity
   a. He has revealed His strength and upset the proud.
   b. He has dethroned the powerful and exalted the humble.
   c. He has fed the hungry and dismissed the rich.
3. God's relationship to Israel
   a. He has remembered His mercy.
   b. He has fulfilled His promise made to Abraham.
   c. He has continued to bless Abraham's descendants and heirs.

The Cantate Domino *(Psalm 98)*

Psalm 98 was offered as an alternative to the *Magnificat* in 1552, perhaps to placate those who had doubts about the suitability of the *Magnificat*. It resembles the *Magnificat* to some extent, especially in its emphasis on God's remembering His mercy and on His victory over heathen forces. It can be analysed as follows:

1. We must sing to the Lord and thank Him because:
   a. He has done great things and defeated the heathen.
   b. He has revealed His salvation and His righteousness.
   c. He has remembered His mercy towards Israel.
2. We must join in a chorus of praise to God:
   a. with musical instruments like the harp, the trumpet and the horn (shawms)
   b. by hearing the sound of the sea and the rivers as they praise God
   c. by listening to the hills as they express their joy.
3. What God is coming to do:
   a. He is coming to judge the world.
   b. He will judge the world in righteousness.
   c. He will judge the world in fairness.

The Nunc Dimittis *(Luke 2:29-32)*

This short canticle was the song of the aged Simeon, who lived in the Temple at Jerusalem in the expectation of the coming Messiah. When he saw Mary and Joseph bringing the baby Jesus to be circumcised, he understood that his prayers had been answered, and prayed to God to allow him to depart in peace for that reason.

The *Nunc dimittis* was used in Compline in the Sarum breviary and was incorporated into the 1549 liturgy. It has remained in place ever since. It is thought that Gregory the Great introduced it into Compline, and its presence in the fourth-century *Apostolic Constitutions* shows that it was popular long before his time.[55] It can be analysed as follows:

1. Mission accomplished
   a. Simeon's hopes have been realised.
   b. Simeon has seen God's salvation.
   c. Simeon can now give up his mission with a clear conscience.

---

55. *Apostolic Constitutions*, 7.49.

2. Mission foretold
   a. The Messiah will be revealed to all people.
   b. The Messiah will be a light to the Gentiles, showing them the way of salvation.
   c. The Messiah will be the glory of Israel, fulfilling the promises made to them.

The Deus Misereatur *(Psalm 67)*

This Psalm was sung at Lauds (i.e. in the morning) in the Sarum breviary. It was introduced into the 1552 prayer book as an alternative to the *Nunc dimittis* and has remained in place ever since. It can be analysed as follows:

1. A prayer for God's mercy and blessing
   a. He is asked to show the brightness of His face.
   b. This will make His ways known on the earth.
   c. His salvation will be revealed to all people.
2. A command for people to praise God
   a. All nations must rejoice and be glad.
   b. God will judge the people in righteousness.
   c. God will govern all the nations (not just Israel).
3. The blessings of God's rule
   a. The earth will be fruitful.
   b. God will bless us.
   c. The whole world will fear Him.

Collects

The Second Collect (for peace)

This collect comes from the Gelasian sacramentary (1472), the Gregorian sacramentary (1343) and the service of Vespers in the Sarum breviary. It was introduced into the 1549 prayer book where it has remained ever since. Although it is a collect for peace, its wording differs from the one found in Morning Prayer. It can be analysed as follows:

1. God is the source of:
   a. all holy desires
   b. all good 'counsels' (ideas, advice)
   c. all just (righteous) works.
2. We pray for Him to give us His peace because:
   a. The world cannot give it to us.
   b. Our hearts must be geared to obey His commandments.
   c. We must be defended against our enemies.

The conclusion is that when we have this peace, we shall live in rest and quietness. Throughout the prayer, the emphasis is on our total dependence on God. What we cannot do for ourselves or find elsewhere, He must give us, and give us in such abundance that it makes a genuine difference to our lives and gives us the assurance that we have nothing to fear in this world.

The Third Collect (for Protection against Danger)

This collect comes from the Gelasian sacramentary (1589), the Gregorian sacramentary (936) and the service of Compline in the Sarum breviary.[56] The language of the collect is reminiscent of many of the Psalms, in particular, Psalm 18:28, Psalm 121:3-4 and Psalm 139:11. There is also an echo of the prologue to the fourth Gospel (John 1:5). It can be analysed as follows:

God is asked to:

a. bring light into our darkness
b. defend us against all the perils and dangers of the night
c. do this for the love of Jesus Christ.

The opening petition is primarily intended to refer to the physical darkness, which in earlier times was always feared because thieves and other evildoers were more active at night. However, there is also a spiritual dimension, since the light that God is asked to bring is a spiritual awareness more than anything else.

The second petition is fairly straightforward, with the emphasis clearly on the physical world. The final phrase is ambiguous. The 'love of Jesus Christ' may be:

a. Christ's love for the Father
b. Christ's love for us
c. the Father's love for Christ
d. our love for Christ.

It might be argued that the second of these is the most likely option but all four are possible and the ambiguity allows us to explore each of them. Love is a many-splendoured thing, manifested in a number of different but complementary relationships, and that is what we find here.

---

56. It can also be found in *The Bobbio Missal*, 565.

Appendices to the Daily Offices

These are three in number. First in order comes the Athanasian Creed, appointed to be said thirteen times in the year at Morning Prayer. Next comes the litany, originally conceived as a separate service but gradually attached to Morning Prayer and often serving as a bridge to Holy Communion. Finally, there are the prayers and thanksgivings for special circumstances, which were meant to be used at Morning and/or Evening Prayer when appropriate.

The Athanasian Creed

The so-called Athanasian Creed, which was said daily at Prime in the Sarum breviary, was restricted to six times a year in 1549 and then expanded to thirteen in 1552 and later.[57] The logic of the 1549 prayer book is clear – the six times chosen were the dates of the great feasts of Christmas, Epiphany, Easter, Ascension, Pentecost and Trinity. The disadvantage of this pattern is that the Creed was frequently said in the Christmas and Easter seasons, sometimes only a week or two apart, but not during the rest of the year. This defect (if that is what it was) was corrected in 1552, when seven other feast days that fall outside those seasons were added. They all occur towards the end of a month and there is a continuous sequence from June to November, which suggests that those dates were chosen in order to ensure that the Athanasian Creed would be said about once a month. There does not seem to be any better explanation:

     24 February: St Matthias
     24 June: St John the Baptist
     25 July: St James
     24 August: St Bartholomew
     21 September: St Matthew
     28 October: St Simon and St Jude
     30 November: St Andrew

The Creed itself is more properly known by its opening words, *Quicunque vult* ('Whosoever will'). It was probably composed in

---

57. For a detailed study of the Athanasian Creed, see J.N.D. Kelly, *The Athanasian Creed: The Paddock Lectures for 1962-3* (London: A. & C. Black, 1964); M. Davie, *The Athanasian Creed* (London: Latimer Trust, 2019).

southern Gaul in the late fifth century, but we cannot now determine who the author was. It certainly has nothing to do with Athanasius (c. 296-373), who as bishop of Alexandria from 328 became famous as the leading defender of Nicene orthodoxy against the Arianism and semi-Arianism of his time. Athanasius was exiled to the West, where he received considerable support for his efforts and where his name became synonymous with correct belief. It is probably for that reason that this Creed was attached to his name.

The reasons why it cannot be Athanasian in origin are straightforward:

1. It was composed in Latin, a language that Athanasius did not use and would not have known sufficiently well to be able to produce the sophisticated document that we now have.
2. It reflects the Christology of the Council of Chalcedon, which was held in 451, nearly a century after Athanasius' death.
3. It mentions the double procession of the Holy Spirit, a doctrine developed by Augustine of Hippo (354-430) and possibly known at Rome by the mid-fourth century, but which Athanasius himself never affirmed.[58]

The liturgical use of the Creed seems to have begun in the tenth century. It was translated into English and published in the *Composite Primer* of John Gough in 1536, followed a year later by the primer of Robert Redman, who improved the style of the translation.[59] It was then incorporated into Morning Prayer in the 1549 Book of Common Prayer.

The liturgical use of the Athanasian Creed has long been problematic, not least because its length and style make it difficult for ordinary worshippers to grasp. However, the more serious objections to it concern its content and perceived theology, especially in the so-called 'damnatory clauses' with which it begins and ends. Theologians know that, when the Creed insists that it is necessary to confess the faith in its terms or face eternal damnation, it is speaking in an intellectual way to people who are capable of absorbing systematic theology. It is certainly not intended to suggest that those without training in that discipline have no hope of getting into heaven. Yet, that is the impression that it is liable to create in many minds, which is bound to compromise its suitability for general use.

---

58. He never denied it either, of course. It was simply not an issue in his time.
59. See Butterworth, *The English Primers*, pp. 124-25, 144.

In the eighteenth century, liberal thinkers began to dispute the claims of the Creed and to argue that its theology was unacceptably narrow. Moved by the spirit of the Enlightenment, they wanted the Creed to be taken out of the prayer book altogether, something that was actually done in the American 1789 text. The Church of Ireland retained it in its 1878 prayer book, but without the accompanying rubric, so that there was no provision for reciting it in public worship. More recently, the 2019 prayer book of the Anglican Church in North America has done the same, with the difference that, in that case, it has reintroduced the Creed into the American Church after an absence of over 200 years.

Analysis
1. The Opening Clauses (vv. 1-2)
Note that the text speaks about *holding* and *keeping* the faith, following 2 Timothy 1:13-14, rather than simply believing it. The idea is that the Catholic faith (i.e. the universal Christian faith) comes as a complete package that must be received and handed on as such. Those who compromise or distort that faith will perish eternally because they have rejected the truth of salvation.

2. The Trinity (vv. 3-6)
The Catholic faith is defined as belief in the Trinity, which proceeds in two directions. We worship the One God in three and the Three in one. Stated like this for symmetry, the formula, nevertheless, represents two distinct ways of confessing the Trinity. We may proceed from the One God and find Him to be a Trinity of Father, Son and Holy Spirit. Or we may start with the revelation of the Father, Son and Holy Spirit and find them to be essentially the same God. The first approach starts with the revealed monotheism of the Old Testament, which the early Christians all accepted. Jesus taught his disciples to pray to God as their Father (Matthew 6:9), and then revealed to them that he was the Son (John 10:30) and that he would send them the Holy Spirit to continue his presence and his work among them (John 15:26). The second approach is rooted in Christian experience. The Holy Spirit dwells in our hearts by faith. He is the Spirit of the Son who gives us the power to pray to the Father in the way that the Son did (Galatians 4:6). Both approaches are equally valid.

To describe the oneness of God we use the word *substance*; to describe his threeness we use the word *person*. Both of these terms were consecrated, if not actually coined, by Tertullian and have remained standard ever since. The appropriateness of these terms has sometimes been questioned, and they must be carefully defined in order to avoid misunderstanding.

By *substance* is meant objective being, or essence. In God, His substance coincides with His nature, because everything about Him is perfect. God has no undeveloped potential; He is what He is, and will always be the same (Exodus 3:14; Revelation 1:8).

By *person* is meant the active agent who owns, governs and controls his substance. However, the word *person* must not be confused with *individual*, as it is in modern speech. An individual is a unit that cannot be further divided – it is indivisible; but a person is an agent who stands in relation to other agents. The name Father implies that there must be a Son, and *vice versa*. This relationality is fundamental to the being of the Trinity.

To confound the persons is to reduce them to mere names that can be swapped around according to circumstances. In the case of God, this means that in one context He may appear as the Father, in another as the Son and in another as the Holy Spirit. This is the ancient heresy of modalism, the word 'mode' meaning 'appearance' or 'role'. It is often attributed to a rather shadowy figure called Sabellius who is supposed to have preached it. It was a real danger, because the Greek word *prosōpon* originally meant 'mask', as worn by actors in the theatre. They could play different parts according to the mask they wore. However, this is not how we are to think of God. Apart from anything else, the New Testament reveals the Son speaking to his Father as to a different person – he is not speaking to himself in a different role (see John 17).

In modern times, the word has been misunderstood because of the development of the concept of 'personality'. In theological terms, what we call 'personality' belongs more properly to the substance because it describes a person's nature. That can change, either naturally over time or as the result of some external intervention like drugs, but personhood is immutable.

To divide the substance is to say that one or two of the persons is essentially different from the other(s). This was the heresy of Arianism, which claimed that the Son was a created being, and therefore inferior to the Father, and also of Macedonianism, which asserted that the Holy Spirit was inferior to the Father and the Son (whom they accepted as consubstantial).[60]

The *glory* of the persons is equal and their *majesty* is co-eternal. These terms are basically synonymous, but a distinction may be made if we think of the glory as their status and the majesty as their power. They are equal in status or rank, and their power is co-extensive. The Arians

---

60. Macedonianism is named for a fourth-century theologian called Macedonius. It has nothing to do with Macedonia.

claimed that there had been a time before the Son came into existence, but this is rejected by the Athanasian Creed.

3. The Divine Attributes (vv. 7-28)

The attributes of the divine *substance* are shared equally by all three persons of the Trinity. They are all uncreated, incomprehensible and eternal. The order is deliberate and significant. It is the first element in the triad of attributes that governs and explains the others. Creation exists in space and time but, because God is the Creator and not a created being, He lacks both of those dimensions. To be 'incomprehensible' is to be limitless – God cannot be grasped (either mentally or physically).[61]

The divine names, or attributes of the persons, are also shared equally among all three. They are all Almighty, God and Lord. Once again, the order is important. In the ancient polytheistic world there were many gods and many lords, but there can be only one Almighty. The term is not meant to be an adjective, as it is in both English and Latin, but a title, corresponding to *El-Shaddai* in Hebrew and *Pantokratōr* in Greek (Revelation 1:8). Unlike the Apostles' and the Nicene Creeds, where the word is applied only to the Father, the Athanasian Creed extends it to all three persons in order to counteract Arianism.

The Creed tells us that the 'Christian verity' obliges us to confess each of the persons as God and Lord but, at the same time, the 'Catholic religion' forbids us to think of three Gods or three Lords. The 'Christian verity' is the New Testament, in contrast to the 'Hebrew verity' (the Old Testament). The 'Catholic religion' is the entire Bible, Old and New Testaments taken together. These terms are used because the Creed was composed at a time when the Scriptures were not described in the way that they are now.

The distinguishing attributes of the divine *persons* may be set out as follows:

	Made	Created	Begotten	Proceeding
Father	No	No	No	[No]
Son	No	No	Yes	[No]
Holy Spirit	No	No	No	Yes

---

61. The Latin word is *immensus* but 'immense' is not a suitable English translation. It would be better to say 'ungraspable' but that is not a term generally used in theology.

The terms 'made' and 'created' are used to distinguish between being made out of something and being created out of nothing. This is an important difference where creation is concerned, but means nothing when speaking about God, since he is neither. The persons are distinguished from each other because the Son is begotten (generated) whereas the Father and the Spirit are not. The Holy Spirit proceeds from the Father and the Son. The Creed does not explicitly say that the Father and the Son do not proceed from anyone else, but that is implied.

The Athanasian Creed is the first document of its kind to confess the double procession of the Holy Spirit, known as the *Filioque* from the addition of the Latin for 'and [from] the Son' to the Nicene Creed sometime around the Third Council of Toledo in 589. This Creed is at least a century older than that. The double procession reflects the theology of Augustine of Hippo, who taught that God is Love. Love, by definition, must have someone who loves and someone who is loved. In the Trinity, it is the Father who loves the Son and the Son who is loved by the Father (the 'Beloved'). However, the love that flows from one to the other and back again is equal. This love is personified as the Holy Spirit, who must therefore proceed equally from both.

This understanding of the matter has never been accepted by the Eastern Orthodox Churches. In their understanding, the Father is the source of Deity, which he shares with the Son by generation and with the Holy Spirit by procession. The Eastern Churches do not define how the Son and the Holy Spirit relate to each other, but they tend to accept the idea that the Holy Spirit proceeds from the Father and rests on the Son, as he did at the baptism of Jesus.

The main objections to the double procession doctrine are:

1. It is not supported by John 15:26, where Jesus speaks of the Spirit's procession from the Father and does not mention himself, except to say that he will send the Spirit to the disciples. Thus, a distinction can be made between the eternal procession of the Holy Spirit (from the Father) and his temporal mission (through the Son).
2. The Augustinian conception reduces the Holy Spirit to a force that is not properly personal. The effects of this can be seen in the frequent tendency of Western Christians to conceive of the Holy Spirit as an 'it', a force sent by God rather than a person dwelling in our hearts by faith.

In reply, the main reasons for accepting the double procession are:

1. The Holy Spirit is the Spirit of the Son (Galatians 4:6).
2. The Holy Spirit brings both the Father and the Son to dwell in our hearts (John 14:20).

Does it make much difference in practice? This is a hard question to answer but perhaps it can be said that, if the Holy Spirit proceeds from the Father alone and that it is he who dwells in our hearts by faith, there is a danger that we might think it possible to go to the Father through the Spirit, bypassing the Son. This appears to be the case in some charismatic movements, which make a great deal of the presence and power of the Spirit but tend to downplay or ignore the Son. That is certainly not the teaching of the Eastern Churches, which believe that the Spirit illuminates the Son and explains him to us. The Western Churches have to live with their own theological inheritance and interpret it accordingly. The Western tradition demands acceptance of the *Filioque* and so the theological divergence with the East remains unresolved.

This section concludes with a resume of the unity of God in Trinity, and a reminder that salvation depends on the right confession of this doctrine.

4. Christology (vv. 29-39)

The second part of the Athanasian Creed concentrates on the doctrine of Christ. Unlike the Apostles' and Nicene Creeds, it focusses mainly on his being rather than on his work, though that is not ignored. However, it is made clear that, in addition to the Trinity, the divinity and humanity of Jesus Christ must also be confessed by those desiring to be saved. In fact, the two doctrines belong together. If Christ were not divine, there would be no need for a Trinity of persons in God and, if there is a Trinity in God, it is only to be expected that the second and third persons will have something to do that makes them important and necessary for us.

The expression 'the Son of God is God and Man' combines both the person and the natures of the incarnate Christ. The Son of God refers to his divine person in relation to the Father. 'God and Man' speaks of his two natures. It is important to understand that, in ancient times, most people did not speak of 'divinity' ('or deity') and 'humanity' but used 'God' and 'Man' instead. So that to confess Jesus as God and Man is not to say that he is two persons rolled into one, but that he is one person, the Son of God, who is both divine and human.

This is made clear in verse 31, which explains that Christ is divine ('God') from the substance of his Father and so is eternal. At the same time, he is human ('Man') from the substance of his mother (who is not named), born in time and space ('the world'). In both his divine and his human nature he is perfect. The Creed specifies that his human nature consisted of both a rational soul and human flesh. This was to counter the teaching of Apollinarius, a wayward disciple of Athanasius, who believed that Jesus Christ was a divine being inhabiting the shell of a human body. He did not have a human mind or will, however, which made it impossible for him to sin. Christians believe that Jesus was sinless, not because he could not sin but because he did not do so. We assert this because, if he could not have sinned, he could not have been tempted, which he was (Matthew chapter 4). Note, however, that the temptations of Jesus are temptations that were only possible for God – human beings cannot turn stones into bread and so would never be tempted to try.

The incarnate Christ is equal to the Father in his divinity but inferior to Him in his humanity. This means that, as a person, he is equal to the Father, but that, in his natures, he is both equal and inferior. By becoming a man, the Son of God gave up the privileges of his divinity but not the divinity itself. It was as Son that he chose to be a servant to the Father, and it was in that servanthood that he became a man (Philippians 2:5-11).

The two natures of Christ are joined in the one person. This statement represents a revolution in ancient thought. Before the Council of Chalcedon in 451, it was generally thought that a 'person' (*hypostasis*) was the manifestation of a nature. According to Nestorius (381-451), Jesus had two natures and therefore two *hypostases*, or 'identities' as we might say today. These two *hypostases* were conjoined in a single person, but they were not inseparably connected. When Jesus was crucified, the Nestorians claimed that the divine *hypostasis* deserted the human one, so that it was only the man who died. They justified this by their interpretation of the words of Psalm 22:1, quoted by Jesus: 'My God, my God, why have you forsaken me?'

The weakness of the Nestorian position was that they could not adequately explain how the two *hypostases* had come together in the first place. Who or what had effected the conjunction between them? The answer given by Chalcedon was that the divine person of the Son added a human nature to himself, giving it his own identity. It was therefore possible for the divine person of the Son to suffer and die in his human nature, but not in his divine one.

This is expressed in the Athanasian Creed by saying that the unity of the two natures in Christ was not achieved by diminishing his divinity in some way (which would have been a quasi-Arian solution) but rather by taking his humanity up into God, not by transforming it into something divine (which would have been 'confusion of substance'), but by uniting it to his person.

There is an analogy between the rational soul and flesh of a human being and the two natures of the incarnate Christ. The difference is that, while Jesus was God and Man at the same time, we humans will acquire a second nature after death, when our body of flesh will disintegrate and be replaced by a 'spiritual body' (1 Corinthians 15:44). Our 'rational soul', however, will be the same – in other words, the resurrection will be a resurrection of the real us, not a transformation into some other being. That is necessary, since otherwise we could hardly claim to be saved here on earth. We are not like caterpillars waiting to be transformed into butterflies but spiritual persons made in the image and likeness of God, waiting for the time when we shall cast off this body and take on a higher, spiritual nature instead.

The verses that describe the work of Christ state that he suffered but do not add that he died. In this, the Athanasian Creed follows the Nicene Creed and early versions of the Apostles' Creed, which helps us to date it to the years around 500. Of course, death is implied in the suffering, as is made clear from what follows. Like the Apostles' Creed (but unlike the Nicene), it affirms Christ's descent into hell and his subsequent resurrection from the dead. It is thought that the phrase 'the third day' was added to make the text conform more closely to the Apostles' Creed – but there is no proof of that.

Following the Resurrection comes the standard sequence of ascension, heavenly session and second coming. Here again, it is thought that the words 'God Almighty' have been added to make the text more like the Apostles' Creed and this makes sense, given that, earlier on, the term Almighty was applied equally to all three persons of the Trinity.

5. The Last Judgement (vv. 40-41)
Here the pattern of Christ's second coming is laid out. When he returns to judge the living and the dead, everyone will rise again. The Resurrection in that sense will be universal and not restricted to believers. However, everyone will be held to account for their deeds, according to which they will be assigned to their eternal destiny. (Matthew 25:45-46; Hebrews 10:26-31).

From the modern point of view, this seems to be advocating a form of salvation by works and, in that sense, it is the most troubling of the verses of the Creed. It represents unfinished theological business that was not fully elucidated until Martin Luther proclaimed justification by faith alone, just over a millennium after this was written. The Creed does not specify what the deeds are that will be judged, but the closing verse makes it clear that what is involved here is faith, not 'works' in the medieval sense. People will be judged by their adherence to the Catholic faith, which they must keep in order to be saved. What was stated as a warning at the beginning of the Creed is here repeated as a declaration of fact and made incumbent on all who would enter into the kingdom of heaven.

6. Conclusion (v. 42)
This repeats the warning issued at the beginning as a reminder to the faithful that they must treat their confession with the utmost seriousness.

The Litany

The origins of the litany are somewhat obscure and probably varied. The word itself means 'prayer' or 'supplication' and could have a fairly general meaning, although it seems to have been particularly used in times of distress. The Emperor Constantine, for example, was said to have spent much time in prayer shortly before his death, presumably pleading for mercy from God.[62] This prayer was called a litany. Soon, however, the word was limited to a kind of responsive prayer in which a minister would ask for something and the people would reply with a set phrase like 'Lord have mercy'. That kind of responsive prayer can be traced back to Psalm 136, which follows a similar pattern and would have been in use in pre-Christian times.

From the fourth century onwards, this kind of responsory prayer became more common and was gradually formalised. Around 467, Mamertus, the bishop of Vienne (Gaul), ordered a series of processional prayers for protection against earthquakes. These prayers were known as 'rogations' and were set for the Monday, Tuesday and Wednesday before Ascension Day. Those days are still celebrated as Rogation Days in the church calendar, though the association with the litany has largely been forgotten now.

Pope Gregory the Great instituted the 'great litany' at Rome, which was celebrated on 25 April, St Mark's Day. It began as a plea for deliverance from the plague but became an annual celebration. Later on, a private form of litany was introduced at Rome by Pope Sergius I

---

62. Eusebius of Caesarea, *Vita Constantini*, 4.61.

(687-701), who brought the custom from his native Syria. It focussed on special devotions to the saints, the Cross and to Christ as the Lamb of God. Over time, the two types of liturgy merged into one and a greatly expanded form was developed for general use. By the later middle ages, there were six parts to the litany, each of which had its own form of response. These can be detailed as follows:

Content of the litany	Words of response
1. Invocations of the Trinity	Have mercy on us
2. Invocations to the saints	Pray for us
3. Prayers for deliverance (deprecations)	Deliver us, Lord
4. Appeals for deliverance (obsecrations)	Deliver us, Lord
5. Intercessions	We beseech thee to hear us
6. Invocations to Christ, the Son and Lamb of God	

In addition to its use on the Rogation Days and on 25 April, the litany was also said or sung at the blessing of the font during the Easter vigil, at the ordination of priests and deacons, and during Lent, when it occurred daily at Terce and on Wednesdays and Fridays after None. It was also used on Wednesdays and Fridays in times of danger.

Interestingly enough, the litany was the first rite to be published in English, in 1544.[63] This was to help Henry VIII's war effort against Scotland and France. It was not a translation of the Sarum litanies but a new composition that drew on a number of sources, not all of which have been identified. In addition to the Sarum texts for rogations and processions, Thomas Cranmer also made considerable use of Martin Luther's litany, the litany from the liturgy of St John Chrysostom, the litany of Gregory the Great and other litanies then in use in England or Germany, possibly including the one found in Cardinal Quiñones' breviary.

Cranmer made a number of innovations in his litany, invoking the Trinity (for example) at the beginning instead of the normal *Kyrie*. In the invocations, he managed to include a line from the Nicene Creed as the third invocation and one from the Athanasian Creed as the fourth, adding the words 'proceeding from the Father and the Son' to the invocation of the Holy Spirit. He also included the words 'miserable sinners' in the opening verse, to describe the petitioners.

---

63. Of course, the Bible had already been translated and published in full, and an English translation of the Apostles' Creed appeared in 1536.

Cranmer reduced the 62 invocations to the saints common in late medieval litanies to only three, one to the Virgin Mary, one to the angels and archangels, and one to the patriarchs, prophets and saints in heaven.

The deprecations were edited and grouped together, being taken in roughly equal measure from Sarum and Luther. The obsecrations and the intercessions came mainly from Luther, with occasional insertions from Sarum. The later parts of the litany tend to follow Luther in organisation, but with material taken from Sarum. One notorious addition was a prayer 'for deliverance from the bishop of Rome and all his detestable enormities', the most obviously Protestant line in the entire text. After the intercessions came a series of suffrages, taken from a tenth-century pontifical somehow connected to Egbert, archbishop of York (734-66). The litany ended with a series of six prayers which would later be incorporated into other parts of the prayer book.

The subsequent history of the litany can be sketched briefly. In 1545 it was ordered to be used in Sunday processions, replacing the one thitherto used before the Mass. The Edwardian Injunctions (1547) ordered that the litany should be said or sung kneeling in the middle of the church. In the 1549 prayer book it was appended to the Holy Communion service and was authorised for use on Wednesdays and Fridays before the ministry of the word. At that time, the invocations of the Virgin Mary, the saints and the angels were omitted and only the first and the last of the six original prayers at the end were retained, although parts of the fifth were incorporated into the first.

In the 1552 prayer book the litany was moved to its present position after the daily offices and authorised for use on Sundays, Wednesdays and Fridays, as well as at other times when commanded by the Ordinary. Two prayers that had followed Holy Communion in the 1549 liturgy, one for rain and the other for fair weather, were printed between the last two prayers of the litany, along with four new prayers for use in times of famine, war or plague.

In 1559 the petition against the bishop of Rome was dropped and the occasional prayers were printed after the litany, rather than within it. They were also followed by the first of the 1544 prayers, which had been omitted in 1549. In addition, there was a prayer for the queen and one for the clergy and people, the second of which had been printed at the end of the 1544 litany. Also added at the end were the prayer of St Chrysostom and the Grace (2 Corinthians 13:14).

In the 1604 prayer book, occasional thanksgivings were added to correspond to the occasional prayers that had been included in 1559. In 1662 petitions for deliverance from rebellion and schism were added, obviously under the influence of the civil war and the consequent disruption of the Church. In the supplication for the clergy, the word 'priests' replaced 'pastors', again in response to Presbyterian and congregationalist claims. The occasional prayers were sectioned off and Church and State prayers were printed at the end of the daily offices, along with the prayer of St Chrysostom and the Grace, although these two latter items continued to be used in the litany too. Another small change was that, whereas previously the minister had said the Lord's Prayer and the *Gloria* by himself, now the congregation were invited to join in with him.

The litany was appointed to be said or sung after Morning Prayer on Sundays, Wednesdays and Fridays but, although that rubric still stands, it is safe to say that the litany has fallen out of general use. It is still sometimes heard in Lent or on special occasions at other times of the year but, for the most part, it has disappeared from ordinary public worship.

Looking at the litany in the light of its original form, this is what we find:

Officiant	Response
1. Invocations to the Trinity	Congregation repeats the officiant's words
2. Confession of sin and plea for forgiveness	Spare us, good Lord
3. Prayers for deliverance from: a. evil, sin, the devil, damnation etc. b. pride, envy, hatred etc. c. the world, the flesh and the devil d. storms, plague, war, sudden death e. sedition, heresy, schism etc.	Good Lord, deliver us
4. Appeals for deliverance: a. by the incarnation and life of Christ b. by the death and resurrection of Christ c. throughout our lives	Good Lord, deliver us
5. Intercessions: a. for the Church b. for the Sovereign's life c. for the Sovereign's faithfulness	We beseech thee to hear us, good Lord

Officiant	Response
d. for the Sovereign's protection	
e. for the royal family	
f. for the clergy	
g. for the government	
h. for magistrates	
i. for all Christian people	
j. for all nations	
k. for a heart of love in us	
l. for grace to obey God's word	
m. for the restoration of those in error	
n. for our strength and protection	
o. for help for those who suffer	
p. for safety for all people	
q. for protection of the weak	
r. for protection for everyone	
s. for forgiveness for our enemies	
t. for plentiful harvests	
u. for true repentance	
6. Invocations:	
a. to the Son of God	Son of God, we beseech thee to hear us
b. to the Lamb of God	Grant us thy peace
c. to the Lamb of God	Have mercy upon us

Next there follows a series of versicles and responses, petitioning God to show His mercy on us. This is then followed by the Lord's Prayer and a further versicle and response.

After that, the litany proceeds as follows:

1. A prayer against persecution and for deliverance from trouble, with a response.
2. A memorial of God's past mercies, with a response.
3. The *Gloria*.
4. Five versicles and responses.
5. A prayer for trust in time of trouble.[64]

---

64. This prayer combines the first and the fifth prayers in the 1544 litany. The first comes from the Gregorian sacramentary, where it is a collect for the feast of St Cornelius and St Cyprian (687). The other was the collect of the Sarum rogation mass, taken from the mass for St Mark's Day

6. A prayer of St Chrysostom.
7. The Grace (2 Corinthians 13:14).

Prayers and Thanksgivings

The early litanies contained a number of prayers for special occasions. Some of these were rewritten for the Book of Common Prayer. Those that date from 1549 were initially placed at the end of Holy Communion but in 1552 they were moved to the end of the litany, where the new prayers added at that time were also put. There were further additions in 1662.

The thanksgivings are of later date, first appearing in the 1604 text and designed to complement the already existing prayers. They were inserted at the request of the Puritans who attended the Hampton Court Conference. Additions were also made to them in 1662. The pattern can be set out as follows:

Prayer	Thanksgiving
	General thanksgiving (1662)[65]
1. For rain (1549)[66]	1. For rain (1604)[67]
2. For fair weather (1549)[68]	2. For fair weather (1604)
3. In time of famine (1552)[69]	3. For plenty (1604)[70]
4. In time of war and tumults (1552)[71]	4. For peace and deliverance (1604)[72]

(25 April) and the great litany appointed for that day in the Gregorian sacramentary (472).

65. Composed by Bishop Edward Reynolds of Norwich.
66. The promise of Jesus refers to Matthew 6:33, quoted here in the Coverdale version of 1535, which is slightly inaccurate.
67. See Acts 14:17.
68. See Genesis 6:5-7; 8:21-22; 9:11.
69. Two forms, the first based on Genesis 1:22, Joel 1:16-20 and Matthew 6:11; the second on 2 Kings 6:25 and 7:1-16. They were omitted from the 1559 prayer book but restored in 1662, with some alterations made by Bishop John Cosin of Durham. There had been a famine in England in 1551, which may explain why these prayers were added a year later.
70. See Psalm 67:5-6.
71. See 1 Chronicles 29:11; Psalm 22:28. The words 'and tumults' were added in 1662.
72. Psalm 124:1-6.

Prayer	Thanksgiving
	4a. For restoring peace at home (1662)[73]
5. In time of plague or sickness (1552)[74]	5. For deliverance from plague (1604)[75]
6. Two collects for the Ember Weeks (1662)[76]	
7. For any occasion (1559)[77]	
8. For Parliament (1662)[78]	
9. For all sorts and conditions of men (1662)[79]	

A thanksgiving service for harvest was prepared by the convocation of Canterbury on 14 February 1862 but it never received royal sanction and so is not included in the prayer book.

---

73. Probably written by Bishop John Cosin of Durham, following suggestions made to him by Bishop Matthew Wren of Ely. See Psalm 65:7; 1 Timothy 2:1-2.
74. See Numbers 16:44-50; 2 Samuel 24:15-25. The wording was slightly altered in 1662. There had been a plague in England in 1551, which may have influenced the inclusion of this prayer a year later.
75. Two forms.
76. The first prayer is based on Acts 6:6, 13:2-3, 20:28, Ephesians 4:7 and 1 Timothy 5:22. The second prayer is based on James 1:17, 1 Corinthians 12:8-10, John 14:16-17 and Ephesians 4:11-16. The prayers assume that the Ember Weeks were times of preparation for ordination, which is true now but was not originally the case.
77. Found in English primers before 1549 at the end of the litany.
78. This prayer first appeared in an order for fasting in 1625 and was repeated three years later in another special service for those dangerous times. On 1 January 1801, the day that Ireland was united with the United Kingdom of Great Britain, an order in council altered the word 'kingdoms' to 'dominions'.
79. Probably composed by John Gunning, then master of St John's College, Cambridge, and subsequently bishop of Chichester (1670-74) and Ely (1675-84). However, some scholars think it was written either by Robert Sanderson, bishop of Lincoln, or by Edward Reynolds, bishop of Norwich.

Chapter 4

Collects, Epistles and Gospels

The 1662 Book of Common Prayer makes provision for collects, Epistles and Gospels to be used at Holy Communion on every Sunday and holy day of the year, as well as during Holy Week and on the Monday and Tuesday after Easter and Whitsun (Pentecost).[1] This makes a total of 90 days that are specially catered for, although in any given year there will only be 87 that are actually used. This is because the prayer book provides for six Sundays after Epiphany and for 25 after Trinity Sunday, whereas there are only 28 such Sundays (taken together), not 31. Thus, if there are six Sundays after Epiphany, there are only 22 after Trinity, and, at the other extreme, if there are 27 Sundays after Trinity, there is only one after Epiphany. In years when there are 26 or 27 Sundays after Trinity, the excess is made up by using unread collects, Epistles and Gospels from Epiphany, though the prayer book does not specify which ones should be preferred.[2]

---

1. See Sargent, *Day by Day*, pp. 16-33; M.R. Dudley, *The Collect in Anglican Liturgy: Texts and Sources 1549-1989* (Runcorn: Alcuin Club; Collegeville, MN: Liturgical Press, 1994).
2. Logically it should be the fifth and/or sixth Sunday after Epiphany, which are both rarely used otherwise, but this is not specified in the rubric. Before 1662 there were only five Sundays after Epiphany in the prayer book. If a sixth Sunday occurred, the collect, Epistle and Gospel for the fifth Sunday were repeated. That actually happened in 1565, 1576, 1603, 1614, 1641 and, possibly, 1660, although the Book of Common Prayer had been abolished in 1645 and was not brought back into general use until the following year.

On other days, the collect of the previous Sunday will be used, except that the Christmas collect is read every day from 29-31 December and the collect for the Circumcision of Christ is read every day from 2-5 January. About 80-90 per cent of the collects, Epistles and Gospels are taken (sometimes with slight alterations) from the Sarum rite and have remained substantially unchanged since 1549.

The title of this section changed over time. In 1549 it read: 'The Introits, Collects, Epistles and Gospels, to be used at the celebration of the Lord's Supper and Holy Communion, through the year; with proper Psalms and lessons for divers feasts and days'. The Introits were Psalms containing something proper to the day and were chanted as the priest made his entrance.

In 1552 the Introits were dropped and the proper Psalms and lessons were printed in a separate table.

In 1662 the title was abbreviated to read: 'The Collects, Epistles and Gospels to be used throughout the year'. The omission of any specific reference to Holy Communion was due to the fact that the collects were also used at Morning and Evening Prayer, and the Epistles and Gospels were read when the service was no more than an ante-Communion.

Collects

The collects are 83 in number.[3] The origin of the word is uncertain and various etymologies have been proposed. The simplest is that it is the Latin *collecta*, meaning 'gathered together', which suggests that they were intended to be a kind of summary of the theme for the day.[4] Another possibility is that it is an elision of *cum lectione* ('with the reading') meaning that it accompanies the reading of Scripture. This would fit the use of the collects here, but not in other places where they occur in the prayer book (as in Morning and Evening Prayer). A third suggestion is that the word conveys the idea that the priest prays on behalf

---

3. The word 'collect' is pronounced on the first syllable. The number is different from that of the Epistles and Gospels (of which there are 90 each) because there are nine days when the collect is that of the previous Sunday or feast day. They are Christmas 1, Monday to Thursday in Holy Week, the Monday and Tuesday after Easter and the Monday and Tuesday after Whitsun (Pentecost). On the other hand, there are three collects for Good Friday, leaving an overall deficit of seven.

4. Collects are unique to the Western (Latin) Church. In the Eastern Churches, prayers are invariably longer and more ornate.

of the people who are gathered together with him, as opposed to the versicles and responses, where the priest and the people pray separately. Whatever the true derivation is, there is no doubt that the collects are brief prayers, densely packed with detail. Many people dislike them and some have objected to their use, for this reason. They believe that prayers should be more expansive, allowing people to absorb them more easily. Opponents of this have always argued that there is virtue in brevity, and it is certainly true that, in an age when few people could read, the collects could be committed to memory by those who wanted to do so. Modern worshippers may find it difficult to enter into the spirit of the collects because they are so condensed; they have to be studied and learned before they are likely to make much of an impression. For the student, however, they are packed with theological observations that provide ready material for teaching and preaching, particularly when they illuminate the scriptural passages that accompany them.

A collect normally has the following structure:

1. The **invocation**. This mentions the name of God, along with one or more of his attributes and often of something connected with redemption. Three collects (those for Advent 3, St Stephen's Day – 26 December – and Lent 1) are addressed specifically to Jesus Christ, but the others are all addressed to the Father. None is addressed to the Holy Spirit.
2. The **doctrine** on which the succeeding petition is based. However, in twelve of the collects no specific doctrine is expressed.
3. The **petition**.
4. The **aspiration**, or purpose for which the petition is offered.
5. The **termination**, which is usually a plea of Christ's merits, but may vary depending on the person of the Trinity involved. This is often accompanied by praise to the Holy Trinity, mentioned by name. There are three types of termination which can be outlined as follows:
   a. the *general* plea: 'through Jesus Christ our Lord'. This occurs, sometimes with very slight modifications, in 52 of the collects.
   b. the *specific* plea: 'through the merits of etc.' There are thirteen instances of this type of ending.
   c. the *extended* plea, which is either doxological ('to whom with thee and the Holy Ghost be all honour and glory, world without end. Amen') or descriptive ('who liveth

and reigneth with thee and the same Spirit, ever one God, world without end'). Seven of the collects have a doxological termination, while ten others have a descriptive one.

One collect (Advent 2) does not have a termination in the usual sense at all.

In the 1662 prayer book all the collects end with 'Amen', as suggested by Matthew Wren, bishop of Ely. Before that time, 'Amen' occurred only intermittently.

Of the 83 Collects, 59 derive to a greater or lesser degree from the Sarum rite. No fewer than 77 were wrought by Thomas Cranmer and they are now regarded as supreme examples of his literary style and genius. Four more were the work of John Cosin, bishop of Durham, and were inserted for the first time in 1662.

Most of the collects in the Sarum rite were taken from earlier sources, in particular, from sacramentaries traditionally linked to the Roman Church. Three of these are of particular importance and collects traceable to them are indicated here, using the numbers assigned to them by their modern editors, as follows:

1. The so-called Leonine or Verona sacramentary, compiled about 600 and edited by L.C. Mohlberg, *Sacramentarium Veronense* (Rome: Herder, 1956).

2. The so-called Gelasian sacramentary, originating in the seventh or early eighth century, edited by L.C. Mohlberg, *Liber Sacramentorum Romanae Aeclesiae Ordinis Anni Circuli* (Rome: Herder, 1968).

3. The so-called Gregorian sacramentary, which claims to date from the time of Pope Gregory I the Great and was sent to Charlemagne by Pope Hadrian I, who intended that it should replace the Gallican sacramentaries then in use in Gaul. It proved to be insufficient to meet the needs of the Gallican Church, and so a supplement was added, probably by Benedict of Aniane sometime shortly after 800. Eventually both the original sacramentary and the supplement were adopted in Rome itself and taken together, they became the basis for later editions of the Roman liturgical books. The combined sacramentary was edited by J. Deshusses, *Le Sacramentaire grégorien*, three volumes (Fribourg: Presses Universitaires de Fribourg, 1971-82). Numbers 1-1018 refer

to the sacramentary proper and numbers 1019-1805 to the supplement.

The Sarum missal was edited by J.W. Legg, *The Sarum Missal: Edited from Three Early Manuscripts* (Oxford: Clarendon Press, 1916).

Advent 1: This collect is read every day of Advent. It was composed in 1549, probably by Thomas Cranmer. It can be analysed as follows:

1. The invocation. This is to Almighty God, putting the emphasis on His sovereign power.
2. The doctrine. This is contained in the phrase 'give us grace', because we cannot do anything spiritually worthwhile without the grace of God at work in our lives.
3. The petition. This is also asking for grace for particular purposes:
   a. to cast away the works of darkness
   b. to put on the armour of light (Ephesians 6:10-20).
4. The aspiration. This asks for the petition to be fulfilled:
   a. now in this mortal life, which Jesus Christ the Son humbled himself to share with us (Philippians 2:7), so that
   b. when he comes again in his glorious majesty, to judge the living and the dead, we may rise to eternal life.
   c. What we receive now are the first fruits and promise of what is to come in eternity.
5. The termination. We pray through him (Christ) who reigns with the Father and the Holy Spirit, now and for ever.

Time and eternity intersect in this collect, reminding us that what is eternally true can and ought to be manifested in our lives here below, right now.

Advent 2: Composed in 1549, it reflects the new emphasis on the Scriptures. For this reason, this Sunday is frequently known as Bible Sunday. The structure is clearer than in the collect for the first Sunday in Advent:

1. The invocation. God is here addressed as 'blessed', not because we have blessed Him, but because He dwells in the

perfect state of blessedness to which we aspire. It may also be understood as our response to the blessing that He has poured out on us.

2. The doctrine. God has caused all the Holy Scriptures to be written for our learning. Note that the collect does not say that God wrote the Bible Himself, nor does it commit itself to anything like a 'dictation' theory. *That* He has caused the Scriptures to be written is sure; *how* He has done it is left unstated.

3. The petition. We pray for the ability to hear them, to read them, to pay attention to them, to learn what they teach us and to commit it to our hearts and minds.

4. The aspiration is that by patience and the comfort that we derive from reading His Word, that we may accept and retain the blessed hope of eternal life. Note the repetition of the word 'blessed' which reflects the divine origin and purpose of the hope that we have received.

5. There is no specific termination.

Advent 3: The Sarum collect was used from 1549 to 1662, when it was replaced by the current one. The third week of Advent is an Ember Week, making the new collect particularly appropriate. It was probably composed by John Cosin, bishop of Durham. The collect is unusual in that it is addressed directly to Christ and also in that no doctrine is given.

1. The invocation. This is to our Lord Jesus Christ, who sent his messenger (John the Baptist) to prepare the way just before his first coming.

2. The doctrine. None is specifically stated.

3. The petition. We pray that the ministers of the Gospel may be like John the Baptist, preparing the way 'by turning the hearts of the disobedient to the wisdom of the just'.

4. The aspiration is that at his second coming in judgement, Christ may accept us as his own.

5. The termination. The three persons are one God, living and reigning in eternity.

Advent 4: Taken from the Gelasian (1121) and Gregorian (805) sacramentaries, as well as from the Sarum missal, where it is similar to one of the *excita* ('stir up') collects, the one used for the first Sunday in Advent. It was slightly revised by Cranmer and again in 1662.

1. The invocation. This is short and to the point, mentioning only the word 'Lord', which links the Father to the Son.
2. The doctrine. This comes as a parenthesis within the petition and at the end of the aspiration. It is a statement that we are held back (from doing God's will) by our sin and wickedness. The words 'in running the race that is set before us' were added in 1662. After the aspiration comes the phrase 'the satisfaction of the Son our Lord', referring to his atoning death for our sins.
3. The petition. The Lord is asked to raise up His power, to come among us, and with that power to help us.
4. The aspiration is that God's bountiful grace and mercy will quickly help and deliver us. The words 'help and' were added in 1662.
5. The termination. Glory is given to the Son, to the Father and to the Holy Spirit in that order (cf. 2 Corinthians 13:14).

Christmas: The second of two collects provided in 1549. The first one was dropped in 1552. The words 'as at this time' were inserted in the Scottish liturgy of 1637 and retained in 1662 to replace the earlier 'this day', because the collect was intended for use throughout the Christmas season.

1. The invocation. This is once again to Almighty God, returning in this respect to the first Sunday in Advent.
2. The doctrine. This collect is strong on doctrine in a way that the Advent collects are not. In particular:
   a. Christ is the only-begotten Son (John 1:14).
   b. Christ took our nature on himself (Philippians 2:7).
   c. Christ was born of a pure virgin (Matthew 1:20-23).
   d. We are born again and children of God by adoption and grace (Romans 8:16). The Epistle and the Gospel are similarly rich in theological content.
3. The petition. We pray that we may be daily renewed by the Holy Spirit.
4. The aspiration. This is contained in the petition.
5. The termination. Similar to Advent 3.

The juxtaposition of three holy days immediately following Christmas has been explained in different ways. For some, it represents different kinds of martyrdom – Stephen in both will and deed, John in will and the Innocents in deed. For others, it commemorates Stephen as the first martyr, John as the beloved disciple and special friend of Jesus, and the Innocents, whose suffering was the direct result of Jesus' birth.

St Stephen (26 December). The collect comes from the Gregorian sacramentary (62) and the Sarum missal, where, however, it is addressed to the Father and not to the Son as it is in the prayer book.

1. The invocation. This is subsumed in the petition and is restricted to the single word 'Lord', as in Advent 3, which is also addressed directly to the Son.
2. The doctrine. This is also contained in the petition. It states that we suffer in this world for the truth of Christ. Doctrine returns towards the end of the collect, where we are reminded that Christ stands at the right hand of God, ready to help all those who suffer for him.[5]
3. The petition. This comes in three parts, all based on Stephen's vision in Acts 7:55-56:
   a. We ask to be given the grace to look up to heaven as Stephen did.
   b. We ask for a vision of the glory to be revealed.
   c. We ask to be filled with the Holy Spirit.
4. The aspiration is that we may learn to love and bless our persecutors as Stephen did. The wording of the original was modified in 1662. From 1549 onwards it had spoken of learning to love our enemies, as Stephen prayed for his persecutors. Here, however, we are asking to pray for our persecutors, while Stephen prayed for his murderers. The change seems to reflect the conditions of 1662, when religious persecution was a living memory for many and still a danger for some.
5. The termination refers to Jesus as our only Mediator and Advocate, an appropriate ending in the context of this commemoration.

St John the Evangelist (27 December). This collect first appeared in the Leonine sacramentary (1283) and then in the Gregorian (67). It was expanded in 1549 and again in 1662.

---

5. This is slightly odd, in that Christ is usually said to be seated at the right hand of the Father. The difference is that seating was the privilege of the king. Everyone else stood in his presence.

1. The invocation. God is approached here as a God of mercy.
2. The doctrine. No specific doctrine is mentioned, though the general teaching of John is.
3. The petition. We pray that God will send His beams of light onto the Church, that it might be enlightened by John's doctrine. In the Sarum missal this enlightenment was confined to individuals; in 1549 it was extended to the whole Church.
4. The aspiration is that we may walk in the light of the truth and so attain the light of everlasting life. The theme of light is a particularly Johannine one and recurs throughout this collect. This entire phrase was added in 1662.
5. The termination is in the standard general form.

Holy Innocents (28 December). This collect from the Sarum missal can be traced back to both the Gelasian (42) and Gregorian (75) sacramentaries. The invocation was partly rewritten in 1662.

1. The invocation. This is to Almighty God. The next phrase, 'who out of the mouths of babes and sucklings hast ordained strength', was added in 1662.
2. The doctrine. No specific doctrine is mentioned.
3. The petition. We pray that God will mortify the sins in us and strengthen us by His grace.
4. The aspiration is that we may glorify God's name:
   a. by the innocency of our life (like that of the children)
   b. the constancy of our faith
   c. until the day we die.

Christmas 1. The collect for Christmas Day is used.

Circumcision of Christ (1 January). This collect is closely connected to one which is found in the supplement to the Gregorian sacramentary (1743). It is not in the Sarum missal.

1. The invocation. This is to Almighty God.
2. The doctrine. Christ was circumcised and made obedient to the law of Moses in order to do all that was necessary for our salvation.
3. The petition. We ask for the true circumcision of the Spirit. The 1549 prayer book had said 'thy Spirit' but it was altered in 1552. The question is whether it was a typographical error

or a deliberate change. If the latter, it would be better to write 'spirit', in order to conform to the aspiration, but it can always be maintained that the accomplishment of our desire can only be by the Holy Spirit.

4. The aspiration is that:
   a. our hearts and bodies may be mortified from all worldly lusts
   b. we may obey God's will in all things.
5. The termination is in the standard general form.

Epiphany (6 January). The collect is taken from the Gregorian sacramentary (87) and the Sarum missal, though with some alterations made in 1549. The original collect presented a parallel between the faith of the wise men leading to their seeing Jesus and our faith leading to the same revelation. This was effectively deleted in the English version, for the very good reason that it is a false comparison.

1. The invocation is extremely simple, mentioning only the word 'God'.
2. The doctrine. God used a star to manifest Himself to the Gentiles.
3. The petition. We pray that in His mercy, God will grant that those who know Him by faith in this life will have the beatific vision of the Godhead in eternity.
4. The aspiration is contained in the petition.
5. The termination is in the standard general form.

Epiphany 1. This comes from the Gregorian sacramentary (1096) and the Sarum missal. The original Latin is extremely concise and difficult to translate, but the English version has managed to provide us with an elegant style, even if the conciseness of the Latin has had to be sacrificed to some extent.

1. The invocation is very simple – to the Lord. That this is the Father and not the Son is clear only from the termination.
2. The doctrine. None is specified.
3. The petition. We ask God in His mercy to accept the prayers of His people.
4. The aspiration. We pray that:
   a. God's people will understand what they ought to do.
   b. God's people will do what they know they ought to.
5. The termination is in the standard general form.

Epiphany 2. This collect appears twice in the Gregorian sacramentary, first among the daily prayers (922) and then in the supplement as the collect for this Sunday (1099). It was also in the Sarum missal.

1. The invocation is full, being addressed to the Almighty and everlasting God. This is in sharp contrast to the previous two collects.
2. The doctrine. God rules over everything in heaven and earth. This emphasises His sovereignty and may be held to include predestination, though that is not specifically mentioned.
3. The petition. Once more, we pray that God in His mercy will hear His people's prayers.
4. The aspiration is that He will grant us peace all the days of our life. In the 1604 text the word 'peace' was replaced by 'grace', but the original was restored in 1662.
5. The termination is the same as in the previous Epiphany collects.

Epiphany 3. Originally from the Gregorian sacramentary (1102) and the Sarum missal, this collect was modified considerably in 1549. Its structure is simpler than the previous Epiphany collects.

1. The invocation repeats the fuller version of Epiphany 2.
2. The doctrine. Nothing is specified.
3. The petition is twofold:
   a. that God will look on our infirmities
   b. that in our necessities He will help and defend us by His right hand (of power). The second part of the petition was added in 1549.
4. There is no specific aspiration.
5. The termination is in the standard general form.

Epiphany 4. This collect has antecedents in the Gregorian sacramentary (1105) and in the Sarum missal. The 1549 prayer book offers a free rendering of it, with some variations, and it was considerably modified in 1662.

1. The invocation reverts to the simple 'God' of the Epiphany collect.
2. The doctrine is:
   a. We are placed in the midst of many great dangers.

b. Because of the frailty of our nature, we cannot 'stand upright', i.e. avoid sin. The force of this is weakened by the introduction of the word 'always' in the English version. In fact, we can never avoid sin and it would be better to omit this misleading qualifier.

3. The petition is for divine strength and protection in all our dangers.

4. The aspiration is that we may be delivered from all temptations. In 1549 the text read: 'that all those things which we suffer for sin by thy help we may well pass over and overcome', which is a slightly modified version of the original Latin.[6] The difficulty is that it is ambiguous, leaving open the suggestion that it might be possible to overcome sin(s) by our own efforts. It was to avoid that ambiguity that the text was revised in 1662.

5. The termination is in the standard general form.

Epiphany 5. Derived ultimately from the Gregorian sacramentary (1108) and the Sarum missal, but very freely translated in 1549:

1. The invocation is again very simple, with 'Lord' instead of 'God'.

2. The doctrine is that the people of God depend entirely on the hope of divine grace.

3. The petition is that the Church may be kept in the profession of an orthodox faith.

4. The aspiration is that the Church may always be defended by God's mighty power.

5. The termination is in the standard general form.

Epiphany 6. This Sunday, which occurs only rarely, was first provided for in 1662 and the collect was written by John Cosin, bishop of Durham. It is much fuller than the other Epiphany collects.

1. The invocation is in the most simple form, mentioning only 'God'.

2. The doctrine is fully stated. The Son of God was manifested in order to:

---

6. The Latin text has 'sins' in the plural and has no equivalent for 'pass over'.

    a. destroy the works of the devil

    b. make us children of God

    c. make us heirs of eternal life.

3. The petition is that we may purify ourselves, even as the Son is pure.

4. The aspiration is that, when the Son returns in power and glory, we may be made like him and dwell in his glorious kingdom.

5. The termination is much fuller than usual, mentioning the eternal reign of the Son along with the Father and the Holy Spirit.

Septuagesima. Taken from the Gregorian sacramentary (144) and the Sarum missal, with minor alterations in 1549:

1. The invocation is simple, referring only to the Lord (the Father).

2. The doctrine is that we are justly punished for our sins.

3. The petition is that:

    a. God will hear the prayers of His people.

    b. God will deliver His people in His mercy and by His goodness. The words 'by the goodness' were added in 1549.

4. The aspiration is that the name of God will be glorified.

5. The termination, which is very full, repeats the standard general ending but adds that the Son reigns eternally with the Father and the Holy Spirit, as one God.

Sexagesima. This collect was taken from the Gregorian sacramentary (147) and the Sarum missal, which both asked for the protection of St Paul, as well as of God. That was naturally removed in 1549.

1. The invocation is simple, but slightly fuller than usual, mentioning the 'Lord God'.

2. The doctrine is that God sees that we do not put our trust in anything that we do.

3. The petition is that by God's mercy we may be defended by His power against all adversity.

4. No aspiration in mentioned.

5. The termination is in the standard general form.

Quinquagesima. This prayer was composed afresh for the 1549 prayer book and is much richer in content than the one found in the Sarum missal.

1. The invocation is simple, referring only to the 'Lord'.
2. The doctrine is that without love we can do nothing worthwhile. It is directly linked to the Epistle reading (1 Corinthians 13). The doctrinal theme is continued in the petition, which states that love is the bond of peace and of all virtues and that without it we are reckoned to be dead in God's sight.
3. The petition is that God will send His Holy Spirit and pour His love into our hearts.
4. There is no distinct aspiration.
5. The termination is unique, in that we ask that our petition may be granted for the sake of Jesus Christ, God's only Son.

Ash Wednesday. Technically known as the first day of Lent, the term 'Ash Wednesday' is derived from the custom of placing ashes on the foreheads of the penitents who come to church on that day. That custom was discontinued in 1548 and the term 'Ash Wednesday' was dropped in 1552.[7] It was, however, restored in the 1637 Scottish prayer book and in 1662. The collect is repeated every day in Lent, after the collect appointed for the day. In 1637 it was directed that the Epistle and Gospel should also be repeated for the rest of the week but that was not carried over in 1662.

1. The invocation is full, repeating the one in Epiphany 2 and 3.
2. The doctrine is clearly stated:
    a. God hates nothing that he has made.
    b. God forgives the sins of those who repent.
3. The petition is that God will create in us 'new and contrite hearts'. To be renewed in our hearts (minds) is to be made repentant.
4. The aspiration is that we might obtain 'perfect' remission and forgiveness of our sins by the intervention of 'the God of all mercy'. However, there are two conditions attached to this:
    a. We must lament our sins 'worthily', i.e. with true repentance.
    b. We must confess our complete helplessness.
5. The termination is in the standard general form.

---

7. In modern times, some churches have revived the custom of 'ashing', usually using ashes left over from burning the palm crosses from the previous year.

Lent 1. This is sometimes called Quadragesima Sunday, a direct reference to the 40 days of Lent which are commemorated in the collect and in the gospel set for the day. The collect was composed by Thomas Cranmer in 1549.

1. The invocation is to the Lord, who in this case is the Son, Jesus Christ.
2. The doctrine is that the incarnate Christ lived his life 'for our sake'. This especially included the 40 days of fasting that he undertook at the beginning of his public ministry. The temptations of the devil are recalled in the gospel of the day but are not mentioned in the collect.
3. The petition is for grace to make good use of abstinence so that:
   a. our flesh will be subdued to the Spirit
   b. we may obey Christ's commands in righteousness and true holiness.
4. The aspiration is that Christ will be honoured and glorified by our behaviour.
5. The termination is full, as in Septuagesima.

The key to understanding this collect is to observe that we are expected to make good use of abstinence in order to grown spiritually. If fasting is too extreme or forced, it is liable to turn our thoughts to eating, rather than to God. It is sometimes observed by Muslims that the month of fasting (Ramadan) is accompanied by excessive eating and drinking after dark, when the fast is relaxed. That is the very opposite of subduing the flesh to the Spirit and is to be avoided by Christians.

Lent 2. A translation from the Gregorian sacramentary (202, 876) and the Sarum missal, the main difference is that, in 1549, the word 'defend' is used to cover both body and soul, whereas the Latin original used 'defend' for the body and 'cleansed' for the mind (soul).

1. The invocation refers to Almighty God but is otherwise fairly simple.
2. The doctrine is that we have no power to help ourselves, and God knows that.
3. The petition is for God to keep us:
   a. outwardly in our bodies
   b. inwardly in our souls.

4. The aspiration is that we may be defended from:
   a. all adversities that may happen to the body
   b. all evil thoughts that may attack and hurt our souls.
5. The termination is in the standard general form.

Lent 3. This collect is taken from the Gregorian sacramentary (229) and the Sarum missal, with the addition of the words 'against all our enemies' in 1549. 'Hearty desires' is the translation offered for Latin *vota* ('vows'), probably because the word developed that sense in medieval times.

1. The invocation is contained within the petition and is 'Almighty God'.
2. There is no doctrinal emphasis.
3. The petition is that God will:
   a. look on the 'hearty desires' of His humble servants
   b. stretch out the right hand of His majesty (power)
   c. defend us against our enemies.
4. There is no separate aspiration.
5. The termination is in the standard general form.

Lent 4. The collect is taken from the Gregorian sacramentary (256) and the Sarum missal. The phrase 'worthily deserve to be punished' was inserted in 1662 to replace the earlier 'are worthily punished' (1549). The change makes the prayer more generally applicable to everyone, whatever their circumstances might be.

1. The invocation is contained within the petition, as in Lent 3.
2. The doctrine is that our sins deserve to be punished.
3. The petition is that by God's grace we may mercifully be delivered from that punishment.
4. There is no specific aspiration.
5. The termination is a slightly expanded version of the standard general form, mentioning that our Lord Jesus Christ is also our Saviour.

The fourth Sunday in Lent was traditionally known as the 'day of refreshment' (*dies refectionis*) when the fast was relaxed and when feasting was (exceptionally) permitted. It seems that some people used this Sunday as a time to visit their cathedral, the 'mother church' of the diocese, with special offerings, or to go to visit their parents with special food ('mothering cakes') and other presents. The Epistle reminds us that the heavenly Jerusalem is 'the mother of us all'. From this grew the idea that this was Mothering Sunday, now largely transformed into Mother's Day, at least in the British Isles and Nigeria.[8]

Lent 5. Sometimes called Passion Sunday. The collect is taken from the Gregorian sacramentary (285) and the Sarum missal. The Latin is hard to translate accurately, but Thomas Cranmer produced a free and elegant version for us in the 1549 prayer book.

1. The invocation is once again included within the petition.
2. There is no specific doctrinal emphasis.
3. The petition is that:
   a. God will look mercifully on His people.
   b. God's people will be preserved, in body and soul, by His goodness.
4. There is no specific aspiration.
5. The termination is in the standard general form.

Palm Sunday. Officially called the Sunday next before Easter. The popular term refers to the triumphal entry of Jesus into Jerusalem just before his crucifixion but, although it is now universally celebrated on that day, neither the collect nor the Gospel makes any reference to it. The collect comes from the Gelasian sacramentary (329), the Gregorian sacramentary (312) and the Sarum missal.

1. The invocation is to Almighty and everlasting God.
2. The doctrine is fully and extensively described:
   a. God has sent His Son into the world out of His love for us (John 3:16).
   b. God sent His Son to be our Saviour by taking our flesh and suffering death on the cross.
   c. God intends that all people should follow the example of his great humility.
3. The petition is that:
   a. we might follow the example of his patience (i.e. suffering)
   b. we might share in his resurrection.

---

8. In other countries, Mother's Day is celebrated at different times, like (for example) the second Sunday in May in North America, Australia, New Zealand and many Commonwealth countries.

    4. There is no specific aspiration.

    5. The termination is a slightly expanded version of the standard general form.

Monday to Thursday in Holy Week. The Book of Common Prayer provides special Epistles and Gospels for each of these days, but the collect is the one used for Palm Sunday.

Good Friday. Uniquely in the prayer book, there are three collects appointed for Good Friday. This is scaled down from the eight that were traditionally used on this day, but their preservation reminds us of the particular solemnity of the occasion. The first two collects come straight from the Gregorian sacramentary (327, 343) and the Sarum missal, and the second one is also found in the Gelasian sacramentary (405). The third collect has antecedents in those sources but is essentially a new composition. The collects can be distinguished as follows: first, for the Church as the family of the redeemed; second, for the Church as a living organism; and, third, for those outside the Church.

First Collect:

    1. The invocation is simply to Almighty God.

    2. The doctrine is contained in the petition:
       a. our Lord Jesus Christ was content to be betrayed
       b. he was given up to wicked men
       c. he suffered death on the cross
       d. he now lives and reigns with the Father and the Holy Spirit.

    3. The petition is that God will look graciously on His family (the Church).

    4. There is no aspiration.

    5. The termination flows out from the doctrinal portion of the petition and is unique to this collect.

Second Collect:

    1. The invocation is full, to the Almighty and everlasting God.

    2. The doctrine is that the whole Church is governed and sanctified by the Holy Spirit.

    3. The petition is that God might accept the prayers we offer for the whole Church.

4. The aspiration is that every member of the Church, in whatever vocation and ministry they may have, may be worthy of their calling.
5. The termination is an expanded version of the standard general form, adding the word 'Saviour' to 'Lord'.

Third Collect:

1. The invocation is to the merciful God. Mercy is a standard theme of these collects, but this is the first one that uses the word in the invocation.
2. The doctrine is that:
   a. God hates nothing that he has made (a repetition of the Ash Wednesday collect).
   b. God does not want sinners to die but wants them to be converted and live.
3. The petition is that God will have mercy on Jews, Muslims (Turks), unbelievers and heretics and:
   a. remove all ignorance from them
   b. soften their hard hearts and their contempt of God's Word
   c. bring them home to the flock.
4. The aspiration is that:
   a. they may be saved as true Israelites
   b. they may be united in one flock under one shepherd, Jesus Christ.
5. The termination glorifies Christ our Lord, who lives and reigns eternally with the Father and the Holy Spirit.

Easter Even. This was traditionally one of the main times for baptising new converts. There was no special collect provided for the day in 1549 but one appeared in the 1637 Scottish prayer book. The one in the 1662 text is a revised version of that, which removes the fanciful notion that our sins are buried with Christ so that we can rise again to holiness of life. Instead, the 1662 collect emphasises the ongoing nature of repentance and sanctification, pointing out that it will not be finally accomplished until we die.

1. The invocation is contained in the petition and is restricted to the single word 'Lord', referring to the Father.
2. The doctrine is that we have been baptised into the death of Christ.

3. The petition is that God will grant that we may be buried with him by constantly mortifying our corrupt affections.
4. The aspiration is that by passing through death we may rise again to eternal joy.
5. The termination is extensive and unique to this collect. It recalls the merits of Christ's death, burial and resurrection on our behalf.

Easter. Easter is unique in the prayer book in that it is the only feast that has preserved something akin to the introits that characterised the pre-Reformation liturgies and the 1549 text. This comes in the form of three anthems, the first of which was appointed for 1662 and the other two of which date from 1549. They are partially derived from the order for the procession to the sepulchre on Easter morning that preceded the Sarum Mass for Easter Day.

The first anthem is 1 Corinthians 5:7-8. The first of the verses was in Gregory's anthem book and formed part of the Epistle in the Sarum missal. The verses portray the death and resurrection of Jesus as the Christian Passover. Jews ate unleavened bread as a sign of purity and spiritual authenticity. The 'old leaven' became a symbol of sin and corruption that had to be thrown out.

The second anthem came originally from one in the Gregorian antiphonary, *In communionem*, and was also found in the Sarum breviary (before Matins) and in the Sarum missal. It is Romans 6:9-11, which talks of baptism and how in it we have died with Christ and risen with him to newness of life.

The third anthem is of similar origin and is 1 Corinthians 15:20-22, where Paul says that what we lost through the sin of Adam we have regained by the triumphal sacrifice of Christ, the second Adam.

In 1549 what are now the second and third anthems were both followed by Hallelujah, a versicle and response, and a collect, as follows:

Priest. Show forth to all nations the glory of God.
People. And among all people his wonderful works.
Priest. Let us pray.

O God, who for our redemption didst give thine only begotten Son to the death of the cross; and by his glorious resurrection hast delivered us from the power of our enemy; Grant us so to die daily from sin, that we may evermore live with him, in the joy of his resurrection; through the same Christ our Lord, Amen.

This entire section, along with the Hallelujahs, was dropped in 1552. In 1662 the *Gloria* was added to conclude the anthems.

The Collect:
The first part of this is taken from the Gelasian sacramentary (463) and the second from the Gregorian sacramentary (383), with both held together in the Sarum missal.

1. The invocation is to Almighty God.
2. The doctrine is that:
    a. Jesus Christ, the only-begotten Son of God, has overcome death
    b. he has opened the gate of everlasting life for us.
3. The petition is that God will go before us with His grace and put good desires into our minds.
4. The aspiration is that He will go on helping us, so that His work may bring good results.
5. The termination picks up the standard general form and extends it with a trinitarian doxology.

In 1549 there were two collects, Epistles and Gospels for Easter, one for the first and the other for the second Communion.

The first collect was to be repeated on Monday in Easter Week. In 1552 it was the only collect appointed for Easter Day, along with the accompanying Epistle and Gospel. It was also the collect to be used on Easter Monday and on the following Sunday. In 1662 this was extended to the whole of Easter Week.

In 1549 the second collect was to be used on Easter Tuesday and on the following Sunday. In 1552 it was to be used on Easter Tuesday only. In 1662 it was moved to the Sunday after Easter.

The second Epistle (1 Corinthians 5:6-8) and Gospel (Mark 16:1-8) appointed in 1549 were dropped in 1552 and were not revived.

Monday and Tuesday in Easter Week. The collect for Easter is to be used.

Easter 1. This collect was originally composed in 1549 for the second Communion on Easter Day, Easter Tuesday and this Sunday. In 1552 its use was restricted to Easter Tuesday but in 1662 it was restored to its earlier place in Easter 1.

1. The invocation is unusual in that it refers to the Almighty Father, instead of Almighty God.
2. The doctrine is that the Father has given His Son:
   a. to die for our sins
   b. to rise for our justification.
3. The petition is that we should put away the leaven of malice and wickedness.
4. The aspiration is that by doing so, we may always serve God in pure living and in truth.
5. The termination appeals to the merits of Jesus Christ our Lord.

Easter 2. This collect was composed by Thomas Cranmer in 1549 to replace the one in the Sarum missal.

1. The invocation is to Almighty God.
2. The doctrine is that God has given His Son to be:
   a. a sacrifice for sin
   b. an example of holy life.
3. The petition is that we may always receive God's gift in a spirit of thankfulness.
4. The aspiration is that we may follow in Christ's footsteps every day of our life.
5. The termination is a slightly expanded version of the standard general form.

Easter 3. This collect is derived from the Leonine sacramentary (75) and the Gelasian sacramentary (546). It is found in the Sarum missal and was translated in 1549.

1. The invocation is to Almighty God.
2. The doctrine is that:
   a. God shows the way of truth to those who are in error.
   b. God intends that those who have gone astray should return to the way of righteousness.
3. The petition is that all those who are 'admitted into the fellowship of Christ's religion' (i.e. who are baptised members of the Church) should reject everything that is contrary to their profession of faith and do what is consonant with it. It is a reminder to us that the Christian life is one of spiritual warfare against sin; to be born again is not to be made perfect.

4. The aspiration is contained in the petition.

5. The termination is a slight rewording of the standard general form.

Easter 4. This collect comes from the Gelasian sacramentary (551), the Gregorian sacramentary (1120) and the Sarum missal. It was slightly altered in 1662.

1. The invocation is to Almighty God.
2. The doctrine as expressed in 1549 was that God makes 'the minds of all faithful men to be of one will'. It was replaced in 1662 with the assertion that only God can correct 'the unruly wills and affections of sinful men'. It is possible that this somewhat depressing change reflects the atmosphere that prevailed in 1662, immediately after the Civil War and Commonwealth period.
3. The petition is that God will grant His people the desire:
   a. to love what He commands
   b. to want to receive what He promises.
4. The aspiration is that in spite of an ever-changing world, our hearts may be fixed on the source of true joy.
5. The termination is in the standard general form.

Easter 5. This is also called Rogation Sunday, though not in the prayer book. The short collect, which derives from the Gelasian sacramentary (556), the Gregorian sacramentary (1123) and the Sarum missal, is suitable to Rogationtide, but was not designed for it.

1. The invocation is simply to the Lord (the Father).
2. The doctrine is that all good things come from God.
3. The petition is that the humble servants of God may be given inspiration:
   a. to think about what is good
   b. to do what is good under God's guidance.
4. There is no distinct aspiration.
5. The termination is in the standard general form.

Ascension. The 1549 collect derives from the Gelasian sacramentary (580), the Gregorian sacramentary (497) and the Sarum missal. However, it represents a return from Sarum to the Gelasian form, which stresses the effort to attain a dwelling place in heaven.

1. The invocation to Almighty God is contained within the petition.
2. The doctrine is that Christ, the only-begotten Son, has ascended into heaven.
3. The petition is that we too may ascend in heart and mind, and dwell continually with him.
4. There is no distinct aspiration.
5. The termination is a trinitarian doxology developed from the heavenly reign of Christ.

Ascension 1. This day was once called 'Waiting Sunday' because it stands in the time between the Ascension and Pentecost (see Acts 1:4-5). The collect was composed in 1549. It includes an antiphon from the ancient Vespers for Ascension Day, that was used by Bede on his deathbed:

> O Lord, King of glory, Lord of virtues, who today didst ascend in triumph above all heavens, do not leave us orphans, but send upon us the promise of the Father, even the Spirit of truth.

The Greek word *orphanous* (John 14:18) is translated as 'comfortless' in the KJV, as it also is in this collect. The antiphon is addressed to the Son, whereas the collect is addressed to the Father.

1. The invocation is to God the King of glory, as in the antiphon.
2. The doctrine is that the Father has exalted His Son with great triumph into the kingdom of heaven (1 Corinthians 15:27).
3. The petition is threefold:
   a. Do not leave us comfortless ('orphans').
   b. Send us the Holy Spirit to comfort us.
   c. Exalt us to the same place where Christ has gone before us.
4. There is no specific aspiration.
5. The termination is a trinitarian doxology.

Whitsun (Pentecost). The collect comes from the Gregorian sacramentary (526) and the Sarum missal.

1. The invocation is extremely simple, consisting of nothing more than the word 'God'.

2. The doctrine is that:
    a. God sent His faithful people the Holy Spirit.
    b. The Holy Spirit came as a teacher to bring light into the hearts of this who believe.
3. The petition is that by the indwelling presence of the Holy Spirit, we may:
    a. have good judgement in everything
    b. rejoice in God's holy comfort for ever.
4. There is no specific aspiration.
5. The termination refers to the merits of Christ Jesus our Saviour and concludes with a trinitarian doxology.

Monday and Tuesday in Whitsun Week. The Collect for Whitsunday is used.

Trinity Sunday. The Sunday after Pentecost. The feast of the Holy Trinity was established in England by Thomas Becket, who was consecrated as archbishop of Canterbury on that day in 1162. It became the benchmark for the remaining Sundays of the year in the Sarum missal and remained such in the prayer book. Recent liturgical revisionists have preferred to regard this Sunday as Pentecost 1, which was the earlier practice, but that is a theological regression in the interest of liturgical primitivism and should be resisted.

The collect is found in the Gregorian sacramentary (1621), where the Sunday after Pentecost was kept in honour of the Holy Trinity, and in the Sarum missal. It was adopted in 1549 and slightly altered in 1662.

1. The invocation is full, addressed to the Almighty and everlasting God.
2. The doctrine reflects the words of the Athanasian Creed. The confession of a true faith acknowledges the glory of the eternal Trinity and gives us the power of the divine majesty to worship God in Unity.
3. The petition is that we should be kept steadfast in this faith and defended from all our adversaries.
4. There is no specific aspiration.
5. The termination is to the one God, who lives and reigns in eternity.

Trinity 1. Derived from the Gelasian sacramentary (566) and the Gregorian sacramentary (1129) as well as the Sarum missal, it was slightly altered in 1662.

1. The invocation is simply to 'God'.
2. The doctrine is:
   a. We can do nothing without God's help.
   b. God is the strength of all who put their trust in Him.
3. The petition is that God will accept our prayers and help us with His grace.
4. The aspiration is that we may please Him in both will and deed by keeping His commandments.
5. The termination is in the standard general form.

Trinity 2. Freely translated from the Gelasian sacramentary (586), the Gregorian sacramentary (1132) and the Sarum missal, it was rearranged in 1662 in order to make it conform to the other collects in style.

1. The invocation is to the Lord, understood as the Father.
2. The doctrine is that God never fails to help and govern those whom He brings up in His steadfast fear and love.
3. The petition is that God will:
   a. keep us under the protection of His good providence
   b. give us a perpetual fear and love of His holy name.
4. There is no specific aspiration.
5. The termination is in the standard general form.

Trinity 3. From the Gregorian sacramentary (1135) and the Sarum missal, the words 'and comforted in all dangers and adversities' were added in 1662.

1. The invocation is to the Lord, understood as the Father.
2. The doctrine is that God has given us a hearty desire to pray.
3. The petition is that we may be defended and comforted in all adversities.
4. There is no specific aspiration.
5. The termination is in the standard general form.

Trinity 4. Taken from the Gregorian sacramentary (1138) and the Sarum missal, the opening phrase is the same as that of a collect found in the Gelasian sacramentary (1548) and the Gallican Bobbio missal.[9]

1. The invocation is simply to God.
2. The doctrine is that:

---

9. Lowe, ed., *The Bobbio Missal*, 442.

    a. God protects all who trust in Him

    b. without God, nothing is strong or holy.

3. The petition is that God will increase and multiply His mercy towards us.

4. The aspiration is that God will be our only ruler and guide through things on earth (temporal), so that we may not lose the things eternal.

5. The termination is an appeal to our heavenly Father, for Jesus Christ's sake.

Trinity 5. Derived from the Leonine sacramentary (633), the Gregorian sacramentary (1141) and the Sarum missal, the Latin word *ecclesia* was translated as 'congregation' in 1549, as 'people' in the 1637 Scottish prayer book and finally as 'Church' in 1662.

1. The invocation is to the Lord, understood as the Father, and is contained within the petition.

2. The doctrine is that God governs all things by His providence.

3. The petition is that God's providence will lead to a peaceful order here on earth.

4. The aspiration is that the Church may serve God with joy and in peace.

5. The termination is in the standard general form.

Trinity 6. This collect comes from the Gelasian sacramentary (1178), the Gregorian sacramentary (1144) and the Sarum missal. Two changes made in 1662 have somewhat altered the sense of the original. The word 'all' was omitted before 'man's understanding', which obscures the link to Philippians 4:7, and the phrase 'above all things' replaced 'in all things', which focussed our attention on seeing God at work in everything that happens to us, or that we come across, in the world.

1. The invocation is simply to God.

2. The doctrine is that God has prepared, for those who love Him, good things that pass our understanding (Philippians 4:7).

3. The petition is that God will pour such love into our hearts that we shall love Him above everything else.

4. The aspiration is that we may obtain the promises of God, which go beyond all our desires.

5. The termination is in the standard general form.

Trinity 7. This collect is freely translated from the Gelasian sacramentary (1182), the Gregorian sacramentary (1147) and the Sarum missal.

1. The invocation is unusual, being to 'the Lord of all power and might' instead of to Almighty God.
2. The doctrine is that God is the source and the giver of all good things (James 1:17).
3. The petition is fourfold. We ask God to:
   a. graft in our hearts the love of His name
   b. increase true religion in us
   c. nourish us with all goodness
   d. keep us in that goodness.
4. There is no specific aspiration.
5. The termination is in the standard general form.

Trinity 8. This collect comes from the Gelasian sacramentary (1186), the Gregorian sacramentary (1150) and the Sarum missal.

1. The invocation is simply to God.
2. The doctrine is that God's never-failing providence orders all things in heaven and on earth.
3. The petition is twofold. We ask God to:
   a. take away everything that is harmful to us
   b. give us what is profitable for us.
4. There is no specific aspiration.
5. The termination is in the standard general form.

Trinity 9. The collect comes from the Leonine sacramentary (638), the Gelasian sacramentary (1190), the Gregorian sacramentary (1153) and the Sarum missal. The 1549 phrase 'that we which cannot be without thee' was altered in 1662 to read 'that we who cannot do anything good without thee'.

1. The invocation is to the Lord (understood as the Father) and is contained within the petition.
2. The doctrine, also contained within the petition, is that we cannot do anything good without the help of God.
3. The petition is that God will grant us the spirit always to think and do the right thing.
4. The aspiration is that we will be enabled to live according to God's will.
5. The termination is in the standard general form.

Trinity 10. This is from the Leonine sacramentary (655), the Gelasian sacramentary (1195), the Gregorian sacramentary (1156) and the Sarum missal. The 1549 Book of Common Prayer follows the Gelasian sacramentary at the beginning and the Leonine at the end.

1. The invocation is contained within the petition and is to the Lord, understood as the Father.
2. There is no specific doctrine.
3. The petition is that God will hear the prayers of His humble servants.
4. The aspiration is that God will make His servants ask things that please Him, so that they may obtain them.
5. The termination is in the standard general form.

Trinity 11. This is from the Gelasian sacramentary (1198), the Gregorian sacramentary (1159) and the Sarum missal. It was significantly altered in 1662. The original 1549 text reads:

> God, which declarest thy almighty power most chiefly in showing mercy and pity; give unto us abundantly thy grace, that we running to thy promises, may be made partakers of thy heavenly treasure.

1. The invocation is simply to God.
2. The doctrine is that God declares His almighty power above all in showing us mercy and pity.
3. The petition is that He will give us such a measure of His grace that:
   a. we shall keep His commandments
   b. we shall obtain His promises
   c. we shall be partakers of His heavenly treasure.

It is the first of the petitions that is the most questionable and that is not found in 1549. We do not partake of God's heavenly treasure by keeping His commandments, which would be a form of salvation by works, but by trusting in His promises.

4. The aspiration is contained in the petition.
5. The termination is in the standard general form.

Trinity 12. This collect is derived from the Leonine sacramentary (917), the Gelasian sacramentary (1201), the Gregorian sacramentary (1162) and the Sarum missal. However, it was greatly enriched in 1549 and somewhat less so in 1662.

1. The invocation is full, being addressed to the Almighty and everlasting God.
2. The doctrine is that:
   a. God is always more ready to hear us than we are to pray.
   b. God is always ready to give us more than we desire or deserve.
3. The petition is threefold. We ask that God will:
   a. pour down on us the abundance of His mercy
   b. forgive us for the things that trouble our conscience
   c. give us those good things that we are unworthy to ask for.
4. There is no specific aspiration.
5. The termination appeals to the merits and mediation of Jesus Christ, God's Son and our Lord.

Trinity 13. This collect comes from the Leonine sacramentary (574), the Gelasian sacramentary (1206), the Gregorian sacramentary (1165) and the Sarum missal. The petition was significantly altered in 1662.

1. The invocation is full, being to the Almighty and merciful God.
2. The doctrine is that we can only please God and serve Him properly if He gives us the power to do so. The English version replaces the Latin *digne* ('worthily') with 'true', because our service to God may be perfectly sincere (i.e. true) but it is never worthy.
3. The petition is that:
   a. we may faithfully serve God in this life
   b. we may not fail to attain the heavenly promises.

The 1549 prayer book, which is more faithful to the Latin sources, reads 'that we may so run to thy heavenly promises, that we fail not finally to obtain the same'. The impression given is that our service to God somehow contributes to the attainment of His promises, which is false.

4. The aspiration is contained in the petition.
5. The termination mentions the merits of Jesus Christ our Lord.

Trinity 14. This collect comes from the Leonine sacramentary (598), the Gelasian sacramentary (1209), the Gregorian sacramentary (1168) and the Sarum missal, omitting the words 'deserve to' (*mereamur*) before 'obtain'. This significant change encapsulates the doctrine of the Reformation, which is that we are saved by grace, not by works.

1. The invocation is full, to the Almighty and everlasting God.
2. There is no specific doctrine expressed – but see the remark on the omission of 'deserve to' above.
3. The petition is that:
   a. God will give us an increase of faith, hope and love (1 Corinthians 13:13).
   b. God will make us love His commandments.
4. The aspiration is that we may obtain His promises.
5. The termination is in the standard general form.

Trinity 15. This collect comes from the Gelasian sacramentary (1213), the Gregorian sacramentary (1171) and the Sarum missal. The words 'from all things hurtful' were omitted in 1549 but restored in 1662.

1. The invocation is to the Lord, understood as the Father, and is contained within the petition.
2. The doctrine is that human weakness will always fail without God's help.
3. The petition is that God will keep the Church by His perpetual mercy, in particular, that He will:
   a. protect us from all things harmful
   b. lead us to all things profitable for our salvation.

The 1549 text altered the Latin *perpetua propitiatione* to 'perpetual mercy', so as to avoid the suggestion that it is by the perpetual propitiation of the sacrifice of Christ in the Mass that God will grant our requests. It is a subtle but clear expression of true Reformed doctrine.

4. There is no specific aspiration.
5. The termination is in the standard general form.

Trinity 16. This collect derives from the Gelasian sacramentary (1218), the Gregorian sacramentary (1174) and the Sarum missal. The word *ecclesia* was translated as 'congregation' in 1549 and as 'Church' in 1662.

1. The invocation is simply to the Lord, understood as the Father.
2. The doctrine is that the Church cannot continue without God's help.
3. The petition is that God will:
   a. cleanse and defend His Church
   b. preserve the Church by His help and goodness.
4. The aspiration is contained in the petition.
5. The termination is in the standard general form.

Trinity 17. This very short collect comes from the Gregorian sacramentary (966, 1177) and the Sarum missal. The word 'prevent' is used in its original meaning of 'go before' but it needs to be changed in modern English because it is too easily misunderstood.

1. The invocation is simply to the Lord, understood as the Father.
2. No specific doctrine is expressed.
3. The petition is that:
   a. God's grace may go before and after us
   b. His grace may make us permanently disposed to do good works.
4. There is no specific aspiration.
5. The termination is in the standard general form.

Trinity 18. This collect comes from the Gelasian sacramentary (1226), the Gregorian sacramentary (1180) and the Sarum missal. Certain phrases in 1549 were altered in 1662: (1549) 'to avoid the infections of the devil' became (1662) 'to withstand the temptations of the world, the flesh, and the devil'; (1549) 'heart and mind' became (1662) 'with pure hearts and minds'.

1. The invocation is simply to the Lord, understood as the Father.
2. No specific doctrine is expressed.
3. The petition is twofold:
   a. for grace to withstand the temptations of the world, the flesh and the devil
   b. for pure hearts and minds to follow the only true God.

The amendments of 1662 are improvements, especially the replacement of the word 'avoid' by 'withstand'. We cannot avoid temptation in this life but we can, and must, withstand it.

4. No specific aspiration is mentioned.
5. The termination is in the standard general form.

Trinity 19. This collect comes from the Gelasian sacramentary (1230), the Gregorian sacramentary (1183) and the Sarum missal. The Latin collect began with the petition and then added the reason for it, but this order was reversed in 1549. In 1662 'the working of thy mercy' was dropped and replaced by 'thy Holy Spirit'.

1. The invocation is simply to God.
2. The doctrine is that we cannot please God unless His Holy Spirit is present in our hearts.
3. The petition is that God will grant us His Holy Spirit and that He will guide and govern our hearts in all things.
4. There is no specific aspiration.
5. The termination is in the standard general form.

Trinity 20. This collect comes from the Gelasian sacramentary (1234), the Gregorian sacramentary (1186) and the Sarum missal. In 1662 the word 'pitiful' was happily altered to 'merciful' as a description of God.

1. The invocation is full, referring to God as Almighty and most merciful.
2. The doctrine is that His goodness is bountiful.
3. The petition is that God will:
   a. keep us from everything harmful
   b. prepare us for His service in body and soul.
4. The aspiration is that we may cheerfully accomplish the things that God wants us to do.
5. The termination is in the standard general form.

Trinity 21. This collect derives from the Gelasian sacramentary (1238), the Gregorian sacramentary (1189) and the Sarum missal. It is well-known because it is authorised for use at Morning and Evening Prayer instead of the absolution, when the celebrating minister is not in priest's orders.

1. The invocation is contained in the petition and is to the 'merciful Lord'.
2. There is no special doctrinal emphasis.
3. The petition is threefold:
   a. for pardon and peace to be given to believers
   b. for believers to be cleansed from all their sins
   c. for believers to serve God with a quiet mind.
4. There is no specific aspiration.
5. The termination is in the standard general form.

Trinity 22. This collect comes from the Anglo-Saxon missal of Leofric, written around 1050. It may have an antecedent in the Gregorian sacramentary (1192) and was in the Sarum missal.

1. The invocation is simply to the Lord, understood as the Father.
2. There is no special doctrinal emphasis.
3. The petition is for God to keep His household (*familia*) the Church in continual godliness.
4. The aspiration is that by divine protection, the Church may be:
   a. free from all adversities
   b. devoutly given to serving God by good works done for His glory.
5. The termination is in the standard general form.

Trinity 23. This collect is from the Gregorian sacramentary (1195) and the Sarum missal.

1. The invocation is to God, who is described as 'our refuge and our strength'.
2. The doctrine is that God is the source of all godliness. It is not a human attempt to imitate Him.
3. The petition is twofold:
   a. that God will hear the devout prayers of His Church
   b. that God will give us what we ask for in faith.
4. There is no particular aspiration.
5. The termination is in the standard general form.

Trinity 24. The collect is from the Gregorian sacramentary (702) and the Sarum missal.

1. The invocation is to the Lord, understood as the Father.
2. There is no special doctrinal emphasis.
3. The petition is that God will absolve His people of their offences.
4. The aspiration is that, through the bountiful goodness of God, we may all be delivered from the bondage of the sins that in our weakness we have committed.
5. The termination is fuller than usual, being addressed to our heavenly Father for the sake of Jesus Christ, our blessed Lord and Saviour.

Trinity 25. A very free translation of one of the *excita* ('stir up') collects found in the Gregorian sacramentary (1198) and in the Sarum missal.

1. The invocation is contained in the petition and is addressed to the Lord, understood as the Father.
2. There is no special doctrinal emphasis.
3. The petition is twofold. We ask that God will:
   a. stir up the wills of His faithful people, that they may be productive in good works
   b. that God may be correspondingly bountiful in rewarding them.
4. The aspiration is contained in the petition.
5. The termination is in the standard general form.

St Andrew (30 November). This collect has the distinction of being the only one composed for the 1552 prayer book.

1. The invocation is to Almighty God.
2. The doctrine is that Andrew received such grace that he readily obeyed the calling of Christ and followed him without delay, as all Christians, who are called by the Word of God, should do.
3. The petition is that we might dedicate ourselves to fulfilling God's commands.
4. The aspiration is contained in the petition.
5. The termination is a slightly modified version of the standard general form.

St Thomas (21 December). Composed in 1549.

1. The invocation is full, to the Almighty and everliving God.
2. The doctrine is that God allowed Thomas to doubt the resurrection of Christ in order to provide greater confirmation of its truth.
3. The petition is that we may be granted the grace to believe in Christ without any doubt.
4. The aspiration is that our faith will never be questioned by God.
5. The termination is very lengthy, asking God to hear us through Christ and concluding with a trinitarian doxology.

Conversion of St Paul (25 January). This collect is based on one from the Saint Gallen sacramentary (169) found also in a corrected version of the supplement to the Gregorian sacramentary (40*) and in the Sarum missal.[10] It was translated with some amendments in 1549 and further amended in 1662. The intention of the amendments was to focus our minds on the teaching of St Paul rather than on his person.

1. The invocation is simply to God.
2. The doctrine is that by the preaching of St Paul the light of the Gospel has spread throughout the world.
3. The petition is that:
   a. we may remember his wonderful conversion
   b. we may give thanks to God for it
   c. we may follow the doctrine that he taught.
4. The aspiration is contained in the petition.
5. The termination is in the standard general form.

The Presentation of Christ in the Temple (2 February). This festival is also called the Purification of St Mary the Virgin, coming as it does forty days after the birth of Christ. The Sarum missal contains a special service for the blessing of candles on this day, which was popularly

---

10. L.C. Mohlberg (ed.), *Das fränkische Sacramentarium Gelasianum in alamannischer Überlieferung* (Münster-in-Westfalen: Aschendorff, 1971). The manuscript with the corrected supplement to the Gregorian sacramentary is now located at Cambrai, Bibliothèque municipale (MSS 162-163). See also the Gelasian sacramentary (927).

known as Candlemas for that reason. The 1549 prayer book maintained the late medieval reference to the Purification of Mary but the 1662 text restored the correct title. The collect derives from one found in the Gelasian sacramentary (829), the Gregorian sacramentary (124) and the Sarum missal. The 1549 text was slightly amended in 1662.

1. The invocation is full, being to the Almighty and everliving God.
2. The doctrine is that the only-begotten Son of God was presented in the temple at Jerusalem in his human flesh.
3. The petition is that we may also be presented to God with pure and clean hearts.
4. There is no specific aspiration.
5. The termination is a slightly modified version of the standard general form.

St Matthias (24 February).[11] The collect was composed in 1549.

1. The invocation is to Almighty God.
2. The doctrine is that Matthias was chosen to replace the traitor Judas among the Apostles.
3. The petition is that the Church may be preserved from false apostles.
4. The aspiration is that the Church will always be guided by faithful and true pastors.
5. The termination is in the standard general form.

The Annunciation of the Blessed Virgin Mary (25 March). More correctly, the Annunciation was not 'of' but 'to' Mary. The feast is also called Lady Day, after Mary, and before 1752 it was celebrated in England as New Year's Day. The collect derives from the Gregorian sacramentary (143) and the Sarum missal, where it is one of the post-Communion collects.

1. The invocation is simply to the Lord, understood as the Father, and is contained within the petition.
2. The doctrine is that we have known the incarnation of Christ by the message of an angel.

---

11. In the old calendar, following Roman custom, the extra day in leap years was added after 23 February, so that this festival then fell on 25 February. This custom lapsed in 1752.

3. The petition is that we may be brought to experience the glory of Christ's resurrection by his cross and passion.
4. The aspiration is contained in the petition.
5. The termination is a slightly modified version of the standard general form.

St Mark (25 April). Composed in 1549 and slightly revised in 1662.

1. The invocation is to Almighty God.
2. The doctrine is that Mark is the inspired author of the second Gospel.
3. The petition is twofold, that:
   a. we may not be carried away by every wind of doctrine (Ephesians 4:14)
   b. we may be established in the truth of the Gospel.
4. There is no specific aspiration.
5. The termination is in the standard general form.

St Philip and St James (1 May). The collect dates from 1549 and was revised to include the name of James in 1662. It had been omitted because of the uncertainty surrounding the identity of James. The Epistle makes it clear that it is the Lord's brother who is intended, but this is guesswork. How Philip and James came to be associated with one another is unknown.

1. The invocation is to Almighty God.
2. The doctrine is that to know God is to have eternal life.
3. The petition is that we may know Jesus Christ as the way, the truth and the life (John 14:6).
4. The aspiration is that we may follow in the footsteps of St Philip and St James, which is the way to eternal life.
5. The termination is a slightly expanded version of the standard general form.

St Barnabas (11 June). He is called the Apostle, following scriptural usage (Acts 14:14), although he was not one of the twelve. The collect was composed in 1549 and slightly revised in 1662.

1. The invocation is to the 'Lord God Almighty', the word 'God' having been added in 1662.
2. The doctrine is that Barnabas was an apostle with special gifts from God.

3. The petition is unusual in that it is expressed negatively. We pray that we shall not:
   a. be left without God's manifold gifts
   b. be deprived of the grace to use those gifts to God's honour and glory.
4. The aspiration is contained in the petition.
5. The termination is in the standard general form.

St John the Baptist (24 June). Unusually, it is the birth of the Baptist, and not his death, that is commemorated, though the latter is marked by a black-letter day on 29 August. The collect was composed in 1549 but the word 'penance' was changed to 'repentance' in 1662, in order to avoid the implications of the word 'penance' for doctrine and liturgical practice.

1. The invocation is to Almighty God.
2. The doctrine is that John the Baptist was:
   a. miraculously born
   b. sent to prepare the way of Christ
   c. called to preach repentance.
3. The petition is that:
   a. we may follow his doctrine and holy life
   b. we may repent according to his preaching
   c. we may follow John's example in preaching the truth
   d. we may boldly rebuke vice
   e. we may patiently suffer for the sake of the truth.
4. The aspiration is contained in the petition.
5. The termination is in the standard general form.

St Peter (29 June). The collect dates from 1549, when the commemoration of St Paul on this date was formally stopped. A variation on this collect is found in the service for the consecration of bishops in the Ordinal.

1. The invocation is to Almighty God.
2. The doctrine is that St Peter received many excellent gifts from God that enabled him to feed the flock of Christ. The collect is notable for what it does not say about Peter. He is not credited with being the chief of the apostles, nor is he acknowledged as having any authority over them or over the Church of the kind claimed by the Roman papacy.

3. The petition is that:
   a. All bishops and pastors may diligently preach God's holy
      Word.
   b. The people will obey the Word thus preached.

The nature of this petition is highly significant. First of all, the primacy of the ministry of the Word is stressed. There is no mention of the sacraments. Secondly, bishops are linked to pastors, not to 'priests'. This may have been an oversight in the 1662 revision but, if so, it was a happy one. Bishops certainly should be pastors as well but not all pastors are bishops. Even so, they share a common ministry. Furthermore, the people are expected to listen to the ministry of the Word, not the words of the minister. It is the message, not the bearer, that counts.

4. The aspiration is that the people may receive the crown of
   everlasting glory.
5. The termination is in the standard general form.

[**St Mary Magdalene** (22 July). This festival was kept in 1549 but omitted in 1662, for reasons that are unclear. Some have thought that the proximity of St James' Day on 25 July influenced the decision to abandon it, but it may also have been because of the undue weight placed on Mary as a sinner, rather than on the fact that she was saved by grace through faith. Modern revisions of the lectionary have restored the festival, but the 1549 collect remains unknown to most people. It reads:

> Merciful Father, give us grace that we never presume to sin
> through the example of any creature; but if it shall chance
> us at any time to offend thy divine majesty, that then we may
> truly repent, and lament the same, after the example of Mary
> Magdalene, and by lively faith obtain remission of all our
> sins; through the only merits of thy Son our Saviour Christ.

1. The invocation, unusually, is to the merciful Father,
   presumably because the emphasis of the collect is on the
   forgiveness of sins.
2. The doctrine is that forgiveness of sin is given to those who
   truly repent.

3. The petition is that:
   a. we should never be led astray by the example of other people
   b. if we sin, we should sincerely repent.
4. The aspiration is that by a living faith we may obtain the forgiveness of all our sins.
5. The termination emphasises the merits of Christ, who has obtained our salvation, something that no merits of ours could ever achieve.]

St James (25 July). This James is the one associated with Peter and John in the Gospels, whose death is recorded in Acts 12:2. That occurred just before Passover, making the date of 25 July for his commemoration clearly wrong, but accuracy in that respect was probably never intended. The collect was composed in 1549, with the word 'holy' before 'commandments' added in 1662.

1. The invocation is to the merciful God and is contained within the petition.
2. The doctrine is that James left his family and followed Christ without hesitation, setting an example for everyone.
3. The petition is that we may forsake all worldly attachments and be ready to follow Christ's commandments.
4. The aspiration is contained in the petition.
5. The termination is in the standard general form.

[**The Transfiguration** (6 August). This festival was dropped in 1549 for unknown reasons but it has been restored in modern times. The Sarum missal contains the following collect (in Latin):

> God, who on this day hast revealed to the fathers of either Covenant thine only begotten [Son] wonderfully transfigured (*transformatum*) in a heavenly manner; Grant us, we beseech thee, by deeds well pleasing to thee, to attain to the continual contemplation of his glory, in whom thou hast testified that thy Fatherhood is well pleased.

1. The invocation is simply to God.
2. The doctrine is that the divine Christ has been revealed to the patriarchs of the Old Testament (Moses and Elijah) as well as to those of the New Testament (Peter, James and John).

3. The petition is that we may do good works pleasing to God and obtain the continual contemplation of Christ's glory.
4. The aspiration is contained in the petition.
5. There is (unusually) no termination.]

St Bartholomew (24 August). Properly known as Nathanael Bar-Tolomaeus. The 1549 collect was based on one in the Leonine sacramentary (1273) and the Gregorian sacramentary (74), where it was regarded as suitable for commemorating any apostle. In the Gallican *Missale Gothicum* (322)[12] it was used on the feast of St John the Evangelist. It was very substantially revised in 1662, which puts more emphasis on Bartholomew as a person. St Bartholomew's Day was well-known to the 1662 revisers because of the martyrdom of the French Huguenots on that day in 1572. It was also the day fixed for introducing the 1662 prayer book and requiring all those who could not accept it to leave their ministry.

1. The invocation is full, to the Almighty and everlasting God.
2. The doctrine is that Bartholomew received grace both to believe and to preach God's Word.
3. The petition is for the Church, that it might:
   a. love the Word that Bartholomew believed
   b. preach and receive that Word.
4. There is no distinct aspiration.
5. The termination is in the standard general form.

St Matthew (21 September). The collect was composed in 1549 and very slightly modified in 1662.

1. The invocation is to Almighty God.
2. The doctrine is that Matthew was called from a worldly profession to be an Apostle and evangelist.
3. The petition is that we may forsake any desire for riches and follow Christ instead.
4. There is no distinct aspiration.
5. The termination is a trinitarian doxology.

St Michael and All Angels (29 September). This collect derives from the Gregorian sacramentary (726) and the Sarum missal. It was embellished

---

12. L.C. Mohlberg (ed.), *Missale Gothicum* (Rome: Herder, 1961).

by the addition of the words 'by thy appointment' in 1549 and slightly modified in 1662.

1. The invocation is to the everlasting God.
2. The doctrine is that God has constituted the services of angels and of human beings in a wonderful order.
3. The petition is that the angels may protect and defend us on earth in accordance with their heavenly service to God.
4. There is no distinct aspiration.
5. The termination is in the standard general form.

St Luke (18 October). This collect was composed in 1549 and revised in 1662.

1. The invocation is to Almighty God.
2. The doctrine is that Luke the physician was called by God to be a physician of the soul as well.
3. The petition is that by the spiritual medicine delivered by him all the diseases of our souls may be healed.
4. There is no special aspiration.
5. The termination is through the merits of Jesus Christ.

St Simon and St Jude (28 October). This collect was composed in 1549 and is based on Ephesians 2:20-22 and 4:3. The word 'Church' replaced 'congregation' in 1662. The association of Simon with Jude is probably based on Acts 1:13, where Simon the Zealot is coupled with Judas (Jude), the son of James. However, Jude may also be the author of the Epistle that bears his name, as Thomas Cranmer evidently thought when he appointed a reading from it for this day.

1. The invocation is to Almighty God.
2. The doctrine is that God has built His Church on the foundation of the apostles and prophets, Jesus Christ being the chief cornerstone (Ephesians 2:20).
3. The petition is that we may be united by their doctrine and made a holy temple acceptable to God.
4. The aspiration is contained in the petition.
5. The termination is in the standard general form.

All Saints (1 November). This collect was composed in 1549 and slightly modified in 1662. The word 'unspeakable' means 'beyond the capacity of human language to express' and ought to be replaced by 'ineffable' or something similar, in order to avoid misunderstanding.

1. The invocation is to Almighty God.
2. The doctrine is that God has bound His chosen people together in the mystical body of Christ.
3. The petition is that we may follow the virtuous and godly living of the saints.
4. The aspiration is that we may inherit the 'unspeakable' joys reserved for those who truly love God.
5. The termination is in the standard general form.

A Table of the Provenance of the Collects

In order to make it easier to see at a glance how dependent the Book of Common Prayer is on earlier tradition, the table indicates where precedents for the collects can be found in the Gelasian sacramentary, the Gregorian sacramentary and the Sarum missal. For the first two, the numbers are those of the most recent editions. The Sarum missal has not been edited in that way, so a simple 'Yes' (or 'No') must suffice. Where a collect can be traced to another source (such as the Leonine sacramentary) that is indicated in a footnote. It should also be borne in mind that the prayer book collect may be a modified version of the precedent cited for it.

Note that the Sarum missal differs from the Gregorian sacramentary in that the Sundays from June to November are calculated from Trinity Sunday, not from Pentecost, although the numbering was retained. Thus, what is Pentecost 10 in the Gregorian sacramentary became Trinity 10 in the Sarum missal, even though, in fact, it was a week later, since Trinity 10 = Pentecost 11.

Collect	Gelasian	Gregorian	Sarum
Advent 1			No
Advent 2			No
Advent 3			Yes
Advent 4	1121	805	Yes
Christmas			No
St Stephen		62	Yes
St John the Evangelist[13]		67	No

---

13. Leonine sacramentary (1283).

Collect	Gelasian	Gregorian	Sarum
Holy Innocents	42	75	Yes
Circumcision of Christ		1743	No
Epiphany		87	Yes
Epiphany 1		1096	Yes
Epiphany 2		922/1099	Yes
Epiphany 3		1102	Yes
Epiphany 4		1105	Yes
Epiphany 5		1108	Yes
Epiphany 6			No
Septuagesima		144	Yes
Sexagesima		147	Yes
Quinquagesima			No
Ash Wednesday			No
Lent 1			No
Lent 2		202/876	Yes
Lent 3		229	Yes
Lent 4		256	Yes
Lent 5		285	Yes
Palm Sunday	329	312	Yes
Good Friday I		327	Yes
Good Friday II	405	343	Yes
Good Friday III			No
Easter Even			No
Easter	463	383	Yes
Easter 1			No
Easter 2			No
Easter 3[14]	546		Yes
Easter 4	551	1120	Yes
Easter 5	556	1123	Yes
Ascension	580	497	Yes
Ascension 1			No
Whitsun (Pentecost)		526	Yes
Trinity Sunday		1621	Yes
Trinity 1	566	1129	Yes
Trinity 2	586	1132	Yes
Trinity 3		1135	Yes
Trinity 4[15]	1548	1138	Yes
Trinity 5[16]		1141	Yes

---

14. Leonine sacramentary (75).

15. Bobbio missal (442).

16. Leonine sacramentary (633).

Collect	Gelasian	Gregorian	Sarum
Trinity 6	1178	1144	Yes
Trinity 7	1182	1147	Yes
Trinity 8	1186	1150	Yes
Trinity 9[17]	1190	1153	Yes
Trinity 10[18]	1195	1156	Yes
Trinity 11	1198	1159	Yes
Trinity 12[19]	1201	1162	Yes
Trinity 13[20]	1206	1165	Yes
Trinity 14[21]	1209	1168	Yes
Trinity 15	1213	1171	Yes
Trinity 16	1218	1174	Yes
Trinity 17		966/1177	Yes
Trinity 18	1226	1180	Yes
Trinity 19	1230	1183	Yes
Trinity 20	1234	1186	Yes
Trinity 21	1238	1189	Yes
Trinity 22[22]		1192	Yes
Trinity 23		1195	Yes
Trinity 24		702	Yes
Trinity 25		1198	Yes
St Andrew			No
St Thomas			No
Conversion of St Paul		40*	Yes
Presentation (Candlemas)	829	124	Yes
St Matthias			No
Annunciation		143	Yes
St Mark			No
St Philip and St James			No
St Barnabas			No
St John the Baptist			No
St Peter			No
St James			No
St Bartholomew[23]		74	No

17. Leonine sacramentary (638).

18. Leonine sacramentary (655).

19. Leonine sacramentary (917).

20. Leonine sacramentary (574).

21. Leonine sacramentary (598).

22. From the Anglo-Saxon missal of Leofric.

23. Leonine sacramentary (1273).

Collect	Gelasian	Gregorian	Sarum
St Matthew			No
St Michael (Michaelmas)		726	Yes
St Luke			No
St Simon and St Jude			No
All Saints			No

Epistles and Gospels

For each of the Sundays and holy days of the year, there is a set reading taken from one of the New Testament Epistles and from one of the Gospels. With respect to the **Epistles**, on 24 occasions, more than a quarter of the total, the reading comes from some other portion of Scripture. There are seven selections from the Old Testament (four from Isaiah), thirteen from the Acts of the Apostles and four from Revelation. Looking at the New Testament Epistles themselves, there is a reasonably significant selection from Romans to Colossians among the Pauline texts, and from 1 Peter, 1 John and Jude. The others are under-represented by modern standards, in particular, the Pastoral Epistles (1 and 2 Timothy and Titus) and the theologically important Hebrews, from which there are only four selections.

With respect to the **Gospels**, Matthew is better represented than any of the others, probably because it was believed in the Early and medieval Church that his was the first Gospel to be written. Mark is hardly used at all, but Luke and John are present in roughly equal amounts. Unlike the Epistles, no other portion of Scripture is ever substituted for a Gospel reading.

Virtually all of the readings are taken from the Sarum missal, occasionally with additions or deletions from the Sarum passages. Leaving aside Epiphany 6, which was a new service introduced in 1662 (and is extremely rare), there are only nine completely new Epistles, six of them appointed for saints' days, and four new Gospels, of which three are in the Easter cycle.

In order best to appreciate the sequencing of these readings, the following table sets them out in order, beginning with the appointed Sundays and fixed holy days, and continuing with the remaining holy days at the end.

Sunday/holy day	Epistle	Gospel
Advent 1	Romans 13:8-14[24]	Matthew 21:1-13
Advent 2	Romans 15:4-13	Luke 21:25-33
Advent 3	1 Corinthians 4:1-5	Matthew 11:2-10
Advent 4	Philippians 4:4-7	John 1:19-28
Christmas	Hebrews 1:1-12[25]	John 1:1-14
St Stephen	Acts 7:55-60[26]	Matthew 3:34-39
St John the Evangelist	1 John 1:1-10	John 21:19-25
Holy Innocents	Revelation 14:1-5	Matthew 2:13-18
Christmas 1	Galatians 4:1-7	Matthew 1:18-25[27]
Circumcision of Christ	Romans 4:8-14	Luke 2:15-21
Epiphany	Ephesians 3:1-12[28]	Matthew 2:1-12[29]
Epiphany 1	Romans 12:1-5	Luke 2:41-52
Epiphany 2	Romans 12:6-16	John 2:1-11
Epiphany 3	Romans 12:16-21	Matthew 8:1-13
Epiphany 4	Romans 13:1-7	Matthew 8:23-34[30]
Epiphany 5	Colossians 3:12-17	Matthew 13:24-30
Epiphany 6	1 John 3:1-8	Matthew 24:23-31
Septuagesima	1 Corinthians 9:24-27[31]	Matthew 20:1-16
Sexagesima	2 Corinthians 11:19-31[32]	Luke 8:4-15
Quinquagesima	1 Corinthians 13:1-13	Luke 18:31-43
Ash Wednesday	Joel 2:12-17[33]	Matthew 6:16-21
Lent 1	2 Corinthians 6:1-10	Matthew 4:1-11
Lent 2	1 Thessalonians 4:1-8[34]	Matthew 15:21-28
Lent 3	Ephesians 5:1-14[35]	Luke 11:14-28
Lent 4	Galatians 4:21-31[36]	John 6:1-14
Lent 5	Hebrews 9:11-15	John 8:46-59a

---

24. Sarum missal, Romans 13:11-14.
25. Sarum missal, 1549, 1552, Hebrews 1:1-13.
26. Sarum missal, Acts 6:8-15.
27. Sarum missal, Sixth Day after Christmas; 1549, Matthew 1:1-25.
28. Sarum missal, Isaiah 9:1-6.
29. Sarum missal, Luke 3:21-4:1.
30. Sarum missal, Matthew 8:23-27.
31. Sarum missal, 1 Corinthians 9:24-10:4.
32. Sarum missal, 2 Corinthians 11:19-12:9.
33. Sarum missal, Joel 2:12-19.
34. Sarum missal, 1 Thessalonians 4:1-8.
35. Sarum missal, Ephesians 5:1-9.
36. Sarum missal, Galatians 4:22-5:1.

Sunday/holy day	Epistle	Gospel
Palm Sunday	Philippians 2:5-11	Matthew 27:1-54[37]
Monday	Isaiah 63:1-9[38]	Mark 14:1-72[39]
Tuesday	Isaiah 50:5-11	Mark 15:1-39[40]
Wednesday	Hebrews 9:16-28	Luke 22:1-71[41]
Maundy Thursday	1 Corinthians 11:17-34[42]	Luke 23:1-49[43]
Good Friday	Hebrews 10:1-25	John 19:1-37[44]
Easter Even	1 Peter 3:17-22[45]	Matthew 27:57-66[46]
Easter	Colossians 3:1-7[47]	John 20:1-10[48]
Monday	Acts 10:34-43[49]	Luke 24:13-35
Tuesday	Acts 13:26-41[50]	Luke 24:36-48
Easter 1	1 John 5:4-12[51]	John 20:19-23[52]
Easter 2	1 Peter 2:19-25[53]	John 10:11-16
Easter 3	1 Peter 2:11-17[54]	John 16:16-22
Easter 4	James 1:17-21	John 16:5-14
Easter 5	James 1:22-27	John 16:23-33
Ascension	Acts 1:1-11	Mark 16:14-20
Ascension 1	1 Peter 4:7-11	John 15:26-16:4a
Whitsun (Pentecost)	Acts 2:1-11	John 14:15-31[55]
Monday	Acts 10:34-48[56]	John 3:16-21
Tuesday	Acts 8:14-17[57]	John 10:1-10

---

37. Sarum missal, Matthew 26:2-27:61;1549, Matthew 26:1-27:56.
38. Sarum missal, part of the lesson for the fourth day in Holy Week.
39. Sarum missal, part of the lesson for the third day in Holy Week.
40. Sarum missal, Mark 14:1-15:46.
41. Sarum missal, Luke 22:1-23:49.
42. Sarum missal, 1 Corinthians 11:20-32.
43. Sarum missal, part of the lesson on the previous day.
44. Sarum missal, John 18:1-19:37; 1549, John 18:1-19:42.
45. Sarum missal, Colossians 3:1-4.
46. Sarum missal, Matthew 28:1-7.
47. Sarum missal, Colossians 3:1-4 on Easter Even.
48. Sarum missal, John 20:1-9 read on the Saturday after Easter.
49. Sarum missal, Tuesday in Easter Week.
50. Sarum missal, Wednesday in Easter Week.
51. Sarum missal, 1 John 5:4-10.
52. Sarum missal, John 20:19-31.
53. Sarum missal, 1 Peter 2:21-25.
54. Sarum missal, 1 Peter 2:11-19.
55. Sarum missal, John 14:23-31.
56. Sarum missal, Tuesday after Whitsun.
57. Sarum missal, Wednesday after Whitsun.

Sunday/holy day	Epistle	Gospel
Trinity Sunday	Revelation 4:1-11	John 3:1-15
Trinity 1	1 John 4:7-21[58]	Luke 16:19-31
Trinity 2	1 John 3:13-24[59]	Luke 14:16-24
Trinity 3	1 Peter 5:5-11[60]	Luke 15:1-10
Trinity 4	Romans 8:18-23	Luke 6:36-42
Trinity 5	1 Peter 3:8-15	Luke 5:1-11
Trinity 6	Romans 6:3-11	Matthew 5:20-26[61]
Trinity 7	Romans 6:19-23	Mark 8:1-9
Trinity 8	Romans 8:12-17	Matthew 7:15-21
Trinity 9	1 Corinthians 10:1-13[62]	Luke 16:1-9
Trinity 10	1 Corinthians 12:1-11[63]	Luke 19:41-47a
Trinity 11	1 Corinthians 15:1-11	Luke 18:9-14
Trinity 12	2 Corinthians 3:4-9	Mark 7:31-37
Trinity 13	Galatians 3:16-22	Luke 10:23-37
Trinity 14	Galatians 5:16-24	Luke 17:11-19
Trinity 15	Galatians 6:11-18[64]	Matthew 6:24-34
Trinity 16	Ephesians 3:13-21	Luke 7:11-17
Trinity 17	Ephesians 4:1-6	Luke 14:1-11
Trinity 18	1 Corinthians 1:4-8	Matthew 22:34-46
Trinity 19	Ephesians 4:17-32[65]	Matthew 9:1-8
Trinity 20	Ephesians 5:15-21	Matthew 22:1-14
Trinity 21	Ephesians 6:10-20[66]	John 4:46-54[67]
Trinity 22	Philippians 1:3-11[68]	Matthew 18:21-35[69]
Trinity 23	Philippians 3:17-21	Matthew 22:15-22[70]
Trinity 24	Colossians 1:3-12[71]	Matthew 9:18-26[72]

58. Sarum missal, 1 John 4:9-21.
59. Sarum missal, 1 John 3:13-18.
60. Sarum missal, 1 Peter 5:6-11.
61. Sarum missal, Matthew 5:20-24.
62. Sarum missal, 1 Corinthians 10:6-14.
63. Sarum missal, 1 Corinthians 12:2-12.
64. Sarum missal, Galatians 5:25-6:10.
65. Sarum missal, Ephesians 4:23-28.
66. Sarum missal, Ephesians 6:10-17.
67. Sarum missal, John 4:46-53.
68. Sarum missal, Philippians 1:6-12.
69. Sarum missal, Matthew 18:23-35.
70. Sarum missal, Matthew 22:15-21.
71. Sarum missal, Colossians 1:9-11.
72. Sarum missal, Matthew 9:18-22.

Sunday/holy day	Epistle	Gospel
Trinity 25	Jeremiah 23:5-8	John 6:5-14
St Andrew	Romans 10:9-21[73]	Matthew 4:18-22
St Thomas	Ephesians 2:19-22	John 20:24-31
Conversion of St Paul	Acts 9:1-22	Matthew 19:27-30[74]
Presentation (Candlemas)	Malachi 3:1-5[75]	Luke 2:22-40[76]
St Matthias	Acts 1:15-26	Matthew 11:25-30
Annunciation	Isaiah 7:10-15	Luke 1:26-38
St Mark	Ephesians 4:7-16	John 15:1-11
St Philip and St James	James 1:1-12[77]	John 14:1-14[78]
St Barnabas	Acts 11:22-30	John 15:12-16
St John the Baptist	Isaiah 40:1-11[79]	Luke 1:57-80[80]
St Peter	Acts 12:1-11	Matthew 16:13-19
[St Mary Magdalene	Proverbs 31:10-31	Luke 7:36-50]
St James	Acts 11:27-12:3a[81]	Matthew 20:20-28[82]
[Transfiguration	2 Peter 1:16-19	Matthew 17:1-9]
St Bartholomew	Acts 5:12-16	Luke 22:24-30
St Matthew	2 Corinthians 4:1-6[83]	Matthew 9:9-13
St Michael (Michaelmas)	Revelation 12:7-12[84]	Matthew 18:1-10
St Luke	2 Timothy 4:5-15	Luke 10:1-7
St Simon and St Jude	Jude 1:1-8[85]	John 15:17-27[86]
All Saints	Revelation 7:2-12	Matthew 5:1-12[87]

---

73. Sarum missal, Romans 10:9-18.
74. Sarum missal, Matthew 19:26-29.
75. Sarum missal, Malachi 3:1-4.
76. Sarum missal, Luke 2:22-32.
77. Sarum missal, Wisdom 5:1-5.
78. Sarum missal, John 14:1-13.
79. Sarum missal, Isaiah 49:1-7.
80. Sarum missal, Luke 1:57-68.
81. Sarum missal, Ephesians 2:19-22.
82. Sarum missal, Matthew 20:20-23.
83. Sarum missal, Ephesians 2:19-23.
84. Sarum missal, Revelation 1:1-5.
85. Sarum missal, Romans 8:28-39.
86. Sarum missal, John 15:17-25.
87. Sarum missal, Matthew 5:5-12a.

Epistles in Canonical Order

[Proverbs 31:10-31	St Mary Magdalene (22 July)]
Isaiah 7:10-15	Annunciation (25 March)
Isaiah 40:1-11	St John the Baptist (24 June)
Isaiah 50:5-11	Tuesday in Holy Week
Isaiah 63:1-9	Monday in Holy Week
Jeremiah 23:5-8	Trinity 25
Joel 2:12-17	Ash Wednesday
Malachi 3:1-5	Presentation of Christ (2 February)
Acts 1:1-11	Ascension
Acts 1:15-26	St Matthias (24 February)
Acts 2:1-11	Whitsun (Pentecost)
Acts 5:12-16	St Bartholomew (24 August)
Acts 7:55-60	St Stephen (26 December)
Acts 8:14-17	Whitsun Tuesday
Acts 9:1-22	Conversion of St Paul (25 January)
Acts 10:34-43	Easter Monday
Acts 10:34-48	Whitsun Monday
Acts 11:22-30	St Barnabas (11 June)
Acts 11:27-12:3a	St James (25 July)
Acts 12:1-11	St Peter (29 June)
Acts 13:26-41	Easter Tuesday
Romans 4:8-14	Circumcision of Christ (1 January)
Romans 6:3-11	Trinity 6
Romans 6:19-23	Trinity 7
Romans 8:12-17	Trinity 8
Romans 8:18-23	Trinity 4
Romans 10:9-21	St Andrew (30 November)
Romans 12:1-5	Epiphany 1
Romans 12:6-16	Epiphany 2
Romans 12:16-21	Epiphany 3
Romans 13:1-7	Epiphany 4
Romans 13:8-14	Advent 1
Romans 15:4-13	Advent 2

1 Corinthians 1:4-8	Trinity 18
1 Corinthians 4:1-5	Advent 3
1 Corinthians 9:24-27	Septuagesima
1 Corinthians 10:1-13	Trinity 9
1 Corinthians 11:17-34	Maundy Thursday
1 Corinthians 12:1-11	Trinity 10
1 Corinthians 13:1-13	Quinquagesima
1 Corinthians 15:1-11	Trinity 11
2 Corinthians 3:4-9	Trinity 12
2 Corinthians 4:1-6	St Matthew (24 September)
2 Corinthians 6:1-10	Lent 1
2 Corinthians 11:19-31	Sexagesima
Galatians 3:16-22	Trinity 13
Galatians 4:1-7	Christmas 1
Galatians 4:21-31	Lent 4
Galatians 5:16-24	Trinity 14
Galatians 6:11-18	Trinity 15
Ephesians 2:19-22	St Thomas (21 December)
Ephesians 3:1-12	Epiphany (6 January)
Ephesians 3:13-21	Trinity 16
Ephesians 4:1-6	Trinity 17
Ephesians 4:7-16	St Mark (25 April)
Ephesians 4:17-32	Trinity 19
Ephesians 5:1-14	Lent 3
Ephesians 5:15-21	Trinity 20
Ephesians 6:10-20	Trinity 21
Philippians 1:3-11	Trinity 22
Philippians 2:5-11	Palm Sunday
Philippians 3:17-21	Trinity 23
Philippians 4:4-7	Advent 4
Colossians 1:3-12	Trinity 24
Colossians 3:1-7	Easter
Colossians 3:12-17	Epiphany 5
1 Thessalonians 4:1-8	Lent 2
2 Timothy 4:5-15	St Luke (18 October)

Hebrews 1:1-12	Christmas (25 December)
Hebrews 9:11-15	Lent 5
Hebrews 9:16-28	Wednesday in Holy Week
Hebrews 10:1-25	Good Friday
James 1:1-12	St Philip and St James (1 May)
James 1:17-21	Easter 4
James 1:22-27	Easter 5
1 Peter 2:11-17	Easter 3
1 Peter 2:19-25	Easter 2
1 Peter 3:8-15	Trinity 5
1 Peter 3:17-22	Easter Even
1 Peter 4:7-11	Ascension 1
1 Peter 5:5-11	Trinity 3
[2 Peter 1:16-19	Transfiguration (6 August)]
1 John 1:1-10	St John the Evangelist (27 December)
1 John 3:1-8	Epiphany 6
1 John 3:13-24	Trinity 2
1 John 4:7-21	Trinity 1
1 John 5:4-12	Easter 1
Jude 1:1-8	St Simon and St Jude (28 October)
Revelation 4:1-11	Trinity
Revelation 7:2-12	All Saints (1 November)
Revelation 12:7-17	St Michael and All Angels (29 September)
Revelation 14:1-5	Holy Innocents (28 December)

Gospels in Canonical Order

Matthew 1:18-25	Christmas 1
Matthew 2:1-12	Epiphany (6 January)
Matthew 2:13-18	Holy Innocents (28 December)
Matthew 3:34-39	St Stephen (26 December)
Matthew 4:1-11	Lent 1
Matthew 4:18-22	St Andrew (30 November)
Matthew 5:1-12	All Saints (1 November)
Matthew 5:20-26	Trinity 6

Matthew 6:16-21	Ash Wednesday
Matthew 6:24-34	Trinity 15
Matthew 7:15-21	Trinity 8
Matthew 8:1-13	Epiphany 3
Matthew 8:23-34	Epiphany 4
Matthew 9:1-8	Trinity 19
Matthew 9:9-13	St Matthew (24 September)
Matthew 9:18-26	Trinity 24
Matthew 11:2-10	Advent 3
Matthew 11:25-30	St Matthias (24 February)
Matthew 13: 24-30	Epiphany 5
Matthew 15:21-28	Lent 2
Matthew 16: 13-19	St Peter (29 June)
[Matthew 17:1-9	Transfiguration (6 August)]
Matthew 18:1-10	St Michael and All Angels (29 September)
Matthew 18:21-35	Trinity 22
Matthew 19:27-30	Conversion of St Paul (25 January)
Matthew 20:1-16	Septuagesima
Matthew 20:20-28	St James (25 July)
Matthew 21:1-13	Advent 1
Matthew 22:1-14	Trinity 20
Matthew 22:15-22	Trinity 23
Matthew 22:34-46	Trinity 18
Matthew 24:23-31	Epiphany 6
Matthew 27:1-54	Palm Sunday
Matthew 27:57-66	Easter Even
Mark 7:31-37	Trinity 12
Mark 8:1-9	Trinity 7
Mark 14:1-72	Monday in Holy Week
Mark 15:1-39	Tuesday in Holy Week
Mark 16:14-20	Ascension
Luke 1:26-38	Annunciation (25 March)
Luke 1:57-80	St John the Baptist (24 June)
Luke 2:15-21	Circumcision of Christ (1 January)
Luke 2:22-40	Presentation of Christ (2 February)
Luke 2:41-52	Epiphany 1
Luke 5:1-11	Trinity 5
Luke 6:36-42	Trinity 4
Luke 7:11-17	Trinity 16

[Luke 7:36-50	St Mary Magdalene (22 July)]
Luke 8:4-15	Sexagesima
Luke 10:1-7	St Luke (18 October)
Luke 10:23-37	Trinity 13
Luke 11:14-28	Lent 3
Luke 14:1-11	Trinity 17
Luke 14:16-24	Trinity 2
Luke 15:1-10	Trinity 3
Luke 16:1-9	Trinity 9
Luke 16:19-31	Trinity 1
Luke 17:11-19	Trinity 14
Luke 18:9-14	Trinity 11
Luke 18:31-43	Quinquagesima
Luke 19:41-47a	Trinity 10
Luke 21:25-33	Advent 2
Luke 22:1-71	Wednesday in Holy Week
Luke 22:24-30	St Bartholomew (24 August)
Luke 23:1-49	Maundy Thursday
Luke 24:13-35	Easter Monday
Luke 24:36-48	Easter Tuesday
John 1:1-14	Christmas (25 December)
John 1:19-28	Advent 4
John 2:1-11	Epiphany 2
John 3:1-15	Trinity
John 3:16-21	Whitmonday
John 4:46-54	Trinity 21
John 6:1-14	Lent 4
John 6:5-14	Trinity 25
John 8:46-59a	Lent 5
John 10:1-10	Whittuesday
John 10:11-16	Easter 2
John 14:1-14	St Philip and St James (1 May)
John 14:15-31	Whitsun (Pentecost)
John 15:1-11	St Mark (25 April)
John 15:12-16	St Barnabas (11 June)
John 15:17-27	St Simon and St Jude (28 October)
John 15:26-16:4a	Ascension
John 16:5-14	Easter 4
John 16:16-22	Easter 3
John 16:23-33	Easter 1

John 19:1-37	Good Friday
John 20:1-10	Easter
John 20:19-23	Easter 5
John 20:24-31	St Thomas (21 December)
John 21:19-25	St John the Evangelist (27 December)

Chapter 5

The Lord's Supper

What's in a Name?

No part of Anglican liturgy has been as controversial as the doctrine and practice of the Lord's Supper, also known as Holy Communion, the Eucharist or the Mass. The range of names given to it often indicates the presence of a particular theological position, although it is not always clear whether that has been consciously adopted by the user or simply taken over from an inherited tradition. The 1549 Book of Common Prayer introduced it as: 'The Supper of the Lord, and the Holy Communion, commonly called the Mass'. In 1552 this was altered to: 'The Order for the Administration of the Lord's Supper, or Holy Communion', in order to downplay any connection with the pre-Reformation doctrine of the sacrament.

The word 'Eucharist' has long been known in specialist theological circles but until recently it was not widely used and is still unfamiliar to most people who are not professional theologians. 'Eucharist' occurs in Early Church writings but is not found in the New Testament, at least not with reference to the Supper. Its basic meaning is 'thanksgiving' and it is used of a particular form of prayer in 1 Timothy 2:1. Thanksgiving is an important introductory part of the Lord's Supper, and so the term 'Eucharist' may be understood as putting an emphasis on a particular aspect of the rite rather than on the service as a whole. It has sometimes been justified by claiming that it is a 'neutral' term, theologically speaking, and does not imply one particular theological tradition. That may be true but its exotic sound in English helps to ensure that few people understand what it means. It has a technical, academic feel to it that will probably ensure that it will never catch on more widely, even though it is now the standard word used by those who are well versed in liturgical theology.

For this *Companion* we have preferred the title of Lord's Supper, derived from 1 Corinthians 11:20, because it was the earliest term in common use. The Church Fathers employed it as a matter of course, and in the middle ages it was frequently referred to by its Latin name, *coena Domini*. It became less common with the development of sacramental theology after the twelfth century, perhaps because it emphasises the corporate nature of the rite over against individual Communion, and by the sixteenth century it had become relatively rare, although it could still be found in liturgical books and the like. In modern times Anglicans have generally preferred other designations for the Supper; but the ancient term still figures in written texts and is often the one preferred by other Protestant churches.

In Anglican circles the Supper is better known as Holy Communion, a term derived from 1 Corinthians 10:16-17. The 1548 interim rite had been titled 'The Order for the Communion' and was meant to be inserted into the existing Sarum rite and, from there, the expression 'Holy Communion' made its first appearance in 1549. As with the interim rite, it referred specifically to the high point of the service, which was the reception of the consecrated elements of bread and wine, and not to the service as a whole, which was the Lord's Supper. The two terms were conflated in 1552 and have remained so ever since. 'Holy Communion' emphasises the partaking of Christ and the resulting fellowship that believers have with one another in him, and it helps us focus on what the Lord's Supper is chiefly about.

The service can also be called the Breaking of Bread, as it was in the New Testament (Acts 2:42; 20:7), and this is the term preferred by the Plymouth Brethren, who were among the first to revive the practice of frequent Communion in the early nineteenth century, but it suffers from its ambiguity. Every meal is a 'breaking of bread' and the expression is sometimes used in that sense, making it less distinctive and therefore less useful as a description of the Lord's Supper.

In a different category is the word 'Mass', which was included in the 1549 prayer book because of its familiarity to most people but which has no justification either historically or theologically. It is unknown in the Eastern Churches, for the simple reason that it is a corruption of a Latin word and was therefore confined to the West. It derives from the dismissal at the end of the Latin service: *Ite, ecclesia missa est* ('Go, the Church is dismissed'). People who did not understand Latin heard *missa* ('dismissed') and attached the word to the service itself, even though it has nothing to do with it. It has, however, come to be associated with the theology of transubstantiation and priestly sacrifice that characterised the late medieval theology of the rite, and it is in that sense that its use has been perpetuated. Anglicans who use the term are invariably Anglo-Catholics who intend to proclaim that medieval theology, modified but not substantially altered by subsequent developments in the Roman Catholic Church. However, it must be stressed that it has no official sanction from any Anglican body and it should not be used – on both historical and theological grounds.

In popular speech, the Lord's Supper is often called simply the 'Sacrament' because it is the one that is most frequently used by Christians generally but, of course, that is ambiguous and misleading. Baptism is also a sacrament – indeed, the word 'sacrament' was applied to it centuries before it was used to describe the Supper – and in medieval theology there were five more sacraments that the Reformed Churches have reclassified or abandoned. No doubt the word will continue to be used in this sense in popular speech and its meaning will be understood, but its inaccuracy is obvious and it should be avoided as much as possible.

Basic Principles

The Lord's Supper traces its origin to the Last Supper that Jesus had with his disciples, which is recorded both in the Synoptic Gospels and in Paul's letters.[1] Paul's testimony is of particular importance because it is the earliest written record, and because it is evidence that the Supper was regularly repeated as a central act of Christian worship from the beginning. Paul does not say so expressly, but it is obvious from the context that the celebrant cannot have been Jesus himself, as it was in the Gospel accounts of the Last Supper. In fact, although the Apostle gives a detailed account of the proceedings, much of which has been incorporated into our liturgy, he never mentions the celebrant at all. Somebody must have presided and maintained order in the congregation, which was one of Paul's main reasons for writing in the first place, but who that was and how he was chosen we do not know.

It is important to say this because much of the discussion that has surrounded the Lord's Supper since medieval times has concerned matters that are not recorded in Scripture. An array of devotional

---

1. Matthew 26:26-29; Mark 14:22-25; Luke 22:19-20; 1 Corinthians 11:23-26.

practices grew up around the Supper which the Reformers either abolished or relegated to a secondary status, and the legitimacy of their continued existence (or revival) has long been one of the major points of controversy over the Lord's Supper within the Anglican world. To appreciate the questions involved we must look at the different parts of the Supper individually.

First come **the materials used for the celebration**, which are bread and wine. At the Last Supper the bread would have been unleavened, as was the Jewish custom at Passover, but it was never stated that this was necessary for the celebration to be valid. In medieval times the Eastern (Greek) Churches used ordinary leavened bread but the Western (Latin) Churches preferred unleavened ('azymes'). This became a matter of controversy, the Greeks (unfairly) criticising the Latins for what they saw as a Judaising practice. The question was finally resolved at the Council of Florence in 1439, when it was decreed that it was a matter of indifference and that either form of bread may be used.[2] This is the official view of every major Church today, including the Anglican Communion. As for the wine, it may have been diluted with water at the Last Supper, since that was a very common practice in ancient times, but, if so, no theological significance can be attached to it. Similarly, it is not necessary for the 'wine' to be fermented; non-alcoholic grape juice can always be used and, in some circumstances, it may be preferable to do so.[3]

What there is no authorisation for is the substitution of other forms of food and drink. Jesus chose bread and wine, partly because they were already in use at Passover and partly because they were visible symbols of his body and blood. To replace them with other things, like doughnuts and coffee for example, may not be absolutely forbidden, and perhaps in exceptional circumstances, where bread and wine cannot be obtained, other kinds of food and drink may have to be used instead, but, if there is no valid reason for changing them, the traditional substances ought

---

2. Session 6 of the Council of Florence, 6 July 1439. The words are: '*Item, in azymo sive fermentato pane triticeo, corpus Christi veraciter confici, sacerdotesque in altero ipsum Domini corpus conficere debere, unumquemque scilicet iuxta suae ecclesiae sive occidentalis sive orientalis consuetudinem.*' ('Likewise, whether in unleavened or in leavened wheat bread, the body of Christ is truly confected, and priests must confect the very body of Christ in either [of them], each one according to the custom of his Church, whether Western or Eastern.')

3. As when giving Communion to an alcoholic, for example.

to be retained. They are true to both Scripture and tradition, as well as being appropriate symbols of what they represent.

Next comes **the blessing or thanksgiving for the bread and wine**. It is clearly stated in all four accounts of the Last Supper that Jesus 'blessed' ('gave thanks' for) the food and drink before giving them to his disciples. An action of this kind was common in Jewish circles and does not imply any kind of transformation in the elements themselves. Exactly the same thing happened when Jesus 'blessed' the loaves and fishes that he distributed to the 5,000 and, although they were miraculously multiplied, there is no indication that they ceased be what they were in material terms.[4] The purpose of 'consecration', as this act is called, is not to change the food into something else, nor to add any special spiritual power to it, but to set it apart for a particular purpose. The bread and wine remain what they were before but they are used to represent something beyond themselves.

Third, Jesus told his disciples that **the bread was his body and that the cup was the new covenant sealed in his blood**. It is obvious that these words cannot be taken literally, since the human body and blood of Jesus were still fully intact at the Last Supper. The emphasis is entirely on the upcoming sacrifice that Jesus would make on the Cross, when his body would be broken and his blood poured out for the salvation of the world. The Last Supper prefigured that but it did not accomplish the work of atonement on the Cross, which still lay in the future. As many have pointed out, if the Last Supper had been efficacious for the redemption of the world, the Crucifixion would have been unnecessary, which was not the case.

Lastly, Jesus told his disciples to **repeat the Supper in remembrance of him**. Here the analogy with Passover is helpful in understanding what he meant. Jewish people do not literally escape from Egypt every year when they celebrate the feast. They remember what God did for them in the past and pledge themselves to love and obey the God who delivered them at that time. Similarly, Christians do not repeat the death of Christ, but remember what he did for us on the Cross and pledge ourselves to the new covenant that he has established with his people. The Lord's Supper is not a re-enactment of Christ's sacrificial death but a memorial of it that is intended to unite us more firmly to him.

Jesus told his disciples that, whenever they celebrated his atoning death, they would be renewing their covenant with him, but there is no indication as to how often that should happen. The Jewish Passover

---

4. Luke 9:16.

was celebrated once a year, which we may assume would have been the minimum envisaged by Jesus, though that is nowhere specified. Over the years, Christian practice has varied enormously. The Church of England traditionally expected its members to communicate at least three times a year, at Christmas, Easter and Whitsun (Pentecost) and the Church of Scotland developed a pattern of seasonal Communion, preceded by a week of preparation, every three months. The Roman Catholic and Eastern Orthodox Churches have always celebrated the Eucharist much more often than that but, in the East, in particular, regular communicants have been relatively few. Many people attend services at which the opportunity to communicate is given but they do not do so. Roman Catholics are generally much better at that than most others are, and a devout few communicate daily. Other Churches have a wide variety of practice that defies easy categorisation but it is fair to say that, thanks to the modern liturgical movement, Communion services are more frequent than they used to be and are more widely accepted as the 'norm' for Sunday worship.

That is certainly true of the Anglican world and marks a significant departure from what was expected in the seventeenth century. In many parishes today weekly Communion is the principal service, though the result has been a corresponding decline in preparation, for which the 1662 prayer book makes ample provision. 'Familiarity breeds contempt', as the saying goes, and it must be feared that, for many, participation in the weekly Eucharist has become a ritual to which little thought is given. Whether we have reached the point where a case can be made for having fewer Communion services, rather than more, is hard to say, but it is at least possible that the pendulum will someday swing in the opposite direction to the one we have seen since the 1960s.

Historical Developments

The 1662 Book of Common Prayer did not emerge in a historical vacuum. The stated intention of the Reformers was to return to the beliefs and practices of the New Testament Church, which they were convinced had been overlaid and corrupted in the course of time. The difference between them and the remaining Roman Catholics was not over the question of whether the Church had developed its teaching further than is apparent in the apostolic writings – everybody agreed about that – but whether that development was legitimate. In the sixteenth century there were many on the Roman side who appealed to 'tradition', by which they meant unwritten customs that had supposedly been handed down from the apostles but had not been recorded in Scripture. That argument was hard to sustain but it was also hard to deny because of lack of sufficient evidence. The Early Church Fathers did not write extensively on the Lord's Supper and what little they did say is hard to interpret within the categories of later thought. For example, Cyril of Jerusalem (fourth century) called the Supper a *mystērion* of faith, using a New Testament term but applying it in a more restricted sense. Was the Supper itself the *mystērion* or did it bear witness to something else – the work of the Holy Spirit in the heart and mind of the believer?

Cyril saw no need to make a hard and fast distinction between these things because he lived at a time when there was still an effective discipline that prevented those who had not been baptised from coming to the Lord's Table. This discipline, the memory of which is preserved in Eastern liturgies to this day as 'the departure of the catechumens', was still a real thing in Cyril's time and had not been reduced to the formality that it is today. It was always possible for someone to eat and drink the Supper unworthily, a circumstance that the Apostle Paul had foreseen and condemned.[5] Paul did not say that the consecrated elements in the Supper had the power to harm those who abused them but in later times that view came to be held by many, even though it was never officially decreed as orthodox doctrine. The reason for that was that the elements were called 'the drug of immortality' (*pharmakon tēs athanasias*), a rhetorical flourish that was meant to be understood in spiritual terms but that could easily be applied by the ignorant and unwary to material ones as well. When that happened, it was inevitable that the consecration of the bread and wine would come to be seen as a transformation of their nature, though it would be many centuries before anyone attempted to explain what that transformation was.

Nature and Grace

The Eastern Churches never reached that point but things were different in the medieval West. Beginning in the twelfth century, Latin theologians developed a complex philosophy of the relationship between matter and spirit, or to use their terminology, between 'nature' and 'grace', that did not do justice to the biblical doctrine of creation. It was this fundamental dichotomy that the Reformers challenged and that explains why the 1662 Book of Common Prayer says what it does. To them, 'nature' meant the material order as it now exists, after the

---

5. 1 Corinthians 11:27-29.

fall of mankind. The original goodness of creation had been marred by sin and the material world no longer reflected the Glory of God in the way that it should have done. It must, of course, be understood that this belief, wrong as it was, was a big improvement on what most pagans had imagined. To the ancient Greeks, matter was essentially evil and those who were caught up in it inevitably sinned because they could not escape from the consequences. The aim of their enlightened philosophy was to get as far away from matter as possible – hence the advocacy of such world-denying disciplines as fasting and celibacy. Something of this legacy survived in the conscience of the medieval Church, with the important difference that it was no longer believed that matter was intrinsically evil. It had fallen into sin, but it could be redeemed, and the message of the incarnation of Christ was that it had been – in him. The Incarnation was the model and the first fruits of the new creation which God was working out in His Church – as the body of Christ and therefore an extension of the Incarnation – and that individual Christians were striving to obtain.

What differentiated the incarnate flesh of Jesus Christ from ordinary humanity was 'grace'. This, it was claimed, had been given to the Virgin Mary, either by the angel Gabriel when he told her that she would become the mother of the Messiah (Christ) or earlier. Gabriel's words to her: 'Hail Mary, full of grace' were interpreted to mean that she was full of the redeeming substance called 'grace' and this is still the teaching of traditional Catholic theology.[6] Grace was thought of as a spiritual substance that was added to nature in order to perfect it. Thus, Jesus could have a genuine human body like that of other people, but it was one that had been perfected by the grace given to his mother before he was conceived in her womb by the Holy Spirit. In Roman Catholic theology it is therefore incorrect to say that the incarnate Christ had an imperfect human nature inherited from his mother and a perfect spiritual nature given to him by the Spirit, because his human nature had been perfected by the spiritual grace given to his mother.

The sixteenth-century Reformers rejected this way of thinking.[7] To them, nature was what God had made it and its character did not

---

6. Luke 1:28.

7. It should also be said that, for them, the witness of the Early Church was problematic, because medieval forgeries had attributed many later doctrines to men like Augustine, who knew nothing of them. Scholarly research has since demonstrated this, and we now know that many texts that Catholics of the sixteenth century cited in defence of their position

change. Adam and Eve had fallen away from God not because of some natural inadequacy but because of their disobedience to His Word, as this had been given to them in the creation mandate. By transgressing the limits set to their power, our first parents rebelled against God and lost the intimacy which they had previously enjoyed (and were meant to enjoy) with Him. God responded to their rebellion by reaching out to them and promising that He would provide a way back into His favour. That way was revealed in progressive steps until the coming of Christ, when the fullness of the divine plan was finally set out in his teaching and in the saving acts of his atoning death and resurrection. Christ took his atoning sacrifice back to heaven, where he now sits at his Father's right hand, pleading for us to be made acceptable in his sight. This truth is revealed to us in the Holy Scriptures and sealed in us by the rites of baptism and the Lord's Supper, conventionally (if somewhat inaccurately) called 'sacraments'. These sacraments are only meaningful (and effective) if they are given and received in faith, which is itself a gift of the Holy Spirit whom the Father has sent to dwell in our hearts.[8]

Grace is not an objectively existing thing that can be applied to 'nature' like a kind of ointment, or like icing on a cake. It is the favour shown by God to those who believe in Him and is therefore the description of a relationship that cannot be quantified. It is for that reason that the believer who is justified by faith is justified completely, even though he is still a sinner. The notion that such a person would need successive doses of 'grace' in order to attain spiritual perfection is alien to such a concept. So, of course, is the idea that 'sainthood' is the achievement of spiritual perfection and therefore reserved to an elite few. In the Christian Church, every believer is a saint because he has been accepted by God as His child, not because he has somehow overcome sin in his life. A Christian is a justified sinner (*simul iustus et peccator*), not a perfect person, and, although we must certainly rely on the power of God in order to live a life pleasing to Him, we can never alter the sinful state in which we have been called and justified, and certainly not by participation in the sacraments or other church activities.

---

were not authentic, but neither they nor the Reformers knew that. We must therefore tread carefully when we examine the arguments of their time and try to interpret them correctly, even if it must sometimes appear that the Reformers themselves were using language whose implications they did not fully appreciate.

8. Galatians 4:6.

Modern readers who fail to understand this fundamental shift in theological thought are liable to be misled into a spurious traditionalism, which seeks to revive medieval concepts and impose them on Anglican liturgy as if nothing really changed at the Reformation. It is a false perception that must be resisted, and nowhere more so than in the Lord's Supper.[9] Frequent Communion cannot by itself bring a believer closer to God, because it is not a medicine designed for that purpose.

All Christians agree that, when Christ ascended into heaven, he took his incarnate nature with him. Seated at the right hand of his Father, he now reigns over the world in the perfection of that glorified incarnation. However, that affirmation raises a host of other questions that cry out for answers. The divine nature is infinite; but human nature is not. Does the ascended Christ dwell in a particular place with a defined (and therefore limited) human nature, or has that human nature been absorbed into the divine, so that it too is infinite? If that is the case, what are the implications for the Lord's Supper, in which Jesus took bread and wine and called them his body and blood? Obviously, they were not extensions of his human body in the purely material sense, but could they be absorbed into the Incarnation by an act of grace that transcended the limitations of time and space? Such an interpretation would have been difficult with respect to the Last Supper but, after the ascension of Christ, it became much more plausible. If his incarnate body had been absorbed into the divine, it could be argued that wherever he is present his glorified body is present with him. Thus, it could be claimed that the consecrated bread and wine of the Supper was the real presence (in objective terms) of Christ in the world, because by the grace of God the material elements had been transformed into his body and blood.

Transubstantiation

This was the philosophical understanding that underlay the development of what came to be called the doctrine of transubstantiation. According to the ancient Greek philosopher Aristotle (or the tradition that had come down under his name) all matter could be analysed in terms of substance and accidents. Thus, bread is a substance but it appears in many different shapes and sizes. These variables are the 'accidents' which can (and do) change without altering the underlying substance of the bread. What was supposed to happen in transubstantiation, however,

---

9. See N. Scotland, *The Supper: Cranmer and Communion* (London: Latimer Trust, 2013).

was that the substance was changed without disturbing the accidents. In other words, if a piece of bread was white and tasted a certain way before being consecrated, it would still be white and have the same taste afterwards, but now it would have become Christ's body and would no longer be bread in the material sense.

What was the point of this? Transubstantiation by itself served no purpose. To be meaningful, it had to be applied to the life of the believer and this is what supposedly took place in the Lord's Supper. The person who consumed the transubstantiated elements was consuming Christ, who was made present to them by the transforming power of grace. It was assumed that the grace that had transformed the bread would also transform the believer, giving him the first fruits of eternal life. The ancient language of 'mystery' could now be redeployed to refer to this 'miracle of the altar' as it came to be known, which was sealed to the believer as a sacrament.

The doctrine of transubstantiation was articulated in the first canon of the fourth Lateran Council in 1215, which decreed:

> There is one universal Church of the faithful, outside which there is absolutely no salvation, in which there is the same priest and sacrifice, Jesus Christ, whose body and blood are truly contained in the sacrament of the altar under the forms of bread and wine, the bread being transubstantiated by divine power into the body and the wine into the blood, so that to realise the mystery of unity we may receive of him that which he has received of us.[10]

The canon recognises that Jesus Christ is the priest and sacrifice, but it goes on to claim that the sacramental action by which bread and wine are transformed into his body and blood are intimately connected with his atonement on the Cross. The words used to expound this are hard to interpret, but the impression is given that Christ somehow receives a sacrifice from us which makes it possible for us to receive his sacrifice

---

10. The Latin original reads: '*Una vero est fidelium universalis ecclesia, extra quam nullus omnino salvatur, in qua idem ipse sacerdos et sacrificium Iesus Christus, cuius corpus et sanguis in sacramento altaris sub speciebus panis et vini veraciter continentur, transubstantiatis pane in corpus et vino in sanguinem potestate divina, ut ad perficiendum mysterium unitatis accipiamus ipsi de suo, quod accipit ipse de nostro.*'

and achieve the spiritual unity which the Supper is meant to produce. The canon then goes on to add:

> And this sacrament no one can effect except the priest who has been duly ordained in accordance with the keys of the Church, which Jesus Christ gave to the apostles and their successors.[11]

Quite apart from the dubious assertion that Jesus Christ gave his apostles and their successors the power to effect this transubstantiation, there is no indication in the New Testament that the word *sacerdos* ('priest') was ever used of a Christian minister.[12] This idea emerged from a typological reading of the Old Testament, according to which the sacrifices of the priests in the Temple prefigured not only the sacrifice of Christ on the Cross but also the sacramental action of properly ordained Christian ministers, who could then be called 'priests' (*sacerdotes*) and whose action in the Supper could be called a 'sacrifice' made on an 'altar'. Typology of this kind had been in existence for several centuries, so its codification in 1215 would not have struck many people as novel, but it has no scriptural basis and, in fact, compromises the uniqueness of Christ's atoning death. Defenders of transubstantiation have always denied this, of course, and claimed that the 'sacrifice of the altar' is no more than a re-presentation of Christ's one eternal sacrifice. However, few people could be expected to understand such subtleties. For the vast majority of worshippers, the celebrant performed a miracle during the consecration and it was this that shaped their devotion more than anything else.

The liturgical consequences were not slow to develop. Much of the consecration was said by the priest *sotto voce* – in a mumble or even in complete silence – so that no one but him could hear what he was saying. Furthermore, he did most of this with his back to the people, so that they could not see what was going on either. It was only when the consecration was complete that he would raise the transubstantiated elements over his head in what became known as 'the elevation of the host', an action that was meant to evoke the worship of those

---

11. The Latin original reads: '*Et hoc utique sacramentum nemo potest conficere, nisi sacerdos, qui fuerit rite ordinatus secundum claves ecclesiae, quas ipse concessit apostolis et eorum successoribus.*'
12. For a full discussion of this, see Chapter 9 on the Ordinal under the section 'The Ordering of Priests'.

in attendance. That only a 'priest' could be the celebrant of this rite was a decision taken by the Church, not a requirement of the Gospel. Presbyters or 'priests' were given the ability to perform the miracle of the altar by the grace that was conferred on them at their ordination. This was obviously something more than was given to ordinary Christians (or even to deacons) and priests were now set apart from the rest of the Church by the requirement of celibacy, which was instituted at the first Lateran Council in 1123. Celibacy had originated in monasticism. It had been imposed on bishops at the Council *in Trullo* held at Constantinople in the winter of 691-92 and it applied in both East and West. The motive seems to have been to prevent the heads of the Church from creating dynasties along the lines of secular rulers. However, the extension of the principle to priests (but not to deacons) in the Western Church went beyond that. A priest was now a person imbued with divine power in a way that was not true of others and his status was elevated accordingly.

Once transubstantiation and the powers of the priesthood were firmly set in place, there developed a range of subsidiary devotions that came to characterise the late medieval Church. Priests could (and often did) consecrate bread and wine for their own benefit, without having to share it with others – the so-called 'private Mass'. They could also consecrate bread and wine and reserve it for other occasions. This was often done by placing the reserved sacrament, as it was called, in a special receptacle that (following Old Testament typology) was called the 'tabernacle', and worshippers were able to adore it in a side chapel of the Church, whether anyone else was there or not. This reserved sacrament could also be paraded around the streets for the general adoration of passers-by, and an entire feast, Corpus Christi ('body of Christ'), emerged for precisely that reason. It was even possible to steal the consecrated elements and use them for occult purposes – the infamous 'black masses'– which witches and sorcerers were regularly accused of celebrating.

Most of these devotional practices continue to exist in the Roman Catholic Church today, which is why many Anglo-Catholics have wanted to reintroduce them into the Anglican Communion, although few people would now fall into the grosser superstitions that were common in medieval times and that were not unknown in Roman Catholic circles much more recently. For example, it is doubtful how many priests nowadays would get down on their knees and lick up any consecrated wine that they happened to spill on the floor! It is also hard to imagine modern theologians of any kind who would debate whether a mouse who had consumed consecrated bread had eaten the body of

Christ, though that question was certainly asked – and answered in different ways – by their medieval forbears.

Another development that occurred in the later middle ages was the withdrawal of the cup from the laity. Communion in one kind only was never officially introduced and its origin is unclear. Some have thought that it was originally a hygienic measure to combat the bubonic plague, and that may be correct, but nobody can say for sure. What is certain is that it spread across the Church and was resisted in Bohemia, where many local clergy insisted that Communion should be in each kind (*sub utraque specie*), from which they came to be known as Utraquists. It was only when this objection was raised that the official Church came down on the side of Communion in one kind only, arguing that, since a body contains blood, the recipient of the consecrated bread also received the blood of Christ. At the same time, the celebrant continued to drink of the cup and it was claimed that he did this on behalf of the people. In this way, the priest became a mediator between God and man, acting out the role of Christ before the congregation. Matters became particularly complicated when a leading Bohemian theologian, Jan Hus (*c.* 1372-1415) was condemned and put to death, at least partly for his Utraquist views. That led to a schism in the Bohemian Church that was never healed and kept the Utraquist question alive. The English Reformers did not have much to say about it, but they obviously sided with the Utraquists and reintroduced Communion in both kinds as a matter of course as soon as they could.[13]

Transubstantiation was at the root of everything else that followed in liturgical practice and, when it was repudiated, the rest of the sacramental edifice constructed on it fell like a house of cards. Of the rejection of transubstantiation by the English Reformers there can be no doubt. Article 28 of the Articles of Religion says quite plainly:

> Transubstantiation (or the change of the substance of bread and wine) in the Supper of the Lord, cannot be proved by Holy Writ; but is repugnant to the plain words of Scripture, overthroweth the nature of a Sacrament, and hath given occasion to many superstitions.

It is important to note that transubstantiation is not merely absent from the Bible; it contradicts its teaching. The Reformers were not disposing of a tradition that had grown up apart from the New Testament but

---

13. See Article 30 of the Articles of Religion in the Book of Common Prayer.

rooting out a teaching that denied it. More than that, the doctrine flouted the basic rule of sacramental theology, which was that material objects were used as signs and seals of spiritual realities, without ever becoming those realities themselves. The sign bears witness to the reality it signifies but is no substitute for it, because matter cannot take the place of spirit, nor can 'nature' be perfected by 'grace'.

The Reformation

It is necessary to rehearse this history in order to understand the Lord's Supper as it is laid out for us, not only in the 1662 Book of Common Prayer, but in all Anglican rites going back to 1549, and even in the interim rite published the year before that. Thomas Cranmer and his associates were dealing not just with the doctrine of transubstantiation but with an entire range of devotional habits and practices that had grown up around it. To understand what happened to the liturgy of the Lord's Supper at the time of the Reformation, we must begin with the doctrinal principles on which the medieval rites had rested and been developed. As far as the Church's worship was concerned, the English Reformers believed that it had been corrupted by false doctrine. What they wanted to do was to scrape that doctrine away and restore what they believed had been the pure, unadulterated worship of the early Christians. This led them to seek out early examples of liturgy, not least in the Eastern Churches, where the effects of transubstantiation and its consequences had not been felt. They were not particularly successful in their quest, and modern research has shown that there never was a 'pure' liturgy of the kind they sought to discover, but they were able to show that the theological principles on which the medieval rites had been constructed did not go back to ancient times and could be altered in the light of what could be shown to have been authentic apostolic teaching.

Some things, like the elevation of the host, depended for their significance entirely on transubstantiation and therefore had to be removed from the liturgy. Other things, like kneeling to receive the elements, had been misconstrued as worship of the consecrated bread, but were not necessarily wrong in themselves. What to do about them divided opinion. Some believed that it was unnecessary to prune practices that had merely been misunderstood, whereas others thought that it was better to be safe than sorry. Kneeling might not be wrong in itself but it was not essential to the sacrament and, if some people were misconstruing it, then it was better to do away with it. On the whole, it was the conservatives who gained the upper hand in controversies of this kind, with the result that Anglican worship retained more of the traditional medieval practices than it might otherwise have done. Nevertheless, it must be admitted that the radicals were not entirely wrong. There was a danger that traditionalists would fail to perceive the new doctrinal emphases that the Reformed liturgies were meant to express and that their thought patterns would gravitate towards what they were already familiar with. Human nature is resistant to change, and nowhere more so than in matters of faith and religion, and many of the Reformers feared that their doctrines would be lost or compromised by the weight of tradition. Greater sympathy with that viewpoint on the part of the authorities might have avoided the upheavals associated with so-called 'puritanism', and it must be admitted that the dogged insistence on certain ritual practices that was to characterise upholders of the establishment in 1662 (and later) was a major cause of division in the Church which could (and should) have been avoided. At the same time, the points of conformity which the bishops were to insist on were not essential to the faith and did not change anything fundamental in the Reformation settlement. The basic structure and doctrine of the Reformation was set in 1549 and confirmed by all subsequent revisions of the prayer book. Whatever appearances might suggest to the contrary, there would be no going back to the medieval world view.

Another important consideration in the Reformers' minds was intelligibility and communication. This comes out most obviously in the translations of medieval texts from Latin into English, but it does not stop there. As the rubrics indicate, there was considerable emphasis placed on the comportment of the minister, who was obliged to position himself in a way that the congregation could see him and to speak in a voice that could be heard. What that would mean in practice might vary from place to place but the principle remained the same. It was also true that no part of the service could be conducted by the minister *sotto voce*; everything had to be clearly articulated so that all those present might hear. That led to a widespread abandonment of those parts of the pre-Reformation rite that were inaudible to the communicants, a move that greatly altered the feel of the service as a whole.

These changes occurred in two stages (1549 and 1552) and there has been considerable disagreement about whether that was deliberately planned in advance or not. Modern scholars have generally concluded that Archbishop Cranmer never intended 1549 to be permanent and that he was already thinking in terms of what became 1552, although, of course, the precise contours of the latter could not have been predicted at the outset. It is possible that the 1552 revision went further than was originally envisaged, in order to make it impossible for conservatives to read it in a pre-Reformation way (as some did with 1549), but the general drift was unmistakable from the beginning and it has even been suggested that Cranmer was planning a second revision that was cut short by the death of King Edward VI in 1553. The 1662 prayer book is sometimes presented as a 'retreat' from 1552 towards the more conservative 1549 version but this is more apparent in the rubrics than anywhere else and does not really affect the text as a whole. What we have in the 1662 book is essentially a version of 1552, the theological emphasis of which is clearly very different from what had prevailed before 1549, however many elements of earlier liturgies had been retained and recycled in the process. The only real question is where the 1549 prayer book should be placed along the spectrum of development that led to 1662. Is it closer to pre-Reformation models, or to what came later? Opinions differ about this but it is fair to say that the general consensus of disinterested scholarship is that there was a real shift from the medieval texts to the 1549 prayer book and that what came later was no more than a logical working through of what had already been stated in principle.

To appreciate what this means in practice, the following comparative table gives the Sarum rite (pre-1549) on the left, 1549 in the middle and the 1552 revision on the right. The items in italics were added to the 1552 prayer book (already slightly revised in 1559 and in 1604) in 1662; those in bold type were originally introduced in the 1548 Communion order.

The Communion office can be logically subdivided into three parts, the Ante-Communion, the Communion and the Post-Communion. At one time it was common for services of Morning Prayer to go on to the Ante-Communion when no celebrant was available but this rarely (if ever) happens now and was not intended when the different services were first composed.

The Ante-Communion

Sarum	1549	1552
Private preparation with:	Introit Lord's Prayer	Lord's Prayer
Collect Antiphons etc.	Collect	Collect

---

14. Put before the Sermon in 1662.
15. Not mentioned before 1662.
16. Placed before Exhortation C in 1662.

Sarum	1549	1552
Lord's PrayerHail Mary etc.		
Introit	Kyrie	
Clergy confession		
Censing, Kyrie etc.		
Gloria	Gloria	
		Ten Commandments
Collect for the day	Collects for the king	Collects for the king
	Collect for the day	Collect for the day
Epistle	Epistle	Epistle
Gradual		
Gospel	Gospel	Gospel
Nicene Creed	Nicene Creed	Nicene Creed
	Sermon	Sermon
		Notices[399]
		Offertory sentences
		Placing of the elements[400]
		Prayer for the Church
	Exhortation A	**Exhortation C**
	Exhortation B	Exhortation B[401]
		Exhortation A
Oblation of the elements		
Censing of the elements		
Handwashing		
Secret prayers		

The Communion

		Invitation
		Confession
		Absolution
		Comfortable Words
Sursum corda	Sursum corda	Sursum corda
Preface	Prefaces	Prefaces
Sanctus	Sanctus	Sanctus
Prayer for the Church	Prayer for the	
Humble access	Church	
Consecration	Consecration	Consecration
	Thanksgiving	

---

17. The 1552 words of administration were completely different from those of 1549; but both were combined in 1559 and retained as such in 1662.

		Invitation
		Confession
		Absolution
		Comfortable Words
Lord's Prayer	Lord's Prayer	
	Versicles	
	Agnus Dei (said)	
	Invitation	
	Confession	
	Absolution	
	Comfortable words	
	Humble access	
	Administration	**Administration**[402]
Agnus Dei	Agnus Dei (sung)	
		Commixture
		The Peace
		Priest's reception
		Ablutions
		Collects

The Post-Communion

	Sentences	
	Versicles	Lord's Prayer
		Thanksgiving
		(Oblation)
		Second thanksgiving
		Gloria
	Blessing	Blessing
		Surplus consumed[403]
Dismissal		
Private prayer		
Last Gospel		

The Sarum rite was more detailed than this table indicates, so that the differences between it and 1549 were actually somewhat greater than appears here. The 1549 prayer book retains a few elements of Sarum that were dropped in 1552 but the most significant alteration was in the position of the items that were introduced in 1548 in order to supplement Sarum. Once the 1549 liturgy was in place, these items could

---

18. Not included in 1552.

be moved and to some extent broken up, as they were in 1552. Concealed in this table is the fact that the consecration of 1552/1662 is quite different in character from that of 1549 and Sarum. The word 'consecration' does not appear either in 1549 or in 1552, where it is more accurate to speak of the words of institution. The traditional term was reintroduced in 1662 but the words were left unchanged, so that what is now regarded as the consecration is not a holdover from 1549, still less from Sarum. It is here, more than anywhere, that controversy has developed in modern times, with liturgical 'experts' advocating a return to 1549 (or something like it) as being, in their view, more satisfactory or 'authentic'.

The Ante-Communion

The Preliminary Rubrics

In the 1662 prayer book the Ante-Communion is preceded by a number of rubrics. There were originally four of these but, following the passing of the Prayer Book (Miscellaneous Provisions) Measure in 1965 and in line with Canon B16 promulged in 1969, the second and third ones were replaced by a new rubric combining them both.[19]

The first rubric requires intending communicants to give notice to the curate (i.e. the officiant) at least sometime the day before. Before 1662 this was supposed to be done immediately before Morning Prayer, but the inconvenience of this was soon noticed and the Presbyterians at the Savoy Conference in 1661 asked for the change, which was granted. It was still very inconvenient, however, and is now entirely disregarded.

The second rubric originally read:

> And if any of those be an open and notorious evil liver, or have done any wrong to his neighbours by word or deed, so that the Congregation be thereby offended; the Curate having knowledge thereof, shall call him and advertise him, that in any wise he presume not to come to the Lord's Table, until he hath openly declared himself to have truly repented and amended his former naughty life, that the Congregation may thereby be satisfied, which before were offended; and that he hath recompensed the parties to whom he hath done wrong, or at least declare himself to be in full purpose so to do, as soon as he conveniently may.

---

19. This alteration does not automatically apply to the prayer book as used outside England, and the new International Version, for example, retains the original texts.

The third rubric originally read:

> The same order shall the Curate use with those betwixt whom he perceiveth malice and hatred to reign; not suffering them to be partakers of the Lord's Table, until he know them to be reconciled. And if one of the parties so at variance be content to forgive from the bottom of his heart all that the other hath trespassed against him, and to make amends for that he himself hath offended; and the other party will not be persuaded to a godly unity, but remain still in his frowardness and malice: the Minister in that case ought to admit the penitent person to the Holy Communion, and not him that is obstinate. Provided that any Minister so repelling any, as is specified in this, or the next precedent Paragraph of this Rubric, shall be obliged to give an account of the same to the Ordinary within fourteen days after at the farthest. And the Ordinary shall proceed against the offending person according to the Canon.

The revised rubric, replacing the previous two, reads:

> If a Minister be persuaded that any person who presents himself to be a partaker of the Holy Communion ought not to be admitted thereunto by reason of malicious and open sin without repentance, he shall give an account of the same to the Ordinary of the place, and therein obey his order and direction, but so as not to refuse the Sacrament to any person until in accordance with such order and direction he shall have called him and advertised him that in any wise he presume not to come to the Lord's Table; Provided that in case of grave and immediate scandal to the Congregation the Minister shall not admit such person, but shall give an account of the same to the Ordinary within seven days after at the latest and therein obey the order and direction given to him by the Ordinary; Provided also that before issuing his order and direction in relation to any such person the Ordinary shall afford to him an opportunity for interview.[20]

---

20. Prayer Book (Miscellaneous Provisions) Measure 1965 (no. 3) (5 August 1965), section 3.1, in *The Public General Acts and Church Assembly Measures 1965* (London: HMSO, 1966).

It seems clear that the New Testament motivation for this rubric comes from Matthew 5:23-24, where Jesus tells his disciples to be reconciled to each other before offering their gifts at the altar (of the Temple, presumably). However, it should be noted that the reconciliation was meant to be between the offended parties themselves, with no mediator or supervisor corresponding to the curate or minister.

The rubrics as they appear in the prayer book are dependent on a long tradition of church discipline that every generation tried to impose, with variable success. After the Restoration in 1660 it became much harder to enforce rubrics of this kind and they are effectively a dead letter nowadays, although they may be invoked in exceptional circumstances.

As it stands at the present time, the minister is expected to tell the Ordinary (almost always the bishop) of cases of notorious sin known to him and await instructions. In the meantime, he is not allowed to refuse Communion to the accused. However, if there is an open breach of order in the congregation, a minister may decide to refuse Communion to the guilty parties but, in that case, he must report the incident to the bishop within a week and await further instructions. In such cases, the bishop is expected to offer the accused an interview before pronouncing judgement, a process that could take a considerable amount of time.[21]

The dilemma here is that, while everyone agrees that some form of church discipline is desirable and that the Lord's Table should not be desecrated by immoral or unseemly behaviour, dealing with it effectively is virtually impossible, especially if legal means must be invoked to do so.

In sharp contrast to the other rubrics, it is the last one that has provoked the most controversy and that still retains some relevance today. The 1549 prayer book contained an elaborate description of the preparation required for the start of the service. It read as follows:

> Upon the day and at the time appointed for the ministration of the Holy Communion, the Priest that shall execute the holy mystery, shall put upon him the vesture appointed for that ministration, that is to say: a white Alb plain, with a vestment or Cope. And where there be many Priests, or Deacons, there so many shall be ready to help the Priest, in the ministration, as shall be requisite: And shall have upon them likewise the vestures appointed for their ministry, that is to say, Albs with

---

21. Linguists will note that the revised rubric combines an archaic style with modern expressions like 'an opportunity for interview' which would not have been used in the seventeenth century.

tunacles. Then shall the Clerks sing in English for the office, or Introit (as they call it) a Psalm appointed for that day.

This rubric placed its entire emphasis on the vesture of the celebrant and his assistants, with nothing said about the Table. The expectation was that there would be a sizable number of clergy accompanied by a choir, which may have been the case in cathedrals and in larger churches but which is unlikely to have been common in most parishes. The vestments themselves were the traditional ones, which soon raised objections among the more advanced Reformers, notably John Hooper (1495-1555), who was even imprisoned for a time because of it. At the same time, the rubric recognises that the service itself had changed considerably. It was to be sung in English and the opening text was to be a Psalm, not the traditional introit.

Real change came in 1552, when the rubric was replaced. The new directions were retained in the 1662 prayer book, with only a few minor changes. The words in grey were dropped (or altered) and those in **bold** type were added, as follows:

> The Table, having at the Communion time **having** a fair white linen cloth upon it, shall stand in the Body of the Church, or in the Chancel, where Morning Prayer and Evening Prayer be **are** appointed to be said. And the Priest standing at the north side of the Table shall say the Lord's Prayer, with the Collect following, **the people kneeling**.

The only significant change in 1662 is that the people are expected to kneel, a concession to traditionalist feeling but one that was without precedent. To appreciate this, we need only look at the rubric as it was modified in the Scottish prayer book of 1637:

> The **Holy** Table having at the Communion time **a Carpet, and** a fair white linen cloth upon it, **with other decent furniture, meet for the high mysteries there to be celebrated**, shall stand **at the uppermost part** of the Chancel or Church, where the **Presbyter** standing at the north side or end thereof, shall say the Lord's Prayer with this Collect following **for due preparation**.

The words in **bold** type were added, with 'presbyter' replacing 'priest' and the position of the Table in the church was considerably altered, but there was no mention of kneeling. In 1662 the repositioning of the Table was retained, but 'presbyter' reverted to 'priest' and the Table was no longer described as 'Holy', though that expression has often been used in the years since, especially by Evangelicals and others who wish to avoid the word 'altar'.

The provisions of the 1637 Scottish prayer book are of interest because they represent what was seen as high church belief and practice at the time of composition. It will be noticed that there is almost no overlap with 1549, which is often regarded as a main source of inspiration for the high church party. On the contrary, the use of the word 'presbyter' is a move in the opposite direction, since it avoids any possible confusion over the meaning of 'priest'. The main emphasis is on decorum, with a 'carpet' to be placed under the linen cloth, 'decent furniture' to be provided and 'due preparation' to be borne in mind. These phrases are ambiguous, and could be held to include such things as the provision of candles, but that is not stated.

More specific is the direction to move the Table to the place where the altar had once stood, making it easy for the unwary to confuse the two. The word 'altar' is studiously avoided in all Anglican prayer books because of its associations with sacrifice and, although it is often heard in popular speech, those who use it should be reminded that it is inaccurate and inappropriate in an Anglican service.

The one recollection of the 1549 prayer book is the use of the term 'high mysteries', which echoes the earlier 'holy mystery'. It is not clear why the plural should have been used instead of the singular, although 'high' is certainly an alternative to 'holy', with which it was often coupled in other contexts. It is true that the Greek word *mystērion* is now used as the equivalent of the Latin *sacramentum*, though this was not its original meaning and it is somewhat forced, especially when anglicised as it is here. The impression given to us is that there is something secret, even something supernatural, taking place, which is false. It is easy to see, however, how this expression could open the door for adopting a doctrine of transubstantiation, which Anglicans explicitly reject. It is, therefore, not surprising that this rubric excited opposition at the time and was not carried over into the 1662 text.

The one change that did survive was the repositioning of the Table, though that is not apparent from the rubric, which makes it hard to understand its original purpose. The word 'north' reflects the fact that most churches were built facing eastwards, so that the chancel stands at the 'east end'. That means that the 'north' is equivalent to the 'left'. In 1552 it was assumed that the table would be placed lengthwise in the nave, or in the chancel between the choir stalls, and that the celebrant would stand to the left so that people could see what he was doing. When the Table was put back into the old altar position, the rubric remained unchanged, so that the celebrant would stand at the left end of the Table.

This rather curious (and sometimes awkward) position was occasionally justified by saying that the true celebrant of the Supper was the Lord Jesus Christ, and that his earthly minister was assuming the role of a servant at his Table. It was a pseudo-theological explanation for something that was never so intended. However, it remained standard in Anglican churches until the Anglo-Catholic movement of the mid-nineteenth century and could be found in Evangelical churches for more than a century after that. It has still not entirely disappeared but is now fairly rare, even in conservative Evangelical parishes.

Anglo-Catholics introduced an eastward facing position for the celebrant, who then had his back to the congregation. This was in obvious imitation of Roman Catholic practice and contradicts the very essence of Anglican worship, which must be visible and accessible to the congregation.

There was great controversy over this in the late nineteenth and early twentieth centuries, with the standard scenario playing out over and over again. Opponents of the Anglo-Catholics would denounce Anglo-Catholic innovations and often secure legal judgements in their favour, but the Anglo-Catholics defied the law and eventually the church authorities capitulated to them in order to preserve the peace. It was disgraceful behaviour in the interest of a cause that lacked all legitimacy, but it left its mark in high church settings and can still be found in some extremely conservative congregations today.

On the whole, however, it must be said that modern reforms have largely superseded the debates of an earlier time. Today the Table can be placed in a number of different positions and it is usual for the celebrant to adopt the 'westward' position – standing behind the Table so as to be seen and heard by the congregation. This is the natural, commonsense approach which comes closest to what Jesus must have done at the Last Supper. It is also almost entirely free of controversy and it is fair to say that its widespread adoption has laid the traditional arguments for and against 'north' and 'eastward' positions to rest.

In summing up these introductory rubrics, the following points should be noted:

1. By and large they are no longer applied (or even applicable) in their original sense.

2. Their main purpose is to ensure decency and order in the celebration of the Holy Communion, a desire that has New Testament support (see 1 Corinthians 14:40) and is generally agreed by everybody.
3. The service of Holy Communion is not a semi-secret rite performed by a specially ordained celebrant while everyone else looks on, but a communal act of worship in which the entire congregation is involved. To that end, what the celebrant says and does should be heard and seen by the people who are present.

The Opening Prayers

The Ante-Communion begins with a rehearsal of the Lord's Prayer in the shorter form, i.e. without the doxology. There is no direction given to the people to join with the celebrant in praying it, but this seems to have been an omission rather than a deliberate decision on the part of the compilers and editors of the subsequent editions. It may also reflect the fact that, prior to the Reformation, the prayer was part of the priest's private preparation for the service. However, a priestly monologue is inconsistent with the rubric covering the prayer in the daily offices, where it is specifically stated that, wherever it is used in divine service, it should be said by the entire congregation. At one time there was a spurious justification for the traditional practice which claimed that the words 'divine service' applied only to Morning and Evening Prayer, but the absurdity of that is too obvious to require comment. It may, however, be necessary for the celebrant to invite the people to pray with him, given that that is not specifically stated in the service itself.

The collect for purity which follows the Lord's Prayer is basically a translation of a Latin prayer that is found in the priest's preparation in the Sarum rite and whose origins can be traced back at least as far as Alcuin (d. 804). In its present form it dates from the 1549 prayer book and its theological richness needs to be appreciated by all who take part in the service.

God is addressed as Almighty, which in this instance includes not only his omnipotence, put also his omnipresence and his omniscience, as can be seen from the opening clauses. He is the one:

1. To whom all hearts are open. God knows what we are thinking.
2. To whom all desires are known. God knows what we want, both good and bad.

3. From whom no secrets are hidden. God cannot be mocked or fooled by our refusal to open up to him in our prayers.

Given this realty, our prayer must be that:

1. God will cleanse the thoughts of our hearts, which are a mixed bag of good and evil.
2. God will do this by the inspiration of His Holy Spirit, who dwells in our hearts by faith (Galatians 4:6).
3. We may be given a pure and perfect love for God.
4. We may magnify His holy Name in a manner that is worthy of Him.

Neither of these last two, it must be said, is possible without the inspiration of the Holy Spirit.

As with the Lord's Prayer, there is no direction to say that the people should pray along with the celebrant, and traditionally the celebrant tended to say this collect on his own. However, this was probably not the original intention of the compilers. The celebrant can, and probably should, invite the people to pray along with him, particularly since the use of 'our', first person plural, indicates that the entire congregation is meant to be praying.

The Ten Commandments

The reciting of the Decalogue follows the opening prayers and is of great theological significance. The Ten Commandments represent the sum of the law of Moses, which is shared by Jews and Christians alike. Their presence in Christian worship is a reminder that the law of God is unchanging and that in the coming of Christ its purpose was not abrogated but fulfilled. Jesus was very clear in his teaching that keeping the Commandments was both necessary and impossible. It was necessary because the Commandments express the character of God and His will for His people. It is impossible, because of our sinfulness. We may think that we have kept them but, if so, it is because we have not properly understood their depth and significance. The story of the so-called 'rich young ruler' indicates this (Matthew 19:16-30), as does Jesus' teaching that those who have thought of adultery or murder in their hearts are just as guilty as those (relatively few) who have committed the sin openly (Matthew 5:17-22, 27-28).

It is important for Christian worship to begin with a rehearsal of God's law because it sets the standard from which we have fallen and explains why the work of salvation, which the service of Holy Communion dramatises and commemorates, had to happen in the way that it did. Worshippers are not meant to congratulate themselves, as the rich young ruler did, by ticking off the Commandments one by one and claiming to have achieved them. Rather they are supposed to be struck with the awesome demands of God's law, their own inability to live up to His requirements and their need for forgiveness and reconciliation. The Commandments by themselves do not go that far but they provide the starting point from which the rest follows.

In liturgical terms, the Decalogue was first added to the prayer book in 1552. The rubric, which was slightly amended and extended in 1662, envisaged the priest rehearsing each of the Commandments individually and the congregation responding after each one with a plea for God's mercy and a desire for Him to incline their hearts to keep that particular law, a desire that could only be fulfilled by the indwelling of His Holy Spirit, for which they had already prayed. The rubric in the 1662 book adds the words 'turning to the people' after 'priest', a concession to a demand made by the Puritans at the Savoy Conference in 1661. It indicates that celebrants were not necessarily doing that, presumably because they were placed at the north end of the Communion Table and therefore facing across the chancel, rather than looking towards the congregation.

Precedent for the inclusion of the Ten Commandments at the beginning of the Communion Office is easy to find in Protestant orders of worship composed for use in the German churches. Martin Luther produced a metrical version of them in 1524, that was translated by Miles Coverdale some years later. The Commandments appear in different places in the order for the church of Frankfurt (1530), Göttingen (1530), Bremen (1534), Pomerania (1535), Calenberg (1536) and Northeim (1539), among others. Thomas Cranmer could have taken any of these as a model but, although it is quite likely that the general idea of including the Decalogue came to him from Germany, it is impossible to point to any single source. The fact that it first appeared in 1552 suggests that he may have been influenced by Martin Bucer or one of the other Continental exiles who took refuge in England at that time. However, it is possible that Cranmer was himself chiefly responsible for the position that it occupies at the beginning of the service, rather than later on, as is the case in most of the German liturgies.

The chief objection to the use of the Ten Commandments has always been their length, and various 'solutions' to this perceived problem have been adopted over time. It is quite usual, when the full text of the

Commandments is used, for the second table of the law (Commandments five to ten) to be strung together as one and concluded by a single congregational response at the end. More common in recent times has been the substitution of Our Lord's Summary of the Law (Matthew 22:37-40) for the Decalogue, a practice that was first suggested in the Non-jurors' liturgy of 1718. No one can object to the use of Jesus' words in this way, and the abbreviation has proved popular in many places, but it has the disadvantage of obscuring the details of commandment breaking. The summary focusses on the positive aspect of the law – we are to love God with our whole being and our neighbours as ourselves – but what this involves in practice is not specified. Here it should not be a case of either/or but of both/and.

We need to understand that the fundamental purpose of the Commandments is that we should demonstrate the love of God both in our relationship to him and in our dealings with one another, but it also helps to have a detailed list of what that entails. Jesus was speaking to people who knew the details but who had often lost sight of their underlying purpose. Today, on the other hand, we are liable to confine ourselves to generalities and lose sight of the ways in which they must be worked out in everyday life. Both approaches are needed and, if the summary is to be permitted, it should not be at the expense of the Ten Commandments.

The Collects for the Sovereign

The addition of two collects for the Sovereign are a clear indication of the nature of the Reformed Church of England. It was a national Church, whose head was the monarch. The title of 'Supreme Head in earth' adopted by Henry VIII was altered in 1559 to 'Supreme Governor in earth', out of deference to the view that Christ alone is head of the Church, but the reality stayed the same. Over time, the role of the Sovereign in both Church and State has evolved considerably, so that today prayers for the monarch are prayers for the government of the state, in general. In countries that do not recognise the British monarch as their Sovereign adjustments have had to be made to reflect this, but the principle that the Church should pray for its secular rulers is well grounded in Scripture and should be maintained (1 Timothy 2:1-2; Romans 13:1-7). The first collect is directed primarily at the obedience of the Sovereign to God and the matching obedience of the people to the Sovereign. The second focusses more particularly on the monarch himself/herself and asks God to bless him/her directly. They may be analysed as follows:

First collect:

1. The sovereignty of God is acknowledged as covering both time (everlasting) and space (infinite). All human power and authority derives from Him.
2. The application of God's sovereignty to the life of the nation is an act of God's mercy.
3. God is asked to govern the heart of the Sovereign so that he/she will recognise the source of his/her authority and seek God's glory above all else.
4. The monarch's subjects must recognise the authority that has been given to him/her and obey him/her as their duty to God, but only according to the lawful limits placed on that authority by God's Word.

Second collect:

1. The Word of God teaches us that the hearts of rulers are controlled by Him and that only He can direct them in the way of godly wisdom.
2. Our prayers must be directed to God, asking Him to give godly wisdom to our rulers, so that they may seek His glory and govern the people committed to them in a way that will preserve their wealth, peace and godliness.

Both collects make valid and important points and one should not be preferred above the other. It might be possible to combine them into one but, if not, then alternating between them is probably the best course to follow.

The Collect, Epistle and Gospel of the Day

There is not much to be said about these that cannot be found in the section devoted to them. In the 1549 prayer book the Gospel was announced and the people were expected to respond: 'Glory be to thee, O Lord.' This was dropped in 1552 but the 1637 Scottish prayer book reintroduced it, adding that the people should stand for the Gospel reading and, when it was over, respond: 'Thanks be to thee, O Lord.' This was not included in 1662 but it has survived in practice. The only difference is that in modern times the response after the Gospel reading has been: 'Praise be to thee, O Christ.' None of this has any warrant in the prayer book and has no status other than that of a popular custom.

The Nicene Creed

The Creed now generally called 'Nicene' was supposedly composed at or shortly after the First Council of Constantinople in 381.[22] It was said to have been the faith of the First Council of Nicaea, held in 325, but that Council issued a different (if broadly similar) Creed of its own. The minutes of the Council of 381 have been lost so we cannot say for sure whether it was really composed there, but it was definitely cited as such at the Council of Chalcedon in 451.

As recognised in the 1662 prayer book, the Creed is in the Western form, with a slight aberration due to mistaken historical 'scholarship'. The Western form, originally in Latin, appeared sometime in the late sixth century in Spain. It is traditionally associated with the Third Council of Toledo, in 589, but the one thing we can say for certain about it is that it was not introduced there. It may already have been in existence or else it appeared shortly afterwards. Its distinctive feature is that it confesses the double procession of the Holy Spirit (*qui ex Patre Filioque procedit*) which was not in the original Greek. The Greek text was taken from John 15:26, which speaks of the procession of the Holy Spirit from the Father, making no mention of the Son, although he is the person speaking.

Whether the Holy Spirit proceeds from the Son as he does from the Father is a question that divides the Western Churches from the Eastern ones to this day.[23] In the late ninth century Patriarch Photius of Constantinople (858-67 and 877-86) insisted that the Holy Spirit proceeds from the Father alone, an interpretation that is not required by the wording of the Creed itself. Later on, Anselm of Canterbury (1033/34-1109) defended the double procession of the Holy Spirit in a full-blown treatise, in which he demonstrated from other texts in John's Gospel and elsewhere that the Holy Spirit is the Spirit of the Son as well as of the Father. The question was debated at the Second Council of Lyons (1274) and again at the Council of Florence (1439), where on both occasions representatives of the Eastern Churches bowed to Roman

---

22. For a detailed history of this Creed, see Kelly, *Early Christian Creeds*.
23. For a fuller discussion of this question, see Appendices to the Daily Offices in Chapter 3 above.

pressure and accepted the Western position, only to be repudiated by their own people when they returned home.

At the time of the Reformation, the Protestant Churches accepted the decisions of Lyons II and Florence without question and that is still their position today. The *Filioque* clause, as the addition to the Creed is known, has been thoroughly re-examined in modern times, but it seems that positions on both sides are now so deeply entrenched that no agreement is possible. Irenic spirits on both sides tend to say that both views are permissible and depend on with whichever model of the Trinity one starts. Many Western Churches, including the Anglican, are prepared to drop the extra clause from time to time, especially when ecumenical relations are at stake, though they have not denied its truth. Some Eastern theologians have reciprocated by saying that belief in the double procession is a possible option for the Orthodox, but that it cannot be regarded as infallible dogma. Rather, it is what the Greeks call a *theologoumenon*, or theological opinion. Whether its presence in the Western Creed should be a barrier to church union is still being debated.

The other oddity about the Nicene Creed in the 1662 prayer book is that, in the clause about the Church, the word 'holy' is omitted. This is because in the most ancient texts available to the Reformers, that word had slipped out. However, there is no doubt that it was in the original version and there is therefore no reason why it should not be restored.

It may be noted that in the Eastern liturgies the Creed is always said, whereas in the West it may be said or sung.

The Notices

Following the Creed there is a brief pause in the service when the officiant ('Curate') is expected to share notices with the congregation.[24] These may be classified as follows:

1. Notice given of holy days and fasting days to be observed in the week following.
2. Notice to be given of an upcoming Communion service.
3. Briefs, citations and excommunications are to be read.

---

24. Before 1662 the notices were given after the Sermon, which is more logical and may still be the practice in some places.

In addition, these notices are circumscribed by the following prohibitions:

1. Only the minister is permitted to read a notice.
2. The minister may read only what is prescribed by the prayer book's rules, enjoined by the monarch or by the 'Ordinary of the place' (normally the bishop).

It is fair to say that most of these requirements are now effectively redundant. There is usually some mention of services to be held during the week ahead, but future Communion services would seldom, if ever, be mentioned, nor is there much call for 'briefs, citations and excommunications'. It is usual for notices to be read by the minister but not compulsory nowadays, nor are his remarks limited to the subjects mentioned here. On the whole, common sense prevails and very often notices given in church will be backed up by a printed leaflet, posted online, or both.

The Sermon

The sermon follows immediately after the notices. It may be taken from one of the 33 officially approved Homilies, of which the first book (containing twelve of them) appeared in 1547 and the second in 1563, and again in 1571. The 1563 version contained 20 homilies, to which one more (on rebellion) was added in 1571. It must be said that the Homilies are seldom if ever read today.

The sermon is placed here because it is meant to be an exposition of one of the Scripture passages read for the day, filtered through the doctrinal prism of the Nicene Creed. In practice, there is a wide variety here and it is hard to generalise. Most sermons today are about 20 minutes long but, with some notable exceptions, the quality of preaching is often low and the sermon may be much shorter – sometimes no more than five to ten minutes long. It is also by no means guaranteed that the sermon will be an exposition of a biblical text, as it ought to be. The Homilies are topical rather than expository, so Anglicans lack a suitable model for their regular preaching. There are, however, many notable Anglican preachers, including men like William Perkins (1558-1602), Charles Simeon (1759-1836) and John Stott (1921-2011), whose works are still widely read and imitated, and not merely by Anglicans.

The Offertory

As found in the 1662 text, the offertory is the remnant of a part of the Communion office that was much more elaborate in pre-Reformation times. Then, it included both alms for the Church (and for the poor) and the presentation of the bread and wine for the Communion itself. In the Anglican tradition, the preparation of the bread and wine was detached from the offertory, which concentrated on the giving of alms, with a special emphasis on poor relief. The minister was expected to recite one or more of 20 verses taken from Scripture. Sixteen of them come from the New Testament, two from the Old Testament and two (remarkably) from the Apocrypha – Tobit chapter 4, to be precise.

In modern times, the minister will seldom read more than one of them, usually the first, which is taken from Matthew 5:16. This part of the service is popularly known as the 'collection' or more formally as the 'offering' and is carried out by lay assistants, who present the alms of the people to the minister. He then blesses them (though this is not specified in the prayer book) and lays them on the Holy Table.

There then follows a short rubric which directs the priest to place enough bread and wine on the table for the celebration of Holy Communion, if such a celebration is to take place. There is no indication that this action should be accompanied by any prayer or ceremony. The directions of 1662 closely follow those of 1552 but are very different from those of 1549, which are far more elaborate. In particular, the 1549 liturgy enjoins the following practices, all of which were abandoned in 1552 and later:

1. Those wishing to receive Communion are to stay behind after the service and gather in the choir. The men are to stand on one side and the women on the other.
2. Those who do not wish to communicate are to leave the church, apart from the ministers and the clerks (who were the singers).
3. The minister is to put the bread in a paten or something similar and the wine into a chalice or cup, if the chalice is too small, mixing it with water.
4. After they are prepared, the minister is to put the bread and wine on the 'altar', a word that was still in use to describe the Lord's Table.

Some of these practices may have survived after 1552 in different places, but they were no longer expected and before long it seems that they were generally abandoned. It should be noted that any suggestion that the bread and wine were offerings (oblations) of some kind is ruled out by the indented rubric, which states that, when there are no alms and oblations, reference to them shall be omitted. It is possible that there would be no monetary gifts, but not that there would be no bread and wine, so the word 'oblations' cannot apply to them.

The Prayer for the Church

Before the Reformation, the prayer for the Church was part of the consecration prayer and came later in the service than it does now. However, in 1552 the consecration prayer was broken up and the first part of it was placed here, before the departure of the non-communicants. It was also specified that the prayer was intended for the Church 'militant here in earth', not for the Church triumphant in heaven, who rest from their labours and do not need our prayers in the same way. It is in the treatment of the latter that the differences between 1549, 1552 and 1662 are most apparent. The 1549 prayer book is especially fulsome in its commemoration of the saints and faithful departed:

> And here we do give unto thee most high praise, and hearty thanks, for the wonderful grace and virtue, declared in all thy saints, from the beginning of the world: And chiefly in the glorious and most blessed virgin Mary, Mother of thy Son Jesu Christ our Lord and God, and in the holy Patriarchs, Prophets, Apostles, and Martyrs, whose examples (O Lord) and steadfastness in thy faith, and keeping thy holy commandments, grant us to follow. We commend unto thy mercy (O Lord) all other thy servants, which are departed hence from us, with the sign of faith, and now do rest in the sleep of peace: Grant unto them, we beseech thee, thy mercy and everlasting peace, and that at the day of general resurrection, we and all they which be of the mystical body of thy Son, may altogether be set on his right hand.

This was greatly trimmed down in 1552:

> And we also bless thy holy name for all those thy servants, who having finished their course in faith, do now rest from their labours. And we yield unto thee most high praise, and hearty thanks for the wonderful grace and virtue declared in all thy

saints, who have been the choice vessels of thy grace, and the lights of the world in their several generations; most humbly beseeching thee, that we may have grace to follow the example of their steadfastness in thy faith, and obedience to thy holy commandments, that at the day of general resurrection, we and all they that are of the mystical body of thy Son, may be set on his right hand.[25]

Unusually, 1662 went farther and shortened the prayer even more:

And we also bless thy holy Name for all thy servants departed this life in thy faith and fear: beseeching thee to give us grace so to follow their good examples, that with them we may be partakers of thy heavenly kingdom.

In 1549 there was still a distinction between the known, or canonised, 'saints' and faithful believers, for whom we hope the best but cannot be absolutely sure. In 1552 that distinction was abolished and the emphasis shifted from them to those still living on earth, that we might be inspired by their example and be found worthy to share in their everlasting bliss. Finally, in 1662 we give thanks for those who died in faith and ask for grace to follow their examples, so that we may share in God's heavenly kingdom. All mention of the general resurrection on the last day is omitted, perhaps in order to allow for the fact that the faithful will go straight to heaven when they die, without a waiting period in between.

Some have claimed that the 1662 wording leaves open the possibility of praying for the dead but it is hard to see how that can be the case. We give thanks for the faithful departed but we pray for ourselves, not for them. Prayers for the dead are wrong because:

1. The dead do not need them. They are in the hand of God. Those who are at rest in Christ do not need any further support.
2. The world of the dead is beyond our jurisdiction as the Church militant here in earth. Our responsibility is for this world, not for the next.
3. Jesus told the thief on the Cross that they would be reunited in Paradise that very same day (Luke 23:43). If that was true

---

25. It may be noted that this form is the one found in the 1637 Scottish prayer book.

of him, how much more must it be true of all believers? Not even death can separate us from the love of God (Romans 8:38-39).

The Exhortations

The 1662 Book of Common Prayer contains three Exhortations which are neither optional nor alternatives. Neither does their positioning reflect their origins. The 1549 book contained only two exhortations, one intended for immediate use (A) and the other for use when the Communion was to be deferred to a later date (B). In 1552 a further Exhortation (C) was added and the first one was placed at the end. In 1662 the order of the first two, both intended for Communion at a later date, was reversed. The pattern may be illustrated as follows:

1549	1552	1662
A	C	B
B	B	C
-	A	A

The first one found in 1662 (B) is meant to be used on the Sunday or holy day preceding the administration of Holy Communion. The second one in 1662 (C) is intended for use in place of the first if there is evidence that the parishioners are slow to come to the Lord's Table and need encouragement. The third one in 1662 (A), and in some ways the most important of them, is meant to be read at the time of Communion and is intended as a warning to the communicants to 'try and examine' themselves before presuming to take the bread and wine in the sacrament.

These exhortations play a key role in the Communion office and it is tragic to think that they are almost never used today. The loss of the first one can perhaps be excused by the changing liturgical pattern, according to which Holy Communion is now offered virtually every Sunday, or at least often enough to make an announcement of this kind seem unnecessary. The loss of the second may also be explained because, with the frequency of Communion nowadays, and the fact that very few churchgoers are likely to avoid taking it, its necessity is less obvious than it once was. The third exhortation comes at the beginning of the Communion section of the service and will be examined in that context.

The First Exhortation (B)

The first exhortation in the 1662 prayer book (B) derives from one that was included in the order for Communion of 1548. In the 1549 liturgy it was expanded and reserved for use when the officiant saw that the people were neglecting their duty to come to Communion. In 1552 it was put in second place and then moved to its present position in 1662. The opening sentence, which was omitted in 1552, is sometimes used by the minister when announcing Communion at some future date, but the frequency of celebration in modern times has virtually eclipsed this.

The exhortation as a whole is almost never heard nowadays and few people are aware of its existence. Nevertheless, to the student of the Book of Common Prayer, it is of considerable interest because of the many changes it underwent between 1549 and 1662. The most important of these were made by Thomas Cranmer himself, in 1552. The 1552 text remained unaltered until 1662, when significant elements from 1549 were reintroduced and other additions were made that appear to have been designed to strengthen the need for congregational discipline.

What strikes the modern reader more than anything else is the concern the Reformers evidently had to encourage frequent communion. This has become so common in modern times that it is easy to forget that for a long time many regular churchgoers hardly communicated at all. Some had scruples about their own worthiness to partake of the consecrated elements; but it appears that many were simply indifferent to the sacrament. Weekly communion was rare, not least because in many parishes it was not on offer. The clergy would therefore announce in advance when the next celebration would take place, evidently hoping that parishioners would make a special effort to attend and participate. It is impossible to know how successful they were in persuading them to do so, but the problem of infrequent communion certainly persisted and over time the exhortations fell into disuse.

In 1549 there was a strong emphasis on the holiness of the Lord's Supper and on the need to repent of sin and amend one's manner of life before presuming to come to the Table. The 1552 revision abbreviates this somewhat but not to the point of diminishing the stress placed on the need to seek forgiveness and restore good relations, not only with God but with other people, before communicating. The other changes made in 1552 served to accentuate the importance of God's Word (i.e. Scripture) in the process of reconciling the penitent and to remind congregations that the celebrant was a servant (minister) of that Word and not a specially gifted person with the power to remit sin himself.

The 1662 revision restored some of the material from 1549 that had been dropped in 1552, particularly in the introduction. It also added a remarkable sentence that addressed the spiritual state of the communicants directly and singled out specific sins for condemnation. Particularly striking is the assertion that those who received the sacred elements unworthily ran the risk that the devil would enter into them, as he entered into Judas at the Last Supper, and bring them to a similar destruction.

In order to make this process of evolution clearer, the exhortation is printed twice. The first time it takes 1549 as its base, indicating by the use of grey what parts were omitted in 1552 and by **bold** type what parts were added at that time. The second time, the exhortation is printed with the 1552 text as its base. Omissions in 1662 are likewise indicated in grey and additions in **bold** type, with portions of the 1549 text that were dropped in 1552 and restored in 1662 are indicated by the use of **grey text in bold.**

The texts of 1549 and 1552 compared:

> Dear friends, and you especially upon whose souls I have cure and charge, on [ ] next, I do intend by God's grace, to offer to all such as be godly disposed, the most comfortable sacrament of the body and blood of Christ, to be taken of them, in the remembrance of his most fruitful and glorious passion: by the which passion we have obtained remission of our sins and be made partakers of the kingdom of heaven, whereof we be assured and ascertained, if we come to the said sacrament, with hearty repentance for our offences, steadfast faith in God's mercy, and earnest mind to obey God's will, and to offend no more. Wherefore our duty is, to come to these holy mysteries, with most hearty thanks to be given to Almighty God, for his infinite mercy and benefits given and bestowed upon us his unworthy servants, for whom he hath not only given his body to death, and shed his blood, but also doth vouchsafe in a sacrament and mystery, to give us his said body and blood to feed upon spiritually. **Dearly beloved, forasmuch as our duty is to render to Almighty God our Heavenly Father most hearty thanks for that he hath given his Son our Saviour Jesus Christ, not only to die for us, but also to be our spiritual food and sustenance, as it is declared unto us, as well by God's Word as by the holy sacraments of his blessed body and blood,** The which sacrament being

so divine and holy a thing, and so comfortable **a thing** to them which receive it worthily, and so dangerous to them that will presume to take the same **receive it** unworthily.[26] My duty is to exhort you in the mean season, to consider the greatness **dignity** of the thing **holy mystery and the great peril of the unworthy receiving thereof**, and **so** to search and examine your own consciences, and that not lightly nor after the manner of dissimulers with God: But as they which **as you** should come **holy and clean** to a most godly and heavenly banquet **feast, so that in no wise you** not to come but in the marriage garment required of God in **Holy** Scripture, that you may (so much as lieth in you) be found **and so come and be received as** worthy to come to **partakers of** such a **heavenly** Table.

The ways and means thereto is:

First, that you be truly repentant of your former evil life, and that you confess with an unfeigned heart to Almighty God, your sins and unkindness towards his Majesty committed, **to examine your lives and conversation by the rule of God's commandments, and wherein soever ye shall perceive yourselves to have offended** either by will, word or deed, infirmity or ignorance, and that with inward sorrow and tears you **there** bewail your offences, and require of **own sinful lives, confess yourselves to** Almighty God mercy and pardon, promising to him (from the bottom of your hearts) the **with full purpose of** amendment of your former life. And amongst all others, I am commanded of God, especially to move and exhort you, **And if ye shall perceive your offences to be such, as be not only against God, but also against your neighbours: then ye shall** to reconcile yourselves **un**to your neighbours **them,** whom you have offended, or who hath offended you, putting out of your hearts all hatred and malice against them, and to be in love and charity with all the world, and to forgive other, as you would that God should forgive you. And if any man have done wrong to any other, let him **ready to** make **restitution and** satisfaction, and due restitution of all lands and goods,

---

26. 1 Corinthians 11:27-29.

wrongfully taken away and withholden, before he come to
God's board, or at the least be in full mind and purpose so to
do, as soon as he is able, or else let him not come to this holy
Table, thinking to deceive God, who seeth all men's hearts.
For neither the absolution of the priest, can anything avail
them, nor the receiving of this holy sacrament doth anything
**according to the uttermost of your powers, for all injuries
and wrongs done by you to any other: and likewise being
ready to forgive other that have offended you; as you
would have forgiveness of your offences at God's hand.
For otherwise the receiving of the Holy Communion doth
nothing else**, but increase their **your** damnation.[27] And
**because it is requisite that no man should come to the
Holy Communion but with a full trust in God's mercy, and
with a quiet conscience: therefore** if there be any of you,
which by the means aforesaid cannot quiet his own whose
conscience, is troubled and grieved in anything, lacking **but
requireth further** comfort or counsel; **then** let him come to
me, or to some other discreet and learned priest **minister of
God's word**, taught in the law of God, and confess and open
his sin and grief, secretly, that he may receive such ghostly
counsel, advice and comfort that **as** his conscience may be
relieved; and that of us (as of the ministers of God and of
the church) **by the ministry of God's Word**, he may receive
comfort and **the benefit of** absolution, to the satisfaction
of his mind **quieting of his conscience**, and avoiding of all
scruple and doubtfulness requiring such as shall be satisfied
with a general confession, not to be offended with them that
do use, to their further satisfying, the auricular and secret
confession to the priest: nor those also which think needful
or convenient, for the quietness of their own consciences,
particularly to open their sins to the priest: to be offended
with them that are satisfied, with their humble confession
to God, and the general confession to the church. But in all
things to follow and keep the rule of charity, and every man
to be satisfied with his own conscience, not judging other
men's minds or consciences, where as he hath no warrant of
God's word to the same.

---

27. Cf. the words of Jesus in Matthew 5:21-24.

The texts of 1552 and 1662 compared:

Dearly beloved, on —day next, I **purpose through** God's **assistance, to administer** to all such as shall be religiously and devoutly disposed the most comfortable sacrament of the body and blood of Christ; to be by them **received,** in remembrance of his **meritorious Cross and** Passion; **whereby alone we obtain** remission of our sins and **be made partakers of the Kingdom of heaven. Wherefore it is our duty to render** most **humble and** hearty thanks to Almighty God **our Heavenly Father, for that he hath given his Son our Saviour Jesus Christ, not only to die for us, but also to be our spiritual food and sustenance in that holy sacrament.** Which **being so** divine and comfortable a thing to them which **who** receive it worthily, and so dangerous to them that will presume to receive it unworthily; my duty is to exhort you **in the mean season** to consider the dignity of the **that** holy mystery, and the great peril of the unworthy receiving thereof; and so to search and examine your own consciences, **and that not lightly, nor after the manner of dissemblers** with God; as you should **but so that ye may** come holy and clean to such a heavenly Feast, so that in no wise you come, but in the marriage garment required of **by** God in Holy Scripture, and so come **and be received as** worthy partakers of such a heavenly **that holy** Table.

The ways and means thereto is:

First, to examine your lives and conversations by the rule of God's commandments; and wherein soever ye shall perceive yourselves to have offended, either by will, word or deed, there **to** bewail your own sinful lives **sinfulness, and to** confess yourselves to Almighty God, with full purpose of amendment of life. And if ye shall perceive your offences to be such as be **are** not only against God, but also against your neighbours; then ye shall reconcile yourselves unto them; **being** ready to make restitution and satisfaction, according to the uttermost of your powers, for all injuries and wrongs done by you to any other; and likewise being **likewise** ready to forgive others that have offended you, as you would have forgiveness of your offences at God's hand: for otherwise the receiving of the holy Communion doth nothing else but increase your damnation. **Therefore if any of you be a blasphemer of God, an hinderer or slanderer of his Word, an adulterer, or be in malice, or envy, or in any other grievous crime, repent you of your sins, or else come not to that holy Table; lest, after the taking of that holy sacrament, the devil enter into you, as he entered into Judas, and fill you full of all iniquities, and bring you to destruction both of body and soul.**[28]

And because it is requisite that no man should come to the holy Communion, but with a full trust in God's mercy, and with a quiet conscience; therefore if there be any of you, which **who** by the **this** means aforesaid cannot quiet his own conscience but requireth further comfort or counsel, then let him come to me, or **to** some other discreet and learned minister of God's Word, and open his grief; that **by the ministry of God's holy Word** he may receive **the benefit of absolution, together with** such ghostly counsel **and** advice, and comfort as his conscience may be relieved, and that by the ministry of God's Word, he may receive comfort and the benefit of absolution, to the quieting of his conscience, and avoiding of all scruple and doubtfulness.

The structure of the exhortation as it stands in 1662 is as follows: First paragraph:

1. The officiant intends to celebrate Communion at some future time and invites all who are 'religiously and devoutly disposed' to communicate.
2. The Communion is a remembrance of Christ's 'meritorious Cross and Passion', the only means by which we can obtain forgiveness of our sins and entry into the kingdom of heaven.
3. It is our duty to thank God, not only for giving us His Son to die for us, but also for making him our spiritual food and nourishment in the sacrament.
4. The sacrament is a 'divine and comfortable thing' to those who receive it worthily, but dangerous to them who receive it unworthily.

---

28. Cf. John 13:27.

5. It is the minister's duty to warn the people of these things so that they can examine their own consciences and come in the right spirit to the Table.

Second paragraph:

6. Intending communicants must first examine their lives according to the Commandments, repent of their sins, confess them to God and intend to lead a new life.
7. Sins against neighbours should lead the communicants to reconcile themselves to them and to make restitution for all wrongs done to them as far as that is possible.
8. Communicants must be ready to forgive others as they want God to forgive them. If they do not, they will bring damnation on themselves by receiving the Communion unworthily.
9. Anyone who has sinned against God must repent. Otherwise, if he receives the Communion unworthily, he will suffer the fate of Judas. The reference here is to Luke 22:3-6.

Third paragraph:

10. No one should come to Communion unless he trusts fully in God's mercy and has a quiet conscience.
11. If anyone has a troubled conscience, he should approach the minister (or some other one) privately and unburden himself, so that he may receive the comfort of God's Word, be absolved from guilt, and be given guidance as to how to acquire and maintain a quiet conscience. Here there is an opening for private confession, which had been compulsory before the Reformation but was discontinued at that time. It is a reminder that there is a place for unburdening the soul, but that it should not be made obligatory or imposed by one particular minister on his congregation.

The Second Exhortation (C)

The second exhortation in 1662 (C) appeared for the first time in 1552 when it was placed first. It may owe its origin to the influence of Martin Bucer or to one of the other Continental exiles, but there is no evidence for that.[29] Its positioning in 1552 means that it may well have been used from then until 1662 in preference to B, but it had effectively disappeared from view by the nineteenth century and is almost never heard today. Like the first exhortation (B), it presupposes that the Communion service will take place at some future time, so that with the recent increase of celebrations it is difficult to imagine when it might be used nowadays. Nevertheless, it is rather different in tone from the first exhortation (B) and contains important theological principles that should not be neglected.

Since it was first introduced in 1552 the changes made to it in 1662 are few and largely cosmetic. The most noticeable feature is the omission of a large section in which the celebrant was expected to denounce those members of his congregation who were reluctant to communicate, something that was attributed to contempt for God. Evidently the 1662 revisers thought that this was taking things too far and they toned it down, though to what effect is impossible to say.

As with exhortation B, words that were omitted in 1662 are indicated in *italic*, whereas those few that were added are in **bold** type.

1552 and 1662 compared:

> We be come together at this time, Dearly beloved brethren, **on — I intend, by God's grace**, to feed at **celebrate** the Lord's Supper; unto the which, in God's behalf, I bid you all that be **are** here present; and beseech you, for the Lord Jesus Christ's sake, that ye will not refuse to come thereto, being so lovingly called and bidden of **by** God himself. Ye know how grievous and unkind a thing it is, when a man hath prepared a rich feast, decked his table with all kind of provision, so that there lacketh nothing but the guests to sit down; and yet they which be **who are** called, without any cause, most unthankfully refuse to come. Which of you in such a case would not be moved? Who would not think a great injury and wrong done unto him? Wherefore, most dearly beloved in Christ, take ye good heed, lest ye, withdrawing yourselves from this holy Supper, and provoke God's indignation against you. It is an

---

29. Martin Bucer deplored infrequent Communion in his *Censura* of the 1549 prayer book but there is nothing to suggest that he advocated an exhortation of this kind. See Whitaker, *Martin Bucer and the Book of Common Prayer*, pp. 146-47.

easy matter for a man to say, I will not communicate, because I am otherwise letted **hindered** with worldly business. But such excuses be **are** not so easily accepted and allowed before God. If any man say, I am a grievous sinner, and therefore am afraid to come: wherefore then do ye not repent and amend? When God calleth you, be **are** you not ashamed to say ye will not come? When ye should return to God, will ye excuse yourself**ves**, and say that ye be **are** not ready? Consider earnestly with yourselves how little such feigned excuses shall **will** avail before God. They that refused the feast in the Gospel, because they had bought a farm, or would try their yokes of oxen, or because they were married, were not so excused, but counted unworthy of the heavenly feast.[30] I, for my part, am here present **shall be ready**; and according to mine office, I bid you in the name of God, I call you in Christ's behalf, I exhort you, as ye love your own salvation, that ye will be partakers of this holy Communion. And as the Son of God did vouchsafe to yield up his soul by death upon the Cross for your health **salvation**; even so it is your duty to receive the Communion together in remembrance of **the sacrifice of** his death, as he himself commanded: Now, if ye will in no wise thus do **which if ye shall neglect to do**, consider with yourselves how great injury ye do unto God, and how sore punishment hangeth over your heads for the same; And whereas ye offend God so sore in refusing this holy banquet, I admonish, exhort and beseech you, that unto this unkindness ye will not add any more. Which thing ye shall do, if ye stand by as gazers and lookers of them that do communicate, and be no partakers of the same yourselves. For what thing can this be accounted else, than a further contempt and unkindness unto God? Truly it is a great unthankfulness to say nay when ye be called, but the fault is much greater when men stand by and yet will neither eat nor drink this Holy Communion with other. I pray you what can this be else but even to have the mysteries of Christ in derision? It is said unto all: Take ye and eat, take and drink ye all of this, do this in remembrance of me. With what face then, or with what countenance shall ye hear these words? What will this be else, but a neglecting, a despising, and mocking of the testament of Christ? Wherefore rather

---

30. Luke 14:18-24.

then you should do so, depart you hence, and give place to them that be godly disposed. But when you depart, I beseech you ponder with yourselves, from whom ye depart: **when** ye depart **wilfully abstain** from the Lord's Table, ye depart **and separate** from your brethren, and from **who come to feed on** the banquet of **that** most heavenly food. These things if ye earnestly consider, ye shall **will** by God's grace return to a better mind: for the obtaining whereof we shall **not cease to** make our humble petitions while we shall receive the Holy Communion **unto Almighty God our Heavenly Father**.

In its 1662 form, this exhortation may be analysed as follows:

1. The minister asks everyone to come to Communion, because the invitation has been given to them by the Lord Jesus Christ himself. To refuse such an invitation is to insult God. The image of the banquet to which those invited refuse to come is taken from the words of Jesus in Luke 14:16-24.
2. Those who refuse to come to Communion risk provoking God's anger. The excuse that they are preoccupied with worldly business is unworthy of God. Those who fear that they are too sinful to attend should repent and amend their lives.
3. Those who made excuses for not following Jesus were regarded as unworthy of the heavenly feast. Nothing is more important than this.
4. The minister will be ready for the celebration and the people should prepare themselves likewise.
5. The Son of God gave his life for his people, and so it is their duty to remember that sacrifice by receiving Communion. To fail to do so is to insult God and invite retribution from Him.
6. Those who take these warnings seriously will be restored by God's grace to a better frame of mind and amend their behaviour.

The Communion

The introductory rubric asks that the intending communicants should be conveniently placed for receiving the sacrament. This is common sense and no specific directions are given because each actual situation is different. The principle is that all the participants should be gathered together (not scattered about a largely empty church, for example) as they would be at a normal meal. Now that Holy Communion is often part of the main service on a Sunday, a special direction of this kind is usually unnecessary, but the principle still applies.

The Third Exhortation (A)

This traces its origin to the order for Communion of 1548 and was placed here in 1549, with the proviso that in cathedrals and places where the Communion office was celebrated daily, it need only be read once a month. This exhortation underwent some significant changes in 1552 but, apart from the loss of a middle sentence, that revision remained essentially the same in 1662. The editing process may be appreciated by comparing the three texts as follows. Grey words were in the 1549 prayer book but later dropped or modified; words in **bold type** were subsequently added, mostly in 1552. The deletions/additions made in 1552, and the few changes that were not made until 1662, are indicated in square brackets.

> Dearly beloved in the Lord, ye that mind to come to the holy Communion of the Body and Blood of our Saviour Christ, must consider what Saint Paul writeth to the Corinthians how [he] **Saint Paul** exhorteth all persons diligently to try and examine themselves, before they presume to eat of that bread and drink of that cup. For as the benefit is great, if with a truely penitent heart and lively faith we receive that holy Sacrament; (for then we spiritually eat the flesh of Christ, and drink his blood; then we dwell in Christ, and Christ in us, we be [made] **are** one with Christ, and Christ with us;) so is the danger great, if we receive the same unworthily. For then we [become] **are** guilty of the Body and Blood of Christ our Saviour; we eat and drink our own damnation, not considering the Lord's Body; we kindle God's wrath [over] **[against]** us; we provoke him to plague us with divers diseases and sundry kinds of death.

The next paragraph was reassigned in 1662 and is no longer in this exhortation:

> Therefore if any here **of you** be a blasphemer **of God, a hinderer or slanderer of his Word, an** adulterer, or be in

malice or envy, or in any other grievous crime (except he be truly sorry therefore, and earnestly minded to leave the same vices, and do trust himself to be reconciled to Almighty God, and in charity with all the world), let him bewail his **your** sins and not come **not** to that **this** holy Table; lest after the taking of that most blessed bread **holy sacrament**, the devil enter into him **you**, as he did **entered** into Judas, to **and** fill him **you** full of all iniquities, and bring him **you** to destruction, both of body and soul.[31]

There then follows the third paragraph, which has been retained:

Judge therefore yourselves, brethren, that ye be not judged of the Lord [Let your mind be without desire to sin]; repent you truly for your sins past, have a[n earnest and] lively [**and steadfast**] faith in Christ our Saviour; [**amend your lives and**] be in perfect charity with all men; so shall ye be meet partakers of those holy mysteries. And above all things ye must give most humble and hearty thanks to God, the Father, the Son and the Holy Ghost for the redemption of the world by the death and passion of our Saviour Christ, both God and man; who did humble himself, even to the death upon the Cross, for us, miserable sinners, [which] **who** lay in darkness and the shadow of death; that he might make us the children of God, and exalt us to everlasting life. And to the end that we should always remember the exceeding [**great**] love of our Master, and only Saviour, Jesus Christ, thus dying for us, and the innumerable benefits which by his precious blood-shedding he hath obtained to us; he hath [left in those] [**instituted and ordained**] holy mysteries, as [a] pledge[**s**] of his love and [a] **for a** continual remembrance [of the same his own blessed body and precious blood for us to feed upon spiritually] [**of his death**], to our [**great and**] endless comfort [and consolation]. To him therefore, with the Father and the Holy Ghost, let us give (as we are most bounden) continual thanks; submitting ourselves wholly to his holy will and pleasure, and studying to serve him in true holiness and righteousness all the days of our life. Amen.

---

31. In the 1662 Prayer Book this entire section was removed from this exhortation and placed in the first exhortation (B).

Of the three Exhortations, this one remains the most accessible today and it has even been included in *Common Worship* as an annex to Order Two.[32] That in itself shows how important it is; and what a pity it is that it has fallen out of general use. There can be little doubt that the spiritual health of the Church would be improved if its use was restored, not least because it provides the necessary preliminary for what comes next.

This exhortation can be analysed as follows:

1. It is addressed to those intending to communicate.
2. Communicants must consider what Paul says in 1 Corinthians 11:27-30.
3. The benefit of the sacrament is that we spiritually eat Christ's flesh and drink his blood, as long as we are truly repentant and come to the Table in faith. Those who do so dwell in Christ and are united with him (and he with them).
4. Those who eat and drink unworthily are in great danger because they are guilty of Christ's body and blood. They provoke God to anger and risk both contracting various diseases and dying in an untimely manner.
5. Communicants must, therefore, judge themselves, repent of their sins, have a lively faith, amend their lives and live in perfect love with everyone.
6. Above everything else, communicants must sincerely thank God the Holy Trinity for the redemption of the world by the Son, who is both God and man.
7. The Son humbled himself to die on the Cross for us sinners, so that instead of dying, we might become children of God and be raised to everlasting life.
8. Jesus Christ has instituted holy mysteries as pledges of his love so that we should always remember the great benefits which his sacrifice has obtained for us.
9. Communicants must therefore thank God the Trinity for this great gift, submit to His will and endeavour to serve Him in holiness and righteousness for the rest of their lives.

---

32. *Common Worship: Services and Prayers for the Church of England* (London: Church House Publishing, 2000), p. 245.

The Invitation

The third exhortation (A) leads naturally into the invitation, which presupposes it, and is sometimes even called the fourth exhortation. Nowadays, it is usually the beginning of the Communion and must therefore do duty as an exhortation, but the loss of the previous one leaves it seriously truncated.

In the 1549 text the invitation and the confession following it were placed after the consecration, so that it appears to be an invitation to receive the already consecrated elements. In the 1552 prayer book both were moved to their present position, indicating that the congregation is meant to participate with the celebrant in the institution of the Lord's Supper. The wording is recognisably the same throughout, but there are some not insignificant variations introduced into the 1662 text, as can be seen from the following:

> Ye[33] that do truly and earnestly repent you of your sins [to Almighty God], and [be] [**are**] in love and charity with your neighbours, and intend to lead a new life, following the commandments of God, and walking from henceforth in his holy ways; Draw near [**with faith**] and take this holy Sacrament to your comfort; [**and**] make your humble confession to Almighty God, [and to his holy church] [**before this congregation**] [here gathered together in his] [**holy**] [**name**][34] meekly kneeling upon your knees.

The two changes introduced in 1552 were cosmetic, though the 'Church' was more carefully defined as those present in the congregation, not the institution represented by the celebrant. In 1662 that whole clause was omitted, presumably because everyone was making the same confession and it was addressed to God, not to the other members of the congregation. In 1662 the words 'with faith' were added, partly because some people were interpreting the phrase 'draw near' literally and crowding around the Table, but mainly in order to emphasise that faith is the indispensable precondition for the right reception of the sacrament.

---

33. In 1552, 'Ye' was (incorrectly) altered to 'you', but 'Ye' was restored in 1662.
34. '[A]nd to his holy church here gathered together in his name' (1549); 'before this congregation here gathered together in his holy name' (1552); both versions omitted in the 1662 prayer book.

The first part of the invitation recapitulates what has already been said in the third exhortation, while the last part of the sentence leads on to the confession.

The Confession

The Confession is without real precedent in the Sarum rite, although the phrase 'thought, word and deed' is found in the mutual confession of the priest and his assistants early on in that service. If there is any source at all for it, it is to be found in Hermann von Wied's order for the church at Cologne, which seems to have influenced much of this part of the service.

The confession first appears in the order for Communion of 1548 and is repeated without significant change in all subsequent revisions.[35] The rubric originally stated that it should be said 'either by one of them, or else by one of the ministers, or by the priest himself' but, at the request of the Presbyterians at the Savoy Conference in 1661, this was simplified to 'by one of the ministers'.[36]

The prayer can be analysed as follows:

1. It is addressed to Almighty God, putting the emphasis on His omnipotence and sovereignty.
2. God is described in three ways:
   a. He is the Father of our Lord Jesus Christ.
   b. He is the Maker of all things.
   c. He is the Judge of all human beings.
3. We confess our many sins and great wickednesses, which progress from thought, to word, to deed. All of our sins are against God only (Psalm 51) and quite rightly provoke His wrath and anger.
4. We confess that we repent:
   a. We are sorry for the wrongs that we have done.
   b. We are grieved when we remember our sins.

---

35. The 1662 text updates the language slightly – 'be' becomes 'are' and 'burthen' becomes 'burden', but that is all.
36. In the 1637 Scottish prayer book it had been simplified to 'by the Presbyter himself, or the Deacon'.

c. We cannot bear to live with the guilt that our misdeeds have brought on us.
5. We cry to God the Father for mercy. He is merciful to us because of the intercession of His Son Jesus Christ. We ask him:
   a. to forgive what we have done in the past
   b. to grant us the grace to live a new life and please Him in the future
   c. to do all this for the honour and glory of His name.

God the Father is our Maker and therefore also our Judge, but this is in time and space. More importantly, He is the Father of Jesus Christ in eternity, and it is that relationship which determines how He will view His creation and how He will judge us. We must recognise that His punishment is justified and confess the burden of our sins, pleading for mercy from the Father of the Son who has given his life for us. Furthermore, we must be prepared to turn away from the past and look towards a future in which we shall magnify God's name by living a new kind of life. Confession of sin is never just a wiping of the slate clean; it also involves the expectation of a transformed existence. Jesus told the woman who was caught in adultery that he did not condemn her, but then he added that she should go and sin no more (John 8:11). That is the pattern for all of us. We are set free from condemnation but we are not affirmed in our sinfulness. On the contrary, we are expected to lead changed lives, which is only possible by the grace of God whose Holy Spirit dwells in our hearts by faith (Galatians 4:6).

The Absolution

The absolution comes originally from the Sarum missal; but there it was used by the ministers who absolved the priest from his sins before he consecrated the elements of bread and wine. In its present sense, it appears for the first time in the order for Communion of 1548, where it is stated: 'Our blessed Lord, who hath left power to his Church to absolve penitent sinners from their sins, and to restore to the grace of the heavenly Father such as believe in Christ.' The role thus ascribed to the Church was removed in 1549. The form of words remained unchanged in 1552 and 1662.

There is some similarity here between the 1549 prayer book and Hermann von Wied's order for the church of Cologne, but von Wied's text retains the declaratory aspect of 1548, whereas that is removed in 1549. Instead of declaring absolution, the priest recalls the promise of God to grant it and then prays that He will do so.

The absolution can be broken into two sections, the first of which expounds the nature and promise of God and the second of which invokes that nature and promise on behalf of the people.

First part:

1. Almighty God is our heavenly Father.
2. God is merciful and has promised forgiveness of sins to His people.
3. All who sincerely repent and turn to God in true faith will receive the promise.

Second part:

4. The merciful God is entreated to:
   a. pardon and deliver the communicants from their sins
   b. confirm and strengthen them in all goodness
   c. bring them to eternal life.

Here, again, we see the connection between the forgiveness of past sins and the expectation of a better future. Wrongdoing is never simply ignored or swept under the carpet as if it does not matter. As Christ died to pay the price for it, so he rose again in order for his forgiven people to be able to lead a new and different kind of life, which is only possible 'through Jesus Christ our Lord'.

The absolution is reserved in the Book of Common Prayer for the priest or for the bishop (if he is present). This is a recognition of a hierarchy in the Church that can only be justified in terms of order, not of power. Neither the bishop nor the priest has any authority to forgive sins and there is no theological reason why the absolution should be reserved to either of them. God's promise is valid and certain, regardless of who proclaims it, because it is God who is at work and not His minister(s). The rubric may be respected for the sake of order in the congregation, but it should not be insisted upon. Sadly, it seems that this is one of those instances where the conservative opponents of the Puritans were determined to preserve some recollection of the pre-Reformation doctrine of priestly absolution even though there was no theological justification for doing so.

The Comfortable Words[37]

These appear to have been taken, with some rearrangement, from Hermann von Wied's order for the church of Cologne. Von Wied placed his quotations from the New Testament between the confession and the absolution, which naturally led the hearers to expect the latter on the basis of the scriptural promises. The position in the 1548 order and, subsequently, in the prayer book serves to confirm the faith of the worshippers by giving biblical support to the promises just mentioned.

Hermann's texts did not include Matthew 11:28, but did make use of John 3:35 and Acts 10:43, which the Book of Common Prayer omits, including instead sayings of:

a. Jesus (Matthew 11:28; John 3:16)
b. Paul (1 Timothy 1:15)
c. John (1 John 2:1-2).

Neither von Wied nor Thomas Cranmer would have interpreted this in a text-critical way, but it is clear from their selection that they understood the message of forgiveness in and by Jesus Christ to be one that was proclaimed by Christ himself and by the two leading authors of the New Testament – Paul and John. Whatever differences they may have had in their approach to the Gospel message, on this central point they were at one. There is, nevertheless, a difference of emphasis that may be noted:

1. The words of Jesus focus:
   a. on those who are burdened by the weight of sin, who will be restored,
   b. on the love of God who sent His Son into the world so that we should not die but have eternal life.
2. The words of Paul focus on the mission of Christ to save sinners.
3. The words of John focus on the mediatorial role of the Son who pleads for us before the Father on the basis of his sacrifice for our sins.

---

37. See J.A. Null, *Divine Allurement: Cranmer's Comfortable Words* (London: Latimer Trust, 2014).

Note that the first of the comfortable words is an invitation by Jesus to those who are burdened, whom he asks to come to him for relief. It is more than a statement of doctrine – it is an application of the most fundamental Christian truth to the lives of those who need to hear it; a proclamation of the Gospel message at the heart of the Lord's Supper.

These different emphases are all essential to the message of the Gospel and should be kept together. It follows from this that the comfortable words should all be used at every celebration, since each of them contributes something special to the overall message.

The Sursum Corda

Named for the Latin meaning 'Lift up hearts', these short phrases are among the oldest that have survived intact in the prayer book. The *Sursum Corda* is found in all the most ancient liturgies of the Church, though not specifically in the New Testament. In 1549 it was placed immediately after the offertory, giving the impression that the worshippers were giving thanks for the sacrament, whereas in fact they were praising God for the promise of salvation that was fulfilled in Christ. Its position here, after the comfortable words, is therefore more appropriate. The *Sursum Corda* begins with a dialogue between the celebrant and the people that proceeds from one step to the next:

1. We are asked to lift up our hearts, a sign of hope in the promise given to us in Christ.
2. We focus this encouragement on the Lord.
3. We are asked to thank the Lord God (for His promise and gift to us).
4. We respond that this is the right thing to do.

The *Sursum Corda* is reserved for the priest because he is the celebrant of the entire service, not because he has any special authority or power to pronounce the words, which in principle could be said by anyone.

The Preliminary Thanksgiving

The opening dialogue then goes on to expound what the nature of our thanksgiving should be. At this point there is a rubric directing that the priest should 'turn to the Lord's Table' before proceeding any further. It is generally assumed that this was inserted in 1662 in opposition to the Puritan demand that the celebrant should always face the congregation and, in the nineteenth century, it was used by Anglo-Catholics to justify the eastward position that they adopted with their backs to the people. If a north end position was adopted, the effect was minimal, since the celebrant would be looking straight ahead of him and the congregation would have a sideways view. Today, the general adoption of the 'westward' position where the celebrant stands behind the Table and faces both it and the congregation at the same time, has made this direction redundant and for most people it is no longer an issue.

The celebrant here picks up the rhythm of the dialogue and takes it to the next level. Not only is it meet and right to thank God, it is our 'bounden duty' to do so – at all times and in all places. God is addressed directly as 'Lord, Holy Father, Almighty' and 'Everlasting'. A note indicates that the words 'Holy Father' must be omitted on Trinity Sunday, presumably because we worship the Trinity and not the Father only, though why that truth should be expressed on only one Sunday of the year is not clear. It might, in fact, be better to reword this as 'O Lord, Almighty, Everlasting God, Father, Son and Holy Spirit', which would do justice to the theological point being made.

In ordinary circumstances this assertion is then followed by a collective response, which culminates in the *Trisagion*, or *Ter Sanctus* ('thrice holy') taken from Isaiah 6:3 and slightly embellished. The observation that we do this along with angels, archangels and 'all the company of heaven' also reflects Isaiah chapter 6, where the Lord is pictured sitting on His throne, surrounded by the seraphim. The use of the *Trisagion* in the liturgy is very ancient and can be found in almost all the pre-Reformation texts that have come down to us. The prayer book does not make it clear whether the congregation is meant to join in with the celebrant in saying (or singing) these words, although, since singing is allowed in 1662, it seems that the revisers envisaged the participation of the choir at least.

Uniquely in the prayer book, the *Trisagion* contains a series of proper prefaces that were meant for use at particular times of the year. These are:

1. Christmas and the following seven days (including New Year's Day)
2. Easter Sunday and the following seven days (including the next Sunday)
3. Ascension and the following seven days
4. Whitsunday (Pentecost) and the following six days
5. Trinity Sunday.

Each of these prefaces draws attention to the events that those festivals commemorate and does so in highly theological terms. Thus, the proper preface for Christmas not only refers to the Father's sending His Son into the world, but adds that he was conceived by the Holy Spirit, made man in the womb of his mother the Virgin Mary and born without sin. The language in which Christ's sinlessness is expressed reflects the standard medieval view that sin is a stain on the soul from which it needs to be cleansed and is a holdover from pre-Reformation times. The Roman Catholic Church still speaks of the 'immaculate' ('spotless') conception, not only of Christ but also of his mother. Anglicans, along with other Protestants, do not subscribe to that interpretation of sin, although they affirm Christ's sinlessness. Sin is a broken relationship with God, which all human beings inherit from their first parents, but it is not a congenital defect that has left a kind of birthmark on the soul.

The proper preface for Easter celebrates the Resurrection, as we would expect, but it also recalls the atoning sacrifice that Christ made on the Cross on the preceding Friday. He is described as the Paschal Lamb, offered for us, who has taken away the sin of the world, destroying death by his death and by rising again, restoring us to everlasting life. On the surface, the language suggests a kind of universalism, but it is not meant to convey the idea that everyone is saved. The description of Christ as the Paschal Lamb places his sacrifice firmly within the covenant context – Christ died for his chosen people, just as the Paschal Lamb was sacrificed for Israel, and the rest follows on from that.

The proper preface for the Ascension rehearses the appearances of Christ to his disciples after his resurrection and reminds us that they were witnesses of his going up to heaven, where he is preparing a place for us to reign with him in his glory.

The proper preface for Whitsunday (Pentecost) emphasises the coming of the Holy Spirit promised by Christ to his disciples. It recalls the miraculous events of the first Pentecost, when tongues of fire sat on the heads of the apostles in order to teach them the fullness of the truth. In addition to that, he gave them the gift of speaking in different languages and the courage to preach the Gospel to all nations in order to bring them out of error and into the light and knowledge of God. It might be said in passing that the preface somewhat misrepresents what Acts chapter 2 tells us about Pentecost. The New Testament does not say that the apostles spoke in different languages, but that people heard them in their own tongues, which is not the same thing.

The proper preface for Trinity Sunday, the Sunday after Pentecost, quotes a line from the Athanasian Creed and reminds us that we worship one God in three Persons, who are fully equal in their divinity.

The Prayer of Humble Access

This prayer is one of the most beloved in the prayer book and has survived every attempt by liturgical purists to remove it. It has no precedent in pre-Reformation liturgies but was introduced in the 1548 order for Communion and then put after the consecration in 1549. In 1552 it was moved to its present position before the consecration so as to avoid any suggestion that the congregation is praying for access to the already consecrated elements of bread and wine. That was the interpretation that had been canvassed by Stephen Gardiner, then bishop of Winchester, who thought that the prayer could be understood to accommodate a doctrine of transubstantiation. By moving it to its present position, that view was made untenable. We pray for access to the atoning death of Christ in which we are united with him from the beginning, and not for access to something already accomplished without our involvement.

Two phrases in the prayer call for special comment. The first is the expression 'in these holy mysteries' that was originally found immediately after the words 'drink his blood'. This was present in both 1548 and 1549 but was dropped in 1552 because of the danger that it might be interpreted in the sense of transubstantiation.

The second is the extended phrase: 'that our sinful bodies may be made clean by his body, and our souls washed through his most precious blood'. The difficulty in deciding what this is supposed to mean has led to its omission from most modern versions of the prayer; and it must be admitted that its obscurity is puzzling.

One theory is that Thomas Cranmer wanted to insist on the necessity of communicating in both kinds – receiving the consecrated bread was not enough, as the late medieval Church insisted it was. However, while it is easy to see how the imagery of the blood could be used as a cleansing agent of the sin-stained soul, it is much harder to see how our bodies can be cleansed by Christ's body (as opposed to his blood). The most reasonable interpretation is that the two things must be taken together. Bread and wine represent Christ's body and blood, and it was by the shedding of his blood in the death of his body that he made atonement for us. Trying to analyse this by saying that the 'body' does one thing and the 'blood' another is pushing the imagery too far. Christ did not die without shedding blood, so the two notions must be held together, but our salvation does not involve a separation of body and soul, and the distinction of the elements must not be interpreted in a way that might suggest that it does.

The prayer may be analysed as follows:

1. We do not approach the Table trusting in any righteousness of our own. We are justified before God by faith alone and not by our works or achievements, however good and noble they might be.
2. We are unworthy even to gather up the crumbs under God's Table. This reflects the statement of the Canaanite woman who pleaded with Jesus to be allowed to eat the crumbs that fell from Israel's table (Matthew 15:27; Mark 7:28) and Jesus' warning to his disciples that, even when they have done all they can do, they are still unprofitable servants (Luke 17:10).
3. God is a God of mercy and does not change, even though we have fallen away from Him. The prayer book correctly states that God's mercy is a 'property' (used in the scientific sense of the word) and not, as in most modern revisions, part of his 'nature'. The difference is that, if it were God's nature to be merciful, no other course of action would be possible. As one of His properties however, it is fully consistent with His nature but not determined by it, so that He is not obliged to be merciful. The grace of God is a wonderful gift, but it cannot be forced out of Him or taken for granted.
4. We must be rightly disposed by God's grace to eat and drink the flesh and blood of Christ in a way that will further our growth in union with him and lead us to everlasting life.

The expressions 'eat the flesh' and 'drink the blood' are startling to those unfamiliar with them, but they must be understood spiritually and not materially. They are taken from the words of Jesus himself in John 6:51-57 but it is quite clear from the context that he was not advocating a form of cannibalism. Such crude misunderstandings, which contributed to the elaboration of the doctrine of transubstantiation, must be avoided at all costs. To eat Christ's flesh and drink his blood is to be united with him, above all, in heart and mind. When that union is achieved, it will affect every part of our being, including our physical nature. Our bodies will not ascend to heaven in their present state but they will be transformed into spiritual bodies (1 Corinthians 15:35-58). The resurrection is not a resurrection of the soul (or spirit) only, but of the whole human being – transformed, yes, but still present in its entirety. We have no way of knowing what our spiritual bodies will be like, other than that they will resemble the bodies of angels, who have no need to marry or procreate (Mark 12:25). Beyond that, it is unwise to speculate.

The Prayer of Consecration

The prayer of consecration is the most contested part of the service and underwent the greatest changes over the course of the various revisions from 1549 to 1662. In 1549 the 1662 prayer was contained in the prayer for the Church and was the second of three parts of the consecration. It came immediately after the *Trisagion* and before the invitation, confession and prayer of humble access. In 1552 the invitation and confession were moved to an earlier place in the service, and the prayer of consecration, as it now stands, was inserted in its present position, immediately after the prayer of humble access. However, the word 'consecration' was not used to describe it. It was not given a name of its own but is nowadays generally referred to as the 'words of institution'. In 1662 it was labelled the prayer of consecration, apparently at the insistence of the Episcopal party at the Savoy Conference, but this was purely symbolic.[38] In fact, there was no change from 1552 and no return to anything that would have been recognised as a 'consecration' before 1549. It is not surprising that many liturgical scholars have found it inadequate, because it does not do what they think a prayer of consecration ought to do. It is no more – but also no less – than a prayer of institution, rehearsing the acts of Jesus at the Last Supper and focussing on that as the model for the memorial of the Lord's Supper in the post-resurrection Church.

The 'consecration' part of the 1549 prayer for the Church may be compared with the 1552 'words of institution' (and 1662 prayer of consecration) as follows. Words dropped in 1552 are in grey; those added are in **bold** type. The symbol ✠ indicates where the celebrant is expected to touch the elements as a sign of their consecration:

> O **Almighty** God, **our** Heavenly Father, which of thy tender mercy didst give thine only Son Jesus Christ, to suffer death upon the cross for our redemption, who made there (by his one oblation **of himself** once offered) a full, perfect, and sufficient

---

38. It reflects the usage of the 1637 Scottish prayer book, where the term 'consecration' is used of this prayer for the first time.

sacrifice, oblation, and satisfaction, for the sins of the whole world, and did institute, and in his holy Gospel command us to celebrate **continue**, a perpetual memory of that his precious death, until his coming again: Hear us, O merciful Father, we **most humbly**[39] beseech thee; and with thy Holy Spirit and Word, vouchsafe to ✚ bless *and* ✚ sanctify **and grant that we receiving** these thy gifts and creatures of bread and wine, that they may be unto us the **according to thy Son our Saviour Jesus Christ's holy institution, in remembrance of his death and passion, may be partakers of his most blessed** body and blood of thy most dearly beloved Son Jesus Christ: who, in the same night that he was betrayed, took bread, and when he had blessed and given thanks, he brake it, and gave it to his Disciples, saying: Take, eat, this is my body which is given for you. Do this in remembrance of me. Likewise after supper he took the cup, and, when he had given thanks, he gave it to them, saying: Drink ye all of this, for this is my blood of the new Testament, which is shed for you and for many, for remission of sins: do this, as oft as you **ye** shall drink it, in remembrance of me.

The 1552 revision, repeated almost verbatim in 1559, 1604 and 1662, de-emphasised the blessing of the elements of bread and wine and stressed the remembrance of Christ's once-and-for-all offering of himself on the Cross. It is that remembrance, and not the consecration of the elements, that allows us to partake of his body and blood.

As it now stands, the 1662 prayer of consecration may be subdivided into three parts. These are:

1. A *declaration* of the relationship of the sacrament to the sacrifice.
2. A *petition* that partakers of the elements may be partakers of Christ.
3. A *recital* of the scriptural account of the original institution.

---

39. Taken from the 1637 Scottish Book of Common Prayer and added in 1662.

The *declaration* may be examined as follows:

> Almighty God, our heavenly Father, who[40] of thy tender
> mercy didst give thine only Son Jesus Christ to suffer death
> upon the cross for our redemption; who made there (by his one
> oblation of himself once offered) a full, perfect, and sufficient
> sacrifice, oblation and satisfaction for the sins of the whole
> world; and did institute, and in his holy Gospel command us
> to continue, a perpetual memory of that his precious death,
> until his coming again.

The text insists on the uniqueness of Christ's atoning death on the
Cross, of which the Lord's Supper can be no more than a memorial, not
a repetition or re-presentation. Some critics have thought that the prayer
labours this point more than is necessary but, while that may be true
nowadays, it must be remembered that the original hearers had been
taught the doctrine of transubstantiation which had to be drummed
out of their heads in any way possible. This explains why in 1552 it was
stated that Christ offered himself once and for all on the Cross and why
the memory of that sacrifice is continued, not celebrated afresh.

The *petition* may similarly be set out as follows:

> Hear us, O merciful Father, we most humbly beseech thee;
> and grant that we, receiving these thy creatures of bread and
> wine, according to thy Son our Saviour Jesus Christ's holy
> institution, in remembrance of his death and passion, may be
> partakers of his most blessed Body and Blood.

This part of the prayer of consecration was substantially altered in
1552, since which time it has remained unchanged, although a serious
attempt to rework it in the direction of 1549 was made in the 1637
Scottish prayer book, where it reads as follows (alterations/additions in
bold type):

Hear us, O merciful Father, we most humbly beseech thee, and **of thy
almighty goodness vouchsafe so to bless and sanctify with thy Word
and Holy Spirit** these thy **gifts and** creatures of bread and wine, **that
they may be unto us the body and blood of thy most dearly beloved
Son; so that we, receiving them** according to thy Son our Saviour Jesus

---

40. This insignificant change, from 'which' in both 1549 and 1552 to 'who',
    was made in 1662.

Christ's holy institution, in remembrance of his death and passion, may be partakers **of the same** his most precious body and blood.

The 1637 text does not deny the remembrance of Christ's sacrifice, but it restores the consecration of the elements as that expressed in 1549 and insists that they are 'unto us' the body and blood of Christ and that we are partakers of 'the same'. It is not a statement of transubstantiation but comes much closer to it than the 1552 version does and may even be said to allow for that interpretation. It is not hard to see why it met with such strong opposition.

There is no suggestion in 1552 that the elements of bread and wine have been specially sanctified. In 1549 the words 'bless' and 'sanctify' were marked with a cross to indicate that the celebrant was expected to make the sign of the cross over the elements at this point. It was a practice that went back to pre-Reformation times and that was meant to signify their transubstantiation. In the 1549 liturgy that doctrine was abandoned but the practice was allowed to continue, perhaps because it was felt that to abolish it at the same time was a step too far. It was, however, discontinued in 1552.

There can be no doubt in the revised wording that the communicants are receiving bread and wine in the same way that the disciples of Jesus received them at the Last Supper. They are meant to remind us of Christ's sacrifice and make us partakers of it by faith, but are in no sense to be regarded as having been transubstantiated into his body and blood.

The *recital* of the original institution at the Last Supper appears as follows in 1549.[41] Only two words were deleted in 1552 and two relatively minor ones were added in 1662:

> Who in the same night that he was betrayed ✛ took bread, and when he had *blessed and* [1552] given thanks, ✛ he brake it and gave it to his disciples, saying: Take, eat, ✛ this is my Body which is given for you, do this in remembrance of me.
>
> Likewise after supper ✛ he took the cup; and, when he had given thanks, he gave it to them, saying: Drink ye all of this; for ✛ this is my Blood of the New Testament, which is shed for you and for many, for **the** [1662] remission of sins: Do this, as oft as you shall drink it, in remembrance of me. **Amen** [1662].

---

41. The crosses mark the places where the celebrant performed the manual acts of taking, breaking and blessing the consecrated elements. These directions were placed in the rubrics from 1552 onwards.

The deletion of 'blessed and' was part and parcel of the determination to remove anything that might lend itself to the doctrine of transubstantiation. The bread was not 'blessed' so as to avoid the idea that it was somehow altered into something more spiritual.

At the same time, and thanks largely to Puritan urgings at the Savoy Conference in 1661, more specific directions were given as to how the celebrant should handle the bread and wine, and when. The five prescribed actions were:

1. 'Took bread'. This had appeared in 1549 but was left out in 1552. It was restored in 1662 on the assumption that the bread would be presented in a paten.
2. 'He brake it'. Here the celebrant was expected to break the bread.
3. 'This is my Body'. Here the celebrant was told to lay his hand on all the bread.
4. 'He took the cup'. Here the celebrant was to take the cup in his hand.
5. 'This is my Blood'. Here the celebrant was to lay his hand on every vessel that contained wine to be consecrated.

It is ironic that these proposals, made by the Puritans in the interests of clarity and to avoid superstition, ended up achieving the exact opposite of what was intended, at least in the eyes of the high church party. The priestly touch could easily be interpreted as a kind of magical act, reintroducing transubstantiation by the back door, though this was the last thing on the minds of those who proposed it. Their aim was to re-enact the Last Supper as accurately as possible and, of course, such a re-enactment was incompatible with any notion of transubstantiation.

As a matter of interest, it may be observed how well this recital blends the four accounts of the Last Supper in the New Testament (Matthew 26:26-29; Mark 14:22-25; Luke 22:19-20; 1 Corinthians 11:23-26):

Who in the same night ... brake it	1 Corinthians
Gave ... disciples	Matthew
Saying	Luke
Take, eat	Matthew
This is my body	All four texts
which is for you	Luke, 1 Corinthians
given	Luke
Do this etc.	Luke, 1 Corinthians

Likewise after supper	Luke, 1 Corinthians
took	Matthew, Mark
cup	All four texts
And when ... to them	Mark
Saying	Luke, 1 Corinthians
Drink ye all	Matthew
For this ... covenant	Matthew, Mark
New	Luke, 1 Corinthians
Shed for you	Luke
for many	Matthew, Mark
for remission of sins	Matthew
Do this etc.	1 Corinthians

The Administration

The rubric governing the administration stipulates that the minister celebrating shall receive the Communion in both kinds before giving it to others. He is then to communicate bishops, priests and deacons if there are any present, also in both kinds, before going on to the rest of the congregation. There is no suggestion that anyone present should abstain from communicating for any reason, and no indication that communicants should fast before coming to the Lord's Table. These and other similar practices are pious inventions with no precedent either in Scripture or in the Book of Common Prayer.

The minister is to give the bread and the cup into the hands of the people, not place them directly in the mouth. There is no provision for intinction (dipping the bread in the wine) either. All who receive are meant to do so kneeling, though this is widely ignored nowadays when many people stand or even sit in order to receive. Nor is there any restriction on who should administer the bread and the cup, though it is assumed that those who do so will be 'ministers'. It is common for deacons to assist in this way and, in recent years, licensed lay people have also done so. There is no theological reason why they should not, but some restriction can be justified on grounds of order.

The words of administration themselves were completely different in 1549 and 1552. However, they were combined in 1559 and have remained so ever since (apart from the 1637 Scottish prayer book, which dropped the 1552 words):

> 1549: The body of our Lord Jesus Christ which was given for thee, preserve thy body and soul unto everlasting life.

1552: Take and eat this, in remembrance that Christ died
for thee, and feed on him in thy heart by faith, with
thanksgiving.

1549: The blood of our Lord Jesus Christ which was shed
for thee, preserve thy body and soul unto everlasting
life.

1552: Drink this in remembrance that Christ's blood was
shed for thee, and be thankful.

It is difficult to say them all to every communicant because of the
time which that takes and, in practice, ministers tend to communicate
several people while saying the words only once. This is not altogether
satisfactory but, as long as everyone can hear what is being said, there
does not seem to be any reasonable objection to the practice. It is better
to do that than to truncate the words to the point where their original
intention is lost or obscured.

The words of 1549 are 'objective' in the sense that they refer primarily
to the elements themselves and describe what they are supposed to do.
They can trace their origin to the Sarum and York missals, which used
similar words for the administration of Communion to the sick, though
there were no words of administration at all in the Mass as celebrated
in church. The addition of the clauses 'which was given for thee' and
'which was shed for thee' are meant to remind the communicant that
the sacrifice of Christ was accomplished on the Cross and is not being
re-presented in the sacrament. Once again, it is an attempt to guard
against false notions of transubstantiation.

The words of 1552 are 'subjective' in that they address the communicant
directly and ask him to remember the death of Christ on his behalf. The
administration of the bread adds that the communicant is expected to
feed on Christ by faith, which is omitted in the words of administration
of the cup.

It may be noted that the 1549 words are a fairly straightforward
translation of an underlying Latin text, whereas the words of 1552 are
not. The expression 'take and eat' is idiomatic in English where two
verbs can easily be combined in this way (compare: 'go and get', 'come
and see' etc.) but is foreign to Latin, where each verb should have its own
object (e.g. 'Take this and eat it').

In the 1549 text there was a provision for the choir to sing the *Agnus
Dei* but this was taken out in 1552 and was never restored, probably
because, yet again, it opened the door to belief in transubstantiation,
which the Reformers wanted to avoid.

This section concludes with two rubrics governing the administration. The first gives directions as to what to do if the supply of bread and wine runs out before all have communicated. In that case, the celebrant is to consecrate further supplies by adapting the final section of the prayer of consecration for the blessing of the bread and of the cup separately.

The second rubric directs the minister to cover any leftover bread and wine with a fair linen cloth to protect them. A further rubric at the end of the service directs that if the remaining bread and wine has been consecrated, the celebrant shall consume it before leaving the church. This is to prevent it being stolen or otherwise abused.

The Post-Communion

The final section of the Communion office is also the shortest. In the 1549 prayer book it consists of 22 verses from the New Testament, of which fifteen are from the Gospels and the rest from the Pauline Epistles. It was expected that one of them would be said or sung as a post-Communion (the term is actually used in the 1549 liturgy). It was then followed by a prayer of thanksgiving and the departing blessing.

In the 1552 text the post-Communion was completely restructured and it was this revised form that prevailed in 1662. The selection of Scripture verses disappeared and was replaced by the Lord's Prayer in its longer form, with the doxology. The rubric states that it should be said by the people 'after' the minister but, although some people have taken this literally, it seems obvious that 'after' should be understood in the sense of 'with' and that is how it is normally used today.

The Lord's Prayer

The introduction of the Lord's Prayer at this point was part of a general trend observable throughout the Book of Common Prayer, where the prayer is almost the 'signature tune' of an authentic Anglican service. Some have criticised it for that reason, thinking that its use is overdone. However, it is always a good text to fall back on and encourages ordinary people, who will usually know it by heart, to join in more readily.

The First Prayer of Thanksgiving (Oblation)

Much more controversial has been the first prayer of thanksgiving which follows immediately afterwards and which had originally been the prayer of oblation in the 1549 text, in which the elements of bread and wine were offered up to God. Its transfer to this point changed its meaning. Now, instead of offering up the elements, we offer up ourselves to the service of God, in thanksgiving for what He has done for us, which is what we have just celebrated in the sacrament. In the course of the transposition the prayer has undergone substantial editing, which can best be appreciated when set out as follows. Words that were dropped or modified in 1552 are in grey and additions are in **bold** type:

Wherefore, **O Lord and heavenly Father,** according to the institution of thy dearly beloved Son, our Saviour Jesu Christ, **we thy humble servants** do celebrate, and make here before thy divine majesty, with these thy holy gifts, the memorial which thy Son hath willed us to make, having in remembrance his blessed passion, mighty resurrection, and glorious ascension, rendering unto thee most hearty thanks, for the innumerable benefits procured unto us by the same, **and we** entirely desiring[42] **desire** thy Fatherly goodness mercifully to accept this our sacrifice of praise and thanksgiving; most humbly beseeching thee to grant, that by the merits and death of thy Son Jesus Christ, and through faith in his blood, we and all thy whole Church may obtain remission of our sins, and all other benefits of his passion. And here we offer and present unto thee, O Lord, our self **selves,** our souls and bodies, to be a reasonable, holy and lively sacrifice unto thee: humbly beseeching thee, that whosoever shall **all we, which** be[43] partakers of this holy Communion, may worthily receive the most precious body and blood of thy Son Jesus Christ: and **be fulfilled with thy grace and heavenly benediction.** and made one body with thy Son Jesus Christ, that he may dwell in them and they in him. **And although we be unworthy, through our manifold sins, to offer unto thee any sacrifice, yet we beseech thee to accept this our bounden duty and service;** and command these our prayers and supplications, by the ministry of thy holy angels, to be brought up into thy holy tabernacle before the sight of thy divine majesty, **not weighing**

---

42. The entire section preceding was restored in the 1637 Scottish prayer book.
43. The 1549 words, 'that whosoever shall be partakers', were restored in the 1637 Scottish rite. Moreover, the 'which be' of 1552 was replaced by 'who are' in 1662.

our merits, but pardoning our offences, through **Jesus** Christ
our Lord; by whom, and with whom, in the unity of the Holy
Ghost, all honour and glory be unto thee, O Father Almighty,
world without end. Amen.

The 1552 text survived unchanged in 1662 but, as the above makes
clear, there was considerable pruning of phrases found in the 1549 prayer
book. The 1637 Scottish version restored some (though not all) of the 1549
text but this modification was rejected in 1662. As we might expect, the
excised phrases are those which could lend themselves to a doctrine of
transubstantiation if they were so interpreted, and it was the desire of
Thomas Cranmer and his colleagues to ensure that that would not happen.
Needless to say, this greatly perturbed the high church liturgists of the late
nineteenth and early twentieth centuries, who made this prayer one of
their principal targets for 'restoration' along 1549 lines. We can only be
grateful that they failed in their aim and that the prayer stands where it
should as a magnificent statement of the self-offering that is expected of
everyone who has met the Lord Jesus in the breaking of the bread.

The prayer may be analysed as follows:

1. We humbly ask God the Father in His mercy to accept our
   sacrifice of praise and thanksgiving.
2. We ask Him to grant us forgiveness of our sins and every
   other benefit of His passion, by the merits of Christ's death
   and through our faith in the power of his blood.
3. We present ourselves, souls and bodies to be a reasonable
   sacrifice (Romans 12:1).
4. We pray that all the communicants may be blessed by God.
5. We confess that we are unworthy to offer any sacrifice but
   ask God to accept what we owe Him.
6. We ask God not to judge us by our (non-existent) merits, but
   to pardon our sins.
7. We pray by, with and through Jesus Christ, who is united
   with the Holy Spirit and the Father in the unity of the one
   God.

What is now the second prayer of thanksgiving was the only one
in 1549 and it was retained as an alternative in 1552, to be used at the
discretion of the minister. It has no clear pre-Reformation antecedents
and, since it was designed to occupy this position, the changes made in
1552 and later were correspondingly slight. They can be appreciated as

follows, with words deleted in grey and words added in **bold** type. The changes were made in 1552, except where otherwise indicated:

> Almighty and everliving God, we most heartily thank thee, for that thou hast **dost** vouchsafed to feed us, in *which* **who** [1662] **have duly received** these holy mysteries, with the spiritual food of the most precious Body and Blood of thy Son our Saviour Jesus Christ; and *hast* **dost** assure*d* us (duly receiving the same) **thereby** of thy favour and goodness towards [1662] us, and that we be **are** [1662] very members incorporate in thy **the** [1662] mystical body **of thy Son** [1662], which is the blessed company of all faithful people; and be **are** [1662] **also** heirs through hope of thy everlasting kingdom, by the merits of the most precious death and passion of thy dear Son. **And** [1662] we therefore **now** most humbly beseech thee, O heavenly Father, so to assist us with thy grace, that we may continue in that holy fellowship, and do all such good works as thou hast prepared for us to walk in; through Jesus Christ our Lord, to whom, with thee and the Holy Ghost, be all honour and glory, world without end. **Amen**.

Once again, anything that might smack of transubstantiation was removed in 1552 and only a few purely cosmetic changes were made in 1662. This prayer may be analysed as follows:

1. We thank God because He has fed the communicants with the spiritual food of the body and blood of Christ.
2. We thank God for the assurance He has given us of His favour and goodness towards us.
3. We thank God that we are incorporated members of Christ's mystical body and heirs of his everlasting kingdom.
4. We ask God to assist us with His grace so that we may continue in His holy fellowship and do the good works that He has prepared for us to perform.

The **Gloria**

This very ancient hymn, which is one of the earliest liturgical texts to have found a home in the prayer book, was originally placed at the beginning of the Communion office and many modern liturgical 'experts' have restored it to that position. Yet the contents of the hymn make it much more suitable as a conclusion, because we are leaving the communion with God with a sense of triumphant joy that takes us out into the world as witnesses of the new life that we have obtained in Christ.

The translation of the ancient hymn is defective in its opening line where it has 'peace, good will towards men' instead of the correct 'peace to men of good will', taken from the song of the angels who appeared to the shepherds in the fields outside Bethlehem (Luke 2:14). In 1552 a second 'Thou that takest away the sins of the world, have mercy upon us' was added to the original text, possibly in order to create a threefold appeal similar to the one found in the *Agnus Dei*. It could be dropped without serious loss.

The *Gloria* has a trinitarian structure similar to that of the creeds. The first section is one of praise and worship to the Father. The second is addressed to the Son, who takes away the sins of the world and sits at the right hand of the Father. The third section is also addressed to Christ but adds a mention of the Holy Spirit, with whom he shares the glory of the Father.

The Blessing

The post-Communion concludes with the final blessing, the first clause of which goes back to the 1548 order for Communion and is taken from Philippians 4:7. The second part, beginning with 'and the blessing' was added in 1549 and the text has remained essentially unchanged ever since. The 'Amen' is printed in italics in order to indicate that the people are to join with the minister in saying it.

The blessing was to be said by the celebrant, or by the bishop if he was present, a provision that is still generally respected today.

Excursus: From the 1637 Scottish BCP to the 1789 American BCP

It has long been recognised that there is a liturgical thread going back in some respects to the 1549 Book of Common Prayer, passing through the 1637 Scottish prayer book and the 1764 Scottish Communion office to the 1789 American Book of Common Prayer and the subsequent American tradition. This liturgical inheritance touches on various services in the English text, but most of these are of secondary importance, being (mainly) alternative lectionaries, canticles in the daily offices and the like. It is in the Communion office that the most important – and most controversial – divergences are found: first, there is the different order in which the various prayers occur; and, second, there is the different content that is apparent in some of the prayers.

The different orders may be set out as follows:

1552	1637	1764	1789
Invitation	Invitation		Invitation
Confession	Confession		Confession
Absolution	Absolution		Absolution
Comfortable words	Comfortable words		Comfortable words
Sursum corda	*Sursum corda*	*Sursum corda*	*Sursum corda*
Prefaces	Prefaces	Prefaces	Prefaces
Sanctus	*Sanctus*	*Sanctus*	*Sanctus*
Humble Access			**Humble Access**
Consecration	Consecration	Consecration	Consecration
	Invocation		
	Oblation	**Oblation**	**Oblation**
		Invocation	**Invocation**
		Prayer for the Church	
	Lord's Prayer	Lord's Prayer	
		Invitation	
		Confession	
		Absolution	
		Comfortable words	
	Humble Access	**Humble Access**	
Administration (b)	**Administration (a)**	**Administration (a)**	**Administration (a/b)**
		Prayer for Grace	
Lord's Prayer			Lord's Prayer
Oblation			
Thanksgiving	Thanksgiving	Thanksgiving	Thanksgiving
Gloria	*Gloria*	*Gloria*	*Gloria*
Blessing	Blessing	Blessing	Blessing

It will be seen from this table that the 1764 Scottish Communion office was much more radical than the 1637 Scottish prayer book and also more radical than the 1789 American prayer book, despite having had some influence on it.

Particular points to note are:

1. The prayer of **humble access**. This precedes the consecration in 1552 and in all subsequent English prayer books. It was moved back to the 1549 position in 1637 and in 1764, but this was not followed by the American prayer book until 1928, since when it has become standard there as well.
2. The **oblation** in 1552 is a prayer of thanksgiving after the administration, in which the communicants offer themselves to the service of God as a living sacrifice (Romans 12:1). In 1637, 1764 and 1789 it is placed after the consecration (as in 1549), where it becomes the offering of the consecrated gifts of bread and wine, as well as the self-offering of the communicants.
3. The **invocation** or *epiclesis* was present in a reduced form in the 1549 prayer of consecration but made more explicit in the 1637 Scottish prayer book. In the 1764 Scottish Communion office it was removed from the prayer of consecration and made part of the prayer of oblation, on the understanding that this was the pattern of most ancient Eastern liturgies. It was accepted as such in the 1789 American prayer book and has remained part of the American tradition ever since, but there is no equivalent in the 1662 text.[44]
4. The words of **administration** in every English prayer book from 1559 onwards combine those of 1549 (a) and 1552 (b). The Scottish rites use only the 1549 words (a) but the 1789 American text follows the English pattern and subsequent American prayer books have done the same.[45] It must, however, be admitted that the length of the words in the 1662 version militates against their use in full, and that there is accordingly a strong tendency to abbreviate them, almost always in ways that would allow them to be interpreted

---

44. The 2019 Book of Common Prayer of the Anglican Church in North America very helpfully points this out on p. 116, presumably with the intention of allowing celebrants to omit it if they wish, although a note adds that 'ecumenical consensus expects its use'.
45. The 1979 American prayer book allows for an abbreviated form of administration in its Eucharistic rite II and the 2019 text of the Anglican Church in North America has also done so.

as affirming transubstantiation. For example, it is not uncommon to hear 'the body of Christ' and 'the blood of Christ' being spoken to each communicant, with no further explanation.

The Appended Collects

The 1662 liturgy has six appended collects which date from 1549, were expanded in 1552 and slightly altered in 1662. They were intended for use immediately after the offertory when there was no Communion and, since that was at one time very common, they may have been frequently heard in churches. Today the Communion office is almost never used in that way and these collects have essentially gone out of regular use, which is a pity. They ought to be relocated to a position following Morning and Evening Prayer where they would be noticed and perhaps employed more often. As it is, they are effectively hidden in plain sight and are easily passed over.

The collects are:

1. For guidance along the pathway towards sanctification in the face of all the challenges of this life.
2. For guidance in keeping God's laws and for preservation in body and soul.[46]
3. For hearing the words of the service in such a way that they will be grafted into our hearts and bring forth the fruits of good living.
4. For our good works, that they may be guided and directed by God and that in everything they may glorify His holy name. Note that the word 'prevent' is used in its original sense of 'go before'.[47]
5. For the omniscient God's compassion on our weaknesses, that He may give us those necessary things that either we feel too unworthy to ask for or are ignorant of.
6. For the fulfilment of God's promise that He will give us what we need and that we have asked for according to His will.

---

46. Based on material from the Gregorian sacramentary and in the Sarum breviary.
47. From the Gregorian sacramentary.

The Closing Rubrics

The Communion office has an exceptionally large number of rubrics attached to the end, which mostly refer to different items that occur earlier on. There are major differences between the rubrics of 1549 and those of 1552, which were only slightly modified later. For purposes of comparison, the 1549 rubrics are set out first (with modernised spelling), followed by the 1552 rubrics, with subsequent modifications indicated as they occur.

The 1549 Book of Common Prayer:

1. Upon Wednesdays and Fridays, the English litany shall be said or sung in all places, after such form as is appointed by the king's majesty's injunctions: Or as is or shall be otherwise appointed by his highness.[48] And though there be none to communicate with the priest, yet these days (after the litany ended) the priest shall put upon him a plain alb or surplice, with a cope, and say all things at the altar (appointed to be said at the celebration of the Lord's Supper) until after the offertory. And then shall add one or two of the collects aforewritten, as occasion shall serve by his discretion. And then, turning him to the people, shall let them depart with the accustomed blessing.

2. And the same order shall be used all the other days whensoever the people be customably assembled to pray in the church, and none disposed to communicate with the priest.

3. Likewise in chapels annexed, and all other places, there shall be no celebration of the Lord's Supper, except there be some to communicate with the priest. And in such chapels annexed where the people hath not been accustomed to pay any holy bread, there they must either make some charitable provision for the bearing of the charges of the Communion, or else (for receiving of the same) resort to their parish church.

4. For avoiding of all matters and occasion of dissension, it is meet that the bread prepared for the Communion be made, through all this realm, after one sort and fashion: that is to say, unleavened and round, as it was afore, but without all manner of print, and something more larger and thicker than

---

48. Edwardian Injunctions 1547, no. 23 (Bray, *Documents*, p. 223). Repeated in Elizabethan Injunctions 1559, no. 18 (Bray, *Documents*, p. 304).

it was, so that it may be aptly divided in divers pieces: and every one shall be divided in two pieces, at the least, or more, by the discretion of the minister, and so distributed. And men must not think less to be received in part than in the whole, but in each of them the whole body of our Saviour Jesu Christ.

5. And forasmuch as the pastors and curates within this realm shall continually find at their costs and charges in their cures, sufficient bread and wine for the holy Communion (as oft as their parishioners shall be disposed for their spiritual comfort to receive the same) it is therefore ordered, that in recompense of such costs and charges, the parishioners of every parish shall offer every Sunday, at the time of the offertory the just valour and price of the holy loaf (with all such money, and other things as were wont to be offered with the same) to the use of their pastors and curates, and that in such order and course as they were wont to find and pay the said holy loaf.

6. Also, that the receiving of the sacrament of the blessed body and blood of Christ may be most agreeable to the institution thereof, and to the usage of the primitive Church: In all cathedral and collegiate churches, there shall always some communicate with the priest that ministereth. And that the same may be also observed everywhere abroad in the country: Some one at the least of that house in every parish to whom by course after the ordinance herein made, it appertaineth to offer for the charges of the Communion, or some other whom they shall provide to offer for them, shall receive the holy Communion with the priest: the which may be the better done, for that they know before, when their course cometh, and may therefore dispose themselves to the worthy receiving of the sacrament. And with him or them who doth so offer the charges of the Communion; all other, who be then Godly disposed thereunto, shall likewise receive the Communion. And by this means the minister having always some to communicate with him, may accordingly solemnise so high and holy mysteries, with all the suffrages and due order appointed for the same. And the priest on the weekday shall forbear to celebrate the Communion, except he have some that will communicate with him.

7. Furthermore, every man and woman be bound to hear and be at the divine service, in the parish church where they be resident, and there with devout prayer or Godly silence and

meditation, to occupy themselves. There to pay their duties, to communicate once in the year at the least, and there to receive, and take all other sacraments and rites, in this book appointed. And whosoever willingly upon no just cause doth absent themselves, or doth ungodly in the parish church occupy themselves: upon proof thereof, by the ecclesiastical laws of the realm to be excommunicate, or suffer other punishment, as shall to the ecclesiastical judge (according to his discretion) seem convenient.

8. And although it be read in ancient writers that the people many years past received at the priest's hands the sacrament of the body of Christ in their own hands, and no commandment of Christ to the contrary: Yet forasmuch as they many times conveyed the same secretly away, kept it with them, and diversely abused it to superstition and wickedness: lest any such thing hereafter should be attempted, and that an uniformity might be used, throughout the whole realm: it is thought convenient the people commonly receive the sacrament of Christ's body, in their mouths, at the priest's hand.

The 1552/1662 prayer books:[49]

1. Upon the **Sundays and other** holy days (if there be no Communion) shall be said all that is appointed at the Communion, until the end of the homily, concluding with the general prayer for the whole state of Christ's Church militant here in earth, and **together with** one or more of these collects, **last** before rehearsed, as occasion shall serve **concluding with the blessing**.

2. And there shall be no celebration of the Lord's Supper, except there be a good **convenient** number to communicate with the priest, according to his discretion.

3. And if there be not above twenty persons in the parish of discretion to receive the Communion; yet there shall be no Communion, except four (or three at the least) communicate with the priest.

---

49. Omissions in 1662 are indicated in grey; additions at that time are indicated in **bold** type.

3a.[50] And in cathedral and collegiate churches, **and colleges,** where be **there are** many priests and deacons, they shall all receive the Communion with the minister every Sunday at the least, except they have a reasonable cause to the contrary.

4. And to take away **all occasion of dissension, and** the superstition, which any person hath, or might have, in **concerning** the bread and wine, it shall suffice that the bread be such as is usual to be eaten; at the table, with other meats but the best and purest wheat bread that conveniently may be gotten.

4a. And if any of the bread or **and** wine remain **unconsecrated,** the curate shall have it to his own use: **but if any remain of that which was consecrated, it shall not be carried out of the church, but the priest and such other of the communicants as he shall then call unto him, shall, immediately after the blessing, reverently eat and drink the same.**

5. The bread and wine for the Communion shall be provided by the curate and the churchwardens at the charges of the parish and the parish shall be discharged of such sums of money, or other duties, which hitherto that have paid for the same by order of their houses every Sunday.

6. And note, that every parishioner shall communicate at the least three times in the year, of which Easter to be one. And shall also receive the sacraments and other rites according to the order of this book appointed. And yearly at Easter every parishioner shall reckon with his **the** parson, vicar or curate, or his or their deputy or deputies, and pay to them or him, all ecclesiastical duties, accustomably due, then and at that time to be paid.

7. **After the divine service ended, the money given at the offertory shall be disposed of to such pious and charitable uses, as the minister and churchwardens shall think fit. Wherein if they disagree, it shall be disposed of as the Ordinary shall appoint.**

It will be seen from the above that the rubrics of 1552 were freshly composed, even if some of the concerns (e.g. that there should be a sufficient number of communicants and that potentially superstitious practices should be avoided) were the same. The only major change after 1552 was that in 1662 consecrated bread and wine was to be consumed immediately after the celebration and not given to the minister for his

---

50. Separated from no. 3 in 1662.

own use, a practice that continues to the present time. There was also an additional rubric concerning the disposal of the cash offerings of the people, a question that had not previously been specifically addressed.

The Black Rubric

This is the best known of all the rubrics. It was attached to the 1552 Book of Common Prayer in order to meet the objection of John Knox to kneeling for the reception of Communion. Knox believed that kneeling implied adoration and wanted it to be ruled out for that reason. Thomas Cranmer refused to go that far but he agreed to add an explanation, making it clear that kneeling does not imply that. It had been thought that it came too late to be printed with the other rubrics in the traditional red, so it was added at the end in black – hence its popular name. However, this interpretation has been shown to be incorrect, partly because all the rubrics in the 1552 prayer book were printed in black and partly because it was not a rubric at all. It was written, probably by Archbishop Cranmer himself, sometime between 7 and 22 October 1552 and was set in a different typeface, usually textura instead of roman, which was used for the actual rubrics. The textura font was known as 'black letter', which explains why in 1688 Abraham Woodhead called it the 'Black Rubric', a name that has stuck.[51]

The Black Rubric was omitted in 1559 but it was restored in an abridged version, with some verbal modifications, in 1662. Few people worry about it now, but it remains a valuable safeguard against possible superstition. The text, with the emendations made in 1662, is as follows (words in grey were dropped in 1662, while words in **bold** type were added at that time.)

> Although no order can be so perfectly devised, but it may be of some, either for their ignorance and infirmity, or else of malice and obstinacy, misconstrued, depraved, and interpreted in a wrong part; And yet because brotherly charity willeth, that so much as conveniently may be, offences should be taken away, therefore, we willing to do the same, **Whereas it is ordained in** *The Book of Common Prayer*, in **this office for** the administration of the Lord's Supper, that the communicants **should receive the same** kneeling should receive the holy Communion; (which thing being **order is**

---

51. See Hefling, *Book of Common Prayer*, pp. 265-69, and Blayney, *Printing and Printers*, pp. 209-12, for a full explanation.

well meant, for a signification of the **our** humble and grateful acknowledging**ment** of the benefits of Christ **therein** given un**to** the **all** worthy receivers, and to **for the** avoide**ing of** such profanation and disorder which about **in** the Holy Communion **as** might else **otherwise** ensue;), **yet**, lest yet the same kneeling might be thought or taken otherwise, we do declare that it is not meant thereby that any adoration is done **should by any persons, either out of ignorance and infirmity, or out of malice and obstinacy, be misconstrued and depraved; It is hereby declared, That thereby no adoration is intended,** or ought to be done, either unto the sacramental bread or wine there bodily received, or unto any real and essential **corporal** presence there being of Christ's natural flesh and blood. For as concerning the sacramental bread and wine they remain still in their very natural substances, and therefore may not be adored, (for that were idolatry, to be abhorred of all faithful Christians;) and as concerning the natural body and blood of our Saviour Christ they are in heaven, and not here; for it is **being** against the truth of Christ's true natural body, to be **at one time** in more places than in one at one time.

The only change of any significance is the one that replaced 'real and essential' with 'corporal' in reference to the presence of Christ's body and blood. This change reflects a controversy that raged between Lutherans and other Reformed Protestants from the time of the Colloquy of Marburg (between Martin Luther and Huldrych Zwingli) in 1529 onwards. One of the problems was that the words 'real and essential' could be given philosophical meanings that were different from the way most people understood them. What the Lutherans and the other Reformed Protestants agreed on was that Christ's body and blood were not present in the sacrament in a material, physical way; and this was best expressed by the word 'corporal' ('bodily'). The Church of England did not subscribe to the Lutheran belief in a spiritual presence of Christ in the sacramental elements of bread and wine but the 1662 revisers did not want to offend or excommunicate the Lutherans who disagreed with them on that point. Without themselves affirming a 'real presence' of Christ in the spiritual sense of 'real', the Anglican divines of the seventeenth century were prepared to accommodate those who thought otherwise, as long as they did not go to the point of believing that the elements themselves changed their nature, as the Roman Catholic doctrine of transubstantiation insisted they did.

Chapter 6

Christian Initiation

Introduction

It appeareth by ancient writers, that the sacrament of baptism in the old time was not commonly ministered, but at two times in the year, at Easter and Whitsuntide, at which times it was openly ministered in the presence of all the congregation: Which custom (now being grown out of use) although it cannot for many considerations be well restored again, yet it is thought good to follow the same as near as conveniently may be: Wherefore the people are to be admonished that it is most convenient that baptism should not be ministered but upon Sundays and other holy days, when the most number of people may come together. As well for that the congregation there present may testify the receiving of them that be newly baptised into the number of Christ's Church, as also because in the baptism of infants, every man present may be put in remembrance of his own profession made to God in his baptism. For which cause also, it is expedient that baptism be ministered in the English tongue. Nevertheless (if necessity so require) children ought at all times to be baptised, either in the church or else at home.

Thus begins the rite of public baptism in both the 1549 and 1552 prayer books and it gives us an excellent introduction to the way that baptism was perceived by the Reformers. They were aware that in ancient times baptism had normally been administered only at Easter and Whitsun

(Pentecost) or, to be more precise, on the eve of those great feasts. They knew that it would be impractical to try to revive the ancient custom and they advocated what to them was the next best thing – baptism ought to be celebrated publicly in church on Sundays and holy days only. This was not for any superstitious reason but because it was at those times that the greatest number of people would be gathered together as witnesses. The Reformers discouraged private baptism, which had become common, though they were not dogmatic about it and recognised that it might be necessary in emergencies. Infant mortality rates were high and many babies did not long survive childbirth and, in those circumstances, their preference for public baptism could not be pressed too far.

The Reformers also understood that, although baptism is administered to individuals, it is an expression of the corporate faith of the Church, to which the newly baptised person is admitted. The surrounding congregation bears witness to this; and the people are encouraged to consider their own profession of faith in their baptism, which almost none of them would remember personally.

From the modern standpoint, the strangest thing about this statement is that it shows no awareness of the fact that the people baptised at Easter and Whitsun would almost all have been adults, or children old enough to answer for themselves. There is no suggestion that it might be a good idea to revive that practice – it was simply assumed that infant baptism was the norm and would remain so. There was apparently also no realisation that, in theological terms, infant baptism is an extension of adult baptism, which is the standard by which the rite ought to be measured. So universal was this attitude that the Reformers made no provision for adult baptism, a defect that was not remedied until 1662. Even then, it was mainly because overseas expansion had led to the conversion of non-Christians who were native to the colonies and (perhaps more importantly) because the disruptions of the Civil War and Commonwealth period (1639-60) had produced a significant number of young adults who had not been baptised in infancy. There was no recognition that adult baptism had once been the norm and that the rite devised for them ought to have been the standard by which the other two were measured – not the other way round.

The result is that the 1662 prayer book has three baptismal rites, one for the public baptism of infants (which is assumed to be the standard), one for the private baptism of infants and a third for the baptism of those who are of 'riper years', which means simply that the candidates were old enough to answer for themselves. Once the backlog of Civil War cases had been cleared, adult baptism was rare in the Anglican world and did not become common until the Book of Common Prayer had ceased to be the Church's usual liturgy, so that to this day that service remains largely unfamiliar.

In addition to the three baptismal rites, this section of the prayer book contains the Catechism, originally composed in 1560 but not included in the prayer book until 1604, and the service of confirmation. Confirmation had originally been seen as the completion of baptism, because it was then that the baptised person ratified the promises that had been made on his behalf by his parents and godparents. In the twelfth century it had been recognised as a sacrament in its own right and, although the Reformers rejected that, they continued to treat it as essentially independent of baptism. Whether this is theologically defensible is still a matter of controversy today, especially when it comes to those who have been baptised on profession of faith. It is easy to see why an uncomprehending infant would be expected to confirm the promises made on his behalf by others. However, do those who are baptised as adults have to be confirmed as well? In Anglican circles, the answer to that is generally yes, partly because (in spite of everything) infant baptism continues to be regarded as the norm for all baptisms and partly because confirmation is reserved to the bishop, who represents the wider Church. It is only in the case of an adult baptism performed by the bishop that the question of whether a further confirmation is necessary would have to be asked again. So far at least, that does not seem to have become much of an issue, perhaps because so few baptisms are now performed by bishops – another great change from antiquity, when it was the bishop who normally presided at the great festal baptisms.

The Forgotten History

Readers of the New Testament will quickly be alerted to the importance of baptism in Christian worship and practice. The rite first appears in the ministry of John the Baptist, the cousin and forerunner of Jesus, who preached a message of repentance and preparation for the coming of the Messiah, and baptised people in the River Jordan as a sign of their commitment to his message. Most famously, John baptised Jesus himself, even though he was the first to recognise that Jesus did not need baptism and that he, John, was unworthy to administer it to him. Nevertheless, Jesus insisted, in order (as he said) to 'fulfil all righteousness', and John acquiesced.[1] Jesus did not have a ministry of baptism but his disciples

---

1. Matthew 3:13-15.

did, presumably in imitation of John.[2] Most importantly, as he ascended into heaven, Jesus commissioned his followers to go into all the world, baptising the nations in the name of the Father, Son and Holy Spirit, which he saw as fundamental to his gospel proclamation.[3]

What is not always understood is that this command was not immediately or universally obeyed. Somebody went to the Samaritans and baptised them in the name of Jesus only, though the reason for that is unknown.[4] There were also Christians who knew only the baptism of John, which they continued to practise.[5] We know about these things because they were aberrations that the apostles corrected as soon as they found out about them. In the case of the Samaritans, the apostles did not rebaptise them but laid hands on them so that they would receive the Holy Spirit, an act that would later contribute to the view that something like that, in addition to immersion in water, was required for baptism to be fully effective. Whether an apostolic (or episcopal) laying on of hands should accompany water baptism became a matter of some discussion and the general consensus was that it should, especially if the baptism was performed by someone of less exalted status or in circumstances that might be open to question.

What those circumstances might be became clearer as time went on. In the New Testament it seems that there was no bar to more-or-less immediate baptism on profession of faith. The Ethiopian eunuch and the Philippian jailer and his household, for example, were baptised in a matter of minutes after making their profession, something that must have posed some logistical problems in the case of the latter – from where did they get water in the middle of the night?[6] The case of the Philippian jailer's household also raises questions to which there is no satisfactory answer. Did every member of the household make an individual profession of faith, or were they included because of their relationship to him? What about children? They are not mentioned, but neither are they specifically excluded, and the Apostle Paul sometimes addresses children (and slaves) when he writes to the churches, evidently because he regarded them as members along with the free adults of the congregation.

---

2. John 4:1-2.
3. Matthew 28:19.
4. Acts 8:14-16.
5. Acts 19:1-5.
6. Acts 8:36-38 and Acts 16:30-33.

It is also not clear whether baptism was necessarily administered by immersion, or specifically in the name of the Trinity.[7] Undoubtedly, those elements were present on many occasions but how essential were they? What we do know is that by the second century what might be termed 'spontaneous' baptism was dying out. Except in cases of emergency, when the recipient was in danger of death, baptisms were usually reserved for the eves of Easter and Pentecost, and occasionally instructions were given that they should not be performed at any other time. Children were never explicitly excluded, as far as we know, but adult converts were subjected to an increasingly rigorous course of instruction known as catechesis, which was taken very seriously. Not only were these catechumens given a solid dose of theology, but they were questioned at periodic intervals about the sincerity of their repentance and their success in leading a new life. These questionings were called *scrutinia* – the candidates for baptism were literally scrutinised, in order to determine whether they were worthy to receive baptism. An increasingly important part of this procedure was exorcism – the devil was chased out of the catechumens, who were specifically required to renounce Satan and all his works.[8]

We cannot say how rigorous the scrutiny was, though we do know that there were considerable variations from one place to another, both in the questions asked and in the amount of time that was devoted to catechesis. Even after Christianity was legalised in the fourth century and the Church was able to impose certain standards of discipline, there remained an enormous variety of practice that was never fully overcome. In the Eastern Christian world, for example, it was standard practice for candidates to be baptised, sealed with oil (chrismation) and communicated – all as part of the same ceremony. The chrismation was an integral part of the rite that was administered by the presbyter in charge of the rest, and that pattern prevails in the Orthodox Churches to the present day. At the same time, the Eastern rites place relatively little emphasis on the Trinity and say nothing about exorcising demons, which seems to have been a Western speciality.

---

7. See, however, Matthew 28:19, where trinitarian baptism is enjoined by Jesus himself.

8. This paragraph and what follows are based on the detailed research of the late Canon J.D.C. Fisher (1909-96), whose pioneering work in the field remains unsurpassed. See J.D.C. Fisher, *Christian Initiation: Baptism in the Medieval West* (London: SPCK, 1965; repr. Chicago, IL: Hillenbrand Books, 2004).

A broadly similar pattern can be found in the West until about 700, when the churches subject to the bishop of Rome were increasingly drawn to the Roman rite. The biggest practical difference between it and the norms that prevailed elsewhere was that the Romans insisted that chrismation should be accompanied by the bishop's laying on of hands. As long as congregations were relatively small, and baptisms were confined to Easter and Pentecost, this was not a big problem but, as time went on, it became increasingly difficult for bishops to be present for every baptism. Practical considerations made it necessary for the rite to be administered in parish churches and the Easter-Pentecost rule became impossible to maintain as numbers swelled. In some places the need for a bishop was met by appointing 'locally ordained' ones (*chorepiskopoi*) but this expedient failed to catch on and was discontinued. Occasionally, the presbyter would anoint the candidates with oil obtained from the bishop but, more often, the chrismation was deferred until a bishop became available. That might take anything from a few days to several years. However, one thing is certain – the newly baptised were communicated immediately, because the presbyter was authorised to do that without requiring any form of episcopal intervention. As a result, most people were baptised and took Communion without being chrismated, and probably many of them never were.

This pattern was designed with adult baptism in mind but children were not excluded from it. A child, even an infant, could be baptised and communicated on the same basis as everyone else, although, obviously, the catechumenate was a very different thing in their case. Children could not be scrutinised but they could be exorcised – and they were. In their case, exorcism amounted to the same thing as scrutiny, because their inability to think or act independently meant that heresy and immorality could only be present in them in an embryonic form. Getting rid of the devil would presumably take care of that, making an infant just as capable of receiving the grace of baptism as someone who could make a conscious profession of faith.

The insistence on episcopal chrismation and its practical displacement from the baptismal rite naturally raised the question as to what its purpose was. It was at this point that confirmation as we now know it came into being. A person who had been baptised but not chrismated needed to be confirmed, partly as a ratification by the wider Church of an act performed in a local congregation, but also (and, in many ways, more importantly) in order for the baptised person to receive the gift of the Holy Spirit, which the bishop supposedly conferred by the laying on of his hands.[9] The question then arose as to whether baptism was sufficient as Christian initiation or whether something was missing as long as episcopal confirmation had not been secured. As confirmation became increasingly detached from baptism, so the need for it was regarded as more essential. In particular, it came to be thought that an unconfirmed person ought not to receive Communion, because the process of his or her integration into the Christian community had not been completed.

No specific time lag was ever decreed for delaying confirmation, though there was a tendency to fix it around seven years of age for those who had been baptised in infancy. We do know of some prominent exceptions, however – the future Queen Elizabeth I was baptised and confirmed when she was three days old and nobody objected. However, the general assumption that there would be a considerable delay encouraged people to think that this was the ideal time for catechesis to take place, so that the questions originally asked of catechumens before their baptism were instead asked of young people before their confirmation. At the same time, the introduction of a doctrine of transubstantiation in the Lord's Supper made the clergy extremely wary of giving Communion to anyone who could not take it with understanding. Babies had a way of spitting it out, which was (to put it mildly) a rather undignified way to treat the body and blood of Christ. So infant Communion not only fell into disuse, it was actually banned and something approaching the modern sequence of infant baptism, followed after several years by adolescent confirmation and participation in Holy Communion, became the norm. That was the pattern familiar at the time of the Reformation which in broad outline has endured to the present time.

It should be noted that these developments occurred over many centuries and were uneven across Western Europe before the thirteenth century, when Rome made great efforts to standardise baptismal rites as much as it could. Very few people bothered to develop theological reasons for the changes as they occurred; in almost all cases, it seems that practical commonsense and even necessity dictated the agenda and that theology caught up later, in an effort to justify what had become accepted practice. This was to have dire consequences, not least because very often the reasons devised to explain the practices were misconceived, making everything that much worse.

The effects of this can be seen most obviously in the thorny question of baptismal 'regeneration'. Is a person born again in baptism? There is much in New Testament language to suggest that he is – but not if the

---

9. Acts 8:17.

rite is divorced from the faith that is meant to precede it, which it never
was in apostolic times. Even when baptism was administered to infants,
it was always in the context of the new covenant and the assumption
was that the parents were believers who were committed to bringing
up their children in the knowledge and fear of the Lord. If that did not
happen, the baptism had no validity, just as circumcision meant nothing
if those who received it when they were eight days old failed to accept its
obligations in adult life. If anything, people in that position were subject
to greater condemnation than others, because they had despised the
covenant promises of God.[10]

The notion that the water of baptism had some magical property that
would produce spiritual rebirth in those who were immersed in it was a
superstition that the Fathers of the Church did not endorse. Tertullian
was the first to make that clear[11] and he was followed by Augustine, who
has left us a detailed argument for the necessity of faith:

> Why does John not say: 'You are clean because of the
> baptism with which you have been washed', but 'because of
> the word which I have spoken to you', unless the reason is
> that even in the water it is the word which cleanses? Take
> away the word and what is the water but (plain) water? But
> when the word comes into association with the material
> element a sacrament comes into being, as though the word
> itself took visible form. ... The cleansing is not to be attributed
> to a fluid and unstable element, unless we add 'in the word'.
> This word of faith works with such efficacy in the Church of
> God that ... it can cleanse even a tiny child, although it is
> not yet able to believe with the heart unto righteousness or
> confess with the mouth unto salvation.[12]

Belief that the water of baptism could be sanctified to the extent
of being able to effect the spiritual cleansing of the recipient was the
result of the development of sacramental theology in the twelfth and
thirteenth centuries. If bread and wine could become the body and

---

10. On this subject, see M. Pickles, 'Doubt Not ... but Earnestly Believe': A
     Fresh Look at the BCP Baptism Service (London: Latimer Trust, 2020).
11. Tertullian, De baptismo, 6.1.
12. Augustine of Hippo, Tractate on John's Gospel, 80.3 (J.-P. Migne,
     Patrologia Latina, vol. 35, col. 1840). Augustine was commenting on John
     15:3.

blood of Christ, then water could become a spiritual cleansing agent and, if that were so, the question of the recipient's faith would not arise. In the Early Church, where adult baptism was the norm, it would have been impossible to claim that catechumens were not Christians or that they would be consigned to hell if they died before being baptised. Had anyone suggested that, the pressure to baptise them sooner rather than later would have been impossible to resist. However, once the rite of baptism was thought to possess spiritual power in and of itself, it became an act of kindness to administer it as quickly as possible. In a society where infant mortality was high, there was no time to waste, and babies were baptised within 24 hours of birth, often by midwives or whoever was available. Those unlucky enough to die without baptism went to the *limbus patrum*, or limbo, a region of hell that was spared the worst torments but that was, nevertheless, cut off from God.

Needless to say, there is no justification for the existence of limbo, and no suggestion anywhere in the New Testament that water baptism is absolutely essential to salvation, but those ideas took hold in the later middle ages and led to many superstitious practices. Even today there are people who think that baptism is a kind of lucky charm and want it for their children, whether they themselves are believers or not. By 1500, infant baptism, complete with the superstitions surrounding it, had become the norm in Western Europe and most people knew nothing else. The earlier history of the rite had been forgotten and if anyone had to be baptised as an adult (like a convert from Judaism, for example) it was the rite used for infants that was adapted to meet the need, not the other way round.

The Reformation

Given the curious development of baptism over the centuries, one might have thought that it would have been a prime target for the Reformers' zeal, but that was not the case – at least, not initially. Martin Luther, for example, at first thought that it was one of the few things that the Church had preserved uncorrupted from ancient times and he saw no need to change it.[13]

---

13. Martin Luther, 'The Babylonian Captivity of the Church', in M. Luther, *Luther's Works: Volume 36: Word and Sacrament II*, ed. A.R. Wentz (Philadelphia, PA: Muhlenberg Press, 1959), p. 57: 'Blessed be God and the Father of our Lord Jesus Christ who according to the riches of his mercy has preserved in his church this sacrament at least untouched and

However, Luther's initially positive endorsement of traditional practice was soon modified by the emphasis he placed on the necessity of faith. He acknowledged that God had declared that whoever believes will be saved but added that it is on the promise that: 'all our salvation depends. But we must so consider it as to exercise our faith in it, and have no doubt whatever that, once we have been baptised, we are saved.'[14] Again: 'The power of baptism depends not so much on the faith or use of the one who confers it as on the faith or use of the one who receives it.'[15] This emphasis was later confirmed in the Augsburg Confession of 1530, which states:

> [M]en must use sacraments so as to join faith with them, which believes the promises that are offered and declared unto us by the sacraments. Wherefore they [i.e. the Protestants] condemn those that teach that the sacraments do justify *ex opere operato*, and do not teach that faith which believes the remission of sins is requisite in the use of sacraments.[16]

Luther's teaching can be summed up in the following:

> It is not baptism that justifies or benefits anyone, but it is faith in that word of promise to which baptism is added. The faith justifies, and fulfils, that which baptism signifies. For faith is the submersion of the old man and the emerging of the new. ... The sacraments are not fulfilled when they are taking place, but when they are believed. It cannot be true, therefore, that there is contained in the sacraments a power efficacious for justification, or that they are 'effective signs' of grace ... unless you should call them effective in the sense that they certainly and effectively impart grace when faith is unmistakably present.[17]

Opposition to infant baptism first raised its head in Zurich, where so-called 'Anabaptists' ('re-baptisers') appeared around 1525. They

---

untainted by the ordinances of men, and has made it free to all nations and classes of mankind; and has not permitted it to be oppressed by the filthy and godless monsters of greed and superstition.'
14. Ibid., p. 59.
15. Ibid., p. 64.
16. *Augsburg Confession*, 13. See Bray, *Documents*, p. 552.
17. Luther, 'Babylonian Captivity', pp. 66-67.

rejected the baptismal practice of their time as false, because it so obviously did not do what the Church claimed, and insisted that only those who professed their faith could be candidates for the sacrament. Moreover, the Anabaptists did not stop there. They were social radicals whose beliefs threatened to overturn society and were therefore rejected by almost everyone, including the mainline Reformers. Yet, they did raise the question of the true meaning and purpose of baptism and those Protestants who wanted to retain the practice of baptising infants were forced to develop a theological rationale for it and not assume that it was self-evident.

Luther defended the baptism of infants on two grounds. First, he claimed that infants are helped by the faith of others, in particular, those who present the child for baptism and the Church, in general. As he put it: 'So through the prayer of the believing church which presents it, a prayer to which all things are possible, the infant is changed, cleansed, and renewed, by inpoured faith.'[18] Second, he said that the validity of baptism is not determined by the faith (or lack of it) in the recipient but depends on God's word and command. In his words: 'My faith does not make baptism; rather, it receives baptism. ... We bring the child with the intent and hope that it may believe, and we pray God to grant it faith. But we do not baptise it on this basis, but solely on the command of God.'[19] He went on to add: 'Where faith is present with its fruits, there baptism is no empty symbol, but the effect accompanies it; but where faith is lacking, it remains a mere unfruitful sign.'[20]

The theological questions that Luther and his followers had to grapple with and find answers to may be summarised as follows:

> 1. The state of unbaptised humanity. From the time of Augustine, if not earlier, it was assumed that all human beings were born in the following of Adam and Eve. That is to say that, even if they had not themselves done anything wrong, they had inherited the sin (and, in Augustinian theology, also the guilt) of our first parents. That sin and guilt

---

18. Ibid., p. 73.
19. Martin Luther, *The Large Catechism*, 4.53, 57, in R. Kolb and T.J. Wengert (eds), *The Book of Concord: The Confessions of the Evangelical Lutheran Church* (Minneapolis, MN: Fortress Press, 2000), pp. 463-64. The *Large Catechism* was composed in 1529, a year before the appearance of the Augsburg Confession.
20. Luther, *Large Catechism*, 4.73, in ibid., p. 465.

could only be removed by the saving grace of Christ, which was given in baptism. To think otherwise was to fall into the heresy of Pelagianism, named for a fifth-century British monk called Pelagius, who taught that the fall of Adam and Eve had not been total. According to him, even fallen human beings retained some ability to resist the power of sin, and the grace of God in Christ could build on that to help them achieve their salvation. By rejecting infant baptism, the Anabaptists incurred the charge of Pelagianism because it was thought (wrongly) that they denied original sin and guilt.

2. If children are born in a state of sinfulness and need the salvation that can only come through Christ, then baptism, which is the sign and seal of that salvation, must be applicable to them as much as to anyone else. To suggest otherwise is to imply that small children are either damned (which nobody wanted to say), or that they are somehow innocent and that responsibility for sin only begins when a child is able to understand the concept for itself. That, in turn, might suggest that it is better to die before reaching the age of discretion, which is not taught anywhere in Scripture and has never been part of the tradition of the Church.

3. If faith is an essential ingredient of baptism, which cannot take effect without it, can a child have faith even if it cannot express what that faith is? In one sense, the answer to this must be yes. Little children are generally trusting of their parents, even though they cannot say why, and that trust is faith. The presence of faith in a person cannot be determined solely by that person's ability to articulate it, especially since some people are much better at expressing themselves than others are. However, at the same time, there can be no guarantee that infant trust will continue into adulthood, and experience shows that often it does not. Part of growing up involves becoming suspicious to some degree, and those who do not mature in that way are regarded as naive.[21] A Christian is expected to do the right thing from conviction, not from ignorance, as a naive person might do, and simple-mindedness is not to be equated with righteousness.

4. The Gospel is meant to be preached to everyone but only some people accept it for themselves. In its practice of infant

---

21. The word 'naive' is French and derives from 'native', referring to birth.

baptism, the medieval Church was giving blanket coverage to the entire population, thereby fulfilling the mandate of Matthew 28:19. Nonetheless, it was perfectly clear that the spiritual life of many people – probably of most, in fact – left more than a little to be desired. How could this be accounted for? Was it necessary to regard everyone as a Christian on the grounds of baptism alone, or was some further evidence of faith required? Many different answers were given to this question; but, whatever people said in theory, in practice just about everyone admitted that baptism was not enough by itself to guarantee salvation, except perhaps to those few who died immediately afterwards. Something further was required, but what? And how was that something to be given? It was in an attempt to answer these questions that confirmation came into its own as a distinct sacrament. What was required was an imparting of the Holy Spirit, whose indwelling presence would bring the promise of baptism to completion. Whether confirmation could effect that imparting, or merely bore witness to it, was left undecided. However, the fact that those desiring to be confirmed were admitted to the Lord's Supper suggests that it was the second view that prevailed, since otherwise they would not have been considered worthy to communicate.

The Reformed Baptismal Rites

When we examine what happened to the baptismal rite during the Reformation, we see that Luther and the English Reformers followed a similar pattern, with the latter drawing heavily on the former's example. In both cases there was a two-stage development.

Both started with a developed medieval rite that laid great stress on exorcism and contained a number of practices related to it. In the first stage of reform, many of these practices, which were considered harmless in themselves, were left untouched, so as not to unsettle people who might otherwise think that there was something defective, either with the baptism that they had received according to the traditional rite, or with the new forms being introduced.

The first stage of reform prepared the way for the second, in which most (if not all) of the traditional practices were swept away, references to exorcism were drastically reduced or eliminated, and the emphasis was placed much more firmly on the faith of the parents and sponsors of the baptismal candidates. It was taken for granted that the candidates would be infants – no provision was made for the baptism of adults, or of persons capable of responding for themselves.

The parallel patterns may be set out as follows:

Luther	England
Magdeburg rite (1497; traditional)	Sarum rite (1543; traditional)
First *Taufbüchlein* ('Baptism booklet') (1523)	1549 Book of Common Prayer
Second *Taufbüchlein* (1526)	1552 Book of Common Prayer

The details differ, not least because the English were working half a generation after the Lutherans and had the benefit of their experience, but the overall approach and its effects were the same. From being a rite focussed on exorcism, baptism became a proclamation of the Gospel and a profession of faith in it, even if that profession was made by sponsors rather than by the candidate. One important difference between the traditional rites and the first set of Reformed ones was that the former continued to reflect a bygone era when baptism was administered to large numbers of candidates at one time, whereas by the sixteenth century it was generally assumed that there would be no more than a few candidates, at most, and probably only one. The traditional rites provided for the separation of men and women, again reflecting a time when adult baptism was regarded as the norm and modesty demanded that each sex should disrobe separately. However, although the prayers used for men and women were similar, they were not identical, a distinction that had no theological basis but had crept in for what were originally purely practical reasons. No trace of that can be found in the 1523 *Taufbüchlein* or in the 1549 prayer book; in the sight of God and in the rite of baptism there would henceforth be no discrimination of any kind between male and female.

What is important to notice is that in 1523 Luther was already preparing people for further change to come. In his inimitably frank style, he addressed them as follows:

> Now remember also that in baptism the least importance attaches to these external things, namely, breathing under the eyes, signing with the cross, placing salt in the mouth, putting spittle and clay on the ears and nose, anointing with oil the breast and shoulders, and signing the top of the head with chrism, vesting in the christening robe, and giving a burning candle into the hand, and whatever else there is that men have added to embellish baptism. For certainly without

all such things baptism may take place, and they are not the kind of devices that the devil shuns or avoids. He despises much greater things than these.[22]

Luther's attitude to the various rituals that had grown up around baptism was dismissive but that was not because he did not take their purported aim seriously. He believed as much as anyone in the need to chase the devil away but took the challenge much more seriously than this. The devil was not going to be impressed by folkloric superstition – for him to take flight, spiritual warfare rooted and grounded in faith was essential, and it is that which he emphasised.

The impact of this was to be felt in the numerous orders for baptism that appeared in Germany in the 20 years following the publication of the second *Taufbüchlein* in 1526. One of the most influential of these, at least in England, was to be the *Einfaltiges Bedencken*, or *Pia Deliberatio*, compiled by Archbishop Hermann von Wied of Cologne, with a great deal of help from Martin Bucer. This text appeared in 1544 and was translated into Latin a year later. A copy of the Latin text was soon acquired by Thomas Cranmer in London, and in 1547 it was translated into English by John Daye and is generally known to us as the *Consultation*.[23] The Latin was a rather loose rendering of the German, but the English translation, touched up and reissued in 1548, stuck very closely to the Latin version and was to prove influential in the composition of the rite in the 1549 prayer book. Cranmer had the ability, and the good sense, to abbreviate Bucer's verbosity, making his text (by common consent) considerably better than the one on which it was based.

English Baptismal Rites

The baptismal rite best known to Thomas Cranmer and his contemporaries was that of Sarum. It had originally been put together in the thirteenth century and reached its final version in 1543, nearly a decade after Henry VIII had broken with Rome and at a time when the Lutheran rites in Germany were already becoming stabilised. In all essentials, the Sarum rite was the same as that of Magdeburg, from which Luther had worked as far back as 1523. That text, and Luther's criticisms of it, would have been readily recognisable to the English, who saw their task of

---

22. Luther, *First Taufbüchlein*, in J.D.C. Fisher, *Christian Initiation: The Reformation Period* (London: SPCK, 1970), p. 7.
23. See ibid., pp. 54-69, for the text of Daye's second translation.

reform very much as Luther did. They too regarded the traditional rite as overloaded with unnecessary accretions that obscured its true meaning and they wanted to prune it, but without unduly disturbing the faith of those who knew nothing else and who might be disconcerted if too much of what they saw as traditional were suddenly to be abandoned.

In the 1549 prayer book, as in the Sarum rite, the service of baptism began at the church door, moving to the font only midway through.[24] Given that the font was usually placed near the door, this was not as dramatic a move as it might otherwise appear to be, but it was important nevertheless, because it signified that there were preliminaries that had to be taken care of outside the church before the baptismal candidate could be admitted.[25] In the Sarum rite these preliminaries were designed to make the candidates catechumens, even though the catechumenate had long ceased to exist in practice. The questions asked of the midwife (not of the parents or godparents) were three in number:

1. Is the child male or female?
2. Has the child already been baptised at home?
3. What name is the child to be given?

In 1549 only the second of these questions was retained and it was asked of the godparents. In both rites it was assumed that the response would normally be negative but it was recognised that, in cases of necessity, a child might already have been baptised at home. In that case, it was incumbent upon the priest to determine whether the baptism had been properly administered. A rubric at the end of the service states that, if a lay person has baptised a child at home, that person is to be asked to give the details. If the words used followed the standard form, then the child would not be rebaptised, but:

> [I]f the priest is in reasonable doubt whether an infant
> presented to him has already been baptised in the required

---

24. For an English translation of the Sarum rite as it stood in 1543, see Fisher, *Christian Initiation: Baptism in the Medieval West*, pp. 178-200.
25. There is however a rubric in the 1549 prayer book that says that, if the number of children to be baptised and of those accompanying them is too great for them all to be able to stand conveniently at the church door, they should be allowed to stand somewhere inside the church, as close to the door as possible. In effect, this probably meant that they would be standing next to the font.

form or not, he must do everything with that child as with
another who is known not to have been baptised, except that
he must use the essential sacramental words conditionally.[26]

It seems likely that in most cases there would have been 'reasonable
doubt', since few lay people had the education needed to be able to
perform the rite correctly. That eventuality is also hinted at in the rubric:

> It is not lawful for a layman or a woman to baptise someone,
> save in the constraint of necessity. But if a man and a woman
> should be present when the need to baptise a child became
> urgent, and no other minister more suitable for this task
> were present, let the man baptise and not the woman, unless
> the woman happened to know well the sacramental words
> and not the man, or there were some other impediment.[27]

The 1549 prayer book resolved this problem by devising a second
form of baptism, intended for those who had been baptised privately. As
in the Sarum rite, those who had performed the private baptism were to
be questioned as to the form and manner in which that had been done
and, if there was any hesitation, the child was to be baptised publicly
according to the standard rite, a practice that was reaffirmed in 1552 and
is still found in 1662.

The first half of the baptismal service in the Sarum rite is the order
for making a catechumen, something that had long been a formality
with no real content. There is no provision for any kind of catechesis and
the service is little more than a rather drawn-out exorcism. During the
course of it, the priest anoints the candidate no fewer than three times,
praying over him or her for three things in the following ascending order:

First anointing	Second anointing	Third anointing
Removal of ignorance	Perseverance in worship	Gift of understanding
Breaking the bonds of Satan	Keeping the commandments	Cleansing of the soul
Making worthy for baptism	Making worthy for baptism	Making worthy for baptism

---

26. Fisher, *Christian Initiation: Baptism in the Medieval West*, p. 196.
27. Ibid., p. 197.

The progression is from deliverance from the power of Satan, through the works of the law to the grace of the Holy Spirit, all of which are intended to prepare the candidate to be a worthy recipient of baptism. Particularly revealing is the prayer that comes immediately after the second anointing, where the priest says:

> O God, who didst create the human race in such wise that thou mightest also restore it, look in mercy upon thine adopted people: and within the new covenant place the children of thy new race, so that that which they could not obtain by nature the sons of promise may rejoice that they have received through grace. Amen.[28]

The medieval distinction between nature and grace is clearly expressed but the description of the former is completely inadequate. First of all, it gives the impression that God created the human race as something less than perfect. The only hint of the fall of Adam is in the word 'restore'; otherwise, there is no mention of sin or disobedience. The language of adoption and the new covenant puts the initiative for salvation firmly in the mind and purpose of God, and it is acknowledged that the blessings of that dispensation are available only to those who have received divine grace. However, there is no expression of any need for repentance and no sign that faith of any kind is required, which would certainly not have been true of the original catechumens.

The 1549 prayer book takes a very different approach, as the opening exhortation to the parents and godparents makes clear:

> Dear beloved, forasmuch as all men be conceived and born in sin, and that no man born in sin can enter into the kingdom of God (except he be regenerate, and born anew of water and the holy Ghost) I beseech you to call upon God the Father through our Lord Jesus Christ, that of his bounteous mercy he will grant to these children that thing, which by nature they cannot have, that is to say, they may be baptised with the holy Ghost and received into Christ's holy Church, and be made lively members of the same.

The scholastic framework of nature and grace is preserved to some extent, but the emphasis is now placed firmly on the work of the

---

28. Ibid., p. 179.

Holy Spirit, which Sarum does not mention. Furthermore, this initial exhortation is followed immediately by a prayer that recalls the examples of Noah and the Red Sea, and also the baptism of Jesus. It is new to 1549 but, after undergoing substantial revision in 1552, survived more or less intact in 1662. The following text takes 1549 as its starting point and indicates deletions and additions made in 1552 in grey and **bold** type respectively:

> Almighty and everlasting God, which of thy justice didst destroy by floods of water the whole world for sin, except eight persons, whom of thy **great** mercy (the same time) thou didst save **Noah and his family** in the ark **from perishing by water**: And when thou didst drown in the Red Sea wicked king Pharaoh with all his army, yet (at the same time) thou **also** didst **safely** lead thy people the children of Israel **thy people** safely through the midst thereof **Red Sea**, whereby thou didst figure the washing of **figuring thereby** thy holy baptism; and by the baptism of thy well-beloved Son Jesus Christ, thou didst sanctify the flood Jordan, and all other waters to this **the** mystical washing away of sin: We beseech thee (for thy infinite mercies) that thou wilt mercifully look upon these children, and sanctify them **and wash them** with thy holy Ghost, that by this wholesome laver of regeneration, whatsoever sin is in them may be washed clean away, **that they, being delivered from thy wrath, may be received into the ark of Christ's Church** and so saved from perishing: And being fervent in spirit **steadfast in faith, joyful through hope,** **and** rooted in charity, may ever serve thee: And finally attain to **so pass the waves of this troublesome world, that finally they may come to the land of** everlasting life, with all thy holy and chosen people. This grant us we beseech thee, for Jesus Christ's sake, **there to reign with thee, world without end, through Jesus Christ** our Lord. Amen.

It will be seen from this that Thomas Cranmer retreated from some of the more extravagant claims for the biblical texts that he made in 1549, deleting references to divine vengeance and instead emphasising the use of water as a cleansing agent. At the same time, he also removed potentially misleading claims that the water of baptism might contain some saving power of its own. The hope that the baptised child will grow into the maturity of a Christian adult is maintained, but its realisation is left open-ended, as it ought to be. The promise of God remains but whether it will be received and acted upon is not assumed.

A few further changes were made in 1662, as shown in the following, which takes as its starting point the 1552 text, with deletions and additions in 1662 shown by grey and bold type respectively:

> Almighty and everlasting God, which **who** of thy great mercy didst save Noah and his family in the ark from perishing by water: and also didst safely lead the children of Israel thy people through the Red Sea: figuring thereby thy holy baptism; and by the baptism of thy well-beloved son Jesus Christ **in the river Jordan,** didst sanctify the flood Jordan, and all other waters, **Water** to the mystical washing away of sin: We beseech thee for thy infinite mercies, that thou wilt mercifully look upon these children **this Child,** sanctify them and wash them **him and sanctify him** with thy **the** holy ghost, that they **he,** being delivered from thy wrath, may be received into the ark of Christ's Church, and being steadfast in faith, joyful through hope, and rooted in charity, may so pass the waves of this troublesome world, that finally they **he** may come to the land of everlasting life, there to reign with thee, world without end, through Jesus Christ our Lord. Amen.

Returning to the Sarum rite, the prayer for grace is followed by the exorcism of salt, which was supposed to act as a kind of stimulus to the candidate who would then go on to seek the wholesome food of regeneration. It was a custom of obscure origin, already mentioned by Luther as something extraneous to the sacrament, and was dropped without trace in 1549. After the exorcism of salt, the Sarum rite distinguishes male candidates from female ones, with a slightly different set of prayers and adjurations to the devil, ordering him to depart from the candidate. In both cases, there are two prayers and two adjurations, followed by an exorcism that is common to both.

The first prayer for the male child recalls the old covenant promises to Abraham, Isaac, Jacob and Moses, setting the catechumenate in the context of the wilderness journey of the people of Israel. This same prayer is repeated, with a slight variation to include the apocryphal heroine Susanna, as the second one used for female candidates.

The second prayer used for males concentrates on God, the fount of all life and goodness, and asks that He will bestow His favour on the candidate. It is not used for females. Instead, the first prayer for girls begins with a long invocation of God as Lord of heaven and earth, including what amounts to a litany of angels, archangels, patriarchs, prophets, apostles, martyrs, confessors, virgins and so on. There is no equivalent used for the males.

This division into male and female has no theological basis, and it would have been possible to use either set of prayers for both. Perhaps that was actually done when there were only a few candidates for baptism, a mixture of males and females – brothers and sisters in the same family, for example. In any case, the whole exercise served no real purpose and was dropped from the 1549 prayer book. It was replaced by a prayer for those being presented for baptism, which was followed by an exorcism that retains the spirit of the Sarum rite but expresses it in different words. The prayer was retained in 1552 and in 1662, but the exorcism introduced in 1549 was dropped. It read as follows:

> I command thee, unclean spirit, in the name of the Father, of the Son and of the holy Ghost, that thou come out, and depart from these infants, whom our Lord Jesus Christ hath vouchsafed, to call to his holy baptism, to be made members of his body, and of his holy congregation. Therefore thou cursed spirit, remember thy sentence, remember thy judgment, remember the day to be at hand, wherein thou shalt burn in fire everlasting, prepared for thee and thy angels. And presume not hereafter to exercise any tyranny toward these infants, whom Christ hath bought with his precious blood, and by this his holy baptism calleth to be of his flock.

A modern reader might be tempted to think that dropping the exorcism represents a decline of belief in the devil and his power but that is not the case. The Reformers were as conscious as those who had gone before them of the dangers of Satan. They were also aware, however, that baptism was not an exorcism and should not be treated in that way. Their concern was to emphasise the promises of the Gospel that would come to fruition in the faith of those who received them, not to perform semi-magical rituals that had no meaning and would have no obvious effect.

After the separate prayers for male and female in the Sarum rite, there came the third anointing, followed by yet another exorcism and a brief quotation from Matthew's Gospel: 'At that time little children were presented to Jesus ... and when he had laid his hand upon them, he departed thence.'[29] Taken out of context and abbreviated to the point where it meant nothing, the verse was replaced in the 1549 book by Mark 10:13-16, quoted in full.

The reading of the Gospel was the culmination of the order for the catechumens; and in the 1549 rite it was followed by a brief exposition, the reciting of the Lord's Prayer and the Apostles' Creed, and a concluding prayer that preceded the procession of the baptismal party into the church. In the Sarum rite, however, although the general pattern was similar, there was no exposition of the Gospel. Instead, the priest performed a strange action known as the *Effeta*, the Latinised form of the Aramaic word *Ephphatha*, which occurs in Mark 7:34. The context is Jesus' healing of a deaf man, when he put his fingers into the deaf man's ears and, after spitting, touched his tongue before saying the word that means 'Be opened'. There is no suggestion that the man was demon possessed, or that his disability had anything to do with sin, but it had been taken over by the Church and was used as yet another form of exorcism. The misappropriation of the biblical passage would have been apparent to Cranmer and the other Reformers and there seems to have been no hesitation in dropping it from the 1549 text. Also dropped in 1549 was the *Ave Maria*, which had traditionally been recited after the Lord's Prayer and before the Apostles' Creed.

The catechumenate portion of the baptismal service ends with the priest taking the candidate by the right hand and leading him or her into the church. The ritual is the same in Sarum and in 1549, but the focus is different. In Sarum, it is on the church as a building but, in 1549, it is on the congregation, as the words addressed to the candidate make clear:

> Sarum: Enter into the temple of God, that thou mayest have eternal life, and live for ever and ever. Amen.
> 1549: The Lord vouchsafe to receive you into his holy household, and to keep and govern you alway in the same, that you may have everlasting life. Amen.

This portion of the rite was dropped in 1552 and subsequently, when the distinction between what happened at the door of the church and what transpired at the font was abolished.

With the procession from the church door to the font a new section of the baptismal rite began. This is much more obvious in Sarum than it is in 1549, where the distinction is deliberately downplayed. In the Sarum rite

---

29. Matthew 19:13, 15.

there is a lengthy introductory section entitled the 'Blessing of the Font' that has no parallel in 1549. It begins with detailed rubric for the preparation of the water, which must be fresh, though not necessarily newly prepared. With our modern sensitivity to hygiene, it seems strange to us that water should be allowed to sit in the font for weeks on end, but the preoccupation of the medieval composers of the rite was different. What concerned them was not cleanliness so much as equality. Hence the statement that 'the water of baptism must not be changed in deference to somebody of distinction, unless it has become stale'.[30] Nor was the consecrated water to be sprinkled around the church. It had been consecrated for the purpose of baptism and purification only and was to be kept for that purpose. So seriously was this taken that offenders were to be punished with the greater excommunication, an extremely severe sanction for what might otherwise appear to be a relatively minor infraction.[31]

In 1549 provision was made for blessing the water in the font if it had been changed, something that was supposed to happen at least once a month. A number of prayers for this were attached to the end of the office for private baptism, from where they were 'rescued' in 1552 and included in the main body of the baptismal rite.

The blessing of the font itself began with an admonition to the godparents, which was delivered in English, not in Latin, and that was followed by a long litany invoking a wide range of saints, many of whom must have been completely unknown to the participants. After that, followed a few short prayers, versicles and responses, before the priest delivered a lengthy consecration address that recalls the one used in the Lord's Supper. Thus far, the ritual was to proceed on Easter Eve and the vigil of Pentecost, whether there was a baptism or not. Only afterwards, if there were actual candidates, would the baptism itself follow.

In the 1549 prayer book this part of the service opens with a word of exhortation to the godparents, which was followed by questions put to them regarding their own faith and intentions for the child whom they were bringing to baptism, before proceeding to baptise the child.

After the baptism, the Sarum rite continues with the anointing of the child with the chrism of salvation, the clothing of the child in his chrismal robe, a second chrismation (if desired), and the giving of a lighted candle to the infant, which must have been a moment of some anxiety for the parents. There is even provision for immediate confirmation and

---

30. Fisher, *Christian Initiation: Baptism in the Medieval West*, p. 186.
31. Holy water could be sprinkled around the church, but not if it had been set aside for baptism.

Communion if a bishop is present, though that was very rare. Instead, the parents and godparents were enjoined to teach the child up to the age of seven, when he was deemed old enough to be presented for confirmation if a bishop could be obtained. In 1549 all this was reduced to a clothing of the child with his christening robe, known as the 'chrisom' and a single anointing. The words for the vesting with the chrisom were:

> Take this white vesture for a token of the innocency, which by God's grace in this holy sacrament of baptism, is given unto thee: and for a sign whereby thou art admonished, so long as thou livest, to give thyself to innocency of living, that, after this transitory life, thou mayest be partaker of the life everlasting. Amen.

The single anointing then followed, accompanied by these words:

> Almighty God, the Father of our Lord Jesus Christ, who hath regenerate[d] thee by water and the holy Ghost, and hath given unto thee remission of all thy sins: he vouchsafe to anoint thee with the unction of his holy Spirit, and bring thee to the inheritance of everlasting life. Amen.

The Sarum rite ended at this point; but the 1549 prayer book concluded with a final exhortation to the parents and godparents, giving them precise instructions about what they should teach the child and asking them to present him to the bishop for confirmation as soon as he was able to say the Apostles' Creed, the Lord's Prayer and the Ten Commandments, without specifying a particular age. In all essentials, this exhortation survived the various revisions and is still found in 1662. The text given below is that of 1549, unchanged in 1552 but slightly revised in 1662, with the words in grey being deleted at that time and those in **bold** type being added:

> Forasmuch as these children have **this child hath** promised by you **his sureties** to forsake **renounce** the devil and all his works, to believe in God, and to serve him; you **ye** must remember, that it is your parts and duty **duties** to see that *these infants* **this infant** be taught, so soon as they **he** shall be able to learn, what a solemn vow, promise, and profession they have **he hath here** made by you. And that they **he** may know these things the better, ye shall call upon them

him to hear sermons; and chiefly you **ye** shall provide, that they **he** may learn the Creed, the Lord's Prayer and the Ten Commandments, in the English **vulgar** tongue, and all other things which a Christian man ought to know and believe to his soul's health; and that these children **this child** may be virtuously brought up to lead a godly and Christian life; remembering always, that baptism doth represent to us our profession; which is, to follow the example of our Saviour Christ, and to be made like unto him; that, as he died, and rose again for us, so should we (which **who** are baptised) die from sin, and rise again unto righteousness; continually mortifying all our evil and corrupt affections, and daily proceeding in all virtue and godliness of living.

From 1549 to 1662

Having looked at the way that Thomas Cranmer reworked the Sarum rite, abandoning most of the exorcism material, we can now look more closely at how he moved on from 1549 to 1552, and to the form that eventually became fixed in 1662. The easiest way to do this is to catalogue the different parts of the 1549 baptismal service and see how it compares with what came later on. Given that 1552 and 1662 were essentially a paring down of 1549, the easiest thing to do is to list the different elements of the latter and put in *italics* those parts that were not carried over into 1552/1662, with material that is new to the latter being indicated in **bold** type:

1549	1552/1662
At the door of the church	**At the font**
1. Preliminary question (*in rubric*)	1. Preliminary question[32]
2. Exhortation	2. Exhortation
3. First of two collects	3. First of two collects
4. *Asking the name of the child*	
5. *Making a cross on the child's forehead and breast*	
6. *The signing formula*	
7. The second of two collects	7. The second of two collects

32. This question was contained in a rubric until 1662 and that pattern was restored by the Prayer Book (Further Provisions) Measure 1968 (no. 2) (18 December 1968), section 3.1, in *The Public General Acts and Church Assembly Measures 1968* (London: HMSO, 1969).

1549	1552/1662
8. *Exorcism of the unclean spirit*	
9. *Suffrages*	
10. The Gospel and the address	10. The Gospel and the address
11. The Lord's Prayer	
12. *The Apostles' Creed*	
13. Thanksgiving and prayer	13. Thanksgiving and prayer
14. *Leading of the child into the church*	
At the font	
15. Formula of reception	15. Address to sponsors
16. Interrogatories	16. Interrogatories
	The four prayers for grace[33]
	Prayer for sanctifying the water
17. Naming/baptising of the child	17. Naming/baptising of the child
18. *Thrice dipping/affusion*	**Once dipping/affusion**
	Reception of the child
	Signing of the child with the cross
19. *Sponsors' laying hands on the child*	
20. *The vesting of the child with the chrisom*	
21. *Anointing of the child's head*	
22. *Formula of anointing*	**Address to the people**
	11. The Lord's Prayer
	Prayer for the child
23. Exhortation to the sponsors	23. Exhortation to the sponsors
	Charge to the sponsors[34]

Public Baptism of Infants (1552/1662)

In the 1552 prayer book the heading was simply 'The Ministration of Baptism to be used in the Church', the word 'Public' (used in 1549) being omitted. It was restored in 1662, along with the addition of the qualifier 'of Infants', made necessary by the inclusion of a service for adult baptism. As structured in the 1552/1662 texts, the rite of the public baptism of infants can be conveniently subdivided into three distinct sections:

    A. The *ante-baptism*, which includes all that in 1549 was celebrated at the church door.

---

33. In 1549 these were in the form for consecrating the font, which was placed at the end of the office for private baptism.
34. In the 1552 liturgy this was mentioned in a rubric, which was transformed into a set form of charge in 1662.

B. The *baptism*, which includes everything from the address to the sponsors to the signing with the cross.

C. The *post-baptism*, which begins with the address to the people and concludes with the charge to the sponsors.

A. The Ante-baptism

There are significant differences in the *introductory rubrics* between those of 1552, 1662 and the 1968 revision of the latter. In 1552 the rubric stated:

1. If there were children to be baptised on a Sunday or holy day, the parents were to give notice the night before, or at the latest, early in the morning, before the beginning of Morning Prayer.
2. The godparents and the entire baptismal party were to be ready at the font immediately following the last lesson read at either Morning or Evening Prayer.
3. The priest was to enquire whether the child had already been baptised.

In 1662 these provisions were for the most part included in the third (and last) of the preliminary rubrics. The only omission was the reference to a Sunday or holy day, but that was because directions concerning them were expanded in the first of the new rubrics introduced at that time. These new rubrics stated:

1. Baptism should not normally be administered except on a Sunday or holy day, though exceptions could be made in cases of necessity. The reasons for this were:
   a. the congregation present at the service could testify to the reception of the newly baptised into the church
   b. all those present would be reminded of the profession of faith made on their behalf at their own baptism. It was added that, for that reason, it was best for baptism to be administered in the spoken tongue.
2. It was specified in the second rubric that every male child should have two godfathers and one godmother, and every female child should have one godfather and two godmothers.

The 1968 revision of the rubrics modified several of the earlier provisions, besides adding new ones.[35] The modifications to the previously existing provisions were:

1. Notice of an upcoming baptism is normally to be given at least a week before the intended baptism. The word 'normally' allows for exceptional cases, but the general understanding is that such cases are unlikely to be frequent, not least because the danger of infant mortality is much less now than it used to be (though that is not stated).

2. The rules regarding godparents are relaxed. In principle the traditional number of three is maintained but, if they cannot easily be obtained, then two will suffice. Parents may also be godparents for their own children, provided that there is at least one other godparent.[36] Godparents must themselves be baptised and confirmed, and promise to bring up the child in their own faith and practice. However, the requirement of confirmation may be waived at the minister's discretion. (This presumably is meant to allow for non-Anglican godparents.)

3. The minister must satisfy himself that the child has not already been baptised, though it is not specified how that should be done.

4. The godparents, parents and baptismal party must be ready at the font for the beginning of the baptismal service, though no particular time is appointed for that.

The new provisions are:

1. Parents and guardians of the child are to be instructed that the obligations undertaken by the godparents apply to them too.

---

35. Prayer Book (Further Provisions) Measure 1968 (no. 2) (18 December 1968), section 3.1, in *The Public General Acts and Church Assembly Measures 1968* (London: HMSO, 1969).

36. This was forbidden by Canon 29 of the 1603 (1604) canons, but the convocation of Canterbury relaxed the rule in 1865. However, the relaxation never received official confirmation and it was not until after the introduction of the new canons in 1969 that this change was legally authorised.

2. No minister may refuse to baptise a child brought to him for baptism, as long as the child resides in the parish and the parents and/or godparents have followed the correct procedures for presenting the child. However, the minister may delay baptism for the purpose of preparing and/or instructing the parents and godparents as to their responsibilities.
3. If a minister refuses to baptise a qualified infant, or delays the baptism for no good reason, the parents or guardians of the child may apply to the bishop of the diocese, who must then consult with the minister and decide how to proceed.

The 1968 revisions reveal a situation in which real understanding of baptism and commitment to the Christian faith cannot be taken for granted. The legal obligation of a minister to baptise those in his parish who are qualified to receive it is respected, but provision is made for introducing the appropriate pastoral discipline. What is not addressed is the traditional habit of holding baptismal services at times when the congregation does not normally meet. That practice has certainly declined in recent years but it has not disappeared completely, and it is surprising that the revised rubrics say nothing about the role of the wider congregation as witnesses (and spiritual beneficiaries) of the service. An important element of the 1662 prayer book rubrics has been omitted and ought to be restored, especially since the situation of the congregation has not changed and the reminder may be more necessary now than ever before.

The *exhortation* that opens the service makes the following assumptions:

1. Every human being is conceived and born in sin. This reflects Psalm 51:5 and Romans 3:23. It should be noted that the sin which is spoken of here is not related to, or dependent on, the sexual act of conception, which is not sinful. Sinfulness is transmitted from parents to children not physically but spiritually, because every human being has inherited the broken relationship with God that occurred when Adam and Eve disobeyed him in the Garden of Eden. Even if that story is a symbolic representation of a historical event that we are now unable to trace, it remains true that all people everywhere are cut off from God by sin, and that this fundamental truth is acknowledged (in one form or another) by every religion and philosophy that has ever existed.

2. Jesus said that no one can enter the kingdom of God unless he is born again of water and the Holy Spirit. This reflects John 3:5-8. Water baptism is the external sign of cleansing and of life, but Jesus makes it clear that the rebirth of which he is speaking is a work of the Holy Spirit. The former represents the latter but is no substitute for it. The exhortation is therefore couched in terms of a promise and an expectation, but not of an accomplished fact.

3. God the Father is merciful and will give the child something that he cannot inherit by nature – but note that baptism by water and the Holy Spirit is a reception into Christ's Church in the hope that the child will become an active ('lively') member of it. This promise can only be adequately fulfilled by spiritual regeneration, but the two things are not identical and the spiritual state of the child will not be known until he reaches an age when he can give voice to it.

The *first collect* reminds us of how God has acted in the past and prepared His people for the Christian understanding of baptism. The examples chosen are taken from Holy Scripture and reflect different aspects of the covenant that God has made with the human race, and more especially with His chosen people.[37]

The first case mentioned is that of Noah and his family. In their case, the water was something that they were protected from, not immersed in, but the Apostle Peter regards this as a type of baptism because baptism is meant to signify cleansing from sin.[38] Without the saving grace of God, such cleansing is effectively destruction, since no human being can justly escape the sentence of death that judgement on our sinfulness brings. We are saved, not by any works of ours, nor even by the earthly life and death of Jesus, but by his resurrection from the dead. This is confirmed by the Apostle Paul who told the Romans:

> Do you not know that all of us who have been baptised into Christ Jesus were baptised into his death? We were buried therefore with him by baptism into death, in order that, just

---

37. This collect traces its origins to Martin Luther's first *Taufbüchlein* (1523), as it was taken up and reused by Hermann von Wied in his *Consultation*. See Fisher, *Christian Initiation: The Reformation Period*, pp. 11, 66, for an English translation of the texts.

38. 1 Peter 3:20-21. The story of Noah is in Genesis 6:9-8:19.

as Christ was raised from the dead by the glory of the Father,
we too might walk in newness of life.[39]

The second case mentioned is that of the crossing of the Red Sea, when the children of Israel escaped from their slavery in Egypt and began a new life as the covenanted people of God, subject to the law of Moses which was soon to be revealed to them.[40] Once again, the water symbolises death, from which the Israelites are delivered. The incident is mentioned by the Apostle Paul as a baptism into Moses but the deliverance was temporary and superficial. The people were indeed rescued, only to die later on in the wilderness, because they did not understand the spiritual significance of what had happened to them.[41]

The Old Testament examples are valid representations of baptism but their true meaning was not revealed until the coming of Christ, who was himself baptised in the Jordan, in order to 'fulfil all righteousness'.[42] By that act, Jesus signified that water would be the outward sign of what the prayer book calls 'the mystical washing away of sin'. Note how the prayer balances the taking away of the old with the promise of the new:

Old Testament	New Testament
wash him/her	sanctify him/her with the Holy Ghost
he/she being delivered from God's wrath	may be received into the ark of Christ's Church

The prayer continues by drawing on the triad of faith, hope and charity in 1 Corinthians 13:13. The newly baptised infant is expected to be:

> *steadfast* in faith: the essential grounding for the Christian life
> *joyful* through hope: the promise of the purpose of the Christian life
> *rooted* in charity: the source of the spiritual power needed for living the Christian life.

---

39. Romans 6:3-4.
40. Exodus 14:1-15:21.
41. 1 Corinthians 10:1-5.
42. Matthew 3:13-17.

Each of these things is coupled with a wish for the child's future life:

> with a *steadfast faith*, he will pass through the waves of this
>   troublesome world
> with *joyful hope*, he will look forward to entering the land of
>   everlasting life
> with *roots grounded in charity*, he will reign with God (who
>   is love) for ever.

In the 1549 rite the naming of the child and the signing with the cross followed at this point, but this was discontinued in 1552, when the naming was placed immediately before the baptism and the signing with the cross afterwards.

The *second collect* shifts the emphasis from what God has done in the past to what He does now in the lives of those who believe in Him. God is:

1. the *aid* of all that need
2. the *helper* of all that flee to Him for succour
3. the *life* of them that believe
4. the *resurrection* of the dead.

These four attributes break down naturally into twos. God is the aid/helper of those who are in need and who turn to Him; He is the life and resurrection of those who believe. In this prayer, the child is offered up to God because he needs salvation and God is able to give him life everlasting. His salvation can be obtained by the forgiveness (remission) of his sins by spiritual regeneration, which is a promise God has made to those who ask in faith. Great reliance is placed here on the words of Jesus in the Sermon on the Mount:

1. *ask* and you shall receive
2. *seek* and you shall find
3. *knock* and it will be opened to you.[43]

The prayer of the minister is on behalf of the baptismal party and the entire congregation, who join with him in it, asking God to fulfil His promise by granting this child the eternal blessing of the 'heavenly washing' and entry into the kingdom promised by Christ.

---

43. Matthew 7:7.

The *Scripture* verses that follow come from Mark 10:13-16 and are applied by extension to the baptism of a child, though that is not the original context.[44] Opinions as to the appropriateness of this text to the occasion are bound to differ but the following points may be made:

1. People brought children to Jesus for a blessing.
2. Jesus' disciples did not think that this was appropriate.
3. Jesus rebuked his disciples and insisted that little children should come to him.
4. The kingdom of God must be received with the spirit of a little child.
5. Jesus took the little children and blessed them.

The point of real theological controversy here is number four – to receive the kingdom of God with the humble and trusting spirit of a little child does not mean that all little children will receive it and, in particular, it cannot mean that a baby who has no idea of what is going on can be put in this position. That does not mean that little children should be kept away from spiritual things, nor does it imply that the blessing of Christ cannot really be given to them. Here, it is important to stress that in baptising the infant, the Church is not claiming that it is saved but is offering its own faith on the child's behalf, in the hope that God will honour His promises to *us* (and not to the children). We pray that God will:

1. *receive* the child favourably
2. *embrace* the child with the arms of his mercy
3. *give* the child the blessing of eternal life
4. *make* the child a partaker of his everlasting kingdom.

As before, these petitions break down easily into two parts. In the first part, we ask that God will receive the child in His favour (grace) and mercy and in the second part we ask that He will bless him with eternal life and a share in His everlasting kingdom. We rely on the belief that God is favourably disposed towards the child and do not doubt that He accepts our loving intentions in bringing that child to baptism. We then follow this up with a final prayer, in which we ask first for ourselves and then for the child.

---

44. The inspiration for this text came from Hermann von Wied's *Consultation*. See Fisher, *Christian Initiation: The Reformation Period*, p. 66.

For ourselves, we thank God that He has called us to knowledge of and faith in Him. We pray that He will increase that knowledge in us and confirm our faith in Him. Then we ask for the child, that he may receive the Holy Spirit, be born again and made an heir of everlasting salvation. All of this rests entirely on our faith, apart from which the prayer has no meaning. At no point is there any suggestion that the act of baptism automatically or necessarily produces the spiritual result that is being prayed for; at all times, we pray in humility and expectation, relying on God's promises but not claiming an entitlement that they must be fulfilled in the way that we expect.

B. The Baptism

The service now moves almost imperceptibly into the baptism itself. In 1549 it was at this point that the candidate and the baptismal party moved from the church door to the font. The priest *addresses the godparents* as follows:

1. They have already prayed that the Lord Jesus Christ would:
   a. *receive* the infant
   b. *release* him from his sins
   c. *sanctify* him with the Holy Spirit
   d. *give* him the kingdom of heaven and eternal life.
2. They have already heard that the Lord Jesus Christ has promised to grant what they have prayed for and that he will keep his promises.

Therefore, the infant must in turn promise by his godparents (until he is old enough to take the promises on himself) that he will renounce:

   a. the devil and all his works
   b. the vain pomp and glory of the world
   c. the carnal desires of the flesh.

This is a tall order and it is hard to believe that a child of seven (the age recommended in the Sarum rite for confirmation) would be able to understand what is involved here. Indeed, it is unlikely that anyone under the age of 21 or so would really understand what it is about. That does not make the renunciations meaningless or inapplicable, but it is a reminder that we are dealing here with some extremely serious things that even mature adults may find hard to grapple with.

This is the only point in the 1552/1662 rite where the devil is mentioned directly and where we come closest to the traditional call for exorcism. There had been a prayer for exorcism in the 1549 prayer book but it was omitted in 1552, probably at the suggestion of Martin Bucer.[45]

The next item in the service is a series of *interrogations* based on the Apostles' Creed. In 1549 they were separated according to the trinitarian division of the Creed, but in 1552 they were combined into one. The question format recalls the pattern of the Early Church and it is probable that our Apostles' Creed emerged from a baptismal interrogation like this one. Needless to say, a confession of this kind is a tall order, even for those who understand what they are saying, and, if it is a requirement for confirmation (as it officially is), this can only mean that confirmation should be delayed well beyond the age at which it is normally administered.

Following the Creed, the infant is asked whether it wishes to be baptised and whether it intends to obey God's will and commandments. The sponsors must respond on its behalf but there is an air of unreality about the form the questions take and modern revisions tend to stress that they are intended for the sponsors, not for the child directly.

After the interrogations come the *four petitions* which were moved from their original position in the 1549 prayer book and placed here. In 1549 there were a total of eight petitions that were appended to the order for the private baptism of infants as a special service for the consecration of the water. The second and eighth (now fourth) of these petitions are unaltered from 1549. The first and the third have been slightly changed and the fourth to the seventh have been omitted. The nature of the changes may be gauged as follows, with words in grey representing those that were dropped in 1552 and words in **bold** type those that were added at the same time.

The first petition:

> O merciful God, grant that the old Adam, in them that shall be baptised in this fountain, **this child** may be so buried, that the new man may be raised up *again* **in him**. Amen.

The third petition:

> Grant to all them which at this fountain forsake the devil and all his works; that they **he** may have power and strength to

---

45. See Whitaker, *Martin Bucer and the Book of Common Prayer*, pp. 92-93.

have victory, and to triumph against him **the devil**, the world and the flesh. Amen.

The four petitions that were dropped in 1552 were as follows:

4. Whosoever shall confess thee, O Lord; recognise him also in thy kingdom. Amen.
5. Grant that all sin and vice here may be so extinct: that they many never have power to reign in thy servants. Amen.
6. Grant that whosoever here shall begin to be of thy flock: may evermore continue in the same. Amen.
7. Grant that all they which for thy sake in this life do deny and forsake themselves: may win and purchase thee (O Lord) which art everlasting treasure. Amen.

There does not seem to be any reason why they were left out in 1552, although they add little to the four which were retained and perhaps there was a perceived advantage in shortening the service overall.

The four petitions are followed by a *prayer for the sanctification of the water*. A prayer of this kind was attached to the service of private baptism in the 1549 rite, where it preceded the above-mentioned petitions. It read as follows:

O most merciful God our Saviour Jesu Christ, who hast ordained the element of water for the regeneration of thy faithful people, upon whom, being baptised in the river of Jordan, the Holy Ghost came down in likeness of a dove; Send down, we beseech thee, the same thy Holy Spirit to assist us, and to be present at this our invocation of thy holy name. Sanctify[46] this fountain of baptism, thou that art the sanctifier of all things, that by the power of thy word, all those that shall be baptised therein may be spiritually regenerated, and made the children of everlasting adoption. Amen.

The prayer now found in the 1662 Book of Common Prayer originated, like the rest of this section, in the form for consecrating the water that was appended to the order for the private baptism of infants in 1549. It was slightly modified in 1552 and more significantly in 1662. The process can be charted as follows, with words in grey being those that

---

46. Here the priest was to make the sign of the cross over the font.

were dropped in 1552 and words in **bold type** those that were added in 1662. Square brackets indicate changes made in 1552 and preserved. Words in grey and bold were added in 1552 and subsequently dropped in 1662.

> Almighty everliving God, whose most dearly beloved Son Jesus Christ, for the forgiveness of our sins, did shed out of his most precious side both water and blood, and gave commandment to his disciples that they should go teach all nations, and baptise them in the name of the Father, **and of** the Son, and [**of**] the Holy Ghost: Regard, we beseech thee, the supplications of thy congregation, **sanctify this water to the mystical washing away of sin**; and grant that all thy servants which shall **this child, now to** be baptised in this water prepared for the ministration of thy holy sacrament **therein**, may receive the fulness of thy grace, and ever remain in the number of thy faithful and elect children, through Jesus Christ our Lord. [**Amen.**]

The only significant alteration, made in 1662, was the addition of the words 'sanctify this water to the mystical washing away of sin'. This means that it has been set aside for a special purpose and does not imply that it has any spiritual power of its own. The key word is 'mystical', which indicates that the washing is spiritual, not physical, which corresponds to the fact that sin is not a stain on the soul that needs to be scrubbed out, but an alienation from God caused by the disobedience of our first parents, and a state into which we are born. The prayer is couched in the language of promise and expectation and is not a statement of what necessarily occurs in baptism. We can hope that the candidate presented at the font will experience the regeneration promised to those who believe, but whether he/she actually does or not is the gift of the Holy Spirit and not the result of a mechanical act. As always, faith is the context in which these words find their meaning and for that we must rely on the grace and goodness of God.

The reference to 'faithful and elect children' must be interpreted in the context of covenant theology. In ancient Israel, Jewish boys were circumcised on the eight day as a sign that they belonged to God's chosen people but that was no guarantee that they would remain faithful or be counted as true children of God on reaching adulthood. The Apostle Paul was very clear about the benefits – and the limitations – of circumcision (Romans 2:25-29) and the same principle applies to the baptised. The children of believers are 'chosen' in the sense that they are privileged to be brought up in the fear and knowledge of the Lord, but whether they are truly elect will only be known if the fruits of the Holy Spirit are manifested in them. We are entitled to pray that it may be so, as we do here, and to trust in the promises of God, but we cannot use earthly and external ceremonies in order to manipulate spiritual power. In the end we must leave the judgement to Him.

The *rubric preceding the actual baptism* directs how the priest is to proceed. In ancient times it seems that candidates were dipped three times, in the name of the persons of the Trinity, and a residue of that was preserved in the 1549 rite. This was abolished in 1552. In the 1662 text the dipping in the water was preceded by a question to the godparents as to the name of the child, something that in 1549 and 1552 had been done at the beginning of the service.

The rubric assumes that a healthy child will be 'dipped' in the water, which may mean a full or partial immersion, though that is not specified. However, if the child is weak in some way, 'affusion' (sprinkling) will suffice and that is the usual practice today, whether the child is capable of being immersed or not. Too much should not be made of this. What matters is the spiritual disposition of those bringing the child to baptism and not the amount of water poured over it. People will doubtless have their preferences but there should be no difficulty in accommodating a variety of practice and no one should question the validity of a baptism conducted in a way that is different from his or her expressed preference.

The baptism concludes with *the signing with the cross*, historically one of the most controversial aspects of the rite. Signing with the cross was a very ancient practice, used in many contexts. In the Sarum rite of baptism it was repeated no fewer than six times. It was originally intended to remind people that their salvation depended on the sacrifice of Christ but over time the ritual had become so banalised that it is doubtful whether anybody reflected very deeply on its significance. In the 1549 prayer book the practice was greatly curtailed, with the baptismal candidate to be signed with the cross on his forehead and breast at the church door, before the exorcism. This unfortunate association led some people to suppose that there was some magical efficacy in the sign of the cross that was connected to the expulsion of the devil, and it became a bone of contention among the Puritans, who wanted to abolish the practice altogether.

In order to meet this objection, Canon 30 of the 1603 (1604) Canons gave a detailed explanation of what the signing meant and why the Church of England had decided to retain it.[47] The reasons were as follows:

1. Despite the abuse of the sign by the medieval Church, its original purpose was good. The abuse of a thing does not mean that the thing itself should be abolished.
2. The sign of the cross is not part of the baptismal service itself, which is valid without it.
3. The baptised person is received into the Church by baptism, not by the sign of the cross, which is merely an external confirmation of that.
4. It is always good and right to remember that the Cross is central to our faith and that the Christian is called to spiritual warfare under its banner.

In other words, the ceremony has a value in reminding people of the nature of their faith and in calling them to uphold it through all the trials and temptations of this life. At the same time, it is not essential to baptism, has no spiritual power in and of itself, and can be omitted without loss or prejudice to the spiritual status of the child. The Irish canons of 1634 (1635) omitted any reference to it and, although it is still widely practised in the Anglican world, it is neither universal nor obligatory.

C. The Post-baptism

After the signing with the cross, the baptismal service enters its final phase. In the 1549 prayer book this was extremely short, consisting of the giving of the christening robe, or 'chrisom', a final anointing of the child, and an exhortation to the godparents, instructing them to ensure that the child should be brought up and instructed in the Christian faith. That exhortation was retained in 1552 but the invitation and prayer preceding it were altered to the pattern which has been retained in the 1662 rite.

The *invitation* has proved to be one of the most contentious parts of the Book of Common Prayer and was even the subject of litigation in the famous trial of George Cornelius Gorham (1787-1857), which concluded in 1850 with the decision of the Judicial Committee of the Privy Council,

---

47. For the complete text in both Latin and English, see Bray (ed.), *The Anglican Canons*, pp. 302-9.

in opposition to the bishop of Exeter and the Court of Arches, that the prayer book does not teach a doctrine of baptismal regeneration. That decision scandalised high churchmen, some of whom left the Church of England for Rome, but it has consistently been upheld by Evangelicals as evidence that the sacramentalist theology of Anglo-Catholicism cannot be justified on the basis of the prayer book. Even so, many Evangelicals (and others) have been disturbed by the wording of the text because they have read it as an affirmation of baptismal regeneration, even though it is not.

The controversial words are those at the very beginning: 'Seeing now, dearly beloved brethren, that this child is regenerate and grafted into the body of Christ's Church.' What does this mean? The correct approach is to interpret this in the context of the covenant theology that underlies the rest of the baptismal rite. Just as a Jewish boy was 'grafted into the body of Israel' by being circumcised, so the Christian child is 'grafted into the body of Christ's Church'. The image of the grafting recalls Romans 11:16-24, where Paul uses the image of an olive tree to make the point that not all the branches bear fruit. Those that do not will be pruned to make room for other branches to be grafted on, which in his case meant that some Jews would be rejected in order to allow some Gentiles to be connected to the living tree.

The parallel with baptism is that, while the children of Christians are privileged, just as the children of Israel were, there is no guarantee that they will bear fruit simply because of that. We present our children to God, trusting in His mercy and in His promises, but not presuming on them, and as the invitation makes plain, we continue to pray that the child will lead the rest of his life according to this beginning. This is a matter for prayer and it cannot be assumed that it will follow on automatically from baptism, or even from a Christian upbringing.

The invitation leads on naturally to the Lord's Prayer, which is then followed by the exhortation to the godparents which remained the same in 1549 and 1552 but was slightly emended in 1662.[48] There the service ended both in 1549 and in 1552, but in the 1662 prayer book there is an *additional charge to the godparents*, which had been relegated to a rubric in 1552. The godparents are to ensure that the child will be brought to the bishop for confirmation as soon as he can say the Apostles' Creed, the Lord's Prayer and the Ten Commandments. That mere recitation of these texts would not be enough is indicated by the final clause, which enjoins the godparents to ensure that the child is instructed in the

---

48. For the precise details, see above.

Church Catechism, which was composed for the purpose of explaining the meaning of the texts in question.

Two *final rubrics* at the end of the service reassure parents that baptised children who die before committing actual sin are 'undoubtedly saved' and that Canon 30 answers any problems that people might have with the signing of the cross. The second rubric should cause no real difficulty, but the first is more problematic. It states that the salvation of the children in question is 'certain by God's Word' but does not quote any text in support of this assertion and it is hard to see what it is based on. It is good to reassure parents who lose a child that the child is safe in the hand of God but to go further than that is to presume on the teaching of Scripture which is not clear. Here, as elsewhere, we are called to walk in faith and to trust in the mercy of God, not to presume that we know the answer to what is hidden in His mind and not revealed to us.

Private Baptism of Infants (1552/1662)

The inclusion in the 1552 and 1662 prayer books of a service for the private baptism of infants was a concession to the necessity of the time in which the rite was composed, though it was clearly not the preferred option of Thomas Cranmer or his colleagues. Already, in 1549, the service opened with the following rubrics:

> The pastors and curates shall oft admonish the people that they defer not the baptism of infants any longer than the Sunday or other holy day next after the child be born, unless upon a great and reasonable cause declared to the curate and by him approved.
>
> *And also they shall warn them* that without *like* great cause and necessity they baptise not children at home in their houses. And when great need shall compel them so to do, that then they minister it on this fashion.

These rubrics were repeated in 1552 and the second is found in the 1662 prayer book with no significant alteration.[49] That the service is not meant to stand on its own but is really just an adaptation of the order for

---

49. The words in italics were altered by the Prayer Book (Further Provisions) Measure 1968 (no. 2) (18 December 1968), section 3.2, in *The Public General Acts and Church Assembly Measures 1968* (London: HMSO, 1969) to read: 'The minister of every parish shall warn the people'. The word 'like' was deleted at the same time.

public baptism is made clear in the opening rubrics of 1662, where the officiant is instructed to say the Lord's Prayer and as many of the collects appointed for public baptism as he thinks are appropriate. The printed service itself begins with the actual baptism which is then followed by a thanksgiving prayer taken from the public baptism order that effectively concludes the first (and most important) part of the service. The pattern of 1549 and 1662 is basically the same:

1549/1552	1662
1. Rubric directing the minister to call on God for His grace and say the Lord's Prayer	1. Rubric directing the minister to call on God for His grace and say the Lord's Prayer
	2. Collects from public baptism at the minister's discretion
3. Naming of the child	3. Naming of the child
4. Dipping in or pouring of water on the child	4. Pouring of water on the child
5. Formula of baptism	5. Formula of baptism
	6. Thanksgiving prayer

The second part of the service is the reception of the child into the Church which basically follows the same pattern in 1549, 1552 and 1662:

1549/1552	1662
1. Certificates and inquiries about the baptism	1. Certificates and inquiries about the baptism
2. Mark 10:13-16 and the address	2. Mark 10:13-16 and the address
3. The Lord's Prayer	3. The Lord's Prayer
	4. The Apostles' Creed
5. Thanksgiving and prayer	
6. Interrogatories	6. Interrogatories
	5. Thanksgiving and prayer
	7. Signing with the cross
	8. Address to the people
	9. Prayer for grace for the child
10. Exhortation to the sponsors	10. Exhortation to the sponsors
11. Hypothetical formula of baptism	11. Hypothetical formula of baptism

The 1662 prayer book provides words of certification to be used by the minister, if he is the one who has baptised the child in private, in the presence of the congregation of his church, to which the child is to be brought as soon as possible. If the baptism was performed by some other minister, or by a lay person, there is a series of questions, originally set out in 1549 and repeated in 1552, that the minister must ask of those who performed the private baptism, after which he certifies it in a somewhat longer form of words that recalls the nature and promises of baptism.

The 1662 format is longer but the contents are taken more or less unaltered from the order for public baptism. The hypothetical words printed at the end of the service are in the wrong place. They should appear at the very beginning as an alternative form of words, to be used by the minister if there is some doubt about whether the child had really been baptised or not.

In the 1549 rite there is a third section, headed the 'Form of Consecration of the Font', which was broken up in 1552/1662 and placed in different parts of the service of public baptism. The service of private baptism was never regarded as 'normal' and modern alternatives to the Book of Common Prayer usually omit it altogether. This does not necessarily mean that private baptisms no longer take place, or that they are disallowed, but merely emphasises what was true all along, which is that private baptism can only be seen as an unwelcome (if sometimes unavoidable) alternative to public baptism, and that, if it is performed, the minister must adapt the service of public baptism as required. That is essentially what he was expected to do in 1549/1552/1662 and is generally thought to make a special form of service unnecessary.

Adult Baptism (1662)

To the modern mind it is curious that, until 1662, the prayer book lacked any provision for the baptism of adults, or as it says 'to such as are of riper years and able to answer for themselves'. Here, more than anywhere else, the Book of Common Prayer reveals that it is a product of its time. The service of adult baptism in the 1662 rite is an adaptation of the public baptism of infants, and the closing rubric states that, if a child has not been baptised in infancy but has not yet reached the age of discretion, it is the service designed for infants that is to be used.

The introductory rubrics in 1662 were considerably altered by the Prayer Book (Further Provisions) Measure 1968 (no. 2)[50] as can be seen from the following comparison of the two texts:

---

50. Prayer Book (Further Provisions) Measure 1968 (no 2) (18 December 1968), section 3.3, in ibid.

1662	1968
When any such persons as be of riper years are to be baptised, timely notice shall be given to the bishop, or whom he shall appoint for that purpose, a week before at the least, by the parents or some other discreet persons, that so due care may be taken for their examination whether they be sufficiently instructed in the principles of the Christian religion, and that they may be exhorted to prepare themselves with prayers and fasting for the receiving of this holy sacrament.	When any such person as is of riper years and able to answer for himself is to be baptised, the minister shall instruct such person, or cause him to be instructed, in the principles of the Christian religion, and exhort him so to prepare himself with prayers and fasting that he may receive this holy sacrament with repentance and faith.
And if they shall be found, then let the godfathers and godmothers (the people being assembled upon the Sunday or holy day appointed) shall be ready to present them at the font immediately after the second lesson, either at morning or evening prayer, as the curate in his discretion shall think fit.	At least a week before any such baptism is to take place, the minister shall give notice thereof to the bishop of the diocese or whomsoever he shall appoint for the purpose.
	The person to be baptised shall choose three, or at least two, to be his sponsors, who shall be ready to present him at the font and afterwards put him in mind of his Christian profession and duties. No person shall be admitted to be a sponsor who has not been baptised and confirmed. Nevertheless the minister shall have power to dispense with the requirement of confirmation in any case in which in his judgement need so requires.
And standing there, the priest shall ask whether any of the persons here presented be baptised or no. If they shall answer, No, then shall the priest say thus:	At the time appointed, the sponsors shall be ready to present the person to be baptised at the font, and standing there the priest shall ask whether the person presented be baptised or no, and if he shall answer, No, then shall the priest say thus:

The opening rubrics differ from those for the public baptism of infants in a number of significant respects. The first, and most important of these, is that the minister is to catechise the candidate(s) before performing the rite of baptism. This reflects the pattern of the Early Church, though that appears to be accidental rather than deliberate. The candidate is also ordered to prepare himself by prayer and fasting, the only place in the prayer book where fasting is actually enjoined. It seems probable that the phrase 'prayer and fasting' was derived from the New Testament, though modern research has shown that in several places the words 'and fasting' were later interpolations.[51] That obviously weakens the case for the practice and, of course, there is no indication of what 'fasting' was supposed to mean. Those familiar with fasting in the Roman Catholic and Eastern Orthodox traditions know that it seldom requires total abstinence from food, usually it involves the adoption of a different and reduced diet, but what that should be in this case is not specified. The lack of clear biblical sanction and the absence of any definition of what is involved have effectively made fasting optional in most cases, and few people would insist on it today.

The minister was also expected to advise the bishop of the diocese, or his representative, of his intention to baptise an adult at least a week in advance. It is interesting to note that a similar period of advance notice has been prescribed since 1968 for the baptism of infants, although in that case it is the parents or godparents who must notify the minister, not the minister who must report it to the bishop.

In 1968 the adult candidates for baptism were also given the liberty to choose their own sponsors as witnesses. As in the case of infants, these sponsors must be baptised themselves, and in normal circumstances also confirmed, though the minister may dispense with that if he thinks it appropriate, as he may also do in the case of infants. It is the sponsors (godparents) who then present the candidate(s) for baptism and the service proceeds along lines that are basically similar to those followed in the case of children. It seems to be assumed that adult baptism will take place in a church service with a congregation, though there is nothing in the order to rule out private baptism, which presumably remained an option in cases of necessity. It can perhaps be assumed that, in those circumstances, the procedures followed would be paralleled by the provisions made for the private baptism of infants, though that is nowhere stated or explicitly allowed for.

The changes made to the service for the public baptism of infants in order to accommodate adults may be listed as follows:

1. In the opening exhortation, mention is made of 'committing many actual transgressions', something that would not be the case with newborn children.

---

51. This is true in Matthew 17:21, Mark 9:29, Acts 10:30 and 1 Corinthians 7:5.

2. The Gospel reading is taken from Jesus' dialogue with Nicodemus (John 3:1-8), which is clearly more appropriate than Mark 10:13-16.

3. The exhortation following the Gospel reading quotes Mark 16:16, Acts 2:37-40 and 1 Peter 3:21 in its teaching on baptism.

4. The questions are put to the candidates themselves and not to the godparents, who are witnesses and not 'sureties'.

5. The priest takes each candidate by the right hand and leads him to the font – another revival of ancient practice.

6. The priest dips the candidate in water or else pours water on him. Immersion, total or partial, is thus permitted but not insisted upon and probably not expected in most cases. There is, however, nothing to prevent it and in recent times it has become more popular than it used to be.

7. The thanksgiving that comes after the address following the reading of the Gospel is repeated, in slightly different words, after the Lord's Prayer. The effect of this is that it is said both before and after the baptism itself. The two texts may be compared as follows:

Before baptism	After baptism
Almighty and everlasting God, heavenly Father, we give thee humble thanks, for that thou hast vouchsafed to call us to the knowledge of thy grace and faith in thee: Increase this knowledge and confirm this faith in us evermore. Give thy Holy Spirit to these persons, that they may be born again, and be made heirs of everlasting salvation, through our Lord Jesus Christ, who liveth and reigneth with thee and the Holy Spirit, now and for ever. Amen.	We yield thee humble thanks, O heavenly Father, that thou hast vouchsafed to call us to the knowledge of thy grace, and faith in thee; Increase this knowledge, and confirm this faith in us evermore. Give thy Holy Spirit to these persons; that, being now born again, and made heirs of everlasting salvation, through our Lord Jesus Christ, they may continue thy servants, and attain thy promises; through the same Lord Jesus Christ thy Son, who liveth and reigneth with thee, in the unity of the same Holy Spirit, everlastingly, Amen.

8. The thanksgiving after the Lord's Prayer used in the public baptism of infants is omitted.
9. The address to the godparents is altered to suit the case of adults.
10. The closing exhortation is addressed directly to the newly baptised and not to the godparents.

The first of the closing rubrics enjoins that the newly baptised should be presented to the bishop for confirmation as soon as possible, so that they may be admitted to Holy Communion. However, since Holy Communion is made available to those who desire to be confirmed, as well as to those who actually are, this rubric would appear to have no force in practice. The second rubric refers to the case of children, already mentioned above, who have passed infancy but who have not yet reached the age of discretion. In such cases, most people today would probably prefer to wait until the child is old enough to answer for itself, but that option was not envisaged in 1662.

The Catechism

From the second century onwards, the Church provided for a period of instruction (catechesis) during which those who wished to be baptised were instructed in the Christian faith. Remnants of the catechumenate, as this period was called, survived for centuries in the liturgies of the Church, long after its existence had become a distant memory. At the time of the Reformation, the ignorance of the laity (and, indeed, of many of the clergy) was a scandal in desperate need of correction. Every Protestant Church made catechesis a priority and, eventually, even Rome took it on board. In England there were a number of primers published, partly for the instruction of young people and partly as aids to worship for those who were familiar only with services in Latin and unsure of what they meant in their own language.

These primers are often very detailed and contain far more material than the Catechism in the Book of Common Prayer, but their basic intention was similar. Three of the more important ones were published by Edward Burton in 1834 and they give us a clear idea of what was intended. The first is *A Goodly Prymer*, published by William Marshall in 1535, the second is *The Manual of Prayers or the Prymer in English*, published by John Hilsey, bishop of Rochester, in 1539 and the third is *King Henry's Primer*, which came out in 1545 and effectively superseded the others.[52] Among many other things, each of these primers contained expositions of the Apostles' Creed, the Ten Commandments and the Lord's Prayer, which were to form the core of the later catechisms.

Instructions to teach these texts to children were quick to make their appearance. The First Injunctions of Henry VIII, issued in 1536, said:

> [In] their sermons and other collations, the parsons, vicars and other curates abovesaid shall diligently admonish the fathers and mothers, masters and governors of youth, being within their cure, to teach or cause to be taught their children and servants, even from their infancy, their Paternoster, the Articles of our Faith and the Ten Commandments in their mother tongue; and the same so taught, shall cause the said youth oft to repeat and understand.[53]

Two years later, in the Second Henrician Injunctions, the same people were told:

> [T]hat you shall every Sunday and holy day through the year openly and plainly recite to your parishioners twice or thrice together, or oftener if need require, one particle or sentence of the Paternoster or Creed, in English, to the intent that they may learn the same by heart … and that done, you shall declare unto them the Ten Commandments, one by one, every Sunday and holy day, till they be likewise perfect in the same.[54]

Further resources for doing this were provided in the so-called *Bishops' Book* of 1537 and its revised version, *The King's Book* of 1543.[55] So valuable was this that Bishop Edmund Bonner, when he composed his own manual of instruction during the Marian reaction, took up the same pattern and expounded the classical texts from a more traditionally

52. Burton, *Three Primers put forth in the Reign of Henry VIII.*
53. First Henrician Injunctions 1536, no. 5, in Bray, *Documents*, p. 155.
54. Second Henrician Injunctions 1538, no. 4, in Bray, *Documents*, p. 158. This was repeated in the Edwardian Injunctions 1547, no. 4 (Bray, *Documents*, p. 219).
55. These are printed together and collated in G.L. Bray, *The Institution of a Christian Man* (Cambridge: James Clarke & Co., 2018).

Catholic point of view.[56] Set against all of these resources, it is clear that the Catechism as it appears in the Book of Common Prayer is but the tip of a much larger iceberg, sufficient perhaps for confirmation but only the beginning of a course of theology that, if fully pursued, would encompass a broad swathe of Christian teaching.

The Catechism, as we now have it, made its first appearance in the 1549 rite, where it was part of the confirmation service. It remained in that position until 1662, when it was detached to form a separate item, though still conveniently placed between baptism and confirmation. The structure of the Catechism is clearly dependent on the order for the public baptism of infants, although the section on the sacraments was not part of the original text. It was added at the request of the Puritans after the Hampton Court Conference in 1604.

The authorship of the Catechism is uncertain but the 1549 text is usually ascribed to Alexander Nowell (1517-1602), who was dean of St Paul's Cathedral from 1561 until his death, and the additional section on the sacraments is thought to be the work of John Overall (1559-1619), Nowell's successor as dean (1602-1614).[57]

The Catechism as it stands in the 1662 prayer book has a fivefold structure that can be broken down into: the Christian covenant; the Apostles' Creed; the Ten Commandments; the Lord's Prayer; and the sacraments.[58]

The child assumes the *Christian covenant*, the promises made on his behalf by his godparents:

1. He acknowledges the name they gave him at his baptism, when he was made a member of Christ,[59] a child of God[60] and an inheritor of the kingdom of heaven.[61]
2. He renounces the world, the flesh and the devil.[62]
3. He confesses the faith contained in the Apostles' Creed.

---

56. Ibid., pp. 239-85, 374-468.
57. The evidence for this is surveyed by M. Davie, *Instruction in the Way of the Lord: A Guide to the Catechism in the Book of Common Prayer* (London: Latimer Trust, 2014), pp. 15-17.
58. See F. Colquhoun, *The Catechism and the Order of Confirmation* (London: Hodder & Stoughton, 1963), p. 15.
59. 1 Corinthians 12:13, 27; Colossians 1:18. See also John 15:1-6.
60. Galatians 3:26; 4:5. See also Hebrews 2:11.
61. Romans 8:17; Galatians 3:29.
62. 1 Timothy 3:6; John 8:44. See also 1 John 3:8.

4. He agrees to keep the commandments of God for the rest of his life.
5. He thanks God, His heavenly Father, for having called him to this state of salvation through His Son Jesus Christ.[63]

The child repeats and expounds the *Apostles' Creed* as follows:

1. God the Father made me and all the world.
2. God the Son redeemed me and all mankind.
3. God the Holy Spirit sanctifies me and all the chosen people of God.

The child repeats the *Ten Commandments* and says that he has learned two principal things from them, as follows:

1. He has a duty towards God, which is:
   a. to believe in, love and fear Him with all his heart, mind, soul and strength
   b. to worship Him
   c. to thank Him
   d. to trust Him
   e. to call upon Him
   f. to honour His holy name and His Word
   g. to serve Him for the rest of his life.
2. He has a duty towards his neighbour, which is:
   a. to love him as myself
   b. to do to others as I would have others do to me
   c. to love, honour and protect my father and mother
   d. to honour and obey the Sovereign and all in lawful authority
   e. to submit to all my governors, teachers, pastors and masters
   f. to be humble towards my betters
   g. to hurt nobody by word or deed
   h. to be true and just in all my dealings
   i. to bear no malice or hatred in my heart
   j. to refrain from stealing
   k. to refrain from lying, slandering or speaking evil of others
   l. to be sober, temperate and chaste

---

63. Acts 2:47; 13:48.

m. to refrain from coveting the goods of others
n. to learn and labour to get my own living
o. to do my duty in the state of life to which God has called me.

The child repeats and expounds the *Lord's Prayer* (not previously mentioned in the Catechism). In expounding the Lord's Prayer, the child prays that God will:

a. send His grace to us and to all people, so that we may worship, serve and obey Him as we ought to do
b. send us everything we need for our souls and bodies
c. be merciful to us and forgive us our sins
d. save and defend us in all dangers, spiritual and physical
e. keep us from sin, wickedness, the devil and everlasting death.

The child expounds the number and meaning of the *sacraments*. This section consists of twelve questions and answers. The first three questions and answers treat of sacraments in general, the next four of baptism and the last five of the Lord's Supper.

In the first section, the child confesses that:

a. There are only two sacraments necessary for salvation.
b. A sacrament is the outward and visible sign of an inward and spiritual grace, ordained by Christ himself as a means and pledge of that grace.
c. A sacrament has two distinct parts – the outward visible sign and the inward spiritual grace.

In the second section, the child confesses that in baptism:

a. Water is the outward and visible sign, in which the candidate is baptised in the name of the Father, Son and Holy Spirit.
b. The inward and spiritual grace is death to sin and a new birth to righteousness.
c. Two things are required – repentance, whereby we forsake sin, and faith, whereby we sincerely believe the promises of God made to us in the sacrament.
d. Infants make the promises through their 'sureties' (godparents) and are bound to perform them when they come of age.

In the third section, the child confesses that the Lord's Supper:

a. was ordained for the continual remembrance of Christ's death and the benefits we receive from it.
b. the outward sign is bread and wine, which the Lord commanded us to receive.
c. the inward part is the body and blood of Christ, which are taken and received by the faithful in the supper.
d. strengthens and refreshes our souls by the body and blood of Christ, just as our bodies are strengthened and refreshed by the bread and wine.
e. requires that those who come to it must repent of their former ways, intend to lead a new life, have a living faith in God's mercy and give thanks for the death of His Son, and to be in charity with everyone.

The closing rubrics repeat the words of the Henrician and Edwardian Injunctions and ordain that, when the children are ready, they shall present themselves to the bishop, accompanied by a godparent, and seek confirmation, according to the order set out for that purpose which immediately follows.

In assessing the Catechism, it must be said that the section dealing with the Apostles' Creed is noticeably weaker than the others. It recalls the trinitarian structure of the Creed but does so in a way that verges on modalism, which is the belief that the persons of the Trinity are determined by their functions – Creator, Redeemer and Sanctifier. Trinitarian theology is more complex and subtle than that. Hard as it is to understand, it ought to be presented in a much fuller way than it is here. There also ought to be some mention of the last phrases of the Creed, following on from the confession of the Holy Spirit, which are not touched on at all.

In stark contrast to this, the exposition of the Ten Commandments is very full. It is clear that the Catechism places its main emphasis on Christian behaviour and, in particular, on the duty of submission to the authorities in home, Church and State. This is an emphasis that is easily lost today and should be retained, though perhaps with additions more appropriate to the responsibilities of adults in a democratic society.

The final section on the sacraments is generally adequate, although the traditional nature-grace dichotomy needs to be re-examined, because it is not equivalent to the distinction between matter (nature?) and spirit (grace?). It could also benefit from a clearer statement regarding Christ's institution of baptism and the Lord's Supper as sacraments of the Gospel and an extension of the ministry of the Word.

It could also be stated that 'sacrament' is a category invented by later theologians and is not found in the New Testament, where baptism and the Lord's Supper are never linked to one another. We may perhaps assume that only the baptised were admitted to the Supper. However, it cannot be taken for granted that baptised children should be admitted to Communion when they do not understand what they are doing. In the case of infants, there is a case to be made for catechesis and confirmation before admitting them to the Table, where they are expected to participate on the same understanding as adults.

Confirmation

The rite of confirmation is intimately connected to baptism and cannot be understood apart from it, although the precise nature of the link between them has been disputed. Some people have thought that it can be traced to Acts 8:15-17 and 19:6, where the apostles laid hands on those who had already been baptised, but, in those cases, the baptism had been inadequate. The Samaritans in Acts chapter 8 had been baptised only in the name of Jesus and the followers in Ephesus in Acts chapter 19 had received only the baptism of John. In other words, the laying on of hands was not confirmation, in the modern sense of the word, but a completion of an inadequate baptism.

It has also been claimed that confirmation was originally the anointing with chrism that came at the end of the baptismal service and, in the Eastern Churches, where that practice continues to the present day, there is no confirmation in the sense that we understand it.[64]

Confirmation in the Western Church grew in importance as infant baptism became the norm and the catechesis that had preceded adult baptism virtually disappeared. The belief that children should make their own profession of faith when they were old enough to do so remained strong and, even though Christian instruction of the young left much to be desired, the principle was maintained.

Another feature of the Western Church was that confirmation was reserved to the bishop of the diocese. In the early days, when dioceses

---

64. For a good introduction to the subject, see J.D.C. Fisher, *Confirmation Then and Now* (London: SPCK, 1978). See also M. Davie, *Defend O Lord: Confirmation according to the Book of Common Prayer* (London: Latimer Trust, 2022).

were small and the bishop was a well-known local figure, this was not a problem but, as dioceses became larger and bishops more remote from their people, episcopal confirmation became much harder to maintain and, to some extent, it must be said that this difficulty has never been properly overcome. The Anglican Church retains episcopal confirmation, but very few bishops have any contact with those whom they confirm and must rely on the assurances given to them by parish priests and parents that the candidates whom they present have been properly instructed.

Confirmation was elevated to the level of a sacrament by Peter Lombard (*c.* 1090-1160) in his *Sentences*, which became the standard theological textbook of the middle ages. Its status was never officially ratified by the Church but it was accepted *de facto* at the eighth session of the Council of Florence (22 November 1439) in the bull of union with the Armenians, and this has never been questioned or superseded.[65] The English Reformers, along with Protestants elsewhere, rejected this and relegated confirmation to a secondary level, though they did not abandon it.[66] On the contrary, as J.D.C. Fisher noted:

> [A] rite of personal commitment such as those in the Reformed tradition envisage by confirmation, is a pastoral and theological necessity in the case of all baptized in infancy. ... In the Prayer Book of 1662 the personal affirmation of faith comes at the beginning of the Confirmation service, when the bishop invites the candidates, who have already learnt the catechism, to ratify and confirm the promises made in their name at their baptism. This is Confirmation as the Reformers understood it.[67]

At the time of the Reformation, it was thought that the godparents of a baptised infant ought to supervise his education until the age of seven, when he would be old enough to answer for himself and could be presented to the bishop for confirmation. That is still often the case in the Roman Catholic Church but Anglicans nowadays usually delay confirmation until much later. In most cases, it will take place in the early teenage years but it can be delayed indefinitely. Confirmation is

---

65. *Conciliorum Oecumenicorum Decreta*, pp. 544-45.
66. Article 25 of the Thirty-nine Articles of Religion.
67. Fisher, *Confirmation Then and Now*, p. 138.

also used to receive members of other churches who become Anglicans and that can happen at any age.

As found in the 1662 prayer book, the rite of confirmation is similar to a coming-of-age ceremony, like the Jewish bar mitzvah, though this is more by accident than by design. The primary purpose of episcopal confirmation in the Western Church was to ratify the decision of a local congregation to baptise a candidate and admit him to Holy Communion. It was a recognition on the part of the wider Christian community that the baptised person was indeed a member of the body of Christ and was understood in that way. Prior catechesis was not required and, in the case of infants, was often ignored. It was understood that a bishop might not be immediately available at the time of baptism, but only a short delay, perhaps of a week or so, was envisaged, which hardly left time for instruction. This primary function of confirmation is the justification for extending it to baptised adults, who must also be confirmed by a bishop, even though they have made their own profession of faith in their baptism.

Given that the baptismal rite in the prayer book is designed primarily for infants, the second use of confirmation has always been more prominent. This is that it should follow a course of catechesis, laid down in the office of baptism and fleshed out in the Catechism, and this is how it is generally understood today. The concluding rubric of the rite states that no one should be admitted to Holy Communion unless he has been confirmed or is 'ready and desirous to be confirmed'. The precise meaning of this last clause is not entirely clear but, in general, it is fair to say that adolescents are not admitted to the Lord's Supper until after confirmation, even if they are not strictly obliged to wait until then.

It should also be remembered that many more infants are baptised than are later confirmed. This may be because many of the parents concerned do not understand that baptism is entry into the visible Church, which requires further instruction, and so never present their children for catechesis later on. It may also be that many leave the Church, either formally or informally, and never bother to pursue matters any further. In a few cases, people may never get around to it or think about it, especially if they come to a living faith in adulthood. There are certainly many communicants in Anglican churches who have not been confirmed and the matter may never be raised unless there are exceptional circumstances that require it. For example, it is not possible to be ordained as a minister of the Church without having been confirmed and there are cases where that has to be done in order to make ordination possible. Obviously, in such a situation, the faith of the candidate ought to be well-established already, and the rite of confirmation will necessarily appear as a formality more than anything else.

As for the rite itself, it opens with an address from the bishop or his appointed representative, who reminds the candidates and the congregation what it requires and what it is for. First of all, it is made clear that only those who can recite the Apostles' Creed, the Lord's Prayer and the Ten Commandments can be presented for confirmation. The candidates are also expected to be able to answer the questions put to them in the Catechism. It is further assumed that they will have reached the age of discretion (which is not specified), that they have learned what their godparents have promised on their behalf, and that they are ready both to ratify those promises and to give an undertaking that they will faithfully observe the things to which they have consented.

Once that declaration is made, the bishop turns to the candidates and asks them whether they are prepared to accept the obligations laid out for them. They must then reply in the affirmative for the service to proceed.

After this, the bishop continues with a short series of versicles and responses, calling on God for help so that the candidates may achieve what they have promised. He then continues with a prayer in which:

1. He acknowledges that the candidates have been born again by water and the Holy Spirit.
2. He acknowledges that the candidates have been forgiven for their sins.
3. He prays that the candidates will be strengthened by the Holy Spirit and that they will continue to grow in grace by receiving:
   a. the spirit of wisdom and understanding
   b. the spirit of counsel and 'ghostly' (i.e. spiritual) strength
   c. the spirit of knowledge and true godliness
   d. the spirit of the fear of the Lord.

The assumptions on which this prayer is based are of course hypothetical. There is (and can be) no guarantee that the candidates are truly born again and the imposition of the bishop's hands cannot produce a spiritual result of that kind. The prayer is meaningful only in the context of a faith that has already taken root in the candidate and the petitions for strengthening can have no effect otherwise.

The bishop next speaks to each candidate individually, laying his hand on them one by one as they kneel before him, asking God to defend them with His heavenly grace, giving them the strength to continue in their faith and to grow in the Holy Spirit until they pass from this life to His heavenly kingdom.

Then, after the versicle and response ('The Lord be with you. And with thy spirit') and the Lord's Prayer (in the shorter form, without the doxology), the bishop goes on to pray, first, for the candidates and, then, for the congregation in general.

In the first prayer, which is for the candidates, he asks that those on whom he has laid hands, in imitation of apostolic practice, may know:

    a. the protection of God's Fatherly hand
    b. the presence of the Holy Spirit
    c. growth in the knowledge of God's Word and obedience to it
    d. eternal life.

In the second prayer, which is for the congregation, he asks that we may all be:

    a. directed, sanctified and governed by God's laws and commandments
    b. be protected and preserved in body and soul, now and for ever.

The service then concludes with the standard benediction.

Chapter 7

Matrimony

Historical Introduction

Along with baptism and burial, matrimony is one of the three great rites of passage celebrated by the Church. Unlike the others, however, it goes back to the origins of the human race and is inscribed in the doctrine of creation. God made human beings male and female, both of them in His image and likeness, and ordained that 'a man shall leave his father and his mother and hold fast to his wife, and they shall become one flesh'.[1] The principle of lifelong heterosexual monogamy is fundamental to the biblical understanding of matrimony, though it must be admitted that the Old Testament records many instances when that ideal was not achieved and other forms of marriage were tolerated, if not actually encouraged. Important figures like Jacob, Moses and David were polygamous, apparently without anyone's disapproval, and others, like Abraham, had concubines – in his case, at the suggestion of his wife.[2] The extreme case was Solomon, the son and successor of David, who had 700 wives and 300 concubines, who were criticised for turning him away from the worship of the one God.[3]

Christians have wrestled with these facts for centuries but have almost never claimed such examples as justification for allowing similar practices in the Church. It is hard to be sure, however, it seems that polygamy had died out in Israel before the Babylonian exile in 586 BC

---

1. Genesis 2:24; see also Genesis 1:26.
2. Genesis 16:2.
3. 1 Kings 11:3.

and, by the time we get to the New Testament, it was virtually unknown. Much the same can be said for the surrounding Graeco-Roman culture, where monogamy was also the norm. Whatever the case, it is clear that the New Testament is much stricter in its marriage discipline than the Old Testament is, and that the subject was taken very seriously by Jesus, as well as by his disciples, at least some of whom were celibate.

Jesus repudiated the Jewish acceptance of divorce, which he regarded as a concession to human weakness, and restricted it to cases of adultery.[4] The Apostle Paul expressed a clear preference for celibacy if possible but was not opposed to marriage, as long as it was between Christians. He recommended that widows should remain as they were but, again, he was prepared to accept their remarriage, and even to encourage it for women under the age of 60.[5] He evidently expected most local church leaders to be married and insisted only that they should be 'husbands of one wife', just as the officially supported widows should have been 'wives of one husband'.[6] Given that polygamy had died out in the Roman world, this probably means that the people concerned should not have been divorced and remarried, though that is not explicitly stated.

Nothing is said in the New Testament about the custom of arranged marriages or betrothals of young children organised by their parents, though the impression given is that marriage ought to be a personal choice, one in which the man takes the initiative.[7] This is presumably because the man is head of the woman, though in principle both are equal and complementary in their relationship.[8] The priority given to the male, such as it is, is grounded in universal custom rather than in any specific command of God, although the Apostle Paul believed that, in commending it, he was speaking with divine authority.[9]

In practice, it is fair to say that the Christian Church, generally, and the Anglican world, in particular, have maintained this pattern. It is very rare for a woman to propose marriage to a man, though a difference of status might occasionally make that inevitable.[10] It is also generally the

---

4. Matthew 19:3-12.
5. 1 Corinthians 7:1-40; 1 Timothy 5:11-14.
6. 1 Timothy 3:2; 3:12; 5:9.
7. 1 Corinthians 7:36-38.
8. 1 Corinthians 11:1-16.
9. 1 Corinthians 7:25-40.
10. The most famous case is the proposal made by Queen Victoria to Prince Albert in 1840. Queen Elizabeth I was in a similar position, though she famously never proposed to anyone!

case that a woman will take the name of her husband, though there is nothing compelling her to do so and she is free to keep her maiden name if she wishes. However, it is rare for a man to take his wife's name, and unusual for a wife to pass her maiden name on to her children.[11] These are customs, not laws, but their widespread observance gives them a certain authority in both Church and society.

There is no suggestion anywhere in the Bible or in the Prayer Book that marriage between persons of the same sex is possible, or even meaningful. The legalisation of 'same-sex marriage' in recent years has put pressure on the Church to recognise it, but to do so would require substantial revision of the service of Holy Matrimony and it is not clear how that would be done. In recent debates it is generally agreed that such a revision would involve a change in the Church's doctrine of marriage, and at the present time there is no consensus on whether that is necessary or desirable. The Prayer Book assumes that lifelong heterosexual monogamy is the norm and the service is designed with that in view.[12]

The practice of matrimony in the Early Church is unclear because of the lack of adequate documentation. There is no evidence in the New Testament that any congregation or church leader preformed weddings, and the official registration of marriages remained the responsibility of the state. It is probable that Christians celebrated their marriages in the churches to which they belonged and in ways that were broadly similar to what was customary among Jews and pagans. No doubt they adapted their prayers and some of their practices to conform to Christian teachings, and there is some indication that they tried to avoid the kinds of excesses that characterised pagan ceremonies, but there is no evidence that they acted in ways that would have shocked or surprised their contemporaries. Family ties probably ensured that non-Christians were often present at Christian weddings, although

---

11. Again, Queen Elizabeth II was an exception to this, in that her children bear the name of Windsor, not Mountbatten (after their father). However, her more distant descendants have the double-barrelled surname Mountbatten-Windsor.

12. See D.W.S. Belousek, *Marriage, Scripture and the Church: Theological Discernment on the Question of Same-sex Union* (Grand Rapids, MI: Baker, 2021).

whether that was common (or even possible) in the centuries of persecution is unclear.[13]

Weddings in church became more frequent in the fourth century, after the legalisation of Christianity. However, it would be many centuries before the Church acquired a virtual monopoly of them. Christian principles mingled with ancestral customs and it could be hard to tell them apart. A case in point is the giving of a ring to the bride as a pledge of the man's commitment to her and of her intention to be obedient to him. There is nothing in Scripture to indicate that a ring is the right way to express this but it became (and has remained) an important part of the marriage ceremony, in spite of occasional protests from Puritans and others. Many other customs – like the tradition that a virginal bride should be married in white to indicate her purity – have persisted for similar reasons, even though there is no theological basis for them and a marriage is not invalidated if they are not followed.

The drift towards ecclesiastical (as opposed to civil) matrimony was accompanied by a countervailing tendency, which was to insist on the celibacy of the clergy. Pope Gregory the Great tried to impose that monastic discipline on his clergy but failed to make it stick. In 692, the Council *in Trullo* decreed that bishops must be celibate but it permitted the ordination of married men to the priesthood. However, if the spouse of a priest died, he would not be permitted to remarry, a discipline that is still maintained in the Eastern Orthodox Churches.[14] It was not until the First Lateran Council in 1123 that celibacy was made mandatory for priests in the Western Church, although it was some time before the decree was universally observed.[15] In the mid-twelfth century matrimony was recognised as a sacrament by Peter Lombard, although it differed in character from the others because it was not specifically Christian. It was therefore classified as a sacrament of creation, not as a sacrament of redemption. It was not intended for all, as five of the other sacraments were (baptism, confirmation, penance, Communion and extreme unction), and was regarded as an alternative to holy orders, which could not normally be held by married men.

---

13. For a review of the evidence, see K. Stevenson, *Nuptial Blessing: A Study of Christian Marriage Rites* (London: SPCK, 1982), pp. 13-32.
14. Canons 6, 12, 13, 26 and 48 of the Council *in Trullo*. (The *troulos* was a domed hall in the imperial palace in Constantinople.) These canons were never officially received in the Western Church.
15. Canon 7. *Conciliorum Oecumenicorum Decreta*, p. 191.

At the time of the Reformation, the compulsory celibacy of the clergy was one of the first traditions of the Church to be questioned and abolished, though in England this did not happen until 1549, the same year that the first English prayer book appeared.[16] In effect, this meant that from 1549 clergy and laity were subject to the same marriage discipline. This gave the clergy a personal interest in the rite that they would not otherwise have had and may have affected the way it was conceived and developed in the Reformed Church.

In 1549 the most commonly used marriage rite was that of Sarum but it was not as dominant as it was in other services of the Church. The rites of Hereford and York were also popular in their respective dioceses and there were numerous local variations, just as there were all over Western Europe. One of the features of these rites that set them apart was that they were mostly in English, made necessary because of the substantial participation of lay people who knew little or no Latin. The English rites differed from many of those in use on the Continent in that the priest played a less prominent role. In other places he was the one who gave the woman to the man but in England he was the witness as the couple gave their consent to one another. The wedding rites were full of blessings, particularly in the first part of the service, preceding the nuptial Mass. However, like the rites in use elsewhere, the English ones put the focus on Holy Communion, which was the apex of devotion and the ultimate sign of the nuptial couple's union with Christ.

This was no accident. The greatest single difference between pagan or Jewish marriage rites, on the one hand, and Christian ones, on the other, was that the Christian rites emphasised the union of Christ the bridegroom with his bride the Church. This is a constant theme of the New Testament, used by Jesus himself to illustrate the nature of his ministry. It reached its highest expression in Ephesians 5:22-33, where the Apostle Paul made a direct comparison between the married couple and Christ.[17] The comparison is particularly striking in that Paul says that the husband is to sacrifice himself for his wife as Christ sacrificed

---

16. 'Act to Take Away All Positive Laws against the Marriage of Priests' (2-3 Edward VI, c. 21), in Bray, *Documents*, pp. 248-49. The law was repealed by Mary I in 1553 and not reinstated until 1603, because Elizabeth I did not approve of married priests either. She was, however, forced to accept them *de facto*. However, it was not until 1691 that a married man was appointed archbishop of Canterbury.

17. See, for example, Matthew 25:1-13; Revelation 21:9 and 22:17.

himself for the Church.[18] In a world where women were frequently devalued and treated as men's playthings, this was a powerful image that overturned prevailing cultural assumptions and put the husband-wife relationship on a different footing. If the man had some priority over the woman, this was not a privilege to be exploited but an obligation to be fulfilled. The stronger partner must sacrifice himself for the weaker, not the other way round, for that was the way in which the law of Christ would be made manifest. Anything less than that would be abusive and devalue the institution of marriage, which was the fundamental building block of the family and, through the family, of society as a whole.

The Reformation

The effect of the Reformation on the marriage rite was to be profound, although less immediately obvious than elsewhere. One reason for that was the fact that much of the service was already in the vernacular and well-known to most people, so that it was difficult to introduce new forms of wording for the vows and so on. In other respects, the exchange of mutual consent, the giving of the ring and the legal requirements regarding possible impediments to the marriage were all taken over from the medieval rites virtually unaltered, leaving the appearance of continuity with what had gone before.

At the same time, the impact of Martin Luther and other continental Reformers could not be ignored. Following Lutheran practice, a number of superfluous ceremonies and blessings were omitted, and more attention was paid to instructing the bridal couple and the congregation regarding the duties of the married state. The Reformers were particularly anxious to suppress the often bawdy festivities that accompanied marriage and to impress upon people the seriousness of what they were undertaking. The use of the Bible and of biblical examples of matrimony was greatly increased, and the theological content of the exhortations, in particular the references to the work of the Holy Spirit, were adopted from the use of Calvin and the other Swiss Reformers. Particularly influential was Hermann von Wied's *Consultation*, which combined Lutheran and Calvinist features and had been translated into English by John Daye in 1548, just as Thomas Cranmer was preparing his 1549 Book of Common Prayer.

It should be noted that the service is called one of 'solemnization' of matrimony because the Church bears witness and ratifies what the

---

18. Ephesians 5:25.

couple have determined to do. It does not create the marriage or confer any sacramental grace upon it.

The Preliminaries to the Marriage Service

The service as it appears in the 1662 prayer book is but a slightly amended version of 1549, with a few changes made in 1552 and none thereafter until 1662. It is effectively subdivided into two parts – the marriage service proper and the post-matrimonial service, with some important preliminary rubrics preceding the former.

According to Canon 51 of the Fourth Lateran Council (1215), a parish priest was obliged to publish banns on three successive Sundays or holy days during the principal service.[19] 'Banns' (not to be confused with 'bans' or 'bands') are a public announcement of the intention of a couple to marry and their purpose was to ensure that they were legitimately qualified to do so. The publication of banns is still a legal requirement in England and Wales, though elsewhere it has often fallen into disuse, or been replaced by some other form of public announcement. The banns must be published in the parishes where the intending bride and groom reside and, if they are to be married in a third parish, there also.

It is very rare for anyone to object to a proposed marriage and many people think that the banns serve no useful purpose, but that is not so. Occasionally, it happens that one of the parties intending to marry is under age or already married and, if someone knows this, the publication of the banns gives them an opportunity to object. It is estimated that there is on average about one case a year in England and Wales. The fact that parish clergy act as registrars gives this a legal significance that it would not otherwise have, and abuse of the privilege can lead to severe punishment, including up to three years' suspension from office, a provision also found in Canon 51 of the 1215 Lateran Council.

The precise point during the service when the banns should be read was not specified in 1549. In 1662 it was meant to be immediately before the offertory sentences and, following the Marriage Act 1753, immediately after the second lesson.[20] Nowadays, it does not much matter when the banns are read. Sometimes this happens at the beginning of the service, sometimes at the end and sometimes along with the other notices. Nor does it matter unduly if a Sunday is overlooked by mistake, as long as

---

19. *Conciliorum Oecumenicorum Decreta*, p. 258.
20. The 1662 prayer book rubric was amended accordingly.

there are three separate readings and that they are recorded in a register that has been provided for that purpose since 1753.

Also connected with this is the prohibition of marriage within certain degrees of consanguinity (kindred) and affinity. Marriage between close blood relations has always been forbidden but the medieval Church added a number of relationships of 'affinity', according to which people who were closely connected, but not related by blood, were also prevented from marrying. In particular, godparents could not marry their godchildren, even if there was no family tie between them. After the Reformation Archbishop Matthew Parker (1559-75) published 'A Table of Kindred and Affinity', based on Leviticus 18:6-18 and on the principle that what applies to the male applies equally, *mutatis mutandis*, to the female. Purely spiritual relationships, like that of godparents, were removed from the list, which first appeared in 1563 and was usually printed at the end of the Book of Common Prayer. It remained unchanged until the twentieth century, when gradually a number of other relations of affinity were removed. The list as given here is based on the one that was in force in 1949, with indications in square brackets of those relations that had been removed up to that time. Relations in italics were removed from the list in 1986 and there have been a few minor changes since then.

In England and Wales the application of the table is governed by statute law, so that it is possible for a prohibition to appear in it but to have no force in practice. In other jurisdictions, the Church must follow the provisions of the civil law, which may be laxer or stricter than that which applies in England and Wales. One particular area of controversy concerns the right of first cousins to marry. This is not forbidden by the traditional table but there are several places (in particular, many American states) where such marriages are illegal. With reference to England and Wales, the table is as follows:

A man may not marry his:	*A woman may not marry her:*
Mother	
Daughter	
Father's mother	Father's father
Mother's mother	Mother's father
Son's daughter	Son's son
Daughter's daughter	Daughter's son
Sister	Brother
Father's daughter	Father's son
Mother's daughter	Mother's son

[Deceased wife's sister]	[Deceased husband's brother][21]
[Deceased brother's wife]	[Deceased sister's husband][22]
[Niece by marriage]	[Nephew by marriage][23]

A man may not marry his:	*A woman may not marry her:*
Wife's mother	*Husband's father*
[Wife's mother's mother]	[Husbands' father's father][24]
[Wife's father's mother]	[Husband's mother's father][25]
Wife's daughter	Husband's son
Father's wife	Mother's husband
Son's wife	Daughter's husband
Father's father's wife	Father's mother's husband
Mother's father's wife	Mother's mother's husband
Wife's father's mother	Husband's father's father
Wife's mother's mother	Husband's mother's father
Wife's son's daughter	Husband's son's son
Wife's daughter's daughter	Husband's daughter's son
Son's son's wife	Son's daughter's husband
Daughter's son's wife	Daughter's daughter's husband
[Father's brother's wife]	[Father's sister's husband][26]
[Mother's brother's wife]	[Mother's sister's husband][27]
[Wife's father's sister]	[Husband's father's brother][28]
[Wife's mother's sister]	[Husband's mother's brother][29]
Father's sister	Father's brother
Mother's sister	Mother's brother
[Wife's sister]	[Husband's brother][30]
Brother's daughter	Brother's son
Sister's daughter	Sister's son
[Brother's son's wife]	[Brother's daughter's husband][31]

---

21. Removed by the Marriage Act 1907, ratified by the convocations of Canterbury and York in 1946.
22. Removed by the Marriage Act 1921, ratified by the convocations of Canterbury and York in 1946.
23. Removed by the Marriage Act 1931, ratified by the convocations of Canterbury and York in 1946.
24. Removed by the Marriage Act 1949.
25. Ibid.
26. Ibid.
27. Ibid.
28. Ibid.
29. Ibid.
30. Ibid.
31. Ibid.

[Sister's son's wife]	[Sister's daughter's husband][32]
[Wife's brother's daughter]	[Husband's brother's son][33]
[Wife's sister's daughter]	[Husband's sister's son][34]

Added by the Children Act of 1975:

Adoptive mother	Adoptive father
Former adoptive mother	Former adoptive father

A man may not marry his:	*A woman may not marry her:*
Adoptive daughter	Adoptive son
Former adoptive daughter	Former adoptive son

Added by the Marriage Act 1986:[35]

Daughter of former wife	Son of former husband
Former wife of father	Former husband of mother
Former wife of father's father	Former husband of father's mother
Former wife of mother's father	Former husband of mother's mother
Daughter of son of former wife	Son of son of former husband
Daughter of daughter of former wife	Son of daughter of former husband

Also prohibited by the Marriage Act of 1986:

Mother of former wife (1)	Father of former husband (2)
Former wife of son (3)	Former husband of daughter (4)

These prohibitions remain in force until after the deaths of the former wife (1), former husband (2), son (3) and daughter (4), as well as of the father of the former wife (1), the mother of the former husband (2), the mother of the son (3) or the father of the daughter (4).

In 2007 a ruling of the European Court of Human Rights was accepted, which removed the ban on marrying a former mother/daughter-in-law or father/son-in-law.

Days and times allowed for the solemnisation of matrimony are determined by statute law, to which the Church is bound. Regulations vary from time to time and from place to place but, generally speaking, marriages must take place in daylight hours and the doors of the church

---

32. Ibid.
33. Ibid.
34. Ibid.
35. Marriages within these degrees are permitted if both parties are over the age of 21 and if neither party lived before the age of 18 as a child of the family in relation to the other party.

must be open, or at least unlocked, allowing unimpeded access to anyone who wishes to witness the wedding. In medieval times there was a prohibition on marriages in Lent but, although some churches continue to discourage weddings at that time, there is no legal restriction on them. In medieval times the opening parts of the service were conducted at the church door but this was stopped in 1549, when the bridal party was instructed to come into the main body of the church.

In the Sarum rite it was decreed that the man should stand on the right and the woman on the left. That direction was omitted in 1549 but restored in 1662. It can probably be assumed that the custom had continued in the interval and it remains general today, although it is not based on any theological principle and failure to observe it does not invalidate the marriage.

The Marriage Service[36]

The service opens with an address read by the officiant, which outlines the purpose of the ceremony, states the reasons why matrimony is practised and gives one last chance for anyone who knows any reason why the couple should not be married to speak up. It is almost unheard of for anyone to object at this point but, if someone does, the service must be stopped, the person who complains must be obliged to prove the justice of his claim, and the validity of his objection must then be investigated. This provision, along with the opening words of the address, were derived from the Sarum rite, with the rest coming most probably from Hermann von Wied's *Consultation*.

In the 1662 prayer book the wording of the address was slightly altered from the 1549 text but not in any matter of substance. Its main points are as follows:

1. The spiritual value of matrimony:
   a. It is an honourable state of life, instituted by God before the fall of Adam.[37]
   b. It signifies the union of Christ and the Church.[38]

---

36. For a detailed commentary, see S. Vibert, *Till Death Us Do Part: 'The Solemnization of Matrimony' in the Book of Common Prayer* (London: Latimer Trust, 2014).
37. Genesis 2:24.
38. Ephesians 5:22-24.

    c. Christ approved of it and performed his first miracle at a wedding in Cana.[39]

    d. The Apostle Paul commends it as honourable and to be respected by all.[40]

2. The seriousness of matrimony:

    a. It is not to be undertaken lightly.

    b. It is not designed to satisfy carnal lust.

    c. It is to be undertaken reverently and in the fear of God.

3. The reasons why matrimony was ordained:

    a. for the procreation of children, to be brought up in the knowledge and fear of the Lord

    b. for a remedy against sin and fornication

    c. for mutual society and support.

From the purely historical point of view, it may be doubted whether God instituted matrimony in any form that we would now recognise in the Garden of Eden before the Fall, or that the first two of the three reasons given for it would have been understood by our first parents. That, however, is not the point of the address. In some modern prayer books the reasons for ordaining marriage have been omitted but the hesitations one might have can be overcome by changing the tense of the verb from the past ('was') to the present ('is'). Whatever the historical evolution of matrimony may have been, within the Christian Church the reasons for its continuance have not changed. A good case however can be made for changing the order, by putting the desire for mutual support first and the other two afterwards. All marriages are intended for the protection of the couple, whether they have children or not. In particular, the inability to have children is not a bar to marriage, although the importance of bringing them up in a stable family environment must not be forgotten.

Before proceeding any further, the officiant addresses the couple directly and asks them whether they know of any reason why they should not be married. It is almost inconceivable that they would say at this point that there is, but the charge is there in order to give added force to the solemnity of the rite. To lie or to mislead the officiant and the congregation is the equivalent of perjury, and this must be brought home to all those who are involved. Having cleared any possible impediment to the marriage, the officiant then proceeds

---

39. John 2:1-11.
40. Ephesians 5:22-23.

to address both the man (first) and the woman in virtually identical terms. They are:

1. to live together
[2. to obey and serve the husband – woman only]
3. to love each other
[4. to comfort the wife – man only]
5. to honour each other
6. to keep each other in sickness and in health
7. to forsake any other attachment of a similar nature
8. to maintain their commitment to one another for life.

Controversy has surrounded the demand that the woman should promise to obey her husband and this requirement is sometimes omitted in modern marriage ceremonies on the ground that it reduces the woman to a lower status. However, this is a misunderstanding. As Ephesians 5:22-36 makes clear, the submission of the woman to her husband is balanced by the sacrifice of the man for his wife, a point that is made later in the marriage service and might usefully be included in the question put to the man at this point.

The officiant then goes on to ask who will give the woman to the man and the rubric indicates that this will normally be the father of the bride. However, provision is made for a friend to perform this function if the bride's father is unavailable. The officiant then joins the right hand of the bridegroom to the right hand of the bride and asks each of them to commit themselves to the other in virtually identical terms. In particular they promise 'to have and to hold' one another:

1. 'for better for worse'
2. 'for richer for poorer'
3. 'in sickness and in health'
4. 'to love and to cherish, till death us do part'.

In addition, the woman is expected to add 'obey' to the promise to love and cherish her husband, though (as already mentioned) this is often omitted nowadays.

Following this, the man places a ring on the service book and the officiant then returns it to him, asking him to place it on the fourth finger of the woman's left hand. This ceremony is a simplification of the one in the Sarum rite, in which the ring was sprinkled with holy water and signed with the sign of the cross. The giving of the ring was retained in the Reformed Church as a sign of commitment but in England it was traditionally restricted to the man. In more recent times the woman has also given her husband a ring, a custom that prevailed in Germany for centuries before the Reformation and which indicates that the commitment is mutual. Today it is usual for a married man to wear a wedding ring but it is not compulsory and some traditionalists do not do so.

It may be said in passing that many Puritans objected to the ring ceremony on the ground that it seemed to them to be a holdover from paganism. However, this concern seems to have died out now and weddings without any rings at all are rare. The pledge of the man to his wife as he gives her the ring expresses the nature of his sacrifice for her. He promises to worship her with his body and to endow her with all his worldly goods – two promises that have far-reaching implications.

Some objected to the use of the word 'worship', because it seemed to them to be blasphemous, but the word must be understood in its earlier sense of 'honour'. It is still used in that way in courts of law, where a judge maybe addresses as 'your worship' or as 'your honour', though admittedly this is now a rather archaic and specialised use and the language here could usefully be updated to 'honour' in order to avoid any possible misunderstanding.

The man's promise to endow his wife with his worldly goods was of particular importance in a society where women did not enjoy the same property rights as men and married women were expected to surrender whatever rights they had to their husbands. That is no longer the case today; but the principle remains the same and has an important part to play in divorce settlements, where the couple's assets must be split fairly between them, even if technically they belong to one and not to the other.

Following the giving of the ring, the officiant prays for a blessing on the couple, using words taken from two prayers in the Sarum rite. This is the only time in the service when direct reference is made to an Old Testament couple, in this case Isaac and Rebecca, who are a rare example in patriarchal times of marital fidelity based on mutual consent.[41]

This prayer is followed by a solemn injunction pronounced by the officiant and taken from the words of Jesus: 'Those whom God hath joined together, let no man put asunder.'[42] It is on this basis that the Church refuses to recognise divorce in spiritual terms, although, of

---

41. Genesis 24:50-67.
42. Matthew 19:6; Mark 10:9.

course, it is obliged to do so legally. Until recently, Anglican churches did not remarry divorced people as long as their former spouse was still living, though that rule has been relaxed somewhat in recent years in order to make allowance for hard cases. Nevertheless, the principle remains valid and the remarriage of such divorced persons is not regarded with much enthusiasm in Church circles.

The service then concludes with a short address by the officiant to the congregation in which he pronounces the couple husband and wife because:

a. they have given their consent to one another in the presence of God and the Church
b. they have pledged their troth to each other by giving a ring and joining hands.

Following this, the officiant pronounces a blessing on the couple, wishing them a happy life in this world and safe entry into the kingdom of heaven when the time for that comes.

The Post-Matrimonial Service

Nowadays the marriage service usually ends at this point, though there may be a short address by the officiant before the final blessing, but the 1662 prayer book provides for a second part that is almost as long as the first. The origin of this was the medieval nuptial Mass which followed the wedding ceremony and for which 1662 continues to make provision. This is indicated by the rubric which directs the minister to move to the Lord's Table, where the remainder of the service is conducted.

The service begins with the recitation of a Psalm, either Psalm 128 or Psalm 67, which is also an alternative at Evening Prayer. This is followed by the Lord's Prayer and a series of versicles and responses, similar in structure to those in Morning and Evening Prayer but directed in content to the newly married couple. After that there is a series of four prayers, which are petitions for divine blessing, physical fruitfulness, a holy married life and divine grace. They may be analysed as follows:

1. The prayer for divine blessing invokes the patriarchs and, in particular, the example of Abraham and Sarah, presumably because they were blessed in old age with a child. The couple's attention is drawn to the Bible as the source of instruction for

them, and the prayer is that they might learn and do what they read in it. The promise to them is that, if they obey God's will and rest in his protection, they will be brought safely to the end of their earthly lives, though nothing is said about their ultimate entry into heaven.

2. The prayer for physical fruitfulness – to be omitted when the woman is past childbearing age – asks for the blessing of procreation and the grace to live happily together in order to bring up their children 'Christianly and virtuously'.

3. The prayer for a holy married life invokes important theological principles that were first mentioned in the opening address. God is praised as the one who has created all things out of nothing and made both man and woman in His own image. Because of their common origin, male and female are to be knitted together in marriage and never be divorced. Moreover, their marriage is called to reflect the spiritual union between Christ and his Church; and the prayer asks for grace that the husband will sacrifice himself for his wife in imitation of Christ and that the wife will respect and obey her husband as the holy women of old supposedly did.

4. The fourth prayer for grace refers back to the creation of Adam and Eve, who are said to have been joined together in marriage, and asks that the couple may be blessed by God and given the spiritual strength to please Him in body and soul and live together in love for the rest of their earthly lives.

After these prayers there is provision for a sermon but, if none has been prepared, the officiant is asked to read a rather lengthy exhortation that outlines what the Bible teaches about the duties of husbands to their wives and *vice versa*. It may be noted that the texts all come from the New Testament epistles of either Paul or Peter. They are simply quoted as they stand and there is no additional exposition. In the 1662 prayer book it is the King James Version of 1611 that is read, that being the most recent and reliable text at the time.

The first quotation is from Ephesians 5:25-33, already frequently used in the marriage service and especially appropriate here because it is addressed to the husbands, who are expected to take the lead in the marriage.

The second quotation is Colossians 3:19, also addressed to the husbands, asking them not to be bitter towards their wives.

The third quotation, again addressed to the husbands, is taken from 1 Peter 3:7, where the Apostle asks the men to honour their wives and respect them as 'the weaker vessel'. Note that the text points out that Peter was himself married and so knew from experience what he was talking about.

The address then moves on to biblical texts that are addressed to the wife, which are quoted in symmetry with those addressed to the husbands. The first of these is taken from Ephesians 5:22-24, where the wife is asked to submit herself to her husband as the Church submits to Christ. This is not a tyranny but a liberation, because Christ is the Saviour of the body just as the husband is meant to be the protector of his wife.

The second text is Colossians 3:18, which says only that wives should submit to their husbands.

The third text is 1 Peter 3:1-6, where the submission of the wife to the husband is couched in evangelistic terms. Peter believes that a non-Christian man will be persuaded by his Christian wife's behaviour to accept Jesus as his Saviour too. Furthermore, women are not to dress up in fancy clothes but to adorn themselves with spiritual virtues, among which obedience occupies a prominent place. Once again, there is a reference to Abraham and Sarah, who called her husband 'lord'.[43]

The two sets of texts may be put side by side like this:

To the man	*To the woman*
Ephesians 5:25-33	Ephesians 5:22-24
Colossians 3:19	Colossians 3:18
1 Peter 3:7	1 Peter 3:1-6

It will be noticed that in the Bible the woman is addressed first and then the man, but here the order is reversed, probably because the man must take responsibility for his wife to a degree that is not true the other way round.

The service concludes with a rubric directing that the couple should proceed to Holy Communion, either immediately or as soon as possible. This is a remnant of the medieval nuptial Mass but it is almost always ignored nowadays, partly because it would make the service inordinately long, but also because the direction is to the couple and not to the wedding guests, many of whom may not be communicants. However desirable it may be for the couple to communicate as soon as they can,

---

43. Genesis 18:12.

it is probably neither appropriate nor convenient for them to do so at this point, and so the effective suppression of the rubric, while perhaps regrettable, is understandable in the context and unlikely to be reversed except in extraordinary circumstances.

Chapter 8

Other Services and Rites

The Visitation and Communion of the Sick

Historical Introduction

Ministry to the sick and the dying is a vital part of church life and a duty incumbent on all its full-time ministers.[1] The order for making deacons specifies it as a diaconal ministry and as such it is often shared by lay people, including volunteers. It was enjoined by Canon 67 of the 1603 (1604) Canons and again, in greater detail, by Canon B 37 of the 1969 Canons of the Church of England.

In liturgical terms, however, it is fair to say that the office for the visitation of the sick has now fallen out of use. The order in the 1662 prayer book is dependent on that of 1549, which it closely resembles, though there were a few changes made in 1552 and in 1662. It was originally a reworked and scaled down version of the visitation found in the Sarum rite, which was closely connected with the sacrament of extreme unction, popularly known as the 'last rites'. Extreme unction was based on James 5:14-15 and was originally intended for healing. However, the high levels of mortality in pre-modern times quickly converted it into a preparation for death, which is what it was at the time of the Reformation and still is in the Roman Catholic Church.

The Reformers abolished extreme unction because it was obviously a corruption of the biblical injunction. Nevertheless, it seems that popular expectation demanded that some sort of rite should take its place and the result was this order of service. Its formal character demonstrates that it was intended for use in a household where one person had fallen ill and the rest of the family were gathered round him (or her) as a mini-congregation. How widely the service was used is impossible to judge but it had largely disappeared by the beginning of the twentieth century

---

1. Matthew 25:36; Luke 10:9.

and had probably gone out of general use long before. The reasons for that are not hard to find. Modern medicine is much more advanced than it was in the seventeenth century and sick people are often treated in hospitals, care homes and other similar facilities, where there are chaplains to attend to their needs. The visitation of the sick, especially at home, is more pastoral and private than it used to be, and the kind of distance between the officiant and the congregation which the formal service assumes is out of place nowadays. Sick Communion has survived but arrangements for that tend to be made to suit the circumstances and are not easily reduced to a set formula.

For all these reasons and more, the official order for the visitation of the sick is now obsolete. Its value today is not liturgical but theological, because the principles that undergird it remain constant, whatever form the actual ministry takes. We can, therefore, disregard the liturgical aspects of the rite as presented in the 1662 prayer book and concentrate on the message which it conveyed and can still convey to those who study it carefully.

The Preliminaries

The service opens with a declaration of peace, based on Luke 10:5. This was a common form of greeting in the ancient world, especially among Jews, who still greet each other with *Shalom* ('Peace'). It is of particular relevance in visiting the sick, because of the natural anxiety which many ill people are bound to have. The uncertainty surrounding their health needs to be addressed and their fears must be put to rest, which is what this opening salutation aims to do.

This is followed by a series of prayers which in their different ways are all petitions for God's mercy. They remind us that we are sinners who deserve God's punishment and that illness is one form which that punishment can take; but they also tell us that God is merciful and that He has redeemed us by the shedding of the precious blood of His Son. It is also the case that illness is a curse brought on by the fall of mankind and that Satan can use it to turn people away from God. It must therefore be regarded as a potential spiritual enemy; and the prayers face it head on. These prayers conclude with one that sums up the petitions as a whole, asking for God to give the sick person:

    a. comfort and sure confidence in God
    b. defence against the danger of the enemy (i.e. Satan)
    c. preservation in perpetual peace and safety.

Finally, there is an additional prayer in which God is asked to:

a. extend his customary goodness to the sick person
b. sanctify the illness as a kind of fatherly correction so that the sick person's physical weakness may encourage him to develop spiritual strength and add seriousness to his repentance for any sins that he may have committed
c. restore him to good health so that he may live the rest of his life in godly fear
d. prepare him to accept the inevitability of death, so that he may be prepared for the eternal life of heaven.

The Exhortation

After the opening sentences there follows an exhortation that is subdivided into two parts. The first (shorter) part is designed to be used in all cases, while the second is an elaboration intended mainly for those whose illness is less debilitating. In its present form, the exhortation is practically unusable today, but its contents are important and may be communicated in different ways to the intended recipients. In particular, it offers food for thought to those who have time to reflect on their eternal destiny as they recover from whatever it is that is ailing them.

The message of the exhortation may be set out as follows:

1. All sickness is a visitation from God. We do not necessarily know why but there are various possibilities to consider:
   a. It may be sent to try our patience and give an example for others to follow. In this case, our faith may stand out on the day of judgement as 'laudable, glorious and honourable' and be the foretaste of endless glory and happiness.
   b. It may be sent to correct whatever in us offends our heavenly Father. In this case, if we repent and endure our suffering patiently, trusting in God's mercy, thanking Him for the warning that He has given us and submitting completely to His will, the experience will turn out for our benefit and help us in the way towards eternal life.
2. Chastening is part of God's love. This is explicitly based on Hebrews 12:6-10. The principal things to consider are:
   a. chastening and correction are essential in the development of parental love

    b. God corrects us so that we may become more like Him in His holiness

    c. suffering makes us more like Christ, who suffered on our behalf.

3. Suffering is a spur to self-examination. In particular, it reminds us:

    a. of the profession made for us in our baptism

    b. of the judgement to come after this life

    c. that we are sinners saved by grace and not by works

    d. of our constant need for God's mercy.

The Confession of Faith

The exhortation is followed by a recitation of the Apostles' Creed, which the sick person is expected to confess as his own and which unites him to the wider Church. This is followed by an extended rubric in which the minister is exhorted to examine the person in question for the following purposes:

1. To see whether he is truly repentant.
2. To discover whether he truly forgives those who have offended him and has sought forgiveness from those whom he has offended.
3. To find out whether he has made amends for any wrongs he has done, at least to the extent that he can.
4. To persuade him to make a will, if he has not already done so.

There are no set words for any of these things but, if the sick person unburdens his conscience, the priest can absolve him in the name of Christ, using the form of words provided for that. This 'absolution' is unusual in that it has the priest say: 'by his [i.e. Christ's] authority committed to me, I absolve thee from all thy sins'. It seems most likely that this is a holdover from the Sarum rite that has slipped into the prayer book, causing interpreters to insist that the priest does not himself absolve the penitent but merely pronounces absolution in the name of God. The Puritans wanted that to be made more specific but they were rebuffed on the ground that absolution depends on the sinner's penitence, not on the words of the priest. In practice, there is very little occasion to use this prayer. However, its wording is unfortunate and should not be used by anyone to claim greater authority for the priest than is warranted by the words of absolution used in Morning and Evening Prayer.

The absolution is followed by a concluding collect in which the priest asks God to:

1. Show mercy on the penitent.
2. Renew whatever has been decayed in him.
3. Preserve the penitent in the unity of the Church.
4. Accept the penitent's contrition and comfort him.
5. Forgive the penitent's former sins.
6. Strengthen the penitent with the Holy Spirit.
7. Receive the penitent into heaven when the time comes.

The Conclusion of the Service

The service then continues with a recitation of Psalm 71, which is a plea for deliverance from suffering. After that comes a short prayer addressed to Christ as the Saviour of the world, asking him to save and bless us. That in turn is followed by two benedictions to be said by the minister over the penitent. The first one pleads that the penitent will know in his heart that there is no one in heaven or on earth who can save him, apart from the Almighty Lord. The second commends the penitent to the mercy and protection of God, using the words of Aaron recorded in Numbers 6:24-26.

In the 1662 rite there then follow four concluding prayers which may be used on special occasions or for particular purposes. They are:

1. for a sick child
2. for a sick person, when there is little hope of recovery
3. for a person on the point of death
4. for persons who are troubled in mind or conscience.

The first of these prayers naturally asks for healing and the gift of a full and complete life but it accepts the reality of death and prays that, if God takes the child, that He will bring him to heaven.

The second prayer asks that the sick person may be strengthened and brought to full repentance of his sins. It asks for healing, if that is possible, but accepts that it is unlikely and prays that the person may be granted eternal life in heaven.

The third prayer commits the soul of the penitent to God, asking that it may be washed in the blood of the Lamb who died to take away the sins of the world.[2] It also addresses those survivors who surround the

---

2. John 1:29; Revelation 13:8.

dying person, reminding them of the frailty of their own condition and praying that they may amend their lives in preparation for what will one day inevitably come to them as well.

The fourth and final prayer asks for God's mercy, quoting Romans 15:4, where we are promised hope through the promises of the Scriptures. It asks that the penitent will have a right understanding of God, will be given strength and grace to withstand temptation and to put his trust in divine mercy and forgiveness. It also asks that the penitent will be delivered from the fear of Satan and be given peace of mind and spirit.

Communion of the Sick

Provision for the Communion of the sick follows ancient precedent and is still to be found today, although the form of service prescribed in the prayer book may not often be used. It presupposes that parishioners will often receive Holy Communion in church, and that sick Communion is in some sense an extension of that in circumstances where he or she is unable to attend regular worship. There is evidence that in the Early Church bread would be taken from the main service and sent to those who were unavoidably absent, so that they could share in the common celebration. Normally this would be done on the same day, following the main service, making it possible for the absentees to regard themselves as part of it. As time went on, however, this became inconvenient and a practice of 'reservation' grew up. This meant that bread consecrated at the main service in church would be held over and distributed to the absent at some convenient time, but not necessarily immediately afterwards.

With the growth of medieval sacramental theology, reservation of the sacrament became an end in itself. Once the bread and wine had been consecrated and become the body and blood of Christ, they could be set aside in the church and adored in a series of devotions designed for that purpose. When the consecrated elements were taken to the house of a sick person, they would inevitably be part of a procession, which would allow passers-by to show due reverence for Christ's body and blood as it passed.

With the rejection of the doctrine of transubstantiation at the Reformation, the logic of reservation largely disappeared. The 1549 rite made some effort to revive the ancient practice of extended Communion. However, it proved impossible to dissociate this from well-established concepts of reservation and in 1552 text the practice was stopped. Instead, the minister was to go to the house of the invalid and there celebrate the sacrament using a greatly abbreviated form of ante-Communion and continuing with the words of invitation in the principal service.

The abbreviated ante-Communion consisted of a collect directed towards the needs of the sick person, followed by Hebrews 12:5 for the Epistle and John 5:24 for the Gospel. It was assumed that there would be other people present to receive Communion along with the priest and the sick person, and they were to be served first. If the sick person was physically unable (or unwilling) to consume the bread and wine, the priest would remind him of what Christ had done for him on the Cross and assure him that, if he repented of his sins and believed in Christ's atoning work for his salvation, he would effectively have communicated, even though he had not taken the physical elements.

If the Communion of the sick was to follow the ordinary visitation, the latter would be cut off before the recitation of Psalm 71 and the priest would continue with the Communion. If no one could be found to communicate with the priest and the sick person, because of fear of contagion or something similar, it would exceptionally be allowed for the two of them to communicate on their own, without anyone else present.

Today the Communion of the sick is practised in a variety of forms, depending on circumstances and churchmanship. Reservation of the sacrament is common in Anglo-Catholic circles but it is contrary to Article 25 and has no place in Anglican worship. The celebrant should always follow the 1662 practice and consecrate what is required for each communicant at the time of Communion. Apart from anything else, this is a reminder to the sick person that he is not receiving some kind of magic potion that has been 'consecrated' elsewhere and distributed for his benefit, rather that he is a full member of the Church and subject to the same spiritual discipline as everyone else.

The Burial of the Dead

Historical Background

Religious ceremonies linked to death and burial are very ancient and widespread. In the Roman world, cremation was frequently practised but the early Christians usually preferred to bury the bodies of their dead. They believed, on the strength of New Testament evidence, that at the general resurrection on the day of judgement people would rise again with their bodies and many took this literally.[3] Christian graveyards were called 'cemeteries' from the Greek word for 'places of sleep' and the

---

3. 1 Corinthians 15:35-57.

usage has stuck. Burial became the Christian custom and remained so until recent times, when cremation has once again become common.[4]

The New Testament says nothing about Christian burial practices, although believers were advised not to grieve excessively, because of the hope of resurrection.[5] In later times forms of burial service were devised, some of which came to include the celebration of Holy Communion, which was intended to remind the living that Christians are united with those who have died as well as with those who are still alive. Over time, this developed into an elaborate system of Masses for the dead, and the emphasis changed. Instead of focussing on the hope of the resurrection, the service came to be more a prayer for the repose of the departed.[6] This was reinforced after purgatory was invented as the place where imperfect souls went to work off their remaining debt of sin before being admitted to heaven. By the time of the Reformation, the original emphasis on resurrection had been totally obscured.

The 1549 rite marked an almost complete departure from what had gone before. Most of the medieval ceremonial was dropped and the rejection of belief in purgatory made it possible to concentrate once more on the hope of resurrection which was impressed on the mourners as a reminder of what the Gospel message was all about. The corpse was still treated with great reverence but the superstitious elements that had surrounded late medieval burials were mostly removed.[7]

There were, however, two exceptions to this. The 1549 rite retained a prayer for the soul of the departed and a celebration of Holy Communion. The first of these made no sense, once belief in purgatory had been abandoned, and the second was open to serious misunderstanding and abuse. The basic thrust of the Reformers' thought was expressed by Martin Luther in the *Ninety-five Theses* that had sparked off the Reformation in the first place. This was that the Church militant here on earth has no jurisdiction beyond the grave. Once a soul has passed from this world to the next, it is in the hand of God and its destiny cannot

---

4. For the history of Christian burial, see G. Rowell, *The Liturgy of Christian Burial* (London: SPCK, 1977).

5. 1 Thessalonians 4:13-14; 1 Corinthians 15:29-58.

6. The Latin word for 'repose' is *requies*; hence the name *Requiem* given to Masses said for the departed. The opening sentence of these Masses was: *Requiem aeternam dona eis, Domine, et lux perpetua luceat eis* ('Grant unto them eternal rest, O Lord, and may light perpetual shine upon them').

7. See A. Cinnamond, *Sure and Certain Hope: Death and Burial in the Book of Common Prayer* (London: Latimer Trust, 2016).

be controlled by those who remain behind. What we are called to do is to preach the Gospel message of hope and that is what the 1552 burial service, slightly modified in 1662, aims to do. The prayer for the departed was accordingly omitted, as was the service of Holy Communion.

The three services may be compared and contrasted as follows:

1549/1552[8]	1662
1. The Scripture sentences	1. The Scripture sentences
	In the church
7. Psalm 39 or 90	
8. The lesson: 1 Corinthians 15: 20-58	
At the grave	At the grave
2. The opening anthem	2. The opening anthem
3. The committal[9]	3. The committal
4. The closing anthem	4. The closing anthem
5. *The first prayer for happiness*	
Part 1	
Part 2	
6. *The second prayer for happiness*	
7. *Psalms 116, 146, 139*	
8. 1 Corinthians 15: 20-58	
9. The lesser litany	9. The lesser litany
10. The Lord's Prayer	10. The Lord's Prayer
11. *Suffrages*	
12. The third prayer for happiness[10]	12. The third prayer for happiness
[13. The collect][11]	13. The collect
14. *Holy Communion*[12]	
	15. The grace

---

8. The sections omitted in the 1552 prayer book are in *italics*.
9. Altered in 1552 to the form used in 1662.
10. Replaced in 1552 with a prayer that, in a slightly modified form, was used again in 1662.
11. Added in 1552.The second part of the collect was the same as the second part of the first prayer for happiness in the 1549 rite. It was repeated in 1662.
12. The Communion collect became the first part of the collect used in 1552 and 1662. The Epistle was 1 Thessalonians 4:13-18 and the Gospel was John 6:37-40. The Communion service began with Psalm 42.

The 1662 Burial Service

The opening rubric, added in 1662 but suppressed in 2018, specified that the service is not to be used for burying the unbaptised, the excommunicate or those who have committed suicide.[13] These all involve theological questions, some of which created considerable difficulty for the officiants at burials, though it can be said that they have ceased to have much relevance today.

The exclusion of the unbaptised was based on the belief that such persons have no hope of the resurrection and that the service is therefore meaningless in their case. That may well be true; but it is often very difficult to determine whether a dead person has been baptised or not. It cannot be left to the officiant to decide this question, except in very obvious cases, as with adherents of other religions. Such people are, however, unlikely to seek Christian burial and so the problem seldom arises.

The exclusion of the excommunicate only ever applied to those who had been condemned to the greater excommunication, which was the complete shunning of the individual concerned from civil society.[14] Such cases were rare, even in the sixteenth century, and have now disappeared completely, so this part of the rubric may be said to be redundant.

The exclusion of suicides is more difficult. It never applied to those who killed themselves in a fit of insanity, only to those who wilfully and knowingly had taken their own lives. One difficulty with this is that it is often impossible to be sure of the state of mind of a suicide and the officiant cannot be expected to be the judge of that. Another is that wilful suicides are unlikely to want a Christian burial, though their relatives may desire it, possibly as a kind of atonement for the sin of self-murder. Here again, it is almost impossible to know what the true situation is; and it is not unknown for relatives to deny that the deceased has committed suicide, preferring a verdict of 'accidental death' instead. In such cases, the officiant has little choice but to give people the benefit of the doubt, which makes enforcement of this rubric virtually impossible.

The second rubric concerns the positioning of the clergy for the burial service. This may be either at the entrance to the church, in the church

---

13. This rubric was removed by Amending Canon 37 passed by the General Synod of the Church of England and promulged on 9 February 2018. This was confirmed by the Church of England (Miscellaneous Provisions) Measure (no. 7) (20 December 2018), section 4.8 in *The Public Statutes and General Synod Measures 2018* (London: HMSO, 2019).

14. The lesser excommunication barred the person from receiving the sacrament but not from social intercourse.

or at the graveside. This flexibility is even greater nowadays, when many funeral services take place at the crematorium. The directions are meant to give guidance so that the service will proceed with dignity and decorum. There is no theological significance attached to any of the positions suggested or adopted.

The Scripture Readings

One of the features of the burial service is its extensive use of quotations from Holy Scripture, which is considerably greater than anything found in other prayer book services. The passages can be analysed as follows:

1. The opening sentences. These emphasise the hope of the resurrection and the vanity of the present world and are directed to the mourners above all. They are:
   a. John 11:25-26 ('I am the resurrection and the life, etc.')
   b. Job 19:25-27 ('I know that my Redeemer liveth, etc.')
   c. 1 Timothy 6:7 and Job 1:21 ('We brought nothing into this world, etc.').
2. The Psalms. In 1662 there are two of these appointed, both of which place an emphasis on the inevitability of death and the desirability of preparing for it as much as possible. They are:
   a. Psalm 39.
   b. Psalm 90. This psalm is well known in its metrical version as the hymn 'O God our help in ages past'.
3. The lesson: 1 Corinthians 15:20-58. The most sustained exposition in the Bible of the meaning and process of death and resurrection.

The Anthem of Lament and Supplication

This consists of four sentences. The first is Job 14:1-2 and emphasises the shortness of human life and the inevitability of death.[15]

The second sentence reminds us that 'in the midst of life we are in death' and that the Lord is our only hope of salvation.

The third sentence is a plea to our mighty and merciful Saviour not to condemn us to the bitter pains of eternal death.[16]

---

15. Taken from the Sarum breviary office for the dead. It was the fifth reading in the Sarum rite and the fourth at Matins for the dead in the Ambrosian rite.
16. This ancient Latin text was translated into German by Martin Luther and then into English metre by Miles Coverdale, before Thomas Cranmer introduced a prose version of it into the Book of Common Prayer.

The fourth sentence is a reminder that God knows the secrets of our hearts and pleads with Him not to abandon us as we approach our death.

It is obvious from the content that these sentences have nothing to do with the deceased but are directed to the living, as a reminder and a warning to them to consider the reality of the shortness of life and to prepare themselves for the inevitability of death. It is a reminder to us that, like the baptismal service, the liturgy is directed more to the bystanders and onlookers than to the professed object of attention, who is unconscious of what is going on.

The Committal and Concluding Prayers

After the anthem comes the committal, which the 1662 prayer book presumes will be a burial. Modern services have to adapt this in the case of cremation, replacing the words 'ground; earth to earth, ashes to ashes, dust to dust' with 'fire' or some suitable equivalent.

The message of the committal is:

1. God in His mercy has taken the deceased to Himself.
2. In material terms, the body is returning to the dust and ashes whence it came.[17]
3. We have a sure and certain hope of resurrection.[18]
4. Christ will change our 'vile' (i.e. perishable) bodies into something resembling his glorious resurrected and ascended body, something which he can do because he is almighty.[19]

Note that the Scriptures quoted in support of the return of the body to earth come from the Old Testament but that those which promise the hope of resurrection are taken from the New. The words 'sure and certain hope' provoked considerable disquiet among the Puritans and, at the Savoy Conference in 1661, they wanted the phrase removed on the ground that notorious and evil livers could not be guaranteed entry into heaven in the next life. The bishops were reluctant to agree to this, because as they said:

> We see not why these words may not be said of any person, who we dare not say is damned; and it were a breach of charity to say so, even of those whose repentance we do not see: For whether they do not inwardly, and heartily repent, even at the

17. Genesis 3:19; Ecclesiastes 12:7.
18. 1 Thessalonians 4:13-14.
19. Philippians 3:21.

last act, who knows? And that God will not even then pardon them upon such repentance, who dares say? It is better to be charitable and hope the best, than rashly to condemn.[20]

Even so, the bishops agreed to drop the words 'sure and certain' but, for some unknown reason, this concession was not acted on and the words have remained unaltered. Funerals are undoubtedly the most sensitive pastoral occasions in the life of the Church, a time when even many unbelievers want to cling to whatever hope they can find. Considering that the words are addressed to them, and not to the deceased, they can serve as a reminder that as Christians we do have a sure and certain hope of resurrection to eternal life. At the same time, that hope can only be realised if there is repentance and faith, and here the bishops' words remind us that we cannot see into the hearts of others. What the Puritans objected to was the danger of giving people false assurance; and that is a very real problem, more so in our time than in the seventeenth century, when most people believed in God, the final judgement and the existence of hell as well as heaven. Today many people simply assume that their loved ones go to heaven when they die and never consider any other possibility. To think that is to err in the opposite direction and we must be as careful to avoid that as we are to refrain from taking God's judgement into our own hands and presumptuously condemning people to hell.

The committal is followed immediately by the saying or singing of Revelation 14:13, a voice from heaven crying that those who die in the Lord are blessed because they are at rest. Next comes the lesser litany followed by the Lord's Prayer (without the doxology), reminding us of the wider context of worship in which the burial service finds its place.

After this comes the prayer for the coming of Christ's kingdom and the consummation of all things, when the living and the dead will be reunited around the throne of grace. It may be analysed as follows:

1. The spirits of the faithful departed dwell with God in blissful eternity.
2. The calling of the deceased to share in that bliss is cause for thanksgiving.
3. We pray for the rapid fulfilment of the calling of the elect to salvation.

---

20. Cited in E. Cardwell, *A History of Conferences and Other Proceedings Connected with the Revision of the Book of Common Prayer: From the Year 1558 to the Year 1690* (Oxford: Oxford University Press, 1849), pp. 361-62.

4. We pray for our reunion with the dead in God's eternal kingdom.

Here again, as always in this service, the target audience is the living, not the dead, and the prayer is designed to remind them of the promises of God to which they can lay claim.

The final collect combines two prayers from the 1549 rite. It is one of the most beautiful in the entire prayer book. It may be noted that it can be used, with little or no alteration, as the concluding blessing for many other services, including Morning and Evening Prayer. It is constructed as follows, with deletions in 1552 in grey and additions in **bold type**:

> O merciful God, the Father of our Lord Jesus Christ, who is the resurrection and the life, in whom whosoever believeth shall live, though he die; and whosoever liveth and believeth in him shall not die eternally; who also hath taught us (by his holy Apostle Saint Paul) not to be sorry, as men without hope, for them that sleep in him:[21] We meekly beseech thee, O Father, to raise us from the death of sin unto the life of righteousness; that, when we shall depart this life, we may sleep **rest** in him, as our hope is this our brother[22] doth, and that, at the general resurrection in the last day,[23] we may be found acceptable in thy sight, and receive that blessing, which thy well-beloved Son shall then pronounce to all that love and fear thee, saying: Come ye blessed children of my Father, receive the kingdom prepared for you before **from** the beginning of the world.[24] Grant this, we beseech thee, O merciful Father, through Jesus Christ, our Mediator and Redeemer. Amen.[25]

---

21. 1 Thessalonians 4:13.
22. Or 'sister', as appropriate. The clause must be omitted if the collect is used outside the burial service.
23. This entire section from 'O merciful God' to 'in the last day' comes from the collect at Holy Communion in 1549. That collect then went on to say: 'both we and this our brother departed, receiving again our bodies and rising again in thy most gracious favour, may with all thine elect saints, obtain eternal joy. Grant this, O Lord God, by the means of our advocate Jesus Christ, which with thee and the Holy Ghost, liveth and reigneth one God for ever. Amen.'
24. Matthew 25:34.
25. This entire section from 'we may be found exceptable' to 'Amen' is taken from the first prayer for happiness in 1549, which began: 'We commend

The collect knits together themes from the entire service and may be analysed as follows:

1. Jesus Christ is the resurrection and the life.[26]
   a. Those who believe in him will survive this present death.
   b. Those who believe in him will not die eternally.
2. God has taught us (via the Apostle Paul) not to grieve as people without hope.[27]
3. We ask God to raise us from the death of sin to the life of righteousness, so that:
   a. when we depart this life, we may rest in Him
   b. we may join the deceased, whom we hope is already enjoying that rest
   c. we may be found acceptable at the judgement of the general resurrection at the end of time[28]
   d. we may receive the blessing that Christ has promised to all who believe in him.[29]

The service then concludes with the words of the grace.[30]

The Thanksgiving of Women after Childbirth

Origin

The service of thanksgiving for women after childbirth, popularly known as the 'churching' of women, can be found in one form or another from very early times. Biblical precedents can be cited from the thanksgiving of Hannah for the birth of her son Samuel and of the Virgin Mary for the birth of Jesus.[31] Just as Hannah went to the tabernacle at Shiloh and Mary

---

into thy hands of mercy (most merciful Father) the soul of this our brother departed N. and his body we commit to the earth, beseeching thine infinite goodness to give us grace to live in thy fear and love, and to die in thy favour: that when the judgment shall come which thou hast committed to thy well-beloved Son, both this our brother, and …'.

26. John 11:25.
27. 1 Thessalonians 4:13-14.
28. 1 Corinthians 3:11-15.
29. Matthew 25:34.
30. 2 Corinthians 13:14.
31. 1 Samuel 1:21-28; Luke 2:22-24. See also Leviticus 12:1-8, quoted in the Gospel passage.

went to the temple at Jerusalem, so Christian women through the ages have been encouraged to go to their parish church and do the same. References to the churching of women can be found in the New Constitutions of the Emperor Leo I (457-74)[32] and also in the correspondence between Pope Gregory the Great and Augustine of Canterbury, concerning the rules to be applied in the newly formed English Church.[33] There is also a decretal of Pope Innocent III, originally a letter sent to the archbishop of Armagh in 1198.[34] Liturgies for the occasion proliferated in the middle ages and the 1549 prayer book adopted a slimmed-down version of the one in the Sarum manual. It was slightly altered in 1552, and more extensively so in 1662, but it remains close to the Sarum rite.

In modern times the churching of women has largely gone out of use, though thanksgivings after childbirth still occur in less formal settings.

The Service

The opening rubric says that a woman should appear in church at the 'usual time after her delivery'. This time is not specified but is often thought to be 40 days afterwards, in line with the feast of the Purification of Mary (Candlemas) which is celebrated 40 days after Christmas (2 February). The service itself begins with an invitation from the priest to the woman to praise God for her delivery. He then goes on to read an appropriate Psalm. In 1549 and 1552 this was Psalm 121; but in 1662 it was changed to Psalm 116, with Psalm 127 as an alternative.

There then follow the lesser litany, the Lord's Prayer and a series of suffrages related to the woman and her deliverance. After that comes a prayer of thanksgiving, though it did not contain any word of thanks until the revision of 1662. Words in grey were deleted at that time and those in **bold type** were added:

> O Almighty God, who hast delivered **we give thee humble thanks for that thou hast vouchsafed to deliver** this woman

---

32. *Novellae constitutiones imperatoris Leonis Augusti*, 17; appended to the *Corpus Iuris Civilis* of the Byzantine Emperor, Justinian I (527-65). English translation by D.J.D. Miller and P. Sarris (eds.), *The Novels of Justinian. A Complete Annotated English Translation*, 2 vols. (Cambridge: Cambridge University Press, 2018).

33. Bede, *Historia ecclesiastica*, 1.27.8.

34. E. Friedberg (ed.), *Corpus Iuris Canonici*, 2 vols (Leipzig: B. Tauchnitz, 1879), X.3.47.1, vol. 2, p. 652.

thy servant from the great pain and peril of childbirth; Grant, we beseech thee, most merciful Father, that she, through thy help, may both faithfully live and walk in her vocation according to thy will, in this life present; and also may be partaker of everlasting glory in the life to come; through Jesus Christ our Lord. Amen.

The closing rubric says that the woman must bring 'accustomed offerings' which, before 1552, was understood to mean the chrism cloth that was placed on her child at its baptism. That was probably what was intended, despite the change of wording in 1552, but it is vague. There is also a direction that she should receive Holy Communion if she appears at the Lord's Supper, though that was probably rare even before the beginning of the twentieth century, by which time the service itself had virtually disappeared.

A Commination

Background

This service, which originally concluded the Book of Common Prayer, has been known by different names in the course of its history. In the 1549 rite it is entitled simply 'The First Day of Lent commonly called Ash Wednesday', which has the commendable advantage of telling us clearly what it was intended for. Martin Bucer thought it should be used more often, so, in 1552, the title was altered to 'A Commination against Sinners with certain prayers to be used divers times in the year'. This in turn was expanded in 1662 to its present form, which is 'A Commination, or denouncing of God's anger and judgements against sinners, with certain prayers, to be used on the first day of Lent, and at other times, as the ordinary shall appoint'. The long-windedness of this is not to modern taste but at least we are left in no doubt about what the service is and when it should be used.

Before the Reformation, the only service that could be compared with the commination was the form of greater excommunication, which was used four times in the year – on Advent Sunday, the first Sunday in Lent, Trinity Sunday and the first Sunday after the Assumption (15 August), presumably because these dates were spread fairly evenly. One of the main features of the service was the signing of the cross with ashes on the foreheads of the people, a custom that is still followed in some places on Ash Wednesday.

The service as we know it now was an adaptation by the Reformers of one that was used between Prime and Mass on Ash Wednesday and was intended to be one of public penitence. Edmund Grindal, archbishop of Canterbury (1575-83), directed that it should be used on Ash Wednesday, on one of the three Sundays immediately before Easter, one of the two Sundays immediately before Pentecost and one of the two Sundays immediately before Christmas. Whether it was or not, it seems fairly safe to say that it was soon confined to Ash Wednesday, as it was in the 1637 Scottish prayer book, and it has remained associated almost exclusively with that day ever since. Having said that, although Ash Wednesday remains an occasion for public penitence, almost nobody now uses the commination. The spirit behind it remains alive to some extent; but the form of words is now thought to be archaic and inappropriate in some respects, and the modern approach to the subject is considerably more subtle than what is found here.

The Service

The service is meant to begin following Morning Prayer and the litany, when the priest is asked to read an introductory address from the pulpit or 'reading pew', a kind of lectern that was once common in churches but that has now largely disappeared.

The address dates to 1549, although there were minor alterations to it in 1552, 1604 and 1662. It can be analysed as follows:

1. The practice of the Early Church:
   a. At the beginning of Lent notorious sinners were forced to do public penance.
   b. The purpose of this penance was that by being punished in this world, their souls might be saved on the day of judgement.
   c. Others might be admonished by this and become more afraid to offend themselves.
2. The second-best option of today:
   a. The primitive discipline has regrettably disappeared.
   b. Until it can be restored, the following service must do duty instead.
   c. The intention here is to read the curses of God on impenitent sinners.
   d. These curses are drawn from Deuteronomy chapter 27 and elsewhere in Scripture.

     e. The congregation is asked to affirm each of them by responding 'Amen'.
  3. The intention of the commination:
     a. to admonish people of God's great indignation against sinners
     b. to move people to earnest and true repentance
     c. to encourage people to live more circumspectly in these dangerous times
     d. to persuade people to avoid the vices that all agree should be cursed by God.

There then follow ten sentences of cursing, after each one of which the congregation is meant to say 'Amen'. The sentences are all taken from Scripture, though most of them were translated by Thomas Cranmer or one of his associates, rather than copied from an existing version.[35] They are:

  1. Deuteronomy 27:15
  2. Deuteronomy 27:16; Proverbs 20:20
  3. Deuteronomy 27:17
  4. Deuteronomy 27:18
  5. Deuteronomy 27:19
  6. Deuteronomy 27:24
  7. Leviticus 20:10
  8. Deuteronomy 27:25
  9. Jeremiah 17:5
  10. Matthew 25:41; 1 Corinthians 6:9-10; Galatians 5:19-21; Psalm 15:3.

It will be noticed that all the cursings except the last are taken from the Old Testament and that most of them come from Deuteronomy 27.

There next follows a lengthy exhortation by the minister. In the printed text it appears as a single paragraph; but that conceals the complex interweaving of biblical verses with accompanying commentary. The text can be broken down and analysed as follows:

  1. First commentary:
     a. Everyone who disobeys God's commands is cursed.
     b. We must remember the judgement hanging over our heads.

---

35. The third and fifth were altered to conform to the King James Version in 1662 but the rest remained as they were.

     c. We must always be ready to turn back to God with humble and contrite hearts.

     d. We must lament our sinful life, confess our offences and try to live as truly repentant people.

2. First set of Scripture quotations:
     a. Matthew 3:10
     b. Hebrews 10:31
     c. Psalm 11:6
     d. Isaiah 26:21
     e. Malachi 3:2
     f. Matthew 3:12
     g. 1 Thessalonians 5:2.

3. Second commentary:
     a. The wrath of God will appear on the day of vengeance.
     b. Obstinate sinners will have heaped judgement on themselves.
     c. They have despised the goodness of God calling them to repentance.

4. Second set of Scripture quotations:
     a. Proverbs 1:28-29
     b. Micah 3:4; Luke 13:25
     c. Matthew 25:41.

5. Third commentary:
     a. Let us beware, while the day lasts and before the night comes.[36]
     b. Let us walk as children of the light.[37]
     c. Let us not abuse the goodness of God but return to him with a true heart.[38]

6. Third set of Scripture quotations:
     a. Isaiah 1:18
     b. Ezekiel 33:11
     c. Ezekiel 36:26
     d. Ezekiel 18:23
     e. Ezekiel 33:13
     f. 1 John 2:1
     g. Isaiah 53:5.

---

36. John 9:4; Luke 13:28.
37. Ephesians 5:8.
38. Hebrews 10:22.

7. Fourth commentary:
   a. God is the merciful receiver of penitent sinners.
   b. God forgives those who come to Him in a spirit of true repentance and submit to Him.
   c. God forgives those who promise to follow Him and take His easy yoke upon them.[39]
   d. God accepts those who are governed by His Holy Spirit and seek His glory.
   e. Christ will deliver us from the curse of the law if we follow him.
   f. Christ will seat us at his right hand and give us the possession of his kingdom.

At this point the congregation is asked to kneel along with the priest and say Psalm 51. That is then followed by the lesser litany, the Lord's Prayer and a series of appropriate suffrages.

Finally, there are three closing prayers, all of which were found in the 1549 prayer book and can be traced to medieval sources in the Sarum missal and elsewhere. The first is a short one, asking that those who confess their sins may be absolved from them. Note that there is no sign of priestly absolution here – everyone, including the clergy, prays the same prayer and asks for the same forgiveness.

The second prayer is longer and is essentially a prayer for pardon. It can be analysed as follows:

1. The character of God
   a. He is mighty and merciful.
   b. He has compassion on everyone.
   c. He hates nothing that He has made.
   d. He does not desire the death of a sinner.
   e. He wants us to turn away from our sins and be saved.
   f. It is characteristic of Him always to show mercy.
   g. He alone can forgive sins.
2. The petitions of the sinners
   a. Forgive our trespasses.
   b. Receive and comfort us.[40]
   c. Spare us.

---

39. Matthew 11:30.
40. By a printer's error, the words 'receive and' were omitted in 1559 but restored in 1604.

    d. Do not judge us.

    e. Turn away your anger from us, who repent.

    f. Hasten to help us in this world.

    g. Give us everlasting life in the world to come.

The third prayer, which is meant to be said by the people along with the minister, is for conversion and restoration. It focusses on the merciful character of God, as follows:

    a. God is asked to turn the people back to Him.

    b. God is asked to show favour to His repentant people.

    c. God is merciful full of compassion and pity.

    d. God spares His people and is merciful, even in His wrath.[41]

The prayer then goes on to ask God to spare His people, so that His inheritance will not be 'brought to confusion' (i.e. destroyed). It asks that God will hear the prayers of the people because His mercy is great. Finally, it asks that all these things may be granted 'through the merits and mediation of thy blessed Son, Jesus Christ our Lord'.

The 1662 rite concludes with the Aaronic blessing, taken from Numbers 6:24 and 6:26. Verse 25 is omitted, apparently because the printer skipped over it by mistake.

Forms of Prayer to Be Used at Sea

Background

As an island, Britain has always been a seafaring nation and at no time more so than in the great age of expansion and exploration that characterised the sixteenth and seventeenth centuries. The need for a special form of ministry to sailors was felt by Parliament as it set about authorising a Directory of Public Worship in 1644 to replace the Book of Common Prayer, which was formally abolished on 3 January 1645. Shortly afterwards, it produced *A Supply of Prayer for the Ships of this Kingdom that want Ministers to pray with them: agreeable to the Directory established by Parliament*.[42] How far that form of service was actually

---

41. Habakkuk 3:2.

42. A facsimile of the original text can be found in Spinks, *Incomparable Liturgy*, pp. 161-69.

used is impossible to know. Nonetheless, its usefulness was appreciated by those who set about revising the Book of Common Prayer in 1660 and the result was the addition of this section. It was envisaged that seafarers would continue to say Morning and Evening Prayer as these were laid down for everyone in the prayer book, with a selection of these additional prayers to be used at the discretion of the minister.

The prayers are of three types. There are general prayers for everyday use in all circumstances; there are prayers to be used in and after storms; and there are prayers to be used in and after battle. They are not grouped together and are presented in a somewhat confusing order, although their different purposes are clearly indicated. For ease of reference, they may be indexed as follows:

1. General
2. General
3. Storms
4. Storms (alternative to 3)
5. War
6. General (for use by individuals)
7. War (for use by individuals)
8. Storms (for use by individuals)
9. Lesser litany
10. Lord's Prayer
11. Confession
12. Absolution
13. Thanksgiving after a storm (Psalm 66)
14. Thanksgiving after a storm (Psalm 107)
15. General thanksgiving
16. General thanksgiving (alternative to 15)
17. Hymn of praise and thanksgiving after a storm
18. The Grace (2 Corinthians 13:14)
19. Hymn of praise and thanksgiving after victory in war[43]
20. Thanksgiving after victory in war
21. The Grace (2 Corinthians 13:14)
22. Alternative committal for the burial of the dead at sea[44]

---

43. This may be followed by the *Te Deum*.
44. This is to be used instead of the committal in the Burial Service.

The General Prayers

The first of these (1) was intended for daily use by ships of the Royal Navy. It asks for preservation from the dangers of the sea and from the violence of enemies and prays for the safety and protection of the Sovereign and his subjects, so that they may live in peace, worship God freely and enjoy the blessings of the land which they have sworn to defend.

The second prayer (2), which is a collect, has been widely used beyond its original purpose. It asks for the guiding hand of God to direct everything we do and to lead us to our inheritance of eternal life. It begins with the phrase 'Prevent us, O Lord, in all our doings', using the word 'prevent' in its original sense of 'go before'. That ought to be changed for modern use but otherwise this is a fine prayer that can be adapted to any time and place.

The prayer to be used by individuals cut off from their fellows (6) is a short form pleading for mercy and deliverance.

The prayers of thanksgiving for deliverance (15-16) recall the terrors of the sea from which the sailors have escaped, thank God for His mercy and ask for the grace to live godly lives in remembrance of His blessing to them.

Prayers for Use in and after Storms

The first of these (3) pleads for safety in the midst of the natural perils caused by storms. The second one (4) emphasises the danger of death and asks God to still the raging of the tempest.

The prayer to be used by individuals cut off from their fellows (8) is a plea for God to still the waves, and recalls the time when Jesus saved his disciples from the raging of the sea (Matthew 8:23-27; Mark 4:35-41; Luke 8:22-25).

The thanksgivings after a storm (13-14) are the words of two Psalms (66, 107). There is also a hymn of praise and thanksgiving for this situation (17) but no special prayer.

Prayers for Use before and after Conflict

The prayer to be said before a conflict (5) asks for strength to fight the battle and for victory. It contains a confession of sin and a recognition of the unworthiness of those who ask.

The prayer to be used by individuals cut off from their fellows (7) is a more poignant plea for victory and deliverance.

There is a hymn of praise and thanksgiving for victory, for which the *Te Deum* may be substituted (19), which is followed by a prayer on the same theme (20), thanking God for His undeserved mercy and asking that those who have fought may live in a godly and humble manner for the rest of their lives.

The Confession, Absolution etc.

Along with these special prayers, there is a confession (11) which is simply the form used at Morning and Evening Prayer, followed by the standard absolution (12) taken from the same services. The Grace is repeated twice (18, 21) and both the lesser litany (9) and the Lord's Prayer (10) are also included. There does not seem to be any particular reason for this, other than perhaps convenience, since the officiant would not have to turn to other services for them.

The State Services

The Disused Services

Political circumstances in the seventeenth century led the revisers of the 1662 Book of Common Prayer to include three state services to commemorate special historical events, all of which were then still in living memory.

In date order, the first special service was held on 30 January to commemorate the execution of King Charles I in 1649. There are churches in England dedicated to 'Charles King and Martyr', which is how he was portrayed at the time, and small numbers of people continue to recall his memory on this day, but the Church of England gives it no official recognition now and most people ignore it. The second state service was held on 29 May, the date of the restoration of King Charles II in 1660. This is now completely forgotten.

The third service was that held on 5 November, the anniversary of the Gunpowder Plot in 1605, when Guy Fawkes and his companions tried to blow up the Houses of Parliament with King James VI and I and the members inside but were foiled. As it happened, the future King William III landed at Torbay on 5 November 1688 and marched from there to London, an act that led to the flight of James II and the so-called 'Glorious Revolution'. After 1689 that was also commemorated at the same time. Nowadays, the landing of William III has been forgotten, but the Gunpowder Plot has entered British folklore and is still widely commemorated as 'Bonfire Night', though the Church officially ignores it.

There was a fourth commemoration in the Church of Ireland on 23 October, in remembrance of the Ulster Rebellion that was nipped in the bud on that day in 1641. When the Church of Ireland was united with the Church of England in 1801, the commemoration was made available in the prayer book to English, as well as to Irish, parishioners, but it is not known whether (or how widely) the day was ever observed outside Ireland.

All these services were discontinued by royal warrant on 17 January 1859.[45]

The Accession Service

The so-called 'Accession Service', properly known as 'Forms of Prayer with Thanksgiving to Almighty God', is the only state service that survives in the prayer book. Properly speaking, it is not a service at all, but a collation of three different sets of prayers and readings for use in Morning and Evening Prayer, at Holy Communion or independently at some other time.

These prayers are seldom used on a regular basis, except in royal chapels, cathedrals and other similar places. However, they can be drawn upon for special royal occasions, like a jubilee or some comparable anniversary. They may be set out as follows:

1. At Morning and Evening Prayer
   a. Psalms 20, 101 and 121 may be said instead of the Psalms appointed for that day.
   b. The first (Old Testament) lesson may be either Joshua 1:1-10 or Proverbs 8:1-17.
   c. The second (New Testament) lesson may be either Romans 13:1-11 or Revelation 21:22-22:4.
   d. There then follow a number of suffrages that focus on the Sovereign before reverting to the normal pattern for Morning and Evening Prayer.
   e. There follows a collect for the Sovereign that is added after the first collect at Morning and Evening Prayer.

---

45. The three special English state services are reprinted in Cummings (ed.), *Book of Common Prayer*, pp. 652-66.

After this there are three prayers which can be said or sung either after the litany, or else instead of the normal prayers for the Sovereign and the royal family. The first concentrates on the health and well-being of the Sovereign himself, the second extends its concern to the government of the kingdom and the third prays for the nation, asking that internal divisions may be taken away and that there may be a godly union and concord among all the Sovereign's subjects.

2. At Holy Communion
    a. The collect of the day is replaced by the collect for the Sovereign, which is the same as the one used at Morning and Evening Prayer.
    b. The Epistle of the day is replaced by 1 Peter 2:11-17.
    c. The Gospel of the day is replaced by Matthew 22:16-22.

However, if the commemoration falls on a Sunday, the regular collect, Epistle and Gospel is retained, with the collect for the Sovereign coming after the collect of the day.

3. Independently
    a. The service begins with the *Te Deum.*
    b. The service continues with the lesser litany, the Lord's Prayer and a few suffrages for the health and safety of the Sovereign.
    c. The service continues with the collect for the Sovereign, the three prayers used at Morning and Evening Prayer, an additional prayer taken from one of the collects provided for use at Morning and Evening Prayer, and the final benediction.

The dates of the accession of the sovereigns since 1558 are:

Elizabeth I	1558	17 November
James VI and I	1603	24 March
Charles I	1625	27 March
Charles II	1649	30 January
James II	1685	6 February
William III and Mary II	1689	13 February[46]

---

46. Mary II died on 28 December 1694, after which the accession service applied to William III only.

Anne	1702	8 March
George I	1714	1 August
George II	1727	11 June[1]
George III	1760	25 October
George IV	1820	29 January
William IV	1830	26 June
Victoria	1837	20 June
Edward VII	1901	22 January
George V	1910	6 May
Edward VIII	1936	20 January
George VI	1936	11 December
Elizabeth II	1952	6 February
Charles III	2022	8 September

---

1. This became 22 June in 1753 after the adoption of the Gregorian calendar.

Chapter 9

The Ordinal

Introduction

The Ordinal is the collective name given to the three distinct services used for the ordination of bishops, priests and deacons. No one can be ordained a priest who is not yet a deacon, nor can anyone who is not yet a priest become a bishop.[2] These three orders are descended from the major orders of the medieval Church, to which they are meant to correspond, at least in formal terms. Before the Reformation there were also five so-called 'minor orders' – subdeacon, acolyte, reader, exorcist and doorkeeper – but these never enjoyed the same status as the major orders and had virtually died out in England by the sixteenth century. The subdeacons did little more than assist the priests and deacons in their ministries. The acolytes were the taper-bearers, who lit the church lamps and prepared the cruets of wine for the priest at Mass. Readers read the lessons, kept the church books and guarded the sacristy. The exorcists cast out demons and made sure that non-communicants did not impede those who wished to approach the altar for Communion. Finally, the doorkeepers prevented the entry of unbelievers and guarded the approach to the altar at Mass time. Subdeacons, acolytes and exorcists have generally disappeared nowadays, although the last of these continues in existence among specialist ministers. Readers are once again to be found in the church but they are licensed lay people who take services from time to time; and the function of doorkeepers is

---

2. There were some cases in Scotland after the restoration of episcopacy in 1610, where men who had not become priests were ordained bishops, but that was recognised as anomalous and has not been repeated. It is technically possible for a person to receive all three orders at the same time, a procedure known as ordination *per saltum*, as was the case of Ambrose of Milan in 374. However, it is safe to say that this has almost never happened in the Anglican world and would be regarded as highly irregular if it did.

now usually the responsibility of the sidesmen. No provision for any of them has ever been made in the Ordinal.[3]

At the time of the Reformation the rites used for ordination were those contained in the Sarum pontifical, which were highly elaborate ceremonies that had been developed over the centuries, though modern research has shown that much of the ritual employed came into use only in the thirteenth century, or even later. It was connected with theological developments that transformed the Lord's Supper into a sacrifice in which the bread and wine were transubstantiated into the body and blood of Christ, and with the elevation of ordination to the status of a sacrament that conferred grace on the recipient. These two things went together – without the special grace, the priest did not have the spiritual power he needed to celebrate the eucharistic sacrifice that was his most important single task. Also connected with this was the imposition of clerical celibacy on bishops and priests, who were thus set apart from the rest of the Church not only by virtue of their office but also in the nature of their identity. They formed an elite corpus within the people of God, set apart by both rituals and law, with their own pattern of life, their own discipline and even their own forms of taxation. Vestiges of that special status survive to this day, not least in the popular imagination, where ordination is often seen as creating a particular class of people, with their own titles (e.g. 'reverend') and dress code, both on and off duty. These things are of no theological significance. However, their influence should not be underestimated and the expectation that the clergy should live differently from ordinary people is still prevalent in many circles.

Theological Questions

The subject of ordination is hedged about with theological questions, which for the sake of convenience may be classified either as 'formal' or as 'functional'. The formal aspect covers the definition of the offices to which people are ordained and the authority which they may (or may not) possess. The functional aspect concerns what those ordained to a particular office are permitted (or required) to do in order to fulfil their responsibilities. Everyone agrees that how a person functions in the life of the Church depends on the office to which he or she has been called. However, it is not clear to what extent (if at all) the functions that a particular office holder can perform are tied to that office. To put

---

3. For the history, see Bradshaw, *Anglican Ordinal*, and idem., *Rites of Ordination: Their History and Theology* (London: SPCK, 2014).

it a different way, a celebrant of Holy Communion must be in priest's orders, but someone in priest's orders is not required to celebrate Holy Communion in order to justify holding that office. A priest who retires, for example, and who ceases to celebrate the sacraments, does not thereby cease to be a priest – there is no concept of 'priest emeritus'.

The question of how form and function relate to one another has been of major importance in dialogue with the Roman Catholic Church. The official Roman position is that Anglican orders are null and void because they suffer from 'defect of intention'.[4] In other words, priests ordained as Anglicans are not being ordained to the priesthood in the Roman sense, because they are not called to offer the 'sacrifice of the altar' in the celebration of Holy Communion. The reply to this, adopted by many Anglicans and even by some Roman Catholics, is that the office is not determined by the function assigned to it. There was a time in the Early Church when the concept of eucharistic sacrifice was unknown (or at least undeveloped) and those ordained as priests were not charged with celebrating it specifically. When it was added in the thirteenth century (or later), those already ordained as priests were not re-ordained – they simply took on board the more developed theology of their time and carried on as before. With that precedent in view, Anglicans and some Catholics claim that Anglican priests are in a similar position. Their ordination may not include a specific command to perform the eucharistic sacrifice but they are commissioned to celebrate the Lord's Supper as the Church intends it to be celebrated. The Church may change its mind but the validity of the ordination remains unimpaired and those in priest's orders do no more than fulfil their calling within the prescriptions of the wider Church.[5]

Also important in this context is the question of the number of orders and their relationship to one another. Anglicans retain the threefold pattern of bishops, priests and deacons, and claim that this goes back to the Early Church, although how far that can be pressed is a matter of controversy. It is generally agreed that it reflects a situation that was

---

4. This was the argument of Pope Leo XIII in his bull *Apostolicae Curae*, published on 13 September 1896. The archbishops of Canterbury and York replied to it with their own statement (*Saepius Officio*) justifying the validity of Anglican orders, which they published on 19 February 1897. For the English-language texts of these statements and a commentary on them, see Franklin (ed.), *Anglican Orders*.

5. For the details of what is often an arcane debate, see Bradshaw, *Anglican Ordinal*, pp. 71-86, 123-57.

in place by the end of the second century and that has continued in Rome, the Eastern Churches and some Protestant bodies down to the present time. For various reasons, most Protestants have broken with this traditional pattern, either deliberately or because they had little choice. In particular, the historic episcopate disappeared from many Protestant Churches for reasons that were often as much political as theological, and account should be taken of that before any pronouncement about the 'validity' of their orders is made.

Historically speaking, it is extremely difficult to reconstruct a coherent and consistent pattern of ordained ministry in the Church before 200. Of the three traditional orders recognised by Anglicans today, the one with the most solid biblical foundation is the diaconate, which was created by the Apostles in Acts 6:1-6 in order to relieve them of administrative and pastoral duties, which were assigned to the deacons. However, the modern diaconate in both Anglican and Roman Catholic Churches is usually little more than an apprenticeship leading to the priesthood and its distinctive character has been obscured. It is also true that many Protestant Churches have 'deacons' but they are not formally ordained and normally serve for fixed terms as lay officers on local church councils. Are they 'deacons' in the Anglican sense? Or, conversely, as some Protestants who have deacons would argue, are Anglican and Catholic deacons a true reflection of what was intended by the Apostles?

There is no easy answer to these questions, but they pale in comparison to the difficulties that surround the priesthood and the episcopate. Today these are regarded as distinct orders and there are functions reserved to the episcopate (like ordination and Confirmation) that are not extended to the priesthood. Nevertheless, there is strong evidence to suggest that the episcopate and the priesthood were originally the same order and that it was only in the course of the second century that one of the priests in a given congregation was elected to be the chairman (as it were) and singled out as the 'bishop', thereby creating what became the universal pattern of monarchical episcopacy that endured unchallenged up to the Reformation. The plurality of presbyters (priests) continued as before; but the priests were seen as agents and representatives of the bishop, working on his behalf rather than alongside him as his equals. It also came to be thought that the bishops were successors to the Apostles, though there is no evidence for that from the first century. Paul appointed Timothy and Titus as his delegates to particular churches, and one of their duties was to examine and appoint bishops, however it was never suggested that they were bishops themselves.[6]

The question of the relationship between the episcopate and the priesthood becomes more sensitive when we realise that the functional distinction between bishops and priests that exists today is not inherent in the nature of their offices. For example, what the Western Churches call 'confirmation' and reserve to the bishop, the Eastern Churches call 'chrismation' and delegate to the priest who administers it at the end of the baptismal service. In recent years there is some evidence that the Roman Catholic Church may be moving towards allowing its priests to confirm candidates, if not immediately following their baptism, then at the time when they would normally be presented to the bishop. If confirmation can be delegated in this way, why not ordination also? If that were to be conceded, Presbyterian ordinations would have to be recognised as 'valid', as it seems that they were in England up to 1662, when the requirement of episcopal ordination was officially imposed, at least partly for political reasons. Anglicans today insist on episcopal ordination and take a negative view of ordinations performed in Protestant Churches that may be seen as offshoots of the Church of England (Methodists, Baptists etc.). However, in the past their approach to foreign Protestants was more ambiguous. At the time of the Reformation, the Church of England insisted on maintaining its own discipline within England, Wales and Ireland, but left other Churches to make their own arrangements, and some would argue that this situation still prevails today.[7]

Another anomaly that is seldom mentioned is that, while both Anglicans and Roman Catholics recognise baptisms performed by other

---

6. Tradition claims that Timothy was the first bishop of Ephesus and that Titus was the first bishop of Gortyn (Crete) but there is no evidence for this. Similarly, the claim that the Apostle Peter was the first bishop of Rome is without solid foundation. Apart from anything else, there is no suggestion anywhere that an apostle could serve as a bishop. The fact that an apostle was supposed to have seen the Risen Christ also made any succession among bishops impossible, since Paul was the last person to have had that privilege and, by his own admission, he was like one who had been 'born out of due time' (1 Corinthians 15:8).

7. Scotland was an independent country at the time of the Reformation and so its Church was regarded as 'foreign'. Attempts to make it conform to the Church of England were made in the seventeenth century but they failed; and the Act of Union in 1707, which united the two kingdoms, specifically excluded the Church, which still remains 'foreign' for legal purposes.

Protestant Churches, they do not allow Protestant ministers to celebrate the Lord's Supper in their churches. In other words, one sacrament is accepted but the other one is not, which seems like a strange position to take.[8]

Whether (or how) Anglicans should recognise non-episcopal ordinations has been one of the thorniest problems in modern ecumenical relations, especially in countries like India, where the local Anglican Church has united with non-episcopal Protestant bodies.[9] These unions have adopted, usually at Anglican insistence, a form of episcopacy, but great care has been taken not to offend non-episcopally ordained ministers by declaring their ordinations 'invalid'. Today, the growth of ecumenism has broken down many of the traditional prejudices and Protestant ministries are increasingly interchangeable, with episcopal 'ordination' limited to the granting of a licence, perhaps accompanied by a ceremonial blessing, to those who were ordained in another Church. At the same time, there is less concern nowadays with the question of Roman or Eastern Orthodox orders in relation to Anglican ones, not least because the ordination of women among Anglicans has ensured that no formal reconciliation with those Churches is now possible. There is also the question of clerical celibacy, which remains compulsory for bishops in both Roman and Eastern Churches, and for Roman Catholic priests, despite growing pressures for change.[10]

The Reformed Church of England

The relationship of form to function comes into stark relief when we consider what happened at the English Reformation. Many of the features surrounding the form of clerical ordination were removed, either by a change of liturgy or by legislation – or both. Clerical celibacy, for example, was brought to an end at the same time as the 1549 Book of Common Prayer was issued – although it was reintroduced under Mary I (1553-58) and priests who had married were deposed.[11] However, as

---

8. It is not always reciprocated either. Baptist and baptistic Churches will not normally accept Anglican or Roman Catholic baptism, especially if it was administered to infants or by aspersion, rather than by total immersion (as is usually the case) but they are less bothered about the Lord's Supper.

9. See Bradshaw, *Anglican Ordinal*, pp. 172-208.

10. Anglican clergymen who convert to Roman Catholicism are, however, allowed to keep their wives if they are ordained into the Roman Church.

11. An Act to take away all Positive Laws against the Marriage of Priests (2-3 Edward VI, c. 21); for the text, see Bray, *Documents*, pp. 248-49. The Act

many of the practices surrounding the doctrine of transubstantiation were abandoned, so the focus of the ministry began to change. From being centred on the sacrifice of the altar, it moved to the pulpit and to the preaching of the Word of God. It was not an easy transition and those who were already ordained were not sent back to study again for their orders. They were allowed to continue as before but were given resources to help them, notably, the book of Homilies which appeared in 1547 and which they were expected to read to their congregations if they were unable to preach themselves.

Quality control, such as it was, was exercised through the granting of preaching licences, which had been compulsory since the early fifteenth century when, in an effort to stamp out Lollardy, the clergy were forced to apply for a licence in order to be allowed to preach. This system, which continues in England to the present time, was used to prevent people who held unorthodox opinions from proclaiming them in the pulpit but, in many cases, it also served to restrict the activities of those who were barely literate and unable to compose sermons of their own.

The new Ordinal was composed to reflect this change of emphasis and to highlight what was required of those who would enter the Church's ministry. It was not ready in time for the publication of the Book of Common Prayer on 9 June 1549, however it was already being drafted and appeared at the end of February 1550, after which it was approved by Parliament and annexed to the prayer book without being part of it. F. Procter and W.H. Frere and F.E. Brightman were of the opinion that Martin Bucer played an important part in its composition and that assumption has survived in some circles to the present day.[12] Bucer arrived in England in April 1549, too late to influence the prayer book, but just in time for the Ordinal, and he was Thomas Cranmer's personal guest at Lambeth before departing for Cambridge. It seems very likely that the two men conferred on the subject. Moreover, we know that Bucer wrote a book about ordination during his time in England. There are also many similarities between what Bucer wrote and what the Ordinal contains, which makes some relationship between them all but certain.

---

was repealed in 1553 and not reinstated until 1603, although in practice clerical marriage was tolerated after the accession of Queen Elizabeth I in 1558.

12. Procter and Frere, *A New History of the Book of Common Prayer*, pp. 662-68; Brightman, *The English Rite*, vol. 1, pp. cxxxi-cxxxiii, and vol. 2, pp. 930-31; Bradshaw, *Rites of Ordination*, pp. 163-64.

The difficulty is knowing what the nature of that relationship was.[13] Did Bucer borrow from Cranmer, or was it the other way round? Did the two men collaborate in a way that produced similar results without one man being dependent on the other? How can we explain the fact that Bucer envisaged only one service to cover all three orders, whereas the Ordinal has a separate one for each of them? Did Cranmer have a theology of ministry different from that of Bucer, which compromised the relationship between them? These questions, and others like them, continue to be debated by scholars and historians and are unlikely ever to be answered to everyone's satisfaction. We may, for example, resolve the problem of the one and the three by saying that Bucer concentrated on the rite that appears in the Ordinal as the 'Ordering of Priests', and that he regarded the other two as variations on that theme – somewhat less onerous for the deacons and somewhat more detailed for the bishops. That might explain certain features that seem to us today to be anomalous, like the failure to invoke the Holy Spirit in the making of deacons. It may also help us to see the insistence of the 1662 prayer book that the episcopate is a separate order to the priesthood as a deviation from Cranmer's original intention, which seems to have been that it was a specialised form of the priestly order, rather than a completely separate one.

Be that as it may, it is impossible to deny the great similarity between the examination questions put to the candidates by both Cranmer and Bucer. In the ordering of priests, all eight questions put to the candidates are the same in both forms. Furthermore, four of the seven questions asked of prospective deacons are also identical, as are three of those put to bishops-elect. This fact fits well with the theory that the ordering of priests was the model rite, modified as appropriate for deacons and bishops. It seems all but certain that Bucer was the originator of these questions. It is much harder to believe that the influence went the other way, since that theory raises the question of why Bucer would have omitted the questions Cranmer addressed specifically to deacons and bishops. There is also the fact that the Ordinal contains a provision for popular objection to the candidate(s), for which Bucer's rite also allowed, and the bishop's allocution to candidates for the priesthood is almost *verbatim* the same as the one found in Bucer, with its emphasis on the teaching office of the minister and the importance of setting a good example in his personal life, neither of which figures in the pre-Reformation Latin rite.

---

13. See C. Hopf, *Martin Bucer and the English Reformation* (Oxford: Blackwell, 1946), pp. 88-94; W. van 't Spijker, *The Ecclesiastical Offices in the Thought of Martin Bucer* (Leiden: Brill, 1996), pp. 345-455.

Like the Book of Common Prayer, the Ordinal had a teaching function and was therefore pitched at the highest level. In many cases, this must have been unattainable in practice, but the bar was set and served as a standard for the future. The real problem, then as now, was spiritual. Education and training can only take a person so far, and the Church can do no more than lay out the ground rules for ministry and hope for the best from those whom it believes have been called to it. In the end, however, it is the Holy Spirit who alone can give the ordinand what is needed to fulfil the ministry to which he or she has been appointed. That is clearly stated in the services of the Ordinal, but as numerous commentators have pointed out, the words 'Receive the Holy Ghost', taken from John 20:22, are a declaration of what must happen if the ministry is to be successful, and not a statement of what has occurred by the laying on of the bishop's hands, although many have mistakenly read it in that sense.

Equally important in the liturgy is the act that is called the *porrectio instrumentorum*, or 'granting of the means', by which the ministry is to be exercised. In the pre-Reformation rites, this meant that the ordaining bishop gave the ordinand a chalice and paten, to indicate the eucharistic sacrifice. In the 1550 Ordinal that practice was continued but to it was added the gift of a Bible, which was intended to underline the importance of preaching. In the 1552 revision, the chalice and paten were omitted, and only the Bible was given, a practice that has endured to the present time. No one can doubt that this represented a change from what had gone before but the significance of that for the Ordinal as a whole has been disputed. Some have argued that the omission of any reference to the sacrament was in order to emphasise the uniqueness of Christ's atoning sacrifice on the Cross and did not imply any downgrading of the Mass. Others have said that the emphasis on the preached Word was a personal prejudice of Archbishop Cranmer that should not be taken as the view of the Church as a whole. Special pleading of this kind was characteristic of Anglo-Catholics, who wanted to believe that Anglican orders were the same as Roman Catholic ones, but nowadays it is generally accepted that their claims cannot be sustained. At the same time, it must also be said that Roman Catholic views of ordination have evolved over time and in some respects are closer to the Anglican pattern now than was the case in the late nineteenth century.[14]

Significantly, modern revisions of the Ordinal, and in particular *Common Worship*, which the Church of England produced in 2000, have enriched the traditional text without departing from it or adding material

---

14. See for example, J.J. Hughes, *Stewards of the Lord: A Reappraisal of Anglican Orders* (London: Sheed & Ward, 1970).

that might make it seem to be more 'Catholic' than it previously was.[15] In all essentials, therefore, the 1662 Ordinal, which like the Book of Common Prayer is a slight revision of its 1552 predecessor, remains the standard reference point for Anglican orders. It may be added that the 1662 text was the first one that actually incorporated the Ordinal, which is why modern editions of earlier prayer books do not necessarily include it.[16]

The Nomenclature

The names given to the three major orders of ministry are derived from the original Greek, not by translation but by direct borrowing. The process by which this occurred can be outlined as follows:

Greek	Latin	English
episkopos	*episcopus*	bishop
presbyteros	*presbyter*	priest
diakonos	*diaconus*	deacon

The Latin terms are almost exactly the same as the Greek, but they have undergone considerable phonetic change as they have passed into the modern European languages. This is particularly noticeable in the case of *episcopus*:

French: *évêque*
Spanish: *obispo*
Portuguese: *bispo*
Italian: *vescovo*
German: *Bischoff*
Dutch: *bisschop*
Polish: *biskup*

15. For a comparison of the two texts, see *Common Worship: Ordination Services: Study Edition* (London: Church House Publishing, 2007); A. Atherstone, *The Anglican Ordinal: Gospel Priorities for Church of England Ministry* (London: Latimer Trust, 2020).

16. This is the case, for example, of Cummings, *Book of Common Prayer*. However, Porter (ed.), *The First and Second Prayer Books of Edward VI*, does contain the earlier texts.

Occasional attempts to translate the Greek *episkopos* as 'overseer' or 'superintendent' can be found in Bible translations but in the life of the Church they have never caught on, perhaps because 'bishop' (formerly *biscop*) is not generally recognised as coming from *episcopus* and is often regarded as a native English word.

The development of Latin *presbyter* is more complicated. It came into English, probably via French, as *prester*, a form that is still found in the name of the semi-mythical Prester John. In Old English the word is *prest* or *preost*, which may indicate a derivation from Latin *praepositus*, the word that has also given us 'provost' (cf. French *prévôt*), meaning 'the man in charge'. Quite possibly the two words were confused in Old English, although virtually every modern writer on the subject has assumed that the derivation of 'priest' is from *presbyter* alone.

In the course of the middle ages, as the sacramental theology of transubstantiation became more prominent, the use of *presbyter* tended to give way to the Latin word *sacerdos*, meaning 'the man who offers sacrifice'. This word corresponds to the Greek *hiereus* and the Hebrew *kohen* but there is no English equivalent to it. Given that *sacerdos* could be used in medieval Latin as the equivalent of *presbyter*, it was translated into English as 'priest', even in contexts where 'priest' was inappropriate. Thus, we find that in English Bibles (and elsewhere) the word 'priest' can be used to mean four quite different things:

1. Old Testament, Jewish priests.[17]
2. Pagan and non-Christian priests.[18]
3. Jesus Christ, our great high priest.[19]
4. The (Christian) people of God, who constitute a 'royal priesthood'.[20]

However, never at any time is the word *sacerdos* or its equivalents used in the Bible or early Christian literature to describe a Christian leader of any kind. They may be called many things in Latin – *episcopi, presbyteri, ministri, pastores* – but never *sacerdotes*. The English Reformers realised that they had a translation problem on their hands and wrote about it. For example, William Fulke (1536?-89) said:

17. Leviticus 1:9 and *passim*.
18. Acts 14:13.
19. Hebrews 4:14 and *passim*.
20. 1 Peter 2:9.

[Y]ou corruptly translate *sacerdos* and *presbyter* always, as though they were all one, a 'priest', as though the Holy Ghost had made that distinction in vain, or that there were no difference between the priesthood of the New Testament and the Old. The name of priest, according to the original derivation from *presbyter*, we do not refuse: but according to the common acceptation for a sacrificer, we cannot take it, when it is spoken of the ministry of the New Testament. And although many of the ancient fathers have abusively confounded the terms *sacerdos* and *presbyter*, yet that is no warrant for us to translate the Scripture, and to confound that which we see manifestly the Spirit of God has distinguished.[21]

Some of the Reformers, apparently including Thomas Cranmer, preferred to speak about 'bishops, pastors and ministers', a formula that is actually found in the litany of the 1550 Ordinal. 'Minister' is a reasonable translation of *diakonos*, and was sometimes used in Latin in that sense, but by the sixteenth century it had come to mean any ordained clergyman or officiant at public worship, and not just a deacon. As the word 'deacon' was not used to mean anything else, it caused no difficulty and was allowed to stand. 'Pastor' was a more complicated question. Its original meaning is 'shepherd' and its Greek form (*poimēn*) can be used of a Christian leader, or even of Christ himself, who is portrayed in the New Testament as the Good Shepherd.[22] English translators tended to avoid the word 'shepherd' when speaking of Christian leaders, but the Latin *pastor* was (and still is) often used in that sense. In recent times it has become the preferred term for Roman Catholic priests who preside over a congregation, and it is common among Lutherans and other Protestants, though less so among Anglicans, who prefer words like 'rector', 'vicar' or 'parish priest', only the last of which terms is directly related to Christian ministry.[23]

In the seventeenth century the main objection to using 'pastor' instead of 'priest' was that it supposedly compromised the position of

---

21. W. Fulke, *A Defence of the Sincere and True Translations of the Holy Scriptures into the English Tongue, Against the Cavils of Gregory Martin*, ed. C.H. Hartshorne (Cambridge: Cambridge University Press, 1843), p.109.

22. John 10:14.

23. A 'rector' was originally the man who received the tithes, whether he was ordained or not, and a 'vicar' was his substitute.

the bishop, who was seen as the chief pastor of his flock. It is doubtful whether many ordinary people would have made that confusion but it must be admitted that 'pastor' is not a translation of *presbyter*, which would have to be rendered in English as 'elder' or possibly 'alderman', neither of which was acceptable, for different reasons.[24] That left 'priest', a word that some argued had been restored to its original meaning at the Reformation.[25] Etymologically speaking, that was true but that argument was not particularly helpful. It would be rather like using the word 'silly' to mean 'blessed' or the word 'ghostly' to mean 'spiritual', both of which can be defended on purely etymological grounds but neither of which would now be generally understood in their original sense. This is the dilemma that confronts English-speakers, some of whom have attempted to resolve it by importing the Latin *presbyter* in its original meaning. That is certainly possible and was done in the sixteenth century, as well as more recently, but 'presbyter' has a somewhat exotic feel, rather like 'Anglophone' in the sense of 'English-speaking'. *Common Worship* compromises by using 'priest' and 'presbyter' interchangeably but whether this practice will enter everyday speech is hard to predict and, on balance, it seems unlikely. Like it or not, 'priest' is probably here to stay, with all the confusion that accompanies it.

Unfortunately, there are Anglicans who revel in this ambiguity and who do not hesitate to use the word 'priest' in its sacerdotal sense when speaking about their own ministers, even though there is no justification for that. It seems likely that, when the 1662 prayer book replaced 'minister(s)' with 'priest(s)', it did so because some high church divines among the revisers wanted to irritate the Puritans, who objected to the latter term because of the confusion that it caused; and a similar motivation can perhaps be discerned today in some Anglo-Catholic circles. If so, it is completely wrongheaded and must be firmly resisted, particularly in serious liturgical and theological writing.

---

24. 'Elder' was (and still is) used by Presbyterians and is generally understood to refer to lay people, despite the fact that elders are ordained. Aldermen are civic officials and the word has never been used in the Church.

25. This was claimed by John Whitgift, *The Works of John Whitgift*, ed. J. Ayre, 3 vols (Oxford: Oxford University Press, 1851-53), vol. 3, p. 351, and also by Richard Hooker, *Of the Laws of Ecclesiastical Polity* (1597), V, 78, 2-3, though Hooker did add: 'in truth the word *Presbyter* doth seem more fit, and in propriety of speech more agreeable than *Priest* with the drift of the whole Gospel of Jesus Christ'.

The Title and Preface

The title of the Ordinal in the 1662 text is: 'The Form and Manner of Making, Ordaining, and Consecrating of Bishops, Priests, and Deacons, according to the Order of the Church of England'. The subsequent pages make it clear that deacons were *made*, priests were *ordained* and bishops were *consecrated*, although whether these different terms have any theological significance is debatable. Given that the diaconate and the priesthood are different orders, it seems that 'making' and 'ordaining' are effectively synonymous and that is certainly how they are understood today. Whether 'consecrated' for bishops is different from 'ordained' is more controversial, because of the uncertainty about the nature of the distinction between priests and bishops. If bishops are merely priests with special functions, they are not 'ordained' because they are not entering a new order. They are rather 'consecrated' because they are being set aside for a particular purpose. Some have argued that 'consecration' is a term better used for things than for people, making it inappropriate in this case. Each term can be taken to mean 'appointed to the office of' and in that sense they are synonymous here.

The Ordinal opens with a short preface which explains its purpose. It originally appeared in 1550 and was repeated with little change in 1552. In the 1662 revision there were a few changes relating to 'lawful authority', which were felt to be necessary after the disruption caused by the Interregnum. Words that were dropped in 1662 are indicated in grey; those that were added are shown in **bold** type:

> It is evident unto all men, diligently reading Holy Scripture and ancient authors, that from the Apostles' time there hath been these orders of ministers in Christ's Church: bishops, priests and deacons, which offices were evermore had in such reverent estimation, that no man by his own private authority might presume to execute any of them, except he were first called, tried, examined and known to have such [e]qualities[26] as are requisite for the same. And also by public prayer, with imposition of hands, approved and admitted thereunto **by lawful authority**. And therefore to the intent these orders should be continued, and reverently used and esteemed in this **the** Church of England, it is requisite that no man (not being at this present bishop, priest nor deacon) shall execute

---

26. The longer form was in the 1550 Ordinal but was 'corrected' in 1552.

any of them **no man shall be accounted or taken to be a lawful bishop, priest or deacon in the Church of England, or suffered to execute any of the said functions**, except he be called, tried, examined and admitted thereunto, according to the form hereafter following, **or hath had formerly episcopal consecration or ordination**.

In examining this statement, the first point that has to be made is that it is not 'evident unto all men' that since the apostles' time there have been three orders of ministry in Christ's Church. As we have already seen, there were at least two (the diaconate and the presbyterate), although the exact definition and status of the second of these is not clear from the New Testament. In particular, the episcopate as we know it today does not appear to have existed in New Testament times. Whether this is because the apostles themselves occupied the office that was later handed on to the bishops is at best uncertain, and too much should not be made of that.

What is clear is that those appointed to offices in the Church had to be tested for their suitability, and that the criteria were more or less the same for everyone.[27] Paul's focus was on the character of those appointed, not on their ability to perform the functions assigned to them, most of which are not mentioned. The main exception is that someone who is to be appointed a 'bishop' must be able to teach – although, if the *episkopoi* and the *presbyteroi* were the same people, not all of them actually did so.[28] Furthermore, the qualities demanded of office-holders were similar to those expected in widows who were on the church roll and receiving financial support from the congregation.[29] Indeed, they were virtues expected from everyone in the Church, regardless of whether they occupied a particular function or not.[30] This does not mean that the qualities enumerated by Paul are unimportant – on the contrary, they are foundational and we must expect them to be manifested in greater degree in those who are called to prominence.

What is missing from the New Testament criteria is what we would now think of as the skills required for the job. It is never suggested that deacons should be trained in finance, for example, or that they should be accredited pastoral counsellors. Nor is there any requirement for

---

27. They are listed in 1 Timothy 3:1-13 and Titus 1:5-9.
28. Compare 1 Timothy 3:2 with 1 Timothy 5:17.
29. 1 Timothy 5:3-16.
30. Titus 2:1-14.

teachers to have a theological degree or the ancient equivalent. Paul himself was a graduate of what might loosely be called the rabbinical school of Jerusalem but the other apostles were not, nor were their disciples. As far as we can tell, men like Timothy and Titus learned on the job and, when Titus was told to appoint 'elders in every town',[31] it is hard to believe that he had a stock of theological graduates to draw on. Hidden behind the general terms of this preface is a list of assumptions that made sense in the sixteenth century, as they still do today, but that cannot have been in the forefront of the Apostle's mind when he was issuing his instructions. Candidates for ordination from the Reformation onwards have been expected to demonstrate an acceptable level of theological training, in addition to the moral and spiritual qualities listed in the New Testament, and this expectation is revealed in the questions put to them in the Ordinal.

Those chosen and appointed to official ministry in the Church must be ordained publicly by the laying on of hands. This has New Testament precedent, as can be seen from the commissioning of the deacons in Acts chapter 6 and of Timothy later on.[32] The 'laying on of hands' is a form of blessing that goes back to very ancient times and was commonly used for solemn ceremonies of many different kinds. It was how the patriarchs blessed their heirs and the practice was continued in both Jewish and Christian circles.[33] It was a powerful statement and not to be taken lightly but it did not mechanically confer 'grace' from one person to another. As with everything else, it was the sign of the promise of future blessing, not a guarantee or confirmation of spiritual power that had not yet been given.

The 1662 Ordinal contains phrases relating to 'lawful authority' that were introduced after the chaos of the Interregnum, in order to emphasise that ordination is an act of the Church and not something (like baptism) which can be performed by anyone independently of the wider body. There was great concern in 1662 that men who had claimed the authority to preach and teach should be properly recognised and, although there was disagreement about how that should be done, the principle was generally admitted. The problem resurfaced in the late eighteenth century when the Methodists began ordaining men for ministry without the participation of the bishops, a practice that eventually led to their secession from the Church of England and their establishment as a

---

31. Titus 1:5.
32. 1 Timothy 4:14; 2 Timothy 1:6.
33. See Genesis 48:14.

separate denomination. In more recent times it has resurfaced again, as Anglicans have crossed provincial boundaries and ordained not only priests but also bishops to serve in what are theoretically other jurisdictions. This has led to the creation of several 'Anglican' Churches that are not recognised as members of the Anglican Communion, even though the orders conferred in this way are regarded as 'valid'.

It should be noted that 'lawful authority' extends to the recognition of episcopal ordination performed in other Churches, though quite what this means is not always clear. In practice, a man ordained by a recognised bishop, who may not be Anglican, can usually be admitted to Anglican ministry without being reordained, although, if he is seeking a post in another province, he will require a licence from the archbishop (or corresponding authority) of that province, and there may be requirements he will have to fulfil before such a licence is granted. In the case of women, the same procedure applies as long as the receiving church ordains women itself; if not, her orders will not be recognised. Similar restrictions apply in the case of clergy who are in same-sex marriages or civil partnerships, who will not be allowed to function in places where those statuses are not accepted. 'Lawful authority' has thus come to be more far-reaching than the revisers of 1662 could have imagined.

The 1550/1552 preface then goes on to specify the minimum age at which a man can be admitted to the different offices. A deacon had to be 21, a priest 24 and a bishop 30 years of age. In the 1662 Ordinal the age for the diaconate was raised to 23, although provision could be made for appointing a younger person in the case of a deacon or priest, but not of a bishop. Generally speaking, this rule is still observed today, which is easy because virtually nobody completes his or her studies before the age of 23. In practice, hardly anyone is consecrated a bishop below the age of 40, though there may be some exceptions in the developing world.

The last part of the preface, now also reduced to a rubric, details the qualifications that a man ought to have if he is to be admitted to the diaconate. As before, the 1552 text is identical to that of 1550, but in 1662 it was amended as indicated below:

> And the bishop, knowing either by himself or by sufficient testimony, any person to be a [man][34] of virtuous conversation, and without crime, and after examination and trial, finding

---

34. This was altered to 'person' after women were admitted to the diaconate in 1987.

him [learned in the Latin tongue][35] and sufficiently instructed in Holy Scripture, may [**at the times appointed in the canon or else, on urgent occasion,** upon a Sunday or holy day],[36] in the face of the Church, admit him a deacon in such manner and form as hereafter followeth.

The requirement to know Latin may seem strange in a Church that was turning the liturgy into the vernacular, however Latin remained the language of university education until the early years of the nineteenth century, so knowing it was necessary for obtaining a theological education. The times appointed in the canon were the Sundays or holy days following the so-called Ember Weeks.[37] These are the Wednesday, Friday and Saturday following: the first Sunday in Lent; Whitsun (Pentecost); Holy Cross Day (14 September); and St Lucy's Day (13 December).

In practice, the first of these Ember Weeks is nowadays generally ignored. Most ordinations now take place at Petertide (29 June) or Michaelmas (29 September) both of which fall well after Whitsun and Holy Cross Day. Very occasionally there may be additional ordinations in Advent, usually on St Thomas' Day (21 December) or thereabouts. Petertide is the most popular time because it falls at the end of the academic year in the northern hemisphere, though south of the equator a date in December may be preferred – for the same reason.

The reduction of these provisions from the main body of the preface to rubrics reflects the fact that they are of little intrinsic importance and can be modified if necessary. Ordinations, in particular, are sometimes held outside the usual canonical times, because of special circumstances that make the usual pattern difficult or inconvenient, and the rubric allows for the flexibility that is needed to make that possible.

---

35. This provision fell into disuse and was replaced by the Clergy (Ordination and Miscellaneous Provisions) Measure 1964 (no. 6) (10 June 1964), section 1.3, in *The Public Statutes and Church Assembly Measures 1964* (London: HMSO, 1965), with 'to possess the qualifications required by law'.

36. This was altered by ibid. to read: 'on the Sundays immediately following the Ember Weeks or on the Feast of Saint Michael and All Angels or of Saint Thomas the Apostle, or on such other days as shall be provided by canon'. Further alterations were made by Amending Canon 10 on 4 July 1988 but these have not been formally included in the Book of Common Prayer.

37. The etymology of the word 'ember' is uncertain but it does not seem to have any theological importance.

The Making of Deacons

This is the first of the three services in the Ordinal, placed here because it is the initial entry-point into the ordained ministry of the Church. In 1550 and 1552 it was called the 'Ordering' of deacons.

The opening rubrics are short but more substantial than they look. The first one states that, before proceeding with the ordination, someone – it is not specified who – shall preach a sermon or give an exhortation in which the following points are to be made:

1. The duty and office of a deacon is to be explained.
2. The need for such an order is to be proclaimed.
3. The people are to be urged to respect the new deacons in their office.[38]

After the exhortation, the archdeacon or his deputy presents the candidates to the bishop.[39] This is because traditionally the archdeacon was the one responsible for theological training and for examining the candidates before they were presented for ordination. Nowadays, the role of the archdeacon is largely formal, because the training for ordination takes place in colleges or on courses designed for that purpose and the examination is carried out by those responsible for the training.

In the 1550 Ordinal the candidates were expected to be robed in a plain alb but this requirement was dropped in 1552. In 1662 it was specified only that they should be decently dressed, which nowadays is usually taken to mean that they should be wearing a cassock and surplice.

The archdeacon (or his deputy) addresses the bishop and informs him that he is presenting candidates for ordination as deacons. The bishop then warns him to make sure that they are 'apt and meet', both in their learning and godly behaviour, to exercise their ministry for the glory of God and the edification of the Church. The archdeacon replies that he has duly examined them and finds that they are suitable for the office to which they have been called. At that point the bishop addresses the congregation and asks them if they know any just cause why one or more of the candidates should not be ordained; if an objection is raised, the service is to be halted until the matter is resolved. This almost never

---

38. The 1550/1552 Ordinal said 'vocation' instead of 'office'.
39. By the Clergy (Ordination and Miscellaneous Provisions) Measure of 1964 (no. 6), section 1.4.1, the words 'or other such person as by ancient custom have the right so to do'.

happens but the existence of this provision is a last-minute safeguard that may be useful in certain circumstances. For example, if a bishop ordains a person who is in debt, he becomes responsible for that debt, but that may have escaped the examination of the authorities beforehand, and this may be the only time that someone who knows the facts will have the opportunity to bring them to their attention.

The examination is followed by a long litany, suffrages, the Lord's Prayer and more prayers, mostly for deliverance from persecution and various forms of oppression. After that comes the celebration of Holy Communion, with a special collect for deacons that mentions the suffering of the first martyr, Stephen (himself a deacon). This is followed by the Epistle, which is either 1 Timothy 3:8-13[40] or Acts 6:2-7.

Before the reading of the Gospel came the oath of the king's supremacy, the precise wording of which was altered several times in the course of three centuries. Since the passing of the Clerical Subscription Act in 1865 it has been moved to a more discreet place before the beginning of the service, where it is joined with the oath of subscription to the doctrine and polity of the Church of England. In other provinces it is normally omitted altogether.

After this, the bishop examines the candidates by asking them several important questions relating to their future ministry. The subjects of these questions may be set out in order as follows:

1. The inward calling by the Holy Spirit
2. The outward calling by the Church
3. Faith in Holy Scripture
4. The ministry of Holy Scripture to the people
5. The specific duties of a deacon
6. The commitment to live a Christ-like life
7. Loyalty to ecclesiastical superiors.

The order of these questions is not arbitrary but follows a logical sequence. First comes the inner calling of the Holy Spirit, without which the rest is meaningless. Then comes the calling of the Church, which is meant to discern the work of the Spirit in a person's life. The chief fruit of that work is a commitment to the supreme authority of Holy Scripture, given by the Holy Spirit for the edification of God's people, with which it is the deacon's privilege to assist. After that come the other

---

40. 1 Timothy 3:8-16 in 1550/1552.

pastoral duties assigned to a deacon, which must be complemented by a blameless personal life. That will be manifested both in the deacon himself and his family, and in his commitment to the authority of those placed above him in the Church.

If the candidates answer positively to all these questions, the bishop will lay hands on each of them individually as they kneel before him. The bishop does this alone, without the assistance of priests or other bishops who may be present. The ordination has two parts to it. In the first part, the bishop invites the candidates to take authority to execute the office of a deacon; and, in the second part, he gives the deacons a New Testament, charging them to read and preach the Gospel as the central act of their ministry.

This is followed by the Gospel reading, which is Luke 12:35-38 in 1662. In the earlier Ordinals, the Gospel of the day was read instead. Following the Gospel, all the newly ordained deacons are expected to receive Holy Communion at the bishop's hands.

The service concludes with the reading of three collects, the first of which is a prayer for strengthening the deacons, with the specific aim that they will be able to progress in due course from their 'inferior' office to the higher ministries of the Church. The second is the well-known 'Prevent us O Lord', taken from the supplementary collects provided for use at Morning and Evening Prayer, and the third is the benediction, taken directly from Philippians 4:7.

The rubric at the end of the service states that the deacons are to remain in that office for at least a year, unless there are good reasons for making the time longer or shorter. After that, if the deacon is satisfactory, he may be ordained to the priesthood. The 1662 Ordinal specified that this should be 'at the times appointed in the canon, or else, on urgent occasion, upon some other Sunday or holy day'. This was expanded in 1964 to read: 'on the Sundays immediately following the Ember Weeks or on the feast of Saint Michael and All Angels (29 September) or of Saint Thomas the Apostle (21 December) or on such other days as shall be provided by canon'.[41]

It is possible to be a permanent deacon and some people have deliberately chosen that option. In other cases, the length of the diaconate has been reduced to six months or so but, on the whole, and certainly in the Church of England, a year remains the norm. What is clear, however, is that the 1662 Ordinal does not intend the diaconate

---

41. Clergy (Ordination and Miscellaneous Provisions) Measure 1964 (no. 6), section 1.4.2.

to be a permanent office on its own – it is explicitly stated that it is an apprenticeship leading to the priesthood. In this respect, it is no longer what it was originally meant to be and this situation is unsatisfactory. Deacons may move on to the priesthood, and virtually all of them do, but that should not be taken for granted and those who choose to remain deacons should be respected for the office they hold.

The Ordering of Priests

The second service in the Ordinal is for the ordering of priests and in statistical terms it is by far the most important. At least 98 per cent of all ordained clergy are (or soon will be) priests and will stay that way for their entire ministry. This figure has not changed in centuries and seems unlikely to do so in the future, unless the permanent diaconate is revived in a serious way. It is not surprising, therefore, that more attention has been paid to this service than to either of the others. There are some differences between 1550 and 1552, but also – and in some ways more surprisingly – between 1552 and 1662. It is not too much to say that the form for the ordering of priests is one of the most significant differences between 1552 and 1662, a circumstance that is most easily explained by the problems arising from the Interregnum, when ordination was conferred without due regard for the traditional forms in use beforehand and maintained in private by the surviving bishops during the years when the Book of Common Prayer was suppressed.

To appreciate the extent of the changes, a comparative table of 1552 and 1662 is useful:

1552	1662
	Morning Prayer
1. Exhortation	1. Sermon (Exhortation)
2. Ante-Communion (to the Gospel)	
3. Epistle	
4. Gospel	
5. *Veni, Creator Spiritus*	
6. Presentation of the candidates	6. Presentation of the candidates
7. Litany and suffrages	7. Litany and suffrages
	2. Ante-Communion
8. Collect for the candidates	8. Collect for the candidates
	3. Epistle
	4. Gospel

1552	1662
9. Oath of king's supremacy	9. Oath of king's supremacy[42]
10. Bishop's address	10. Bishop's address
11. Examination of the candidates	11. Examination of the candidates
12. Bishop's prayer for the candidates	12. Bishop's prayer for the candidates
13. Silent prayer of the congregation	13. Silent prayer of the congregation
	5. *Veni, Creator Spiritus*
	Thanksgiving and prayer
14. Ordination of the candidates	14. Ordination of the candidates
15. Remainder of the Communion service	15. Remainder of the Communion service
16. Prayer for the new priests	16. Prayer for the new priests
	Collect 'Prevent us'
17. Benediction	17. Benediction

The main differences are two:

1. The position of the presentation of the candidates, which comes much earlier in 1662.
2. The position of the *Veni, Creator Spiritus* which comes much later in 1662.

The *Veni, Creator Spiritus* comes before the presentation of the candidates in 1552 but is placed almost immediately before the Ordination in 1662, which has the effect of focussing the invocation of the Holy Spirit on the ordination itself, rather than on the more general presentation of the candidates. Other differences between 1552 and 1662 are concealed in this schematic presentation. For example, the Scripture readings are not the same, nor is the translation of the *Veni, Creator Spiritus*, the current version of which was introduced in 1662 and is generally thought to have been the work of John Cosin.

Much of the service for the ordering of priests parallels that for the making of deacons and it is not uncommon for the two to be combined into one, for which provision was made in a closing rubric as early as 1550. When that happens, the collects for the making of deacons and the ordering of priests are both meant to be used, along with the Epistle from the service for priests and a choice of Gospel from either service.

---

42. Removed to a position before the beginning of the service in 1865 and now generally abandoned outside England.

In 1662 the service was meant to be preceded by Morning Prayer, which was not mentioned in 1550 or 1552, both of which began with the exhortation. What that consisted of was not specified but it must be assumed that it was essentially the same as the one provided for the making of deacons. In 1550 the exhortation was followed by a Psalm, which could be either Psalm 40, 132 or 135, but this provision was dropped in 1552. In 1662 the contents of the sermon or exhortation are sketched out and are identical to those provided for the making of deacons, but there is no mention of a Psalm.

The 1662 service then proceeds directly to the presentation of the candidates, which is basically the same as that used for deacons, the only difference being that the word 'priest(s)' replaces 'deacon(s)' as appropriate.[43] After that starts the Communion, with the same collect as the one used in 1550/1552, the only difference being the addition in 1662 of the words 'and adorn them with' before 'innocency of life'.

Next come the Epistle and Gospel readings, which are different in the 1662 service:

	1550/1552	1662
Epistle	Acts 20:17-35 or 1 Timothy 3:1-16[44]	Ephesians 4:7-13
Gospel	Matthew 28:18-20 or John 10:1-16	Matthew 9:36-38 or John 10:1-16

After this comes a long address by the bishop, which may be analysed as follows:

1. The importance of the office to which the candidates are called:
   a. This is taught in the Scripture passages that have just been read.
   b. The candidates are called to be messengers, watchmen, [pastors] and stewards of the Lord.[45] The word 'pastors' was omitted in 1662, because it was thought to apply primarily to bishops.
   c. Your duties are:

---

43. In 1964 the words 'or such other person as by ancient custom have the right so to do' were added to the prefatory rubric after 'in his absence, one appointed in his stead'; Clergy (Ordination and Miscellaneous Provisions) Measure 1964 (no. 6), section 1.5.
44. In 1662 these readings were transferred to the service for the consecration of bishops.
45. The images are taken from Isaiah 52:7, Ezekiel 33:7 and 1 Corinthians 4:1-2.

   1. To teach, advise, feed and provide for the Lord's family.
   2. To seek out Christ's lost sheep so that they may be saved.
2. The treasure that has been entrusted to you:
   a. The people are the sheep of Christ, for whom he shed his blood.[46]
   b. The Church is Christ's bride and his body.[47]
   c. If anyone is harmed by your negligence, you know how serious the fault is and what punishment will result.
3. The call to consider your ministry:
   a. It is to the people of God, the bride of Christ.
   b. You must do all you can to bring those in your care to maturity in Christ.
   c. You must exclude heresy and evil living.
4. The qualifications required for the work:
   a. You must be dutiful and thankful to the God who has called you.[48]
   b. You must not give offence or be the cause of stumbling to others.
   c. You must pray earnestly for the Holy Spirit.
   d. You must be diligent in studying the Scriptures.[49]
   e. You must live according to the Scriptures yourself.
   f. You must avoid worldly cares and entanglements as much as possible.
5. The need for self-consecration:
   a. You must be single-minded in your devotion to God.
   b. You must continually pray to God the Father for the mediation of our Saviour Jesus Christ and the heavenly assistance of the Holy Spirit.
   c. You must study the Scriptures daily in order to:
      1. Grow stronger in your ministry.
      2. Sanctify your own life and that of your family in order to set an example for others.[50]

Of particular importance in this address is the classification of the ordinands as future messengers, watchmen and stewards of the Lord. These terms, along with 'pastors', which was unfortunately omitted in

---

46. John 10:11.
47. Isaiah 54:5; Revelation 19:7.
48. 2 Timothy 2:12-13.
49. 2 Timothy 3:16-17.
50. 1 Timothy 4:12.

1662 because of a misunderstanding, are biblical images with special significance.[51] In the sixteenth century it was generally accepted that preachers were the modern descendants of the ancient prophets, and the word 'prophecy' was frequently applied to their sermons. Thus, we find that the designation 'messenger' was used of both Haggai and Malachi and was given special prominence by Isaiah in the run-up to the famous passage about the suffering servant, which Christians have always applied to Christ.[52] The Apostle Paul also associated himself with this tradition, when he called himself a 'herald' of the Gospel and an 'ambassador' for Christ.[53] Obviously, the messenger must understand his message and deliver it faithfully. His success cannot be measured by the response of those who hear him, but only by the degree to which he fulfils his primary task of communicating it clearly and correctly.

Another important function of the priest is that he is called to be a 'watchman', someone who is constantly on guard for signs of danger and on the lookout for God's message in addressing the situation. Habakkuk was such a watchman and the theme is particularly prominent in Ezekiel, who spells out the dire punishments that await the watchman who fails in his task.[54] The theme recurs in the New Testament, if somewhat more obliquely.[55]

The Christian minister is also called to be a steward of God's house, who can be relied upon to handle the treasure entrusted to him.[56] Their pastoral role is part of this and is brought out in the Scripture readings assigned for the service, even if the word 'pastor' itself is omitted.[57]

After concluding his exhortation, the bishop goes on to say that he must examine the candidates so that the congregation can bear witness that they intend to do what they are expected to promise. This examination takes the form of eight questions to which the candidates must answer in the affirmative. The questions are:

1. Are you persuaded of your calling from God?
2. Do you believe in the authority and sufficiency of Holy Scripture for salvation?

---

51. For a full exposition of this, see Atherstone, *Anglican Ordinal*, pp. 8-20.
52. Haggai 1:13; Malachi 2:7; Isaiah 52:7.
53. 1 Timothy 2:7; 2 Corinthians 5:20.
54. Habakkuk 2:1; Ezekiel 3:16-21; 33:1-9.
55. Acts 20:31; Colossians 1:28: Hebrews 13:17.
56. 1 Corinthians 4:1-2; 1 Timothy 6:20; 2 Timothy 1:14; Titus 1:7.
57. See Ephesians 4:7-13; Matthew 9:36-38; John 10:1-16.

3. Will you be faithful to your duty?
4. Will you resist heresy and warn people against evil?
5. Will you give yourself to prayer and the study of Scripture?
6. Will you live a godly life and be an example to others?
7. Will you strive for peace and unity among Christians?
8. Will you obey your bishop and those in authority over you?

Next, the bishop prays that the God who has given the candidates the will to do the above will also give them the strength to accomplish their desire.[58] The congregation is then asked to pray for the same thing in silence.

After that comes the singing or saying of the *Veni, Creator Spiritus*, which is printed in two different translations. The first of these appeared for the first time in John Cosin's *Private Devotions* (1627) and is the one generally sung today. The second is much longer and is carried over from 1550/1552, with some slight modernisation of the wording.

The original hymn was composed in Latin but is anonymous, appearing first in the pontifical of Loisson (eleventh century) and can sometimes be found in breviaries as a hymn to be sung at Terce on Pentecost.

This is then followed by a prayer taken mainly from the Sarum pontifical. It rehearses the ongoing work of the ascended Christ, including his sending into the world apostles, prophets, evangelists, doctors and pastors, among whom may be numbered those currently being ordained. The prayer expresses thanks to God for His great blessings and asks that we may all continue to grow in the knowledge and faith of Christ, so that both those who are called to be ministers and those who benefit from their ministry may glorify God in all they do.

This prayer is followed by the laying on of hands on each of the candidates, which is performed by both the bishop and the other priests who are present. The words of the bishop vary from 1550/1552 to 1662, when the words printed in **bold** type were added:

> Receive the Holy Ghost **for the office and work of a priest in the Church of God, now committed unto thee by the imposition of our hands**. Whose sins thou dost forgive, they are forgiven; and whose sins thou dost retain, they are retained. And be thou a faithful dispenser of the Word of God, and of his holy sacraments, in the name of the Father, and of the Son, and of the Holy Ghost. Amen.

---

58. In the 1662 Ordinal he is to stand up to say this.

This formula has been extremely controversial. It is not of ancient origin and did not appear in any Ordinal before the thirteenth century. In the sixteenth century the objections of the Puritans were such that Archbishop John Whitgift (1583-1604) was obliged to explain:

> The bishop, by speaking these words, doth not take upon him to give the Holy Spirit, no more than he doth to remit sins, when he pronounceth the remission of sins; but by speaking these words of Christ ... he doth show the principal duty of a minister, and assureth him of the assistance of God's Holy Spirit, if he labour in the same accordingly.[59]

In the 1550 service this was followed by the *porrectio instrumentorum*, when the bishop gave the newly ordained priest a Bible in one hand and a chalice and paten in the other. In 1552 this was reduced to the giving of a Bible only. The words spoken were altered slightly in 1662, as indicated here by grey for deletions and **bold** type for additions:

> Take thou authority to preach the Word of God, and to minister the holy sacraments in the congregation, where thou shalt be so **lawfully** appointed **thereunto**.

In line with the general tenor of the 1662 revision, the stress was placed on 'lawfully' in view of the chaos that had resulted from the Interregnum.

After this, the service continues with the Nicene Creed and the remainder of the Communion. At the end, there is a prayer of blessing for the new priests, followed in 1662 by the collect 'Prevent us', as in the order for the making of deacons, and the benediction taken from Philippians 4:7, which also concludes the service in 1550 and 1552.

The Consecration of an Archbishop or Bishop

It is specified that the consecration of an archbishop or bishop is always to take place on a Sunday or holy day. In 1964 this rule was relaxed by adding the words 'unless for weighty and urgent reasons some other day be appointed'.[60] Nowadays consecrations are often held on holy

---

59. Whitgift, *Works*, vol. 1, p. 489.
60. Clergy (Ordination and Miscellaneous Provisions) Measure 1964 (no. 6), section 1.6.

days during the week, so as not to disrupt the normal pattern of Sunday worship and to allow as many clergy as possible to be present.

The requirements for a consecration are that at least three bishops, including the archbishop of the province, must be present. The archbishop is assisted by two other bishops who must present the bishop-elect to him. In addition, the Epistle and the Gospel must be read by different bishops. There are no specific directions for the consecration of an archbishop, as opposed to a bishop, although normally it would be expected that the archbishop of the other province would preside, assisted by two bishops of the province receiving the new archbishop.

In the Ordinal of 1550, the pre-Reformation custom of anointing the bishop-elect's head and hands, and the delivery of the ring and mitre, were dropped. The delivery of his pastoral staff, the wearing of the cope and the laying of the Bible on his head, which were retained at that time, were dropped in 1552.

The order of service broadly follows that for the ordering of priests, with the appropriate modifications where necessary. The forms used in 1550 and 1552 are much the same, with greater differences appearing in 1662, as follows:

1550/1552	1662
	Morning Prayer
1. Holy Communion	1. Holy Communion
	Collect for a bishop
2. Epistle	2. Epistle
3. Gospel	3. Gospel
4. Nicene Creed	4. Nicene Creed
	Sermon
5. Presentation of the bishop-elect	5. Presentation of the bishop-elect
6. Royal mandate read	6. Royal mandate read[61]
7. Oath of royal supremacy	7. Oath of royal supremacy[62]
8. Oath of obedience to the archbishop	8. Oath of obedience to the archbishop[63]
9. Invitation to congregation to pray	9. Invitation to congregation to pray
10. Litany (modified)	10. Litany (modified)

61. This is still done in England but not elsewhere.
62. Removed to the beginning of the service in 1865 and mostly dropped outside England.
63. Omitted when it is an archbishop being consecrated. However, archbishops customarily declare their deference to the see of Canterbury when they are elected.

1550/1552	1662
11. Concluding prayer	11. Concluding prayer
12. Examination of the bishop-elect	12. Examination of the bishop-elect
13. *Veni, Creator Spiritus*	13. *Veni, Creator Spiritus*
14. Thanksgiving and prayer	14. Thanksgiving and prayer
15. Consecration	15. Consecration
16. Giving of the Bible[64]	16. Giving of the Bible
[17. Giving of the pastoral staff][65]	
18. Remainder of the Communion	18. Remainder of the Communion
19. Prayer for the new bishop	19. Prayer for the new bishop
	Collect 'Prevent us'
20. Benediction	20. Benediction

It will be seen from the above that the 1662 rite is considerably longer than the earlier ones because of the addition of Morning Prayer and a sermon, although the rest looks much the same. The major differences are in the Scripture portions read and in the *porrectio instrumentorum* following the Consecration (16-17).

The collect for the bishop introduced in 1662 is a modified version of the one used for St Peter's Day (29 June). Epistle and Gospel readings were as follows:

	1550/1552	1662
Epistle	1 Timothy 3:1-6	1 Timothy 3:1-6 or Acts 20:17-35
Gospel	John 21:15-17 or John 10:1-16	John 21:15-17 or John 20:19-23 or Matthew 28:18-20

After the reading of the Gospel come the recitation of the Nicene Creed and the sermon, though neither the preacher nor the subject is specified. Then the two supporting bishops present the bishop-elect to the archbishop, assuring him that the candidate is 'godly and well-learned'. Given that the candidate will already be a priest of some standing, there does not seem to be a need for a detailed examination of his beliefs at this point, though he must swear an oath of allegiance to the archbishop before proceeding any further.

Next the archbishop turns to the congregation and reminds them that Jesus and the apostles both spent long periods in prayer before he chose

---

64. In 1550 the Bible was laid on the bishop-elect's neck but in 1552 it was simply handed to him.

65. Omitted in 1552.

his apostles and they, too, spent a long period praying before they went forth into the world. The archbishop invites the congregation to follow the same practice before the consecration of a new bishop, though obviously the time period available for this is much shorter. The specific incidents cited are the occasion when Jesus went up a mountain and spent an entire night praying before calling his disciples (Luke 6:12-16) and the time when the church at Antioch fasted and prayed before commissioning Paul and Barnabas for their first missionary journey (Acts 13:1-3).

After this comes the litany, which is the same as the one used in the making of deacons, except that the suffrage 'That it may please thee to bless these thy servants, now to be admitted deacons etc.' should be replaced by the following:

> That it may please thee to bless this our brother elected, and to send thy grace upon him, that he may duly execute the office whereunto he is called, to the edifying of thy Church, and to the honour, praise and glory of thy name.

At the end of the litany there is a concluding prayer which is the same as the one used as the Communion collect for the ordering of priests, adapted as necessary for a bishop. This prayer, like the alternative suffrage in the litany, is taken from the Sarum pontifical.

After this, the archbishop addresses the bishop-elect in the following words, emended in 1662 by certain deletions (in grey) and additions (in **bold** type):

> Brother, forasmuch as **the** Holy Scripture and the old **ancient** canons commandeth that we should not be hasty in laying on hands and admitting of any person to *the* government of **in** the congregation **Church** of Christ, which he hath purchased with no less price than the effusion of his own blood: afore that **Before** I admit you to this administration whereunto ye are called, I will examine you in certain articles, to the end **that** the congregation present may have a trial, and bear witness, how ye **you** be minded to behave yourself in the Church of God.

The only alteration of any significance is the change from 'congregation' to 'Church', which probably reflects the high church proclivities of the 1662 revisers. Note that the archbishop addresses the bishop-elect in the plural forms of ye/you, a sign of polite respect at a time when thou/thee were much more common in liturgical use.

Following this come the questions, which are similar to those asked of candidates for the priesthood, apart from the seventh one, added in 1662, which deals with the ordination of others that is specially entrusted to bishops. The questions asked are:

1. Do you believe that you have been truly called by Christ and by the powers that be?
2. Do you believe in the authority and sufficiency of the Holy Scriptures and will you teach them faithfully to your people?
3. Will you be faithful in your study of the Scriptures?
4. Will you diligently banish error and encourage others to do the same?
5. Will you live a godly life and set an example to others?
6. Will you pursue all that makes for peace and unity in your diocese?
7. Will you be faithful in ordaining others?
8. Will you be gentle to poor people and strangers who need help?

The archbishop then repeats the same prayer as is asked for candidates for the priesthood, asking that God, who has given the bishop-elect the will to fulfil these tasks will also give him the strength he will need to accomplish them.

At this point the bishop-elect puts on his full episcopal vestments and the service proceeds with the *Veni, Creator Spiritus.* This is then followed by a prayer for the new bishop, which was slightly altered in 1662, as is shown by the deletions in grey and the additions in **bold** type:

Almighty God and most merciful Father, which **who** of thy**ine** infinite goodness hath given to us thy **thine** only and most **dearly** beloved Son Jesus Christ, to be our Redeemer and **the** author of everlasting life; who after that he had made perfect our redemption by his death, and was ascended into heaven, poured down his gifts abundantly upon men, making some apostles, some prophets, some evangelists, some pastors and doctors, to the edifying and making perfect of his congregation **Church**: Grant, we beseech thee, to this thy servant such grace that he may be evermore **be** ready to spread abroad thy Gospel, and **the** glad tidings of reconcilement to God **reconciliation with thee**; and to use the authority given unto him, not to destroy **destruction**, but to save **salvation**, not to hurt, but to help: so that he as a wise and a faithful servant, giving to thy family meat **their portion** in due season, **he** may at the last day be received into **everlasting** joy, through Jesus Christ our Lord, who with thee and the Holy Ghost liveth and reigneth, one God, world without end. Amen.

There then follows the formula of consecration, which in 1662 starts off the same as that used for the ordering of priests but then cuts off and adds the words originally used in 1550 and 1552:

Receive[1] the Holy Ghost for the office and work of a bishop in the Church of God, now committed unto thee by the imposition of our hands, in the name of the Father, and of the Son, and of the Holy Ghost, Amen. [1550/1552:] And remember that thou stir up the grace of God which is given thee by this imposition of our hands, for God hath not given us the spirit of fear, but of power and love and soberness.[2]

After this comes the *porrectio instrumentorum*, reduced in 1552 to the giving of the Bible, accompanied by a short exhortation to the new bishop in which he is told to:

1. Pay attention to reading, exhortation and doctrine.
2. Meditate on the Scriptures.
3. Be diligent in studying the Scriptures.
4. Guard himself and his doctrine, in order to save others.
5. Be a shepherd to the flock of Christ.[3]
6. Protect and succour the weak, the sick, the outcasts, the lost.
7. Be merciful in ministering discipline.

After that, the archbishop resumes the celebration of Holy Communion, concluding with a collect for the new bishop, praying that he may be given strength to be an example to his flock and receive the crown of righteousness at the end of his life.

There then follows the collect 'Prevent us' and the benediction, taken from Philippians 4:7.

---

1. In 1550 and 1552 the word used was 'take'.
2. 2 Timothy 1:6-7.
3. It was at this point that the archbishop gave the bishop his pastoral staff in 1550.

Chapter 10

The Articles of Religion

The Thirty-nine Articles of Religion, as fixed in 1571 and ratified by King Charles I in 1628, are normally attached to the Book of Common Prayer but do not form an integral part of it. As there are many good expositions of them, it is not necessary to go into them in detail here, but some indication of how they are structured and which ones are of particular relevance to the prayer book may be useful.

As to structure, the Articles are best grouped as follows:

A. 1-8. The Catholic Articles, referring to the universal faith of all Christians.

B. 9-33. The Reformed (Protestant) Articles, dealing with the controversies of the Reformation era. They may be subdivided as follows:
   (i) 9-18. The Way of Salvation.
   (ii) 19-33. Church, Ministry and Sacraments:
      a. 19-22. Church
      b. 23-24. Ministry
      c. 25-33. Sacraments.

C. 34-37. The Local or 'Anglican' Articles, covering matters specific to the Church of England.

D. 38-39. Miscellaneous Articles, constituting an appendix to the rest.

This division is unofficial and some Articles might be classified differently. For example, Article 34 on tradition leads from the general subject of the Church to the particular circumstances of England, and could fit under either heading. The following list of the Articles indicates how and where each of them is applied in the Book of Common Prayer.

The Catholic Articles

1. *Of Faith in the Holy Trinity.* The Trinity is central to the prayer book. The Triune God is prayed to in every doxology and benediction, as well as in a number of prayers. Also, Trinity Sunday is a major festival and the Sundays following it are numbered accordingly until Advent.
2. *Of Christ the Son of God.* Mentioned in almost every prayer.
3. *Of his going down into Hell.*
4. *Of his Resurrection.* There are special prayers and readings for Easter. This is also a prominent theme of the service for the burial of the dead.
5. *Of the Holy Ghost.* He is celebrated on Pentecost Sunday and for seven days thereafter and is mentioned in almost all of the prayers.
6. *Of the Sufficiency of the Scriptures.* The Scriptures are widely read and quoted in every service and a lectionary is provided to take people through the text in the course of a year.
7. *Of the Old Testament.* The Old Testament is frequently quoted (e.g. in the invitation to Morning and Evening Prayer) and the Psalms are read every day.
8. *Of the Three Creeds.* The Apostles' Creed is read at Morning and Evening Prayer, and also features in the Catechism. The Nicene Creed is used in the Lord's Supper. The Athanasian Creed is said at Morning Prayer on thirteen occasions in the course of the year.

The Reformed Articles I: The Way of Salvation

9. *Of Original or Birth Sin.* Mentioned in prayers of confession and prominent in the baptismal rites.
10. *Of Free Will.*
11. *Of Justification.* The main theme of the Lord's Supper.
12. *Of Good Works.* Prayers for the strength to perform them are found at the end of the baptismal services, the Lord's Supper and elsewhere.
13. *Of Works before Justification.* Alluded to in the general confession in Morning and Evening Prayer and also in the Lord's Supper.
14. *Of Works of Supererogation.*

15. *Of Christ alone without Sin.* A prominent theme of the Lord's Supper.
16. *Of Sin after Baptism.* Assumed in every prayer of confession and repentance.
17. *Of Predestination and Election.* Mentioned in baptism and in the burial service and assumed in the Lord's Supper.
18. *Of Obtaining Salvation by Christ.* A prominent theme of every service.

The Reformed Articles II: Church, Ministry and Sacraments

19. *Of the Church.* Prayers for the Church occur in Morning and Evening Prayer and in the Lord's Supper.
20. *Of the Authority of the Church.* This is emphasised most clearly in the prefaces but can also be found (at least implicitly) in the words of absolution pronounced by the priest and throughout the Ordinal.
21. *Of the Authority of General Councils.*
22. *Of Purgatory.* The things condemned in this Article are omitted from the prayer book.
23. *Of Ministering in the Congregation.* Alluded to in the Ordinal.
24. *Of Speaking in the Congregation.* Implied by the fact that the prayer book is in the vernacular.
25. *Of the Sacraments.* Implied by the shape and content of the sacramental services.
26. *Of the Unworthiness of Ministers.* Alluded to in the Ordinal.
27. *Of Baptism.* Worked out in the baptismal rites.
28. *Of the Lord's Supper.* Worked out in the Lord's Supper.
29. *Of the Wicked which eat not the Body of Christ.* Alluded to in the Lord's Supper.
30. *Of Both Kinds.* Worked out in the Lord's Supper.
31. *Of Christ's One Oblation.* The theme of the institution in the Lord's Supper.
32. *Of the Marriage of Priests.* Alluded to in the Ordinal.
33. *Of Excommunicate Persons.* Alluded to in the Lord's Supper, the commination and the burial of the dead.

The Local or 'Anglican' Articles

34. *Of the Traditions of the Church.* Found in the preface to the 1549 prayer book, now printed as 'Of Ceremonies' at the beginning of the 1662 book.
35. *Of the Homilies.* A sermon must be preached at the Lord's Supper.
36. *Of Consecrating of Ministers.* A reference to the Ordinal.
37. *Of Civil Magistrates.* The Sovereign, the royal family and the civil magistrates are prayed for in Morning and Evening Prayer, and the Sovereign is prayed for or mentioned many times elsewhere – in the Lord's Supper and in the Ordinal especially.

The Miscellaneous Articles

38. *Of Christian Men's Goods.* The clergy are meant to encourage almsgiving, according to the Ordinal.
39. *Of a Christian Man's Oath.* Ordinands take an oath of allegiance to the Sovereign and of obedience to the bishop or archbishop.

For Further Reading on the Articles of Religion, see:

Bicknell, E.J., *A Theological Introduction to the Thirty-nine Articles of the Church of England*, 2nd edn (London: Longmans, Green & Co., 1925) A classic work, written from a conservative high church (though not Anglo-Catholic) standpoint and still useful for details.

Bray, G.L., *Anglicanism: A Reformed Catholic Religion* (Bellingham, WA: Lexham Press, 2021) A brief introduction to the Articles intended mainly for lay people and interested outsiders.

———, *The Faith We Confess: An Exposition of the Thirty-nine Articles* (London: Latimer Trust, 2009) A study guide to the Articles intended mainly for church groups. Contains scriptural references and discussion questions.

Griffith Thomas, W.H., *The Principles of Theology: An Introduction to the Thirty-nine Articles* (London: Church Book Room Press, 1963) A detailed examination of the Articles from an Evangelical standpoint.

Hardwick, C., *A History of the Articles of Religion*, 3rd edn (London: George Bell & Sons, 1881) The best account of the history of the Articles.

O'Donovan, O., *On the Thirty-nine Articles: A Conversation with Tudor Christianity* (Exeter: Paternoster, 1986) Somewhat convoluted and hard to follow, but interesting for those prepared to engage in intellectual gymnastics.

Rodgers, J.H., *Essential Truths for Christians: A Commentary on the Anglican Thirty-nine Articles and an Introduction to Systematic Theology* (Blue Bell, PA: Classical Anglican Press, 2011) A well-presented study of the Articles written from a conservative Episcopalian (now ACNA) standpoint.

Rogers, T., *The Catholic Doctrine of the Church of England: An Exposition of the Thirty-nine Articles* (Cambridge: Cambridge University Press, 1854) Published by the Parker Society, it was originally written in 1616.

Bibliography

Adam, P., *The 'Very Pure Word of God': The Book of Common Prayer as a Model of Biblical Liturgy* (London: Latimer Trust, 2012)

Anderson, R.D., Jr, 'The Division and Order of the Psalms', *Westminster Theological Journal* 56 (1994), pp. 219-41

Atherstone, A., *The Anglican Ordinal: Gospel Priorities for Church of England Ministry* (London: Latimer Trust, 2020)

———, *Charles Simeon on* The Excellency of the Liturgy, Alcuin/GROW Joint Liturgical Study 72 (Norwich: Hymns Ancient and Modern, 2011)

———, *Scarf or Stole at Ordination? A Plea for the Evangelical Conscience* (London: Latimer Trust, 2012)

Belousek, D.W.S., *Marriage, Scripture and the Church: Theological Discernment on the Question of Same-sex Union* (Grand Rapids, MI: Baker, 2021)

Blayney, P.W.M., *The Printing and Printers of the Book of Common Prayer, 1549-1561* (Cambridge: Cambridge University Press, 2022)

Blunt, J.H., *The Annotated Book of Common Prayer* (London: Rivingtons, 1888)

Boersma, H., and M. Levering, *The Oxford Handbook of Sacramental Theology* (Oxford: Oxford University Press, 2015)

Booty, J.E., *The Book of Common Prayer, 1559: The Elizabethan Prayer Book* (Washington, DC: Folger Shakespeare Library, 1978)

Bosher, R.S., *The Making of the Restoration Settlement: The Influence of the Laudians, 1649-1662* (London: Dacre Press, 1951)

Bradshaw, P.F., *The Anglican Ordinal: Its History and Development from the Reformation to the Present Day* (London: SPCK, 1971)

———, *Rites of Ordination: Their History and Theology* (London: SPCK, 2014)

———, and M.E. Johnson, *The Origins of Feasts, Fasts and Seasons in Early Christianity* (London: SPCK; Collegeville, MN: Liturgical Press, 2011)

Bray, G.L., (ed.), *The Anglican Canons, 1529-1947* (Woodbridge: Boydell & Brewer, 1998)

———, (ed.), *The Books of Homilies: A Critical Edition* (Cambridge: James Clarke & Co., 2015)

———, (ed.), *Documents of the English Reformation*, 3rd edn (Cambridge: James Clarke & Co., 2019)

———, (ed.), *The Institution of a Christian Man* (Cambridge: James Clarke & Co., 2018)

———, (ed.), *Records of Convocation*, 20 vols (Woodbridge: Boydell & Brewer, 2005-06)

Bray, S.L., and D.N. Keane, *The 1662 Book of Common Prayer: International Edition* (Downers Grove, IL: InterVarsity Press, 2021)

Brightman, F.E., *The English Rite*, 2nd edn, 2 vols (London: Rivingtons, 1921)

Brook, S., *The Language of the Book of Common Prayer* (London: Andre Deutsch, 1965)

Bucer, M., *Martin Bucers Deutsche Schriften*, 19 vols, ed. R. Stupperich (Gütersloh: Gerd Mohn, 1960-2016)

Buchanan, C.O., *An Evangelical among the Anglican Liturgists* (London: SPCK, 2009)

———, *The Savoy Conference Revisited*, Alcuin/GROW Joint Liturgical Study 54 (Cambridge: Grove Books, 2002)

Burkill, M., *Dearly Beloved: Building God's People through Morning and Evening Prayer* (London: Latimer Trust, 2012)

Burton, E., *Three Primers Put Forth in the Reign of Henry VIII* (Oxford: Oxford University Press, 1834)

Butterworth, C.C., *The English Primers (1529-1545): Their Publication and Connection with the English Bible and the Reformation in England* (Philadelphia, PA: University of Pennsylvania Press, 1953)

Buxton, R.F., *Eucharist and Institution Narrative: A Study in the Roman and Anglican Traditions of the Consecration of the Eucharist from the Eighth to the Twelfth Centuries* (Great Wakering: Mayhew-McCrimmon, 1976)

Cardwell, E., *A History of Conferences and Other Proceedings Connected with the Revision of the Book of Common Prayer: From the Year 1558 to the Year 1690* (Oxford: Oxford University Press, 1891)

Cinnamond, A., *Sure and Certain Hope: Death and Burial in the Book of Common Prayer* (London: Latimer Trust, 2016)

Colquhoun, F., *The Catechism and the Order of Confirmation* (London: Hodder & Stoughton, 1963)

Common Worship: Services and Prayers for the Church of England (London: Church House Publishing, 2000)

Common Worship: Ordination Services: Study Edition (London: Church House Publishing, 2007)

The Communion Office for the Use of the Church of Scotland, as far as Concerneth the Ministration of that Holy Sacrament (Edinburgh: Drummond, 1764)

Conciliorum oecumenicorum decreta (Bologna: Istituto per le scienze religiose, 1973); English translation: N. Tanner (ed.), *Decrees of the Ecumenical Councils*, 2 vols (London: Sheed & Ward, 1990)

Cranmer, T., *An Answer unto a Crafty and Sophisticall Cavillation, devised by Stephen Gardiner* (London: R. Wolfe, 1551)

——, *A Defence of the True and Catholic Doctrine of the Sacrament of the Body and Blood of Our Saviour Christ* (London: R. Wolfe, 1550; repr. Eugene, OR: Wipf & Stock, 2004)

Cuming, G.J., *The Durham Book: Being the First Draft of Revision of the Book of Common Prayer in 1661* (London: Oxford University Press, 1975)

——, *The Godly Order: Texts and Studies relating to the Book of Common Prayer* (London: SPCK, 1983)

——, *A History of Anglican Liturgy*, 2nd edn (London: Macmillan, 1982)

Cummings, B., (ed.), *The Book of Common Prayer: The Texts of 1549, 1559 and 1662* (Oxford: Oxford University Press, 2011)

Dalby, M., *Anglican Missals and Their Canons: 1549, Interim Rite and Roman*, Alcuin/GROW Joint Liturgical Study 41 (Cambridge: Grove Books, 1998)

Davie, M., *The Athanasian Creed* (London: Latimer Trust, 2019)

——, *Defend O Lord: Confirmation according to the Book of Common Prayer* (London: Latimer Trust, 2022)

——, *Instruction in the Way of the Lord: A Guide to the Catechism in the Book of Common Prayer* (London: Latimer Trust, 2014)

Day, J., and B. Gordon-Taylor, *The Study of Liturgy and Worship* (Collegeville, MN: Liturgical Press, 2013)

Dennison J.T., Jr, *Reformed Confessions of the Sixteenth and Seventeenth Centuries in English Translation*, 4 vols (Grand Rapids, MI: Reformation Heritage Books, 2008-14)

Deshusses, J., (ed.), *Le Sacramentaire grégorien: Ses Principales formes d'après les plus anciens manuscrits*, 3 vols (Fribourg: Presses Universitaires de Fribourg, 1971-82)

Dickinson, F.H., *Missale ad usum insignis et praeclarae ecclesiae Sarum* (Burntisland: Pitsligo Press, 1861-1883)

Dix, Gregory, *The Shape of the Liturgy* (London: Dacre Press, 1945; and New York: Seabury Press, 1982)

Donaldson, G., *The Making of the Scottish Prayer Book of 1637* (Edinburgh: Edinburgh University Press, 1954)

Dowden, J., *The Scottish Communion Office, 1764* (Oxford: Oxford University Press, 1922)

——, *The Workmanship of the Prayer Book in Its Literary and Liturgical Aspects* (London: Methuen, 1899)

Dudley, M.R., *The Collect in Anglican Liturgy: Texts and Sources 1549-1989* (Runcorn: Alcuin Club; Collegeville, MN: Liturgical Press, 1994)

Faulenbach, H., and E. Busch (eds), *Reformierte Bekenntnisschriften*, 3 vols (Neukirchen-Vluyn: Neukirchener Verlag, 2002-16)

Fawcett, T.J., *The Liturgy of Comprehension 1689: An Abortive Attempt to Revise the Book of Common Prayer* (Southend-on-Sea: Mayhew-McCrimmon, 1973)

Feltoe, C.L., *Sacramentarium Leonianum* (Cambridge: Cambridge University Press, 1896)

Fisher, J.D.C., *Christian Initiation: Baptism in the Medieval West* (London: SPCK, 1965; repr. Chicago, IL: Hillenbrand Books, 2004)

———, *Christian Initiation: The Reformation Period* (London: SPCK, 1970)

———, *Confirmation Then and Now* (London: SPCK, 1978)

Franklin, R.W., (ed.), *Anglican Orders: Essays on the Centenary of Apostolicae Curae 1986-1996* (London: Mowbray; and Harrisburg, PA: Morehouse Publishing, 1996)

Frere, W.H., *Graduale Sarisburiense: A Reproduction in Facsimile of a Manuscript of the Thirteenth Century*, 2 vols (London: Plainsong and Medieval Music Society, 1891 and 1894)

———, *Some Principles of Liturgical Reform: A Contribution to the Revision of the Book of Common Prayer* (London: John Murray, 1911)

———, *The Use of Sarum*, 2 vols (Cambridge: Cambridge University Press, 1898 and 1901; repr. Forgotten Books, 2018)

Friedberg, E., (ed.), *Corpus Iuris Canonici*, 2 vols (Leipzig: B. Tauchnitz, 1879)

Fulke, W., *A Defence of the Sincere and True Translations of the Holy Scriptures into the English Tongue: Against the Cavils of Gregory Martin*, ed. C.H. Hartshorne (Cambridge: Cambridge University Press, 1843)

Gant, A., *O sing unto the Lord: A History of English Church Music* (London: Profile Books, 2015)

Gardiner, S., *An Explicatio and Assertion of the True Catholique Faythe* (Rouen: Robert Caly, 1551)

Gasquet, F.A., and E. Bishop, *Edward VI and the Book of Common Prayer* (London: John Hodges, 1890; repr. Milton Keynes: Alpha Editions, 2020)

Gordon, B., *Zwingli: God's Armed Prophet* (New Haven, CT: Yale University Press, 2021)

Gould, G., (ed.), *Documents Relating to the Settlement of the Church of England by the Act of Uniformity of 1662* (London: W. Kent & Co., 1862; repr. Scholar Select, 2016)

Gray, D., *The 1927-28 Prayer Book Crisis*, Alcuin/GROW Joint Liturgical Studies 60 and 61, 2 vols (Norwich: SCM/Canterbury Press, 2005 and 2006)

Grisbrooke, W.J., *Anglican Liturgies of the Seventeenth and Eighteenth Centuries* (London: SPCK, 1958)

Harford, G., and M. Stevenson (eds), *The Prayer Book Dictionary* (London: Sir Isaac Pitman & Sons, 1912; repr. Forgotten Books, 2018)

Hatchett, M.J., *Commentary on the American Prayer Book* (New York, NY: Seabury Press, 1980)

Hefling, C., *The Book of Common Prayer: A Guide* (Oxford: Oxford University Press, 2021)

———, and C. Shattuck (eds), *The Oxford Guide to the Book of Common Prayer: A Worldwide Survey* (Oxford: Oxford University Press, 2006)

Henry VIII Fid. Def., *His Defence of the Faith and Its Seven Sacraments* (Sevenoaks: Ducketts Booksellers/Fisher Press, 2008)

Hicks, Z., *Worship by Faith Alone: Thomas Cranmer, the Book of Common Prayer and the Reformation of Liturgy* (Downers Grove, IL: InterVarsity Press, 2023)

Hopf, C., *Martin Bucer and the English Reformation* (Oxford: Blackwell, 1946)

Hughes, J.J., *Stewards of the Lord: A Reappraisal of Anglican Orders* (London: Sheed & Ward, 1970)

Jagger, P.J., *The Alcuin Club and Its Publications 1897-1987* (Norwich: Hymns Ancient and Modern, 1986)

Jasper, R.C.D., *The Development of the Anglican Liturgy, 1662-1980* (London: SPCK, 1989)

———, and G.J. Cuming, *Prayers of the Eucharist: Early and Reformed*, 4th edn, ed. P.F. Bradshaw and M.E. Johnson (Collegeville, MN: Liturgical Press, 2019)

Jeanes, G.P., *Signs of God's Promise: Thomas Cranmer's Sacramental Theology and the Book of Common Prayer* (London: T. & T. Clark, 2008)

Johnson, M.E., *Sacraments and Worship: The Sources of Christian Theology* (Louisville, KY: Westminster John Knox Press, 2012)

Kelly, J.N.D., *The Athanasian Creed: The Paddock Lectures for 1962-3* (London: A. & C. Black, 1964)

———, *Early Christian Creeds*, 3rd edn (Harlow: Longman, 1981)

Kolb, R., and T.J. Wengert (eds), *The Book of Concord: The Confessions of the Evangelical Lutheran Church* (Minneapolis, MN: Fortress Press, 2000)

Laud, W., *The Works of the Most Reverend Father in God, William Laud, D.D.*, ed. W. Scott and J. Bliss, 7 vols. (Oxford: John Henry Parker, 1847-60)

Lee, F.G., *The Altar Service Book* (London: Chiswick Press, 1867)

Legg, J.W., *Cranmer's Liturgical Projects: A Complete Edition of British Museum MSS* (London: Harrison & Son, 1915)

———, *The Sarum Missal: Edited from Three Early Manuscripts* (Oxford: Clarendon Press, 1916)

———, *Second Recension of Quignon's Breviary*, 2 vols (London: Henry Bradshaw Society, 1912; reissued Woodbridge: Boydell Press, 2010)

Lietzmann, H., *Liturgische Texte*, 8 vols (Bonn: A. Marcus und E. Weber, 1909-10)

Lowe, E.A. (ed.), *The Bobbio Missal: A Gallican Mass Book*, 2 vols. (London: Henry Bradshaw Society, 1920 and 1924)

Luther, M., *Luther's Works: Volume 36: Word and Sacrament II*, ed. A.R. Wentz (Philadelphia, PA: Muhlenberg Press, 1959)

MacCulloch, D., *Thomas Cranmer*, rev. edn (New Haven, CT: Yale University Press, 2016)

Maltby, J., *Prayer Book and People in Elizabethan and Early Stuart England* (Cambridge: Cambridge University Press, 1998)

Martos, J., *Doors to the Sacred: A Historical Introduction to Sacraments in the Catholic Church* (Liguori, MO: Triumph Press, 2001)

Maxwell, W.D., *An Outline of Christian Worship: Its Development and Forms*, 9th edn (London: Oxford University Press, 1963)

Medd, P., *The Priest to the Altar* (1861), 2nd edn (London: Rivingtons, 1859); 5th edn (Oxford: Oxford University Press; and London: Longmans, 1904)

Miller, D.J.D. and P. Sarris (eds.), *The Novels of Justinian. A Complete Annotated English Translation*, 2 vols. (Cambridge: Cambridge University Press, 2018).

Milton, A., *England's Second Reformation: The Battle for the Church of England, 1625-1662* (Cambridge: Cambridge University Press, 2021)

Mohlberg, L.C., (ed.), *Das fränkische Sacramentarium Gelasianum in alamannischer Überlieferung* (Münster-in-Westfalen: Aschendorff, 1971)

———, (ed.), *Liber Sacramentorum Romanae Aeclesiae Ordinis Anni Circuli* (Rome: Herder, 1968)

———, (ed.), *Missale Gothicum* (Rome: Herder, 1961)

———, (ed.), *Sacramentarium Veronense* (Rome: Herder, 1956)

Neil, C., and J.M. Willoughby (eds), *The Tutorial Prayer Book: For the Teacher, the Student, and the General Reader* (London: The Harrison Trust, 1913)

Null, J.A., *Divine Allurement: Cramer's Comfortable Words* (London: Latimer Trust, 2014)

Page, W., 'The First Book of Common Prayer and the Windsor Commission', *Church Quarterly Review* 98, no. 195 (1924), pp. 51-64

Parker, J., *An Introduction to the History of the Successive Revisions of the Book of Common Prayer* (Oxford: Oxford University Press, 1877)

Patrick, T., *Anglican Foundations: A Handbook to the Source Documents of the English Reformation* (London: Latimer Trust, 2018)

Pfaff, R., *The Liturgy in Medieval England: A History* (Cambridge: Cambridge University Press, 2009)

Pickles, M., *'Doubt Not ... but Earnestly Believe': A Fresh Look at the BCP Baptism Service* (London: Latimer Trust, 2020)

Porter, J.R., *The First and Second Prayer Books of Edward VI* (London: J.M. Dent & Sons, 1910; repr. Prayer Book Society, 1999)

Procter, F., and W.H. Frere, *A New History of the Book of Common Prayer, with a Rationale of Its Offices* (London: Macmillan & Co., 1958)

Procter, F., and C. Wordsworth, *Breviarium ad usum insignis ecclesiae Sarum*, 3 vols (Cambridge: Cambridge University Press, 1879-86)

The Public General Acts and Church Assembly Measures 1964 (London: HMSO, 1965)

The Public General Acts and Church Assembly Measures 1965 (London: HMSO, 1966)

The Public General Acts and Church Assembly Measures 1968 (London: HMSO, 1969)

The Public General Acts and General Synod Measures 1974 (London: HMSO, 1975)

Public Statutes and General Synod Measures 2018, London: HMSO, 2019

Quiñones, F. de, *Breviarium Romanum a Francisco Cardinali Quignonio: Editum et Recognitum: Iuxta Editionem Venetiis A.D. 1535 Impressum*, ed.

J.W. Legg (Cambridge: Cambridge University Press, 1888; repr. Farnborough: Gregg International, 1970)

Rattray, T., *The Ancient Liturgy of the Church of Jerusalem: Being the Liturgy of St. James* (London: James Bettenham, 1744)

Richter, A.L., *Die evangelischen Kirchenordnungen des sechszehnten Jahrhunderts: Urkunden und Regesten zur Geschichte des Rechts und der Verfassung der evangelischen Kirche in Deutschland*, 2 vols (Weimar: Landes-Industriecomptoir, 1864)

Robinson, H., *Original Letters Relative to the English Reformation*, 2 vols (Cambridge: Cambridge University Press, 1846 and 1847)

Rowell, G., *The Liturgy of Christian Burial* (London: SPCK, 1977)

Sargent, B., *Day by Day: The Rhythm of the Bible in the Book of Common Prayer* (London: Latimer Trust, 2012)

Scotland, N., *The Supper: Cranmer and Communion* (London: Latimer Trust, 2013)

Segger, G.J., *Richard Baxter's* Reformed Liturgy: *A Puritan Alternative to the Book of Common Prayer* (London: Taylor & Francis, 2016)

Sehling, E., *Die evangelischen Kirchenordnungen des sechszehnten Jahrhunderts*, 24 vols (Leipzig: O.R. Reisland, 1902-13)

Shipley, O., *The Ritual of the Altar* (London: Longmans, 1870)

Simeon, C., *The Excellency of the Liturgy: In Four Discourses, Preached before the University of Cambridge, in November, 1811* (Cambridge: J. Smith, 1812)

Spijker, W. van 't, *The Ecclesiastical Offices in the Thought of Martin Bucer* (Leiden: Brill, 1996)

Spinks, B.D., *The Rise and Fall of the Incomparable Liturgy: The Book of Common Prayer, 1559-1906* (London: SPCK, 2017.)

Stanton, A.H., *Catholic Prayers for Church of England People* (London: W. Knott, 1880)

Stevenson, K., *Nuptial Blessing: A Study of Christian Marriage Rites* (London: SPCK, 1982)

Stone, D., *A History of the Doctrine of the Holy Eucharist*, 2 vols (London: Longmans, Green & Co., 1909)

Taylor, N.H., *Lay Presidency at the Eucharist? An Anglican Approach* (London: Mowbray, 2009)

Thompson, B., *Liturgies of the Western Church* (Philadelphia, PA: Fortress Press, 1980)

Timms, G.B., *Dixit Cranmer: A Reply to Dom Gregory Dix* (London: Mowbray & Co., 1946)

Vibert, S., *Till Death Us Do Part: 'The Solemnization of Matrimony' in the Book of Common Prayer* (London: Latimer Trust, 2014)

Whitaker, E.C., *Martin Bucer and the Book of Common Prayer* (Great Wakering: Mayhew-McCrimmon, 1974)

Whitgift, J., *The Works of John Whitgift*, ed. J. Ayre, 3 vols (Oxford: Oxford University Press, 1851-53)

Wilkins, D., (ed.), *Concilia Magnae Britanniae et Hiberniae*, 4 vols (London: Various Printers, 1737)

Wilson, H.A., (ed.), *The Gelasian Sacramentary: Liber sacramentorum romanae ecclesiae* (Oxford: Clarendon Press, 1894; repr. Forgotten Books, 2018)

——, (ed.), *The Gregorian Sacramentary under Charles the Great* (London: Harrison & Son, 1915; repr. Forgotten Books, 2018)

——, (ed.), *The Order of Communion, 1548* (London: Harrison & Son, 1908; repr. Forgotten Books, 2012)

Wordsworth, J., *The* Te Deum: *Its Structure and Meaning and Its Musical Setting and Rendering: Together with a Revised Latin Text, Notes and Translation*, rev. edn (London: SPCK, 1903)

Wotherspoon, H.J., and G.W. Sprott, *The Second Prayer Book of King Edward the Sixth (1552) with Historical Introduction and Notes; and the Liturgy of Compromise Used in the English Congregation at Frankfort* (Edinburgh: William Blackwood & Sons, 1905)

Index

Holy Scripture and Early Christian Writings

Apocrypha

New Testament

Early Christian Writings

Names and Places

Subjects

Liturgies and Rites

Anglican

Eastern Orthodox

English (pre-Reformation)

Western Catholic

Western Protestant

Church Councils

Parliamentary Statutes and Measures